D1234017

Race to Pearl Harbor

The Failure of the Second London Naval Conference

and the Onset of World War II

Race to Pearl Harbor

The Failure of the Second London Naval

Conference and the Onset of World War II

STEPHEN E. PELZ

Harvard University Press   Cambridge, Massachusetts   1974

FOR MY MOTHER AND FATHER   Lois A. Pelz and Kurt S. Pelz

Acknowledgments

Because the research for this book was conducted in Japan, the United States, and Britain, I have incurred a debt that is international in scope. The work has drawn into its vortex a number of people who have given generously of their time and resources. Unfortunately I cannot mention all of them, but I would like to acknowledge my major obligations.

I owe special thanks to Professor Hosoya Chihirō of Hitotsubashi University, who first pointed out the importance of the naval problem for the history of Japanese-American relations and led me to the proper documents. Professor Usui Katsumi of Kyushu University helped me sort out various problems of Sino-Japanese relations and discussed with me the nature of Japanese public opinion formation. Professor Tsunoda Jun of the National Diet Library shared with me his great knowledge both of the Japanese navy and of international politics in the thirties, as well as showing me some of his work in progress.

I must also thank Professor Kurihara Ken and the archival staff of the Japanese Ministry of Foreign Affairs. They used their knowledge of the records to answer questions and spent a great amount of time unearthing materials for me. In particular, I wish to thank Baba Akira, who guided me in the use of the documents. I fear that on more than one occasion my questions impeded his work, and I shall not forget his kindness. Other patient men helped me with the Japanese language, such as Itasaka Gen and Yamashita Shinichi of Harvard University and the staff of the Inter-University Center in Tokyo; their efforts went far beyond the call of duty.

Others were of assistance in acquiring research materials. In England, Professor Stephen W. Roskill of Cambridge University gave me many useful hints on the rich resources at the Public Record Office in London. In Japan, Professor Itō Takashi of Tokyo Metropolitan University showed me the Katō Kanji papers, which proved most useful. Baron Admiral Tomioka Sadatoshi and Commander Sekino Hideo provided information on the Japanese Navy that was indispensable, and Admiral Suekuni Masao spent many hours describing Japan's strategic plans and weapons development. Professor Asada Sadao of Dōshisha University shared his valuable work on the Japanese Navy with me. The staffs of the National Diet Library in Tokyo, the Library of Congress, the National Archives and Records Service, the Franklin D. Roosevelt Library, and the Public Record Office in London also were extremely helpful.

Professor Waldo H. Heinrichs of the University of Illinois was a constant source of encouragement. He joined Professors Robert A. Hart, John M. Maki, and Richard H. Minear of the University of Massachusetts at Amherst and Professor Akira Iriye of the University of Chicago in reading and commenting on early drafts. Throughout my work, Professor Albert M. Craig of Harvard University was a wise and penetrating critic, and Professor Edwin O. Reischauer, also of Harvard, provided detailed comments on the manuscript. Professor Ernest R. May of Harvard took a steady interest in my work, and I am indeed grateful for his balanced direction. I would also like to thank the members of the United States-Far Eastern Policy Studies Committee of the History Department of Harvard for their constant financial support, as well as the Fulbright-Hays Foreign Studies Program for funding a year of language study in Tokyo.

I am also obligated to Professor William M. Berg for permission to publish quotations from his thesis, ''The United States and the Breakdown of Naval Limitations, 1934–1939''; to Harvard College Library for permission to publish quotations from the diary of J. Pierrepont Moffat and the journal of William Phillips; to the President and Fellows of Harvard College for permission to publish quotations from *Franklin D. Roosevelt and Foreign Affairs,* vols. 1–3; to Her Majesty's Stationery Office for permission to reproduce material from S. W. Roskill's *The War at Sea,* vol. 1; to Tokyo daigaku shakai kagaku kenkyūjo for permission to publish quotations from the papers of Admiral Katō Kanji; to Misuzu shobo for permission to publish quotations from *Gendai shi shiryō,* vols. 8–11; to the Taiheiyō sensō genin kenkyūbu of the Nihon kokusai seiji gakkai for permission to publish quotations from *Taiheiyō sensō e no michi,* vols. 1–8. Quotations from Crown copyright records in the Public Record Office appear by permission of the Controller of Her Majesty's Stationery Office.

Finally, I would like to thank my wife, who has fulfilled her manifold duties as editor, typist, teacher, and homemaker with verve and style in Cambridge, Tokyo, Washington, London, and Amherst.

SEP

Amherst, Massachusetts
Summer, 1973

Contents

Illustrations

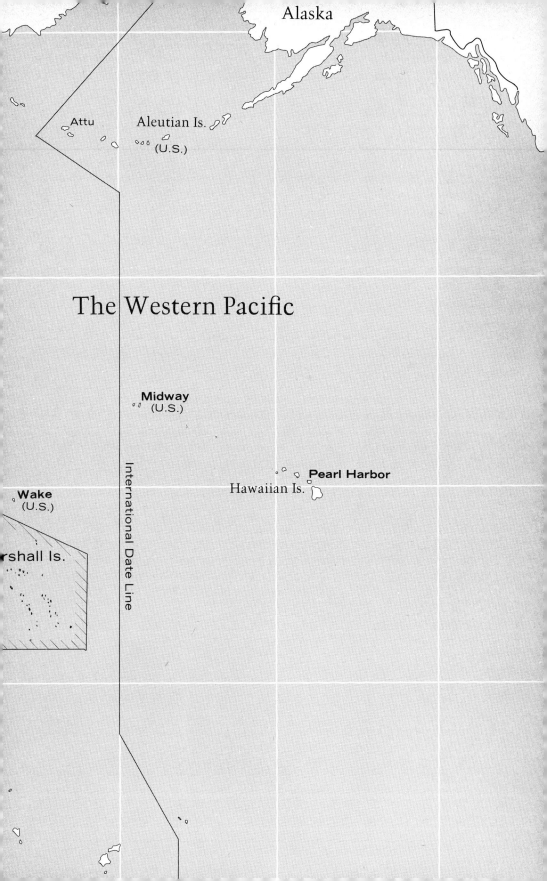

Alaska

Attu

Aleutian Is.
(U.S.)

The Western Pacific

Midway
(U.S.)

Pearl Harbor
Hawaiian Is.

Wake
(U.S.)

rshall Is.

International Date Line

Race to Pearl Harbor

Harvard Studies in American-East Asian Relations   5

The Harvard Studies in American-East Asian Relations are sponsored and edited by the Committee on American-Far Eastern Policy Studies of the Department of History at Harvard University.

Introduction

Viewed from the present, the decade of the twenties seems like a golden interlude, bracketed by decades of war and depression. At least in one way, those years were indeed unique: the great powers were able to make and maintain a system of international naval disarmament. At the Washington Conference in 1921, representatives of the United States, Japan, Great Britain, France, and Italy created a set of naval limitations and, building on that foundation, established a stable political arrangement that was to preserve the peace for more than a decade. The system rested on a series of treaties that together comprised the Washington settlement. In the Four-Power Pact, the United States, Japan, Britain, and France promised to respect each other's Pacific possessions; in the Nine-Power Treaty, these four countries joined five others in pledging to honor China's territory and to help it modernize. These international agreements replaced the old order that had produced gradual economic penetration of China, imperial rivalries, and the race in naval arms.

THE NAVAL DISARMAMENT SYSTEM

During the Washington Conference, the diplomats also tried to build a naval balance that would provide security for each of the signatories. The result was the Five-Power Pact or Washington naval treaty, a set of formulas, tonnage restrictions, and gun limitations that froze the navies of the five great powers at new, low levels. First, each nation agreed to a tonnage ceiling for battleships, battle cruisers, and carriers. These limitations on total tonnage of capital ships were not enough by themselves to produce a naval balance, however, since one nation might still gain a decisive advantage by building fewer ships that were larger and more heavily gunned; consequently, the representatives also agreed that new battleships would be limited to 35,000 tons in displacement and to sixteen-inch guns. The negotiators also restricted the tonnage and guns of aircraft carriers. These overall tonnage agreements provided for parity between the United States and Great Britain, whereas Japan received only a 6/10 ratio vis-à-vis each of the Anglo-Saxon countries. As compensation for this inferiority, the Americans and British agreed not to fortify their western Pacific bases, so as to make operations in Asian waters more difficult. This five-power naval pact with its nonfortification clause provided the girders which supported the whole Washington treaty edifice.

Through these treaties, the powers brought to an end their competition in capital ships, but immediately a new race started in cruiser construction. After one fruitless try for a truce in 1927, the Americans, Japanese, and British met at London in 1930 to complete the system of naval restrictions. During these talks, the Japanese insisted that they needed more cruisers than a 6/10 ratio would provide, and the American Secretary of State, Henry L. Stimson, accepted a complicated arrangement to satisfy the Japanese. The United States, Stimson promised, would not build the last three of its eighteen heavy cruisers until 1936, 1937, and 1938. Consequently, Japan would have a 7/10 ratio in cruisers until 1936, when the treaty would be renegotiated. Japan also got a 7/10 ratio in destroyers and parity in submarines, although tonnage levels in these classes were set at such low levels that Japan's gains were minimal. In addition, the London Treaty reduced capital ship tonnage by about ten percent and set the number of battleships at fifteen for the United States and Great Britain and nine for Japan. Thus, in 1930 the system of naval disarmament was complete, with each nation knowing not only what number of ships the other countries would have, but also how powerful each capital ship would be. The incentive for naval competition was gone.

Although naval disarmament was popular with politicians and with their constituents, professional navy men in all three countries were outraged. The London settlement differed from the Washington naval treaty in that it did not reflect the actual strengths of the three navies. In 1921, Great Britain had forty-three completed battleships, including a number approaching obsolescence, and the British had no desire to add to their enormous fleet. The United States at that time had thirty-three capital ships either finished or in the process of being built, while the Japanese had eighteen afloat or under construction. Therefore, the 10/10/6 American, British, and Japanese ratio reflected reality. But the 10/7 ratio established at London meant that Japan would have to stop cruiser construction and allow the United States to catch up. As a result, the Japanese navy was unhappy with the London Treaty.[1]

The American navy had a similar response. During Senate hearings on the London Treaty, twenty-two active and retired naval officers testified against it. The roots of their dissatisfaction were similar to those that inspired Japan's admirals to protest, for professional naval men in all countries thought in surprisingly similar terms. Both the American and Japanese admirals believed that a force attacking across the wide reaches of the Pacific needed at least twice the strength of a defending fleet. In fact, the General Board of the United States Navy had asserted in 1921 that "Great Britain's former ratio of 2 to 1 is the only safe ratio for the United States to maintain . . . toward Japan."[2] The navy had therefore settled for the 10/6 figure at Washington with reluctance.

The London Conference brought this issue to a head. On May 27, 1930, Captain J. R. Taussig told the Senate Foreign Relations Committee that "The 5–3 ratio combined with our agreement to limit fortifications in the Far East gave us only a sporting chance for victory. [Given any] advance in the Japanese ratio beyond the 60 percent I feel . . . our chances for victory would be very slim.'' There was a similar reaction in Britain. The Admiralty Board, which was the high command of the Royal Navy, protested the limit of fifty cruisers on the grounds that England had long sea lanes which it had to protect against surface raiders. A maverick Tory, Winston S. Churchill, charged that the treaty would make Britain "an inferior sea power," but the milder leader of the Tories, Stanley Baldwin, confined himself to a brief inquiry on the cruiser settlement. By the end of 1930, the British and American governments had accepted the London Treaty, in spite of the discontent.[3]

On the other side of the world, the General Staff of the Japanese navy insisted that an overall 7/10 ratio was the minimum necessary to ensure victory, and it therefore tried to prevent ratification of the treaty. A tenet of Japan's strategic doctrine had long been that a defending force needed to be seventy percent as strong as an attacking fleet to make certain of success. At the Washington Conference, Japan had agreed to accept a 6/10 ratio in capital ships because it was allowed to build an unlimited number of cruisers, destroyers, and submarines. By using these craft to deliver repeated torpedo attacks, Japan's admirals planned, if necessary, to reduce the American fleet as it advanced across the Pacific until the strengths of the two fleets were equal. Although the London naval treaty did give Japan a 7/10 ratio in auxiliaries, the General Staff considered the authorized numbers of these light craft to be too small to ensure the success of its attrition strategy.[4] Japan's politicians, however, were able to override the admirals, and Japan ratified the London Treaty.

The alarm of the admirals in the three countries highlighted the strengths of the system. Each country accepted a certain amount of risk, since absolute security for one meant peril for the others. The British and Americans placed in trust with Japan both their trade in Asia and their possessions in China and the Philippines. In return, Japan accepted a naval ratio that created a naval balance in the mid-Pacific. Since the British and Americans could not fortify their harbors at Hong Kong and Manila, they could advance into the western Pacific only by placing their fleets in danger. Conversely, the unfavorable ratio made very difficult a Japanese advance on Singapore, India, Australia, or Hawaii. Thus, while the English and American admirals feared for their nations' trade and possessions in East Asia, their Japanese counterparts worried about the Anglo-American preponderance in ships of the line. Such was the base on which the Washington treaties rested.

If the Nine-Power Treaty on China had remained intact, the navalists' fears might have been of little consequence, but one year after the London Conference the Japanese army invaded Manchuria. In the late twenties, the Chinese Nationalists had begun a drive to unify their country and to recover full sovereignty over the provinces like Manchuria in which the great powers had established spheres of interest. Japan's Kwantung army reacted to the Nationalists' initiative by creating the puppet state of Manchukuo.[5] Japan's action was clearly a breach of the Nine-Power Treaty, and the Washington system implied that, in case of a violation of the treaties by one signatory, the remaining powers would consult and possibly even discipline the offender. Although in combination the United States and Britain certainly had enough naval strength in 1931 to threaten Japan with reprisals, the Western countries lacked the will to fight. The Americans and British simply sent diplomatic protests and refused to recognize Manchukuo.

Frustrated by the ineffectiveness of these measures, Secretary of State Stimson warned Japan that further transgressions against the nine-power guarantees to China might force the United States to scrap the disarmament sections of the treaties. In a public letter to Senator William E. Borah, the Republican chairman of the Senate Foreign Relations Committee, Stimson declared that all three of the Washington treaties were "interdependent." He warned: "The willingness of the American government [at the Washington Conference] to surrender its then commanding lead in battleship construction and to leave its positions at Guam and in the Philippines without further fortification, was predicated upon, among other things, the self-denying covenants contained in the Nine Power Treaty." [6] Thus, when the administration of Franklin Delano Roosevelt took office, the house built at Washington had collapsed.

Although the prospects for disarmament seemed poor, Roosevelt did not give them up as hopeless. Great Britain's leaders, hard-pressed in Europe, also sought to preserve restrictions on naval building. Yet their efforts failed, for reasons that this study will show, and disarmament came to an end at the Second London Naval Conference of 1935. This study will also demonstrate that the breakdown of disarmament led to an exhausting naval race, which in turn influenced Japan's decision for war. This thesis naturally challenges some widely shared assumptions about the causes of the Pacific war, although I am not attempting a comprehensive reinterpretation of that much contested question, for the naval race was only one among many reasons for the war.

THE PEARL HARBOR DEBATE

One group of historians, the revisionists, lay most of the blame for the war at the feet of Franklin D. Roosevelt, whom they portray as a lying politician who was determined to entangle the United States in war, in order to save the British Empire. And they argue that Roosevelt's aggressive attitude toward Japan began during his first administration when the new President rejected Japan's offer to tighten naval limitations further at the London Naval Conference of 1935 and decided instead to build a huge fleet. In 1941, they argue, Roosevelt finally destroyed the peace by denouncing Japanese expansion in China and Southeast Asia, holding the American fleet in a threatening position at Pearl Harbor, and embargoing strategic materials.[7]

The hinge on which the revisionists' case hangs is their interpretation of Japanese foreign policy. In fact, some students of Japan's prewar policy argue that the United States forced Japan down the path toward war. They portray Japanese policy makers as rational men, who sought the traditional, limited goal of building a strong and secure nation, but found themselves resisted at every turn by the Western powers. While these writers are critical of Japan's actions in China, they also assert that the United States' oil embargo of July 1941 drove Japan into a war of desperation in which it had "almost no hope of victory." In these works, the Japanese navy usually appears as a force for moderation.[8]

In the course of this book, however, it will become clear that Japan's admirals wanted to build a great fleet and to expand into China and Southeast Asia, even at the risk of war with the United States. Consequently, they attacked the Washington and London naval treaties, drew the Pacific powers into a violent naval race, and helped bring conflict where peace had reigned. Thus, this book lends support to those who still maintain that the Japanese military establishment was primarily responsible for the Pacific war.[9]

This book should also modify the often caricatured portraits of Franklin D. Roosevelt and Neville Chamberlain.[10] Roosevelt was neither an evil conspirator nor a far-sighted statesman, but rather a hard-pressed politician whose difficulties with Congress led to a fateful delay in American naval building. Similarly, Chamberlain did not appease the aggressors solely because of his own stupidity, arrogance, or anticommunism. The British Prime Minister was trapped between Britain's economic frailty and its need to rearm; appeasement was a policy of necessity, not preference.

In sum, a thorough investigation into the origins of the Pacific war requires that one dig beneath the mounds of diplomatic detritus cast off by the negotiators in 1940 and 1941. This book considers one of the less proximate, but more fundamental, causes of the war, namely, the breakdown of the disarmament negotiations, the ensuing spiral of armament building that finally snared the leaders of Japan, the United States, and Great Britain in a trap of their own making. In a world of revolutionary nationalism and runaway technology, this account should serve as a cautionary tale.

PART ONE   Japan's Decision

1   The Background of Japan's Disarmament Policy

In 1934, the Japanese government demanded naval equality with the two strongest naval powers, Great Britain and the United States. This decision seems surprising for an island nation poor in natural resources and new to the ranks of the great powers. The reasons for the demand were numerous, stemming from both external developments and internal changes that occurred during the turbulent four years from 1930 to 1934.

In the fall of 1931, the Japanese army invaded Manchuria and set Japanese diplomacy on a new course. Newspapers and radio brought the welcome news of these victories to a people distracted by economic depression and political assassinations, and in the general election of February 1932, Japanese voters gave overwhelming support to the Seiyūkai party, which advocated a "positive policy" for both economic and foreign problems. At the request of the army, the Diet decided unanimously to develop Manchuria as a state under Japanese suzerainty.[1]

The execution of this policy in 1932 and 1933 brought Japan and the West into conflict. When the League of Nations began to investigate the Manchurian question, Japan countered by formally recognizing Manchukuo, its new puppet state, and by embarking on a new course of "independent diplomacy." To support this new policy, Japan's armed services decided on a major rearmament effort. If the military buildup were carried far enough, of course, it might require an end to naval limitations. Before Japan's leaders decided to risk the solitary path of armed isolation, they decided to try a diplomatic offensive. But by 1933 the diplomats had failed to blunt Western criticism, and Japan had withdrawn from the League.[2] Once again, Japan's isolation required a reassessment of its security policy. To understand the reaction of the Japanese cabinet under these circumstances, it is necessary to understand both the men who determined the policies and the institutions in which they worked.

THE JAPANESE POLITICAL PROCESS

At the pinnacle of the state was the Emperor—in theory the source of all power, in practice the holder of none. To the masses, according to the official doctrine of the Education Ministry, he was both the embodiment of all that was good in the world and a link to the power of the universe; to government officials, he was the symbol of the state. Hirohito, the holder of the title since

1925, was a reserved, scholarly man who frequently protested the more danger-ous proposals of the military. Such protests sent his courtiers, including the Lord Privy Seal, the Chamberlains, and the Imperial Household Minister, into fits of worry over possible military reprisal, for there were imperial princes who were eager to take the throne in a coup.[3]

In the military services, a few officers considered themselves "double patri-ots," since they were willing not only to offer their lives in battle for the Em-peror, but also to die removing traitors from around the throne. During the feudal period, an inferior had been able to make a public protest only on pain of death; therefore, when conditions became intolerable, the loyal samurai would commit suicide, thereby hoping to induce his master to self-reflection. Some of these young officers combined this tradition of protest with emulation of the romantic leaders of the Meiji restoration, who left their immediate superiors to serve a transcendent lord, the Emperor. From 1930 on, these officers sought to effect a Showa restoration in which the army and navy would take government out of the hands of the corrupt political parties. Their aim was not to replace the old gov-ernment with their own group, but rather to induce self-reflection and change on the part of the established authorities. Between 1930 and 1932, two abortive rightist coups took place and four major politicians were assassinated, two of them Prime Ministers. As the young officers had expected, the reaction of the responsible military ministers was to call for self-reflection on the part of the authorities rather than to enforce discipline in the ranks. As the Army Minister, Araki Sadao, said when the second Prime Minister was assassinated, these "pure youths . . . did not act for fame or publicity. They acted believing sincerely it was for the good of the country." And the Navy Minister echoed, "When we consider what caused these pure-hearted youths to make this mistake, reverent reflection is proper." The culprits went virtually unpunished.[4]

In the fall of 1933, the Emperor's advisers were again alarmed by reports of an abortive conspiracy, the *shimpeitai* (Divine Soldiers) affair. This outbreak had occurred in a capital already made nervous by the trial of the young naval officers who had assassinated the Prime Minister during the May 15 incident in 1932. The Divine Soldiers leader planned a combined jail break, mass demon-stration, assassination spree, and coup d'état with the help of a naval air officer, other army officers, and an Imperial Prince. While the mass demonstration was creating a diversion, the naval flier would bomb the cabinet session at the Prime Minister's residence; men on the ground would release the assassins, carry out further murders, and install a new cabinet under the leadership of the Imperial Prince. Only after the first demonstrators had arrived in Tokyo did the police dis-cover the plan. Naturally, political leaders around the Emperor were constantly afraid that General Staff officers would join one of these plots and destroy the Meiji constitutional structure.[5]

A less romantic, more sensible image of the samurai was the model for the

great majority of Japanese politicians, who believed that the role of the loyal servant was to carry out his lord's wishes in the daily affairs of government. Endur-
ance and faithfulness in the face of mundane problems were the mark of these
"bureaucratic" servants. Yet the feudal tradition also inspired these men with
considerable bravery, for they made and implemented the government's policies
under a constant threat of assassination. They accepted foreign policies that they
considered dangerous, not because they lacked the courage to oppose them, but
because of their higher duty to the Emperor. This transcendent loyalty motivated
the last of the genro, Prince Saionji Kimmochi.

As a power holder in the Meiji government, Saionji had built up factions in the
bureaucracy and Diet, and after the original leaders of the restoration had died,
he assumed one of their major functions: the selection of new Prime Ministers
when cabinets fell. By 1930, however, he was old and frail, living in Okitsu,
seventy miles from Tokyo, and keeping in touch with the political situation
through his secretary, Baron Harada Kumao. Although Saionji had served as
Prime Minister a number of times, his sense of duty seems to have been at war
with his loyalty to the older ideal of the court noble, for in his early years, he was
well known and loved in the geisha quarters, and he was a great traveler and litterateur. His travels had impressed him with the need to cooperate with the West,
but his desire for a contemplative old age also led him to a horror of crisis. By
1933 Saionji no longer intervened in the daily affairs of government, conserving
his energies for the task of selecting a Prime Minister when the cabinet fell.[6]

Saionji, various attendants in the Imperial Household, and the Chamberlains'
staff had decided in 1912 that the Emperor should not intervene in the making of
public policy. After the young officers' coup attempts, they also resolved that the
military should not be unduly antagonized. These maxims led to the establishment of governments that would pacify the armed services and contribute to the
restoration of discipline. In November 1933, Harada warned a powerful party
politician who was planning a public defense of the London naval treaty that such
a speech would be a mistake when "the government in various ways and at great
pains is quietly not antagonizing the military and is gradually, skillfully succeeding." While urging this low posture, Harada kept alert for rumors of trouble
from the young officers and made weekly reports of their activities to Saionji.
Other men around the Emperor also approved of this general wariness: both
Marquis Kido Kōichi, head of the Secretariat in the Imperial Household Ministry, and Konoye Fumimarō, President of the House of Peers, kept track of the
right wing for Saionji.[7]

Thus, the influential group around the Emperor was determined to keep their
lord safe by appeasing the military. Behind the scenes, Saionji, Harada, Kido,
and Konoye maneuvered to prevent Hirohito from intervening in politics on the
side of internationalism, and sought to avoid a political confrontation between
the party men and the military. To this end, they decided to build a buffer be-

tween the parties, the Emperor, and the military in the form of a cabinet of elders who represented the whole nation. The man they selected to create such a government in 1932 was Saitō Makoto, a retired admiral.

Saitō was a wise choice, since as a soldier he might appeal to the military, and yet he had also proved his ability to work with party politicians during the abortive Geneva Naval Disarmament Conference in 1927. He also came from a samurai family, so that Saionji could appeal to his soldierly traditions. Although in 1932 Saitō was seventy-six and suffering from rheumatism, he kept at his task much longer than anyone had expected. Because he had been a Navy Ministry bureaucrat rather than a fleet officer, he had learned the virtues of patience, caution, and tenacity. Moreover, he was acceptable to both the right wing, for he was one of three directors of the Kokuhonsha, a right-wing society, and to the navy, for as a former Navy Minister and president of the Navy League, he had fought for armament expansion.[8] Despite all these qualifications, the nature of his cabinet and the complexion of the Japanese Diet meant that Saitō would face many difficulties in pacifying the military.

In the cabinet the Prime Minister was simply first among equals. When considering changes in major foreign policies, he had to meet with the Army, Navy, War, and Finance Ministers, in order to seek a consensus. In opposing the more extreme budget demands of the military, Saitō could expect support from Takahashi Korekiyo, the Finance Minister. Takahashi was a former party president and Prime Minister. Descended from a poor artist of the Kano school, he had studied English abroad, and then become a government financial expert after failing in business. Although seventy-eight when entering the Saitō cabinet, he was still extremely vigorous. Cabinet meetings frequently ended in a confrontation between Takahashi, who had public support because of his inflationary policy, and the military ministers. In 1932, under Takahashi's leadership, the Finance Ministry vainly opposed increased naval expenditures, arguing that Japan actually had a 7/10 ratio in existing tonnage and that this ratio would gradually improve as the United States scrapped its overage light craft.[9]

Saitō could also expect some help from Hirota Kōki, his Foreign Minister. As a brilliant student, Hirota had wanted to be a soldier, but when Japan was humiliated diplomatically by the West after the Sino-Japanese War, he decided to enter the Foreign Office. He served his apprenticeship under some of the more internationalist officials in Japan's Foreign Service. His diplomatic training made him very smooth, and he was usually able to round off his statements with enough conditional clauses to make them meaningless. As a student, he had been a member of the Genyōsha, the ancestor of Japanese nationalist and expansionist groups, and he had married the daughter of one of the Genyōsha leaders.[10] In 1933 he accepted expansion in China as desirable, provided it did not involve danger of collision with Russia or the Western powers.

Although both the Finance and Foreign Ministers favored a pacific policy toward Russia and the West, the majority party in the Diet supported a strong diplomatic posture. The Seiyūkai had won a major electoral victory in 1932, but in forming the two subsequent cabinets in 1932 and 1934, Saionji had passed over Suzuki Kisaburō, leader of the majority Seiyūkai faction, because of the latter's violent attitude toward China and the West. Using the power of the purse, the Seiyūkai could have brought down these cabinets, but this action would have alienated Saionji and ruined Suzuki's chances for the succession. Moreover, the Seiyūkai was split into rival factions, with each politician loyal to his leader, and Suzuki's primary rival would not let him challenge the government. The Seiyūkai therefore took a position of "spiritual cooperation" because of the "time of emergency." Yet if the government should make the mistake of opposing the military on an issue that the soldiers considered vital, the Suzuki wing of the Seiyūkai could be expected to cooperate. The minority party, the Minseitō, went along with some of the Seiyūkai's aggressiveness in foreign policy, but it also defended its former policy of disarmament and fiscal responsibility. In the fall of 1933, the Minseitō's defense of their disarmament policy was so vigorous that Harada warned one of the Minseitō leaders against antagonizing the military further. Thus, the Prime Minister and his allies in the cabinet could not expect much help from the parties in the Diet.[11]

To deal with the military ministers, then, Saitō, Takahashi, and Hirota needed a great deal of tact and patience, but the character of the military men did not make the task easy. Representing the army was Araki Sadao, a mercurial general who stressed publicly both the identity of the soldier with the soul of Japan and the need to prepare economically and militarily for a rapidly approaching war with Russia. He gradually strengthened his position in the army by transferring officers hostile to his policy away from Tokyo. By the fall of 1933, he was at the height of his power. The Navy Minister, Ōsumi Mineo, was a less flamboyant figure than Araki, who cooperated with the antidisarmament faction of the navy in such a bumbling way that he antagonized others in government. Pulling in tandem, Araki and Ōsumi frequently threatened to run away with Saitō's "slow motion" cabinet.[12]

SAITŌ AND THE NAVY

Saitō had to fight the military ministers from a vague legal position. Under the ambiguous Meiji Constitution, two governments had grown up: military and civilian, separate and equal. As long as the Meiji leaders had remained strong, there were relatively few problems, since they controlled both governments. As the genrō's grip had slackened, however, there was a struggle over the powers of each government, in which the civilians successfully asserted the cabinet's right to set general military policy on troop strength and organization, while the military retained the right to run actual operations independently. In the twenties, civilian governments were able to force disarmament policies on the military, but with the crisis of confidence in 1930, the soldiers reasserted their "right of supreme command." According to the military interpretation, the Chief of the

General Staff of the army or navy was an equal to the Army or Navy Minister and, on matters concerning national defense, could block the government's policy. Moreover, if the services were displeased with any government action, they could recall their minister from the cabinet and refuse to supply a new one until their demands were met.[13]

The right of supreme command became a political issue in 1930 during the debate over the London Treaty. Although the army and the Seiyūkai gave support, a large group in the navy, known as the "fleet faction," led the attack against the government. The struggle over the London Treaty helped to determine the course of navy politics after 1930, in which Japan's growing isolation encouraged the preparedness advocates of the fleet faction, as opposed to the internationalists of the "treaty faction," culminating in the victory of the fleet faction in 1934.

The fight over the London naval treaty within the Japanese navy was complicated and angry. The Washington naval treaty of 1922 had limited capital ships and aircraft carriers. Japan had then built a new fleet of heavy cruisers and submarines, which gave it superiority over the American fleet in the western Pacific. With the failure of the Geneva Conference in 1927, the United States also began to build in the cruiser category, and in 1930 the limits on heavier ships ended. To avoid a naval race, Japan sought an extension of the 10/6 ratio in capital ships and the establishment of a 10/7 ratio in cruisers and auxiliaries (excluding submarines). After much backing and filling, America and Britain agreed to give Japan a ratio of 10/6.975 in auxiliary categories.

Although this compromise met the Japanese demand for a 10/7 ratio, it did not please the Japanese navy, since for heavy cruisers the 10/6 ratio remained in principle. Moreover, Japan would have to stop all cruiser building for five years to allow the United States to catch up in that category, and Japan also had to reduce its submarine tonnage below what the navy considered to be a safe minimum. Although the responsible ministers in the respective countries had agreed that the new treaty did not compromise national security, navalists in each of the countries were outraged.[14]

The outcry was particularly fierce in Japan, since the government had made public the empire's demand for a 10/7 ratio in cruisers at the outset of the conference. The cutting edge of the attack against the compromise was the fleet faction, whose members had always opposed disarmament. Katō Kanji, as Chief of the Navy General Staff, was the central figure in this attack. He had opposed the Washington naval treaty, and he maintained that the "inferior" ratio system invited Chinese contempt. He urged the naval representatives at the London Conference to make no compromise, assuring them that if the conference broke up, "not only would the world's sympathy be attracted to Japan, even America itself would be ashamed because of the Kellogg Pact, and it would probably fall into the dilemma of not being able to undertake any great naval expansion in the future. Even if they build a 'top fleet' and expand their navy to a size many times that of Japan . . . the result will be a Japanese-English rapprochement, and America will probably become another Germany.'' [15] Katō was supported in this position by Admiral Suetsugu Nobumasa, Vice Chief of the General Staff, and a member of various nationalist groups. The fleet faction also had an Imperial Prince on its side, Prince Fushimi Hiroyasu. When the army gained prestige by appointing Prince Kanin as the Chief of the General Staff, the navy responded by appointing Fushimi to the same position in the navy. Although Fushimi was old and somewhat vague, he proved an able advocate for the fleet faction when given proper direction. [16]

The treaty faction included Admirals Saitō Makoto, Okada Keisuke, Takarabe Takeshi, Yamanashi Katsunoshin, and Hōri Teikichi. Saitō could lend only occasional support during the treaty fight, since he was absent as Governor General of Korea. Saionji and the Emperor's advisers therefore turned to Okada to mediate between the determined Prime Minister, Hamaguchi Osachi, and the angry Chief of Staff, Katō. The fact that the large metropolitan papers supported the compromise aided Okada; even more important, however, was a smashing election victory by Hamaguchi's party over the belligerent Seiyūkai in February 1930. Through his determination and popular support, Hamaguchi, who was known as "The Lion," overcame the navy's initial objections to the compromise. As a sop, Hamaguchi agreed to have the new limits run out in 1936 and to secure greater appropriations for naval air development. Admiral Katō then tried to block imperial approval of the instructions with a direct appeal to the throne, but the Emperor's attendants found the calendar of appointments conveniently full. [17]

The fleet faction did not give up easily. When the Diet opened, Admiral Katō claimed in another appeal to the throne that the "right of supreme command" had been infringed, since the opinions of the Chief of Staff had not been taken into account. But Hamaguchi refused to debate the constitutional question with the Seiyūkai, and the Diet accepted the agreement. The London Treaty also had to be ratified by the main imperial advisory board, the Privy Council. The *éminence grise* of this body, Hiranuma Kiichirō, was president of a major nationalist group, the Kokuhonsha. An ally of Katō, he believed in the inevitability of war between the Anglo-Saxons and the Japanese. But in the Privy Council, Hamaguchi maintained that the naval authorities supported the treaty, and he refused to answer questions about the right of supreme command. Katō and Suetsugu then resigned, and a meeting of the fleet commanders demanded the resignation of the Navy Minister, Takarabe. Finally, all the major leaders of the treaty faction were swept away: Takarabe, Yamanashi, and Hōri. The government promised supplementary naval appropriations and agreed to put followers of the fleet faction into positions vacated by the treaty faction. Although their initial venture into the political arena had failed, the members of the fleet faction increasingly made their views public, thereby breaking their oath as soldiers and sailors of the Emperor.[18]

By the fall of 1933, the leaders of the fleet faction had succeeded in placing Fushimi at the head of the Navy General Staff; subsequently, they moved to strengthen his powers. The Navy Minister had always been stronger than his army counterpart, but in September 1933, he lost his former powers to determine the strength of the navy, to protect citizens abroad, and to dispatch warships; these powers went to the Chief of the Navy General Staff. The General Staff had long sought this reform, and the fleet faction was able to press it on an unwilling Emperor and his advisers because of the continuing danger of military revolt. The navy warned that it was necessary to change the regulations because of the dispute over the "right of supreme command" and because of the abortive coup of May 15, 1932; moreover, Navy Minister Ōsumi claimed that the reform was an internal matter of the navy and not a concern of the cabinet. Saitō and Harada chose not to resist, since the navy was not demanding complete clemency for the group of young naval officers involved in the coup attempt. Saitō argued that the new regulations would simply confirm the fact that the navy's attitude toward the disarmament treaties should be determined cooperatively by the Navy Ministry and the General Staff.[19]

After their success in revising the navy regulations, the fleet faction continued to purge the Navy of their opponents. They sent Admiral Taniguchi Naomasa to the reserve list and moved Admiral Terashima Ken out of the Bureau of Military Affairs of the Navy Ministry. In November, they made their own Admiral Suetsugu commander of the combined fleets. In this post he was in close contact with the young officers of the line and could therefore encourage demonstrations of support for the fleet faction's proposals.[20] By 1933, then, opponents of the disarmament system had taken the helm in the Imperial Navy.

The Saitō government had little strength with which to oppose the military. Each participant in the political process was loyal to the Emperor, but also loyal to the head of his own subgroup and to its aims. The modulation of these aims was a risky business: if Saitō angered the military too greatly, they might depose him by a coup; and even a well-timed threat of a coup by the military might bring a warning from Saionji to conciliate the armed forces. Saitō could expect some help from his Finance and Foreign Ministers in the cabinet, but the leading party in the Diet was not sympathetic. Moreover, the Prime Minister was in a weak constitutional position, because of the whole debate over the London Treaty and "the right of supreme command." In ordinary times, Saitō, as a former admiral, might have appealed to his own followers in the navy, but the London treaty debate and the Manchurian crisis had allowed the fleet faction to take command. Because of his weak position, Saitō's only option was "slow motion." But there were certain problems, such as defense policy, on which he could not postpone action. The decision to establish Manchukuo in the face of Russian and American hostility seriously complicated the calculation of Japan's defense spending, with the army arguing for the necessity of building forces against Russia, and the navy claiming that increased tension with the United States made it necessary to withdraw from the naval treaties and to build a large number of new ships.

By 1933, with Japan's withdrawal from the League of Nations having increased its isolation and the acquisition of a long border with the Soviet Union having complicated the problem of defending Manchukuo, Japan needed a new foreign policy. The debate, which began in the spring of 1933 and continued into the fall, brought into sharp relief the aims of the various ministers and the routes by which they thought Japan ought to proceed. The controversy also showed the weakness of the Saitō government when faced with military intransigence. The arguments about Japan's future foreign policy, which would have been bitter enough by themselves, were further exacerbated by budget problems.

Because of the importance of the issue, Saitō convened a series of meetings of the inner cabinet, composed ordinarily of himself, the Army and Navy Ministers, the Foreign Minister, and the Finance Minister. Despite long discussions and clouds of position papers, Saitō failed to achieve a complete compromise between Japan's diplomatic, military, and financial needs. The government and the military were able to agree on a policy of diplomatic initiatives to ease Japan's isolation and on a new policy for China, but Saitō would not sanction the destruction of the naval disarmament system. During the debate, however, it became clear that the military's ambitions were growing.

THE ARMY'S AMBITIONS

In 1933, the Japanese army made a series of fateful suggestions for dealing with Japan's isolation. In sum, the generals proposed to build a greater Japanese Empire, which would have both the strength and the security of a major world power. Since 1932 the Imperial Army had been establishing a buffer region in North China, building up its military strength, and waiting for the diplomats to secure recognition of Manchukuo. But the drive for recognition had failed, and by 1933 the generals were growing nervous. Stalin's economic plans were progressing, and a stronger Russia might soon want to regain its sphere in North Manchuria. Throughout the debate in the fall of 1933 the Army Minister, Araki Sadao, stressed the need to build forces against Russia, to end the propaganda of the Third International, and to reduce Soviet military strength in the Far East. If necessary, army leaders argued, Japan would have to settle these problems "by drastic measures." Although these proposals seemed defensive in the short term, their overall tone was belligerent.

Japan's generals were more confident about the future of relations with China. If a Russo-Japanese war occurred, Japan would need to have friendly Chinese regimes on its flank. Consequently, they suggested that Japan build buffer zones in China's northern provinces. From the outset, Japan would have to discourage

Western aid to China. Then, by playing one Chinese leader against the other, Japan could exclude Nationalist influence from North China, encourage leaders there who were friendly to Japan, and integrate the economies of North China and Manchukuo.[21]

According to the Army Minister, economic mobilization was absolutely necessary for Japan's future security. To this end, he asked that the Saitō cabinet adopt an internal policy that would purify national thought and lay the economic foundation for national defense. Araki also argued that, "In order to have enough of the raw materials . . . which will be lacking in wartime, we should plan to acquire and use foreign resources existing in our expected sphere of influence, such as Sakhalin, China, and the Southern Pacific." [22]

Despite the size of their ambitions, Japan's generals were not overly concerned about probable Western resistance. The army leaders argued that neither Great Britain nor the United States had the military strength to stop Japan's advance on the continent, and in any case, the Western powers lacked the will to fight. Japan's generals believed that concern for their large Chinese investments and their European flank would check the British, and that public opinion would stay the United States hand. Nevertheless, the generals argued, Japan should continue to build a navy sufficient to deter the Americans, even if such construction threatened the limitation system. If a favorable revision of the naval treaties were not possible, they maintained, "we will preserve our national security without taking to heart the breakup of the [naval disarmament] conference, if that becomes inevitable." Throughout the debate, the army representatives admitted that skillful diplomacy might influence the West to accept Japan's ambitions, but if a diplomatic settlement were not possible, then it was clear that the Japanese navy should be ready to fight.[23] To conduct "independent diplomacy" in China and to deter Russia, both the army and the navy would have to grow stronger. If necessary, then, the army was willing to see the navy end the limitation system and embark on a naval race.

THE NAVY AND PREPAREDNESS

The leaders of the Japanese navy were as concerned as their counterparts in the army with the need for a firm foreign policy, and their recommendations closely resembled the army's proposals. But on one point they were wary: the army's proposed Russian policy. Japan's admirals warned that a war against Russia might raise up a hostile coalition that would be impossible to defeat, for Britain and the United States might seize on a Russo-Japanese war to intervene.

The admirals were less concerned about Chinese intervention, since they believed that the army's tactics of divide-and-rule would solve the China problem. Gradually Japan could separate North China from Chiang Kai-shek's influence and integrate it economically with the Japanese Empire. In addition, the admirals argued that Japan should "suppress foreign aid" to China and keep Western influence out of South China by devising "positive measures" of its own toward this region at a later date. On China policy, then, the navy not only stood with the army but appeared even more ambitious.

But the danger of Anglo-American intervention in a continental war remained. The Navy Minister, Ōsumi Mineo, urged his colleagues to seek British and American recognition of the new realities in East Asia. While the diplomats talked, however, Japan would have to continue its naval buildup. If war came with the United States and Britain over the issue of Japan's continental policy, Japan must be ready, and the navy leaders argued that full preparedness would mean the end of the existing naval ratios.[24]

During the weeks when they were proposing new foreign policies, Japan's admirals were also beginning a major drive for increased arms spending. In late September 1933, Ōsumi asked the cabinet to adopt a new naval policy before the next disarmament conference. Japan, he said, should either seek a large increase in its naval ratio or perhaps even full equality. The smallest ratio that the navy would consider was 10/7 in capital ships, 10/8 in heavy cruisers, and complete equality in light cruisers, destroyers, and submarines.[25] Such would be the naval cost of the ambitious foreign policy proposals being debated by the military.

The civilian members of the government resisted the idea of demanding a larger ratio or full equality, but Ōsumi refused to give up. Throughout October 1933, he asked his colleagues for permission to explain in public the need for equality in the right to arms and for an end to the unfavorable treaty limits. If the powers would not accept Japan's quest for a just disarmament agreement, he argued, then the Japanese people must realize that "we will face a situation in which there will be no pact." [26] But the cabinet and the Foreign Office were not ready to condemn the limitation treaties without a full hearing, and Ōsumi had to be content with success on another front.

Throughout 1933, Ōsumi had also been pressing for a larger naval budget, and he increased these efforts when it became clear that the administration of Franklin D. Roosevelt was channeling funds into a new American building program. By the late fall of 1933, Prime Minister Saitō was in a receptive mood, for he feared that a refusal to increase military spending would lead to trouble with the young officers. But the Finance Minister Takahashi Korekiyo, who was worried about deficit spending and aid for the suffering farm villages, tried to cut the navy's budget request in half. Outraged, Ōsumi threatened resignation and a full cabinet crisis. In the end, the government agreed to float more bonds, to ignore the plight of the farmers, and to raise the military's share of the budget from 36 to 45 percent of the total outlay.[27]

Thus, the seizure of Manchuria had thrown Japan into isolation and increased its defense problems. The military proposed to deal with the situation by further expansion in China, in order to become self-sufficient and secure. In the process of this expansion, however, Japan would necessarily anger its neighbors, the Russians and Chinese, as well as the more distant naval powers, the United States and Britain. If the advance were to succeed, therefore, the Japanese might first have to overthrow the naval limits. Before making such a fateful decision, Saitō, Hirota, and the other civilians in the government wanted to try for a diplomatic settlement.

THE DIPLOMATIC CAMPAIGN

The Foreign Ministry was concerned that military meddling in China and an attack on the naval limitation system might produce a severe crisis with the West. Consequently, it proposed to reassure the British and Americans that Western interests in Asia would not suffer even if Japan continued to improve its position. Hirota hoped to secure tacit Western approval of Japan's new role in Asia by making bilateral agreements with Britain and the United States. Then, having eased Japan's isolation, he might be able to convince the navy to abandon its campaign against disarmament.

In a strong statement in early 1933, Tōgō Shigenori, head of the European-American desk at the Foreign Ministry, explained the need for an accommodation with the United States, Britain, and Russia. Since Japan had alarmed the powers by advancing into Manchuria, he argued, it had to restore its international reputation in order to secure the capital needed to develop Manchukuo. Tōgō believed that an understanding was possible. Since British and American interests in East Asia were mainly economic, the Western nations would welcome a Japanese pledge to maintain an open door for both trade and investment in Manchuria and China. In return, Tōgō hoped that the Americans would end their "moral guardianship" of China.[28] If a Pacific understanding could be achieved on these terms, then Japan might avoid a naval race.

Tōgō's superiors did not share his hopeful view of relations with the West, but they did agree that a diplomatic campaign was in order. Vice Foreign Minister Shigemitsu Mamoru believed that the Americans were encouraging Russia to send troops to the Far East and that the Americans and Russians might unite against Japan during the revision of the naval treaties in 1935. Foreign Minister Hirota shared Shigemitsu's worries about the United States and Russia. As he told Harada: "I want to work diplomatically so as to avoid a time of difficulties. . . . Won't there come a time when America, recognizing Russia and bringing along China, may make Japan say 'uncle'? I want to do something vis-à-vis Russia, China, and America in order to avoid facing such a situation." A détente would ease diplomatic isolation, avoid a crisis over China, and strengthen the civilians' hands on disarmament. Ultimately, Hirota and Saitō were able to secure permission from the military to seek a détente with the West.[29]

After a number of meetings, the inner cabinet produced a new foreign policy for Japan. Essentially it was a compromise between the military's desire to expand and the civilians' wish to negotiate, for the Japanese government decided to do both. The inner cabinet agreed that the empire would seek its goals by diplomatic means, but that it would also increase its military strength to deter any threat from the United States, Britain, or Russia. The diplomats did accept an advance on the continent, in that China would be asked to agree to tripartite economic cooperation between itself, Manchuria, and Japan, with the latter in control. However, the diplomats were allowed to reassure the Americans about their interests in Manchukuo.[30] Most important, the Foreign Ministry secured leeway to seek a negotiated settlement of the disarmament question. But the time for diplomatic maneuver was limited, for the admirals continued to agitate against the naval treaties. The diplomats would have to achieve an understanding with the West before the army resumed its China advance and before the naval talks began.

In early 1934, Hirota started his campaign to improve relations with Washington. At first he considered sending a goodwill mission to the United States, but both his own ambassador and the American Secretary of State, Cordell Hull, opposed the idea. Hirota settled for an "informal" greeting to be delivered to the Americans by Saitō Hiroshi, his new and enthusiastic ambassador to Washington. Hirota phrased his note in lofty generalities: there had been years of friendly relations between Japan and the United States, and no problems existed that could not be solved by peaceful means and mutual understanding. More significantly, Hirota added that Japan had no designs on any other country. Hull replied that the United States also wanted to settle all problems in a friendly spirit and that he was happy that neither country had aggressive designs on the territory of others. On March 3, 1934, to indicate the fine state of Japanese-American relations, Hirota published these notes.[31]

From the start, however, Japan's attempt to improve relations with the United States and Britain had no firm basis. The government's decision to establish tripartite cooperation between Japan, China, and Manchuria in economic and defense matters, and the army's plan to separate North China from Nationalist control, could not be realized without undercutting Hirota's promise of peaceful diplomacy. Furthermore, the decision to exclude Western aid from China promised to raise another troublesome issue. Western aid to China was in fact growing, if only slowly. Before 1934, the League of Nations and the United States had been providing some technical and financial assistance to China. In early 1934, the Western nations also began to give military aid to the Nationalists. A German military mission undertook to reorganize the Chinese army, and Americans and Italians began to train the fledgling Chinese air force. The Japanese Navy General Staff became concerned by the reports of Chinese air development and urged both the exclusion of foreign "infiltration" from China and the substitution of Japanese influence and advisers.

Western intervention in China continued on the financial front as well. In early March 1934, Consul Suma Yakichirō returned from China with a request from Jean Monnet, the director of China's new Development Bank, for Japanese participation in an international loan to China. Hirota asked Finance Minister Takahashi whether Japan had the financial ability to take part and was told that it did not. Hirota then informed Monnet that China had misused such aid in the past for the purpose of setting one power against another and waging internal wars. For these reasons, Hirota asserted, Japan opposed the loan, which he added would fail without the support of the "stabilizing power" of the East.[32]

Hirota also advised Japan's diplomats abroad that Japan's China policy had taken a new turn. In all problems the diplomats were asked to take the following line: because the situation in China was extraordinary, international law did not apply there, and because Japanese power was the sole foundation for the maintenance of Asian peace, Japan would take the lead in handling the China problem. For its part, China must stop playing power against power. The Western nations could continue to trade with China, but they should not supply planes, advisers, or military goods. Thus, while seeking an understanding with the West, Hirota was also implementing Japan's new China policy.[33]

The first public hint of the new China policy came in Hirota's opening address to the Diet in January 1934, in which he used phrases that were later to become axiomatic in the press: "The empire, as the cornerstone supporting peace in Asia, bears that entire burden, and we must not forget it for a single day." [34] Then on April 17, 1934, Amō Eiji, the Foreign Office press secretary, made the mistake of revealing the new line to the public. Japan, he said, had a duty to preserve order in East Asia, which it would share only with a reunified China. Western aid would lead to spheres of influence in China and would encourage the Chinese to play one power against another. Although Hirota had Amō reassure the West that Japan would not meddle with China's independence or the open door, the damage was done.[35] The diplomats' hopes for an atmosphere of good will at the naval talks lay in ruins.

Because of Amō's indiscretion, Hirota feared that the Americans and the British would raise the whole question of China at the coming naval talks. During the Amō incident, Morishima Gorō, head of the first section of the Foreign Ministry's Asia desk, warned that public discussion of the security pledges contained in the Washington treaties would stir up the Chinese. Hirota immediately instructed his ambassadors in the West to keep the question of Chinese security off the agenda for the naval talks, and he made clear that Japan would not sacrifice its China policy to the cause of détente: "It is natural that the empire, which was forced to withdraw from the League when its opinions unfortunately differed from those of the powers concerning East Asian problems . . . cannot recognize the consideration of East Asian problems at an international conference, today when it is reaffirming its determination to carry out its mission in Asia independently." [36]

The Japanese ambassador to Washington, Saitō Hiroshi, also feared that Amō's indiscretion would undermine his determined efforts to establish a Pacific détente. As a result, while trying to ensure that China would remain off the disarmament agenda, he also made a personal bid to set Japanese-American relations on an entirely new foundation. At a secret meeting in Hull's apartment, Saitō argued that China's failure to reform had invalidated the Washington treaties and that it would be "worse than useless" to consider Oriental problems at the naval conference. On this point Hull remained noncommittal.

As a first step toward real Pacific harmony, Saitō continued, Japanese-American relations would be simplified if both countries pledged jointly to preserve the open door for trade, to abjure aggressive designs, and to recognize that the United States in the eastern Pacific and Japan in the western Pacific "are principal stabilizing factors and [that] both Governments will exercise their best and constant efforts so far as lies within their proper and legitimate power to establish a reign of law and order in the regions geographically adjacent to their respective countries." Such a statement, Saitō argued, would end American suspicion about Japan's continental ambitions and, at the same time, convince the Japanese people that the United States would neither interfere with Japan's efforts to establish order in East Asia nor block Japan's "progress externally." [37]

In effect, Saitō had asked the Americans to recognize that Japan would police Asia, just as the United States oversaw Latin America; he wanted the Americans to make a fundamental reassessment of their Asian policy, give up their support of China, and end the historic dispute that had troubled Japanese-American relations for three decades. But he was unsuccessful. Hull replied that Roosevelt had abandoned the troublesome policies which previous Presidents had applied to Latin America, and that Americans did not believe they had a right or a duty to maintain order in neighboring lands. Furthermore, progress in weaponry meant that "the more highly civilized nations" like America and Japan should cooperate to maintain peace, whereas Japan appeared to want to establish an "overlordship of the Orient" or " preferential trade rights." If Japan in fact had no aggressive plans, Hull suggested, then the Japanese would not need to increase their arms spending. President Roosevelt congratulated Hull on his "magnificent" stand. [38]

The ambassador to London, Matsudaira Tsuneo, a more experienced and cautious diplomat than the newly appointed Saitō, was in time able to secure assurances that the powers would not raise East Asian questions during the negotiations. He waited until the British had urged Japan to send representatives to London for preliminary conversations. Matsudaira then indicated that Japan was in no hurry to comply, stating that the Japanese would oppose "to the bitter end" a discussion of East Asian security problems. After consulting with the Americans, Prime Minister J. Ramsay MacDonald assured Matsudaira that both Britain and the United States thought it best to exclude political problems from the conference. On this basis, Japan accepted Britain's invitation to send negotiators to London. [39] Matsudaira had gained only a token victory, however, for the evil effects of Amō's statement and Saitō's initiative remained. Rather than being reassured, the Americans approached the disarmament talks with heightened concern about Japan's ultimate intentions.

By the spring of 1934, the future of naval limitations seemed bleak indeed. Because of the terrorist incidents, civilian rule was in abeyance in Japan. Saionji, fearful of a successful coup by the right and the military, had stopped selecting party leaders to head the government. The new administrations were bureaucratic cabinets, which had a seemingly simple task: to pacify the right wing and appease the military. If the military leaders were satisfied, Saionji reasoned, they would not join with the radical right to overthrow the constitution. The defensive policy of the government meant that a strong drive mounted by the military and the right might well be effective. Thus, the winds of international and internal politics blew ill for the advocates of naval disarmament.

Through the winter of 1933–1934 the military had kept the civilian authorities cowed, strengthened their hold on China policy, and secured more money for arms to meet the problem of diplomatic isolation. In early 1934, in order to avoid a crisis at the disarmament talks, the civilian ministers had tried to secure tacit Western approval of Japan's new role in Asia, hoping that, with Japan's diplomatic isolation eased, the navy might forgo an attack on the naval treaties. But Hirota's campaign for a détente, begun in an atmosphere of hope, had ended in failure. By the middle of 1934, the Saitō government was floundering, and Saionji selected as Prime Minister another moderate admiral, Okada Keisuke. During these same spring months, the leaders of the Japanese navy bided their time, cemented their understanding with the army, and planned an offensive against the treaties.

2 New Weapons, New Strategy, and No Limitations

In the spring of 1934, the leaders of the Japanese navy confirmed their decision to end the era of disarmament, and their motives for this decision were numerous. The lessons of history and their own analysis of the international situation played a part in their decision. The development of new and better weapons, however, provided the main reason for their new course, for they believed that technological progress gave them the ability to build a navy that could successfully defend an empire in the western Pacific. New weapons opened a seemingly broad highway to imperial glory, beside which the footpaths of peace and disarmament seemed tame and unworthy.

During the years of disarmament, Japan had built its navy up to treaty limits, while the Americans had not. Consequently, Japan had eighty percent of America's total naval tonnage, and the Japanese expected to maintain that level through December 1936. This figure of eighty percent was well above the 7/10 ratio on which the Japanese naval experts had insisted at the Washington and London Conferences. But in 1933, the Roosevelt administration began to threaten this comfortable arrangement by renewed building. And in the spring of 1934, the Vinson Bill authorized the President to bring the American navy up to treaty limits by 1942.[1] This projected building, linked with actual new American construction of two carriers and nine cruisers, threatened the Japanese navy with a possible loss of their reassuring 8/10 ratio. Under these circumstances, continuation of the naval restrictions naturally became less attractive to Japan's admirals.

ALFRED THAYER MAHAN AND THE LESSONS OF HISTORY

Admirals Okada and Saitō would probably have pointed out that the Americans would build to treaty limits only if Japan refused to continue naval limitation. But Katō Kanji and his followers, not Okada and Saitō, were in charge of the naval establishment, and they believed that the future progress of the Japanese Empire required the end of disarmament. Katō, Suetsugu, and the rest of the fleet faction were outspoken sailors, whose thoughts on navies and disarmament followed certain pseudoscientific strategic formulas. They based these so-called ''principles'' on their own experience and on the writings of the American naval theorist, Captain Alfred Thayer Mahan.

In his work on naval history and strategy, Mahan argued that sea power was the key to the rise of empires. In order to control the sea, he continued, a growing empire had to defeat its rival's fleet in a decisive sea battle. Tactically, the commander who concentrated his ships and firepower against a part of the enemy's strength would be the victor. At the turn of the century, the Japanese navy's major strategic thinkers, Satō Tetsutarō and Akiyama Shinshi, adopted Mahan's arguments as their own, and these ideas continued to dominate Japanese strategic thinking in the 1930s. In 1932, the Navy General Staff published a new translation of Mahan's *Naval Strategy,* and in 1935, one of its officers produced a study on strategy that repeated Mahan's principles. Moreover, at the Navy War College, all officers studied Mahan and Western military history.[2]

Mahan's model, of course, was the British Empire. The English had attained their preeminent international position by seizing the narrow places of the world and by defeating the fleets of rival empires in decisive sea fights. Such battles had been rather scarce in the nineteenth century, raising the fear that accelerating technological progress had made the battleship obsolete. But Great Britain's enormous battle fleet proved its worth during the First World War. England defeated the German High Seas Fleet at Jutland, retained command of the sea, and enforced a blockade against Germany. Thus, despite a century of technological development that produced the torpedo, the mine, the submarine, and the airplane, fleets of capital ships once again proved decisive, and Mahan's star shone forth with renewed luster.

More important, perhaps, than the theoretical influences of Mahan or the example of England were Japan's actual experiences in its wars with China and Russia. In spite of its youth, the Japanese Empire had won two decisive sea battles which had paved the way for its expansion. At the outset of its war with China, the Japanese navy had only two-thirds of China's overall tonnage. Using fewer and smaller ships, but better firepower and tactics, the Japanese navy destroyed China's fleet in 1894. Japan was even more of an underdog against Russia in 1904, when the Japanese admirals had only one-half the number of capital ships that their Russian counterparts had, and less than one-third of the tonnage. A surprise attack and a close blockade led to the destruction of Russia's Far Eastern Fleet. When Russia's Baltic Fleet arrived at Tsushima in the Japan Sea, the Japanese again found themselves outnumbered ten to four. By using superior speed and greater firepower, Japan's commander, Admiral Tōgō Heihachirō, was able to concentrate his fleet's fire on the head of the Russian column. After night fell, his destroyers and torpedo boats attacked the Russians repeatedly, and when the sun rose, ten of the twelve Russian capital ships had sunk or surrendered. Again, superior quality of ships and tactics had overcome quantity, and the Japanese had been able to concentrate superior firepower successfully against parts of the enemy force.[3]

Mahan's geopolitical axioms and the lessons of the Russo-Japanese War ran through the thoughts and words of the doyen of the fleet faction, Katō Kanji. Katō seems to have been a straightforward type of sailor. He had a traditional background: his father had commanded a squad of samurai spear bearers in the feudal domain of Fukui, and Katō had received training in the traditional warrior virtues. Furthermore, he was influenced as a youth by a samurai teacher who had taken part in the Meiji restoration. On one occasion, he recommended a book on *The Meaning and Nature of Bushidō* to a group of students, and at the time of the London Conference, Katō threatened to commit *seppuku* (ritual suicide) if his demands were not met.[4]

Mahan's argument that sea power was the basis for empires evidently appealed to Katō, and he believed that the old empires were holding back young Japan through disarmament restrictions. On June 19, 1926, he gave a formal lecture to the Emperor on the status of arms and national influence in the Pacific. He declared that the urge to dominate was basic to human nature and that the rise and fall of empires comprised the whole history of the Pacific. The United States and Britain had replaced Spain and Portugal while Japan had been idle. After 1868, Japan started catching up. With its naval power existing in 1898, Japan could have prevented the United States from taking Hawaii, he claimed, but the Japanese people and government had lacked an awareness of the value of such places. Even worse, Japan let the United States advance to Guam and the Philippines on the empire's very "doorstep." At the Washington Conference, Japan had compounded these "failures" by agreeing to limit battleship construction and to end the Anglo-Japanese Alliance. America, he declared, imposed this naval inferiority on Japan, sought to monopolize communications in the Pacific, and fortified Hawaii in an attempt to achieve "capitalistic, imperialistic domination" of China and the Orient.[5]

Katō had gone as an adviser to the Washington Conference. During the conference he argued that it was unfair for the West to freeze Japan's naval influence at one point in time. In the specialists' committee, Katō had fought so strenuously for a 7/10 ratio in capital ships that the chiefs of the delegations had had to adjourn the committee and settle the matter themselves. A few years after the conference, Katō wrote that the Western nations had ganged up against Japan and secured an "Anglo-American hegemony." A new treaty was necessary, he said, but he predicted that it would be difficult to make an agreement which would conform to every country's defense needs and economic abilities. Therefore, he concluded that naval equality was best, especially since it matched the modern ideal of human equality. A new naval treaty, Katō argued, should establish a common international standard for the five great powers; this standard would be as low as possible, and all countries would then determine what weapons they needed within that tonnage limit.[6] This proposal, written in the mid-twenties, became the position of the Japanese navy in the spring of 1934.

Katō evidently thought that Japan could compete successfully with Western navies through skillful technological development and superior morale. He attributed Japan's victories over China and Russia to a combination of careful naval preparation and the ''Japanese spirit.'' After the victory over China, he explained, Japan had built up its fleet as a ''nation united,'' while the navy had made sure that each Japanese ship was superior in all weapons and machinery. He told a meeting of reservists on May 26, 1935, ''We always had what the enemy did not have, and even though we were inferior to the enemy in numbers, our ships were a little superior in quality.'' The result was a victory over Russia that astonished the world.[7]

Thus, the axioms of Mahan and the lessons of history dominated the thought of Katō Kanji. He believed that the struggle for empire was eternal because of the nature of man, and he accepted Mahan's dictum that sea power was the key to imperial success. He pointed to the fact that battles for empire comprised the history of the Pacific and that Japan was very late in entering the contest. Both his own experience during the decisive sea battle at Tsushima and the subsequent British victory at Jutland confirmed Mahan's argument that a single fleet battle could make or mar the fortunes of an empire. Because Japan had twice been victorious in its quest for empire, Katō argued, the two principal sea powers, Britain and the United States, had combined to block the Japanese Empire's growth by establishing the Washington disarmament system. But the lessons of history showed that Japan need not fear naval competition with the West; Japan could always be superior in quality, if not in numbers.

Katō's chief lieutenant, Suetsugu Nobumasa, also disliked the treaties, especially on strategic grounds. After the victory over Russia, the Japanese navy had taken the United States as its hypothetical enemy. At the same time, the navy adopted an ''ambush strategy'' based on the model of the Russo-Japanese War. Japan's admirals would wait for the enemy to arrive in Japanese waters and then sink his fleet in one decisive blow. After the disarmament treaties were signed, the navy modified its strategic plans to include an initial ''attrition stage.'' First, in order to ensure that the American fleet would cross the Pacific, Japan would attack the Philippines in the early stages of the war. Then, in order to make up for Japan's inferior ratio, its submarines and destroyers would wear down the American fleet as it crossed the Pacific. The attrition caused by these light forces would equalize the strength of the two fleets before the decisive battle.[8]

Suetsugu feared that this initial attrition stage of the strategy would not work and that the enemy would arrive in the western Pacific in too much strength. In 1927, during a lecture at the Navy War College, he pointed out that Japanese submarines would have to find the American fleet as it left Pearl Harbor and, in order to succeed in that initial task of reconnaissance, they would have to spread out; yet to carry out their subsequent attacks, they would have to concentrate, and the American fleet might slip undamaged through their net. Suetsugu was also afraid that Japan's destroyers would be ineffective, since he had witnessed the battle of Jutland during the First World War in which both German and British destroyers had suffered great losses when they advanced within range of the capital ships. Suetsugu wanted more ships in order to ensure victory in both the attrition stage and the decisive battle. The navy's greatest duty, he maintained, was to find solutions to the problems that Japan would encounter in its attrition strategy.[9]

ACCELERATING TECHNOLOGICAL DEVELOPMENT

Between 1927 and 1934, Japan's technicians produced a number of new and improved weapons, which laid Suetsugu's doubts to rest. The influence of technological development was a relatively new factor in the practice of naval warfare. From the battle of Salamis in 480 B.C. to the sea fight at Lepanto in 1571 A.D., sea battles took place in galleys, and the decisive weapon was the boarding party. The long-range cannon, however, brought about a great change in tactics. Between 1588 and 1815, captains of sailing ships tried to use speed and rapid fire to concentrate the weight of their broadsides on a part of the enemy's fleet.[10]

It was only after 1860 that technological progress once again began to change the whole outward appearance and tactical theory of naval warfare. During the first half of the nineteenth century, steam power took over from sail, and from 1860 to 1900, a contest developed between improved guns and thickening armor. Rifled steel guns were matched against wrought iron and steel armor. At the same time, the invention of the self-propelled torpedo made possible the evolution of the torpedo boat and destroyer. These developments threw tactical theories based on big ships and big guns into confusion. Steam power led many tacticians to advocate ramming by capital ships, but the increasing range of the new cannon disposed of that theory. Torpedo warfare also gained proponents, but the large cannon on the great warship again proved superior because of its longer range and improved rate of fire.[11]

By 1900, the standard types of ships and the proper tactics for employing them had again been set. Big guns in big ships were the core of naval power, just as they had been since 1600. Cruisers and destroyers would screen this main fleet from attack by the enemy's lighter forces. The tactical goal was still to cross the enemy's battle line with your own, so as to concentrate your fire on a few of his ships. But technology was increasing the pace of naval competition: between 1900 and 1922, battleships tripled in size; gun calibers increased from twelve to sixteen inches; and the use of carbon and nickel steel improved armor. Engineers developed many new types of warships: the battle cruiser was built to destroy enemy cruisers and run from battleships; the submarine was constructed to strike at the enemy's battle fleet below its armor; and the aircraft carrier was developed for scouting purposes. Finally, conversion from coal to oil as fuel greatly increased the range of a battle fleet.[12]

Despite the quickening pace of technological development, the lessons of the First World War were thought to confirm once again that big guns in big ships were the decisive element in sea power. The British Grand Fleet met the German High Seas Fleet at Jutland and sent it back into hiding. Tactically, the action showed the worth of an advanced body that would scout for the enemy and engage him if necessary. Technically, the battle indicated the usefulness of heavy armor and speed.[13] Since the great majority of these technological developments took place between 1870 and 1920, the Japanese navy was able to absorb them as it grew. With the aid of the navy, Japanese shipbuilders imported foreign techniques and rapidly improved the quality of their ships. By 1905 Japan was building its own cruisers, and by 1910 it was constructing its own battleships. By 1920, Japan's technicians were beginning to plan for superiority in all types.[14]

TECHNOLOGICAL ADVANCES IN THE JAPANESE NAVY, 1928–1934

Japanese naval technology came of age in the late twenties and early thirties. It was the rule of the navy's shipbuilding division to provide quality rather than quantity. Japan's technicians not only were able to bring existing types of ships to the highest level of development in the world, but were also able to produce new types of armament. These technicians produced the ships and weapons that laid Admiral Suetsugu's doubts about strategy to rest.

Until 1920, Japan had imported submarines from the West. In 1919, Japanese builders secured plans for the most advanced German submarine and built the craft on their own. In 1932, they laid down the first completely Japanese submarine, the Fleet Type 6. Japan also ceased buying diesel engines from the West and used one of its own improved design, which pushed the submarine at a surface speed faster than that of the American battle fleet. Japanese builders also solved the scouting problem that had worried Suetsugu by attaching a scout plane and catapult to each of their largest submarines. These 2,000-ton craft had a cruising range of 20,000 miles, which meant that they could reach the California coast. Between 1931 and 1934, the Japanese navy acquired eight such ships. In 1933, work also began on a secret project, the midget submarine, which could launch torpedoes at the enemy fleet from short range. Japanese shipbuilders also started construction of mother ships, each of which would carry twelve of these midget craft to the scene of battle.[15]

Japanese technicians led the world in some types of aircraft as well. Japan had begun airplane construction with British aid during the First World War, but after the end of the Anglo-Japanese Alliance in 1922, the British left Japan on its own. By 1929, Japanese developers were planning and building their own aircraft. In 1932, Mitsubishi produced a prototype for a long-range scout plane, which turned out to be the fastest plane in the world at that time. In May 1934, tests of the new model were so successful that the navy decided to convert the plane into a long-range, land-based bomber. The plane had an effective bombing range of six to seven hundred miles, and eventually became the Type 96 Mitsubishi medium attack bomber. In 1932, Japan also built the first Japanese-designed fighters for carrier use, and in 1933 they built a dive bomber based on German plans.

Naval strategists in these years were also concerned with developing carriers, which they considered important for scouting before a battle, spotting gunfire during an action, harassing the enemy's fleet and bases at long range, and most important, defending the battle line against air attacks. But only a few mavericks in the navies of the three powers predicted that carriers would play a truly decisive role in the future, and ranking admirals universally dismissed their advice. Japan was no exception. Although Japan had followed Britain's lead and built carriers in the twenties, Japanese strategists believed the carrier to be merely an important auxiliary to its battle fleet.[16]

Japanese cruisers and destroyers had already reached a high level of development before the London Treaty of 1930. In the twenties, these types of ships were faster and more heavily gunned than their American counterparts. After 1930, the London Treaty permitted the United States to have eighteen heavy cruisers and Japan to have twelve. Japan responded by planning the Mogami class light cruiser, which was designed to fight heavy cruisers; it had armor capable of withstanding an eight-inch shell, and its gun turrets were constructed for rapid mounting of eight-inch guns in time of war.[17] Japan's strategists planned to use their heavy cruisers and destroyers in attacks against the enemy's battle line, as Admiral Tōgō had done against the Russians in 1905. But Jutland had raised doubts about the ability of such craft to approach within torpedo range of capital ships without suffering prohibitive losses. If Japan's lighter ships could not do damage to the enemy's battle line, then the attrition strategy would not work, and Admiral Suetsugu's fears were justified.

In order to overcome this problem, Japan's technicians developed an extremely high-speed, long-range, large torpedo designated Type 93. This torpedo developed 500 horsepower in an engine fueled by compressed oxygen and kerosene; because it used this kind of fuel, the weapon left almost no trace when running toward its target. At a speed of 39 knots, it had an extreme range of twenty-four miles; at 49 knots, it had a range of twelve miles. The weapon also carried an extremely powerful warhead, almost twice the strength of older Japanese torpedoes. The long range of this new weapon meant that Japan's destroyers and cruisers could choose their distance and carry out their night torpedo attacks in relative safety.[18]

These ships and weapons were only accessories, however. After Tsushima and Jutland, the Japanese navy put primary emphasis on the battleship and its big guns. As a result of the lessons of Jutland, Japanese technicians strengthened the armor on Japan's older battleships; they also increased the speed of their battleships by streamlining and conversion to oil. Before the Washington Conference, the Japanese navy had hoped to leap ahead in the naval race by building a 47,500-ton battleship mounting eighteen-inch guns. Although these cannon would only be two inches larger in caliber than the weapons on the battleships of other nations, their increased size permitted the use of a projectile that had thirty percent more power on impact. One of the planners claimed that this gun would be able to knock out older types of battleships with a single shell. Production difficulties were solved, and the gun was successfully tested in 1931.

The Japanese builders began to draw blueprints in October 1934 for their new, post-treaty battleship. The proposed Yamato class battleship had armor capable of withstanding an eighteen-inch shell above the waterline, although the largest caliber gun on American battleships was only sixteen inches. Below the waterline, the Japanese superbattleship had a three-foot bulge and three separate layers of armor against torpedoes. Laden with all this artillery and armor, these ships displaced at least 62,000 tons, almost twice the size of any American warship. With a top speed of thirty knots and a cruising range of 8,000 miles, the new craft combined the virtues of a battleship and battle cruiser. Its speed would allow its commander to choose the occasion for action, and its armor and armament would make it invincible.[19]

Thus, Japan's naval engineers had developed a large number of new and improved arms between 1928 and 1934. Submarines and cruisers had been made more effective. Japanese technicians had added new weapons to Japan's arsenal, such as the midget submarine, the compressed oxygen torpedo, the long-range bomber, and the carrier. Finally, they had showed the practicability of building a battleship that was incomparably superior to Western types.

THE FLEET FACTION AND THE TECHNICIANS

The technicians and junior officers sympathetic to the fleet faction did not hesitate to put their views on disarmament and security before their superiors. They argued that the naval treaties were distorting Japanese shipbuilding efforts and that progress in battleship technology would give Japan an insurmountable lead in any naval race.

An incident in the spring of 1934 gave weight to the argument that treaty limits were dangerous. Japan had attempted to steal a march on the other naval powers by building its 600-ton torpedo craft to have the fighting capabilities of a 1,000-ton destroyer. But four torpedo tubes and three five-inch guns made the late models of this ship unstable, and on March 12, the *Tomotsuru*, a newly launched torpedo ship, capsized in a storm. Because of their instability, many Japanese warships had to have weight added below the waterline, usually in the form of antitorpedo armor.[20]

On September 10, 1934, Commander Yamashita Chisaku and Lieutenant Commander Shiotani Eisaku (the latter a specialist in naval construction) told their superiors that the treaties were the fundamental cause of the *Tomotsuru* incident. They urged an early decision on construction programs to match American building after the treaties had come to an end, and they described the ships that would be most suitable for Japan's defense. Central to their proposed program was a new battleship, somewhat smaller than the Yamato class battleship, which would be "unsinkable by the existing types of capital ships" and would mount incomparably greater offensive power. They concluded: "If the Empire withdraws from the restraints of the disarmament conference and builds two of these ships, we firmly believe that they, together with our existing ships, will be able to oppose both the American and British navies adequately and also be able to destroy them . . . Moreover, if in our future plans we always try to build ships that use the progress of weaponry in this way, we need have no fear no matter how large the other countries make their building plans." [21]

This type of thinking was not an isolated phenomenon. On October 21, 1933, a former member of the ship construction division of the Japanese navy, Commander Ishikawa Shingo, sent Admiral Katō a memorandum that went into detail concerning the new superbattleship and Japan's ability to cope with a naval race. He argued that the treaty limitations forced Japan to build planes and other such expensive weapons in order to make up for Japan's lack of submarines, whereas if Japan would withdraw from the treaty system, it could save money by building more efficient weapons. The empire could withstand a naval race against the United States, he argued, because the relative economic strengths of the two countries had changed. Japan had greatly increased its industrial power and was dominating the resources of Manchuria and Mongolia, while the American economy had fallen on hard times. He expected that "the empire's economic strength in ten or more years, coupled with our strategic position in the Pacific, will be sufficient to build armaments which will cause us no uneasiness . . . no matter how much America increases the level of competition." A naval race would not "drastically increase" Japan's level of expenditure, he argued, and Japan had sufficient economic resources for ten years of foreseeable competition.

Ishikawa presented a detailed chart of the ten-year building plans that he considered necessary to ensure Japan's security. He advocated building two battleships mounting twenty-inch guns (even larger than those actually used on the Yamato class) and armored to withstand ten torpedoes. He added, "When we complete these battleships, the scale of our relative battleship strengths will change fundamentally and our present sixty percent strength vis-à-vis America will change in one bound to an absolute predominance for us." According to Ishikawa's plans, these first two battleships would be built in the 1937–1940 period, and Japan would add three more similar ships in the following six years. [22]

Actually, Ishikawa doubted that the United States would build ships to match Japan's. He argued that the extreme cost of widening the Panama Canal and dredging harbors to accommodate these craft would further increase the great expense of the weapons themselves. Moreover, by the time the United States had planned, developed, and constructed a battleship comparable to the *Yamato* with its eighteen-inch guns, Japan would probably already be building even larger ships mounting twenty-inch cannon. Ishikawa also claimed that Japan could end

America's superiority in heavy cruisers by constructing "a battle cruiser strong enough to destroy the value of the American navy's existing heavy cruisers." This ship would be twice the size of existing heavy cruisers, be capable of a speed of forty knots, mount twelve twelve-inch guns, and have full armor against the eight-inch shells and the torpedoes of America's heavy cruisers. He suggested building four of these craft over the following ten-year period.[23]

Ishikawa concluded that Japan could ensure its security in a period of free competition. And in any case, he argued, there was no hope for a disarmament agreement, because America would not grant Japan a real defensive capability. Since Japan would then have to walk out of the conference, the navy should prepare opinion at home and appeal to smaller countries and peace groups abroad. The way to accomplish these tasks would be to demand publicly the abolition of offensive weapons such as capital ships and carriers and the establishment of naval equality for all. If by any chance, he added, the Western powers should grant Japan such equality, Japan would have the advantage, since its aircraft based in the mandated islands could attack the American fleet as it crossed the Pacific.[24]

Japan's technicians thought a naval race feasible for another reason: they might not have to face it alone. Germany had withdrawn from the Geneva Disarmament Conference in October 1933, and the same Yamashita and Shiotani who had argued that Japan should withdraw from the treaties and build a super-battleship suggested that Japan also cooperate militarily with Germany. By using Germany, they argued, Japan could check other European powers and keep them from concentrating their forces in the Pacific. They pointed out that German industry was highly developed and that the Germans had been building naval weapons in Russia. Technical cooperation would have great advantages for Japan as well; it was very important, for example, to get a German device that rotated gun turrets and set the elevation of cannon automatically, and to procure a German fire direction device that could replace the more complicated Japanese model. They also wanted to arrange for more purchases of optical equipment from Zeiss through the German navy to be used for range finders. Finally, Yamashita and Shiotani emphasized the benefit of obtaining German technical data on diesel engines, aircraft, machine guns, and submarines.[25]

JAPAN'S NAVAL STRATEGY

The Japanese navy continued to develop a strategy that would take advantage of these new weapons. In the early thirties, Japan's admirals still assumed that Japan would have to fight the United States alone, since they thought that Britain would stay out of a Japanese-American war in order to save British colonies and interests in Asia. Prince Fushimi explained the basic strategy, vis-à-vis America, in this way: "The policy of operations against America (which occupies the most important position in the strategies of the Imperial Navy) is first, at the outset of war . . . to clear out the enemy's seaborne military power in the Orient and at the same time, in cooperation with the army, attack their bases, thereby controlling the western Pacific; then, while protecting the empire's trade, to harass the operations of the enemy's fleet, and thereafter await the assault of the enemy's home fleet and defeat it through surprise attack.'' [26] This plan followed the basic axiom of accepted naval strategy, namely, the wartime purpose of a navy was to protect its nation's seaborne trade and to grasp control of the sea in a decisive fleet battle. The United States' only bases in the western Pacific were Guam and the Philippines. An attack on the Philippines had two purposes: first, it would allow Japan to control the resources of the South Seas, particularly oil; second, it would lure the American fleet across the Pacific into a decisive battle for the relief of the Philippines.

American maneuvers off Hawaii in 1925 led the Japanese admirals to believe that the Americans would come to the relief of the Philippines, since the United States Navy appeared to be rehearsing a decisive battle for the distant waters of the western Pacific. If the Americans came, Japan would be in a very advantageous position, since it would be standing on the defensive. Moreover, a strategic principle of Japanese naval doctrine was that an attacker, to be successful, must have at least twice, if not three times, the strength of the defender; yet the American fleet would probably be at only a 10/7 rather than a 10/5 ratio.[27]

Japan's General Staff officers divided their strategy into two parts: the attrition stage and the decisive battle. Japan's admirals planned to use their newly developed submarines and bombers to grind the American fleet down as it crossed the Pacific. When the American ships left Pearl Harbor, Japan's large new submarines (Fleet Type 6) would launch their scout planes to make and maintain contact with the Americans. Packs of these large submarines would use their top speed of 23.5 knots to move ahead of the slower American ships, which had a cruising speed of only 20 knots. The submarine packs would then launch their long-range oxygen torpedoes and dive, well before the American advance body came within gun range. After surfacing, the subs would again use their superior speed to get ahead of the American fleet and attack. They would then repeat this process until their torpedoes were exhausted. The Japanese planners expected that these attacks would wear down the Americans both materially and psychologically.[28]

As the American fleet drew nearer the Philippines, it would come into range of the navy's air power based on Japan's mandated islands, the Marshalls and Carolines. The new long-range bomber (Mitsubishi Type 96) would then make torpedo attacks on the American ships. Although this plane carried a smaller torpedo than the submarine did, it could deliver a weapon that would sink capital ships; on December 10, 1941, for example, these aircraft sank the British ships *Prince of Wales* and *Repulse* off the Malay coast by torpedo attacks. According to Japan's strategic doctrine, such auxiliary weapons as submarines and aircraft could be sacrificed to give the main fleet an edge in the decisive battle. Japan's admirals expected that these submarine and air attacks would wear the American fleet down to at least a level of equality with the Japanese main body. Then, the superior quality of Japan's ships would win the day.

Somewhere between the Marshalls and the Philippines, the struggle would enter its second, decisive phase. Late in the day, the Japanese advance body, comprising fast battleships, cruisers, and forty-six destroyers, would make contact with the enemy fleet. The Americans would pursue this advance body, just as the Germans had done at Jutland. After darkness fell, this fast fleet would turn and launch two hundred or more of the long-range (Type 93) torpedo. Japan's strategists believed that twenty-five percent of these torpedoes would strike their targets. If enemy cruisers attacked the Japanese destroyers, they would be warded off by fire from the fast battleships and cruisers in this advanced body. The Japanese planners expected that this massive torpedo attack, launched at night, would throw the enemy into confusion. Using the enemy's discomfort, the Japanese advanced body would turn, reform and deliver perhaps two more such attacks before the night ended.[29]

When the sun rose, the battle would enter its final phase. Japan's carriers would launch air strikes against the American carriers. The Japanese planes would not try to sink the carriers; rather, they would attempt to hit the decks of the American ships, so that the Americans would be unable to launch planes for the duration of the battle. Since planes were the main scouting force, the American fleet would be blinded for the rest of the battle.

The combined Japanese advance and main fleets would then approach parallel to the head of the American fleet. The mother ships would advance and launch thirty-six midget submarines along the American line of advance (Fig. 1). As the two fleets drew closer, the Japanese advance body would launch an attack at the extreme range of the Type 93 torpedo's capabilities, about twenty miles. As the American fleet maneuvered and suffered under the impact of this attack, the thirty-six midget submarines would move in and hit the American ships with small torpedoes, at a close range of one to two thousand yards (Fig. 2).

Both the Japanese advance body and the main fleet would then execute turns that would bring them into cannon range of what was left of the American fleet. Although the older Japanese battleships and cruisers would have to trade blows with their American counterparts at a range of twenty to thirty thousand yards, the Yamato class battleships would be able to fire their salvos from forty thousand yards, well out of range of the American shells (Fig. 3). Consequently, the Yamato class battleships would begin firing first and the other Japanese capital ships would close within effective range of the American ships when the Japanese advantage had become overwhelming. Because of their great speed, the Yamato class battleships could stay at the proper range and destroy the enemy's ships at leisure (Fig. 4). Since this battle would start in the morning, Japan's fleet would have all day to pursue and destroy the enemy ships. The ten older Japa-

AMERICAN FLEET

MIDGET SUBMARINES

JAPANESE FLEET

Fig. 1. Attrition by Japanese midget submarines

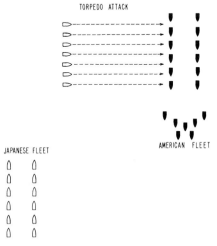

TORPEDO ATTACK

AMERICAN FLEET

JAPANESE FLEET

Fig. 2. Attrition by advanced body of Japanese fleet

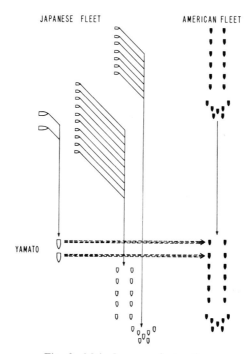

Fig. 3. Main Japanese fleet action

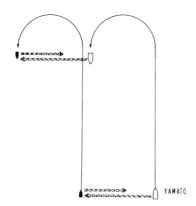

Fig. 4. Superior range of Yamato cannon

nese battleships would consequently have an easy contest against their counter-parts, which would certainly by this time be numerically inferior.[30]

The Japanese planners could not expect that everything would follow this pattern precisely, and they made ample allowance for the unexpected disasters of battle and the possibility that the Americans would discover defenses against some of their modes of attack. But they estimated that if this plan were fifty percent successful (one half of the enemy force sunk or seriously damaged), it would take the Americans at least two years to rebuild, refit, retrain, and mount another attack.[31] In that time, Japan's defensive strength would have further increased. Actually, the Japanese planners probably hoped for close to ninety percent results, as at Tsushima. Such a victory, in addition to the Japanese technological lead in battleships, would have made the situation hopeless for the Americans, who, rather than spending five to eight years and considerable money to build a fleet of super battleships, would probably negotiate a satisfactory peace settlement. Presumably, the United States would finally recognize Japan's predominant position in the western Pacific and East Asia.

THE VICTORY OF THE FLEET FACTION

On June 8, 1934, the Navy Minister called a meeting of the navy's Military Council at his official residence. The military councillors were the highest ranking active and retired admirals who comprised the ultimate sanctioning authority in the navy. Admiral Suetsugu carefully summed up the position of the fleet faction. The treaties were dangerous, he argued, because their restrictions took away the freedom to build the types of weapons necessary for Japan's defense. The treaties were also expensive, since they forced the navy to build many inefficient weapons that were outside the treaty limits. There were those, he declared, who wanted to preserve eternal peace through disarmament, but their hope was "nothing more than the dream of fools." Those who argued for the treaties were playing into the hands of the United States and Britain, whose leaders had forced "our newly advancing, energetic empire to swallow [the disarmament restrictions] whole." Japan's naval power had made the Manchurian advance possible, whereas continuing the limitations would make the support of Manchukuo difficult, would invite the contempt of Russia and China, and would bring further economic pressure by the powers. With Mahanian resonance, he proclaimed that economic strength went hand in hand with national strength and that "trade follows the flag."

Suetsugu also reassured his listeners that there was no need to fear free competition in building. The leaders of the Japanese navy, he stated, were "confident" that they could provide an effective defense using "weapons which have the greatest capacity to fit [Japan's] special national situation and that they shall absolutely not fall prey to the evils of competition." They were confident, he said, for two reasons. First, "we are separated from the great powers of Europe and America . . . we predominate in the Far East and . . . our unique geographical

position . . . gives us an extremely favorable position for national defense.''
And second, ''the authorities in Tokyo have been piling up a considerable
amount of research concerning what types of independent armaments we ought
to produce if a treaty is not signed.'' The best policy, Suetsugu continued, would
be for Japan to ''abrogate the existing treaties and have no treaties and no restrictions.'' As the next best policy, Japan should propose a common upper limit on
tonnage, with each country remaining free to choose any type of weapon within
these limits. Japan should also announce that it intended to abrogate the Washington naval treaty by the end of the year. The instructions to the delegates
should be very clear, and the government ''should control public opinion and
manage it completely.'' If the delegates to the conference did compromise with
the West, he warned, ''we cannot guarantee that, with the military and people
angered, a misfortune even greater than the May 15 incident would not occur.'' [32]
As Commander of the Combined Fleets, Suetsugu had direct control over the
younger officers, and he could easily carry out his threat of a coup. The military
councillors agreed to the fleet faction's demands: the navy would insist that the
government abrogate the Washington naval treaty and seek parity with the West.

In sum, the leaders of Japan's navy decided to end naval restrictions for a
number of reasons. Renewed building by the United States certainly threatened
the favorable 8/10 ratio that had prevailed at the time of the Manchurian incident.
Efforts to overcome the treaty restrictions had caused costly accidents, such as
the *Tomotsuru* incident, which in turn damaged the prestige of the navy. Japan's
continued economic advance and the United States' financial collapse made a
naval race seem feasible. More important, perhaps, was the general background
of theory and experience that dominated the minds of the fleet faction's leaders:
Mahan, Tsushima, and Jutland had demonstrated conclusively that sea power
was the key to the rise and fall of empires. The Japanese navy's own experience
in battle had shown the value of better tactics, surprise, night attacks, faster
ships, and superior firepower. From 1928 to 1934, Japan's naval engineers and
technicians developed new and improved weapons which gave the leaders of the
navy confidence that they could defeat the American fleet. In particular, new
submarines, torpedoes, and aircraft made the attrition strategy attractive. Especially important was the fact that the new Yamato class battleship promised the
Japanese navy an insurmountable lead over its rivals. Japan's admirals would
begin the contest for empire in the greatest battleship of all time. Finally, there
was the new role in East Asia that Japan's leaders had decided to assume in October 1933 and which Amō had proclaimed in April 1934. The arbiter of the
Orient needed a great fleet.

3   Public Opinion and the Navy's First Moves

When Japan's delegates to the first London Naval Disarmament Conference returned to Tokyo in the spring of 1930, a large, friendly crowd filled the square in front of Tokyo station to greet them. The delegation was bringing back a treaty that ensured the continuance of naval disarmament until 1936. Yet in 1934, the Japanese government announced that it was withdrawing from the disarmament system, and it did so to the cheers of a seemingly united public opinion.[1] In large part the activities of Japan's navy were responsible for this abrupt reversal of public sentiment. The admirals were able to exploit the changes that had taken place in the mood of the Japanese public after the Manchurian incident, to suppress most dissent, and to engineer a rousing campaign for naval parity.

NEW ATMOSPHERE IN THE MEDIA

Between 1930 and 1934, a number of events, both internal and external, undercut the strength of the disarmament party, the Minseitō, and increased the strength of the military. As the party in power from 1929 to 1931, the Minseitō bore the blame for the depression and its attendant woes of unemployment and starvation. Consequently, in February 1932 the Minseitō lost its majority in the Diet to the Seiyūkai.

At the same time, external events helped to change the tone of the media from internationalism to militarism. Japan's victories in Manchuria seemed like a ray of light in the dark depression days. The press supported the government eagerly, with the Japanese Newspaper Association declaring its endorsement of the Manchurian action, and editorials explaining that Chinese crimes had made the invasion necessary.[2] International economic events reinforced Japan's sense of isolation in a hostile world. Almost all countries were raising tariff barriers against Japanese goods, and efforts to lower these barriers were uniformly unsuccessful. Many said that Japan's only alternative was to build up its own economic sphere in Manchuria, China, and the South Seas so as to match those of Britain and America. In 1933, the September issue of *Kaizō* published maps and graphs to show that the United States, Britain, and the European nations were monopolizing world trade. In July 1934, *Nihon oyobi Nihonjin* assured its readers that a "rising Japan" was forcing the West out of its economic bloc in the eastern and southern Pacific; the magazine also promised that Japan would develop the resources of the South Seas in order to produce inexpensive goods for the use of the peoples native to the region. Other newspapers and magazines also carried reports of trade warfare and economic bloc building.[3]

The battles on the continent combined with international and economic isolation to produce a crisis psychology in the media. Heroes were in demand. When fighting spread from Manchuria to the streets of Shanghai in 1932, "three heroic sappers" became stars of stage, screen, and the magazines. According to news reports, three Japanese soldiers had made human bombs of themselves in order to blow a hole in the Chinese barbed wire entanglements. Stories about similar heroes continued to appear. Much attention was also given to the pure youths who had taken part in the coups against the party cabinets. During the trial of the defendants arrested after the May 15 incident, the government received about 700,000 letters appealing for clemency. The media implied that the citizen should follow the example of these "heroes" and make sacrifices for the nation in its time of emergency.[4]

During the second half of 1933, the Japanese military began using the atmosphere of crisis publicly to justify its large budget demands, and it warned the nation of an even greater emergency in 1935–1936. On November 18, 1933, a reserve officers' group argued for preparedness in a memorial that explained the coming crisis in typical fashion. China was building arms with British and American aid; Japan's membership in the League of Nations would run out at the same time as a crisis would develop over the naval treaties; and Russia would complete its economic and military preparations by 1935. Major General Tōjō Hideki, head of the Army Research Bureau, also gave these arguments in an article published in December 1933, adding that it was the traditional policy of the United States to advance to the East in search of markets. Japan, he concluded, would have to prepare for the coming emergency.[5]

The changing international situation and the military propaganda about an emergency brought an outpouring of war scare literature. Books about imaginary wars had enjoyed a vogue from 1910 to 1922, but they had almost disappeared during the twenties. After the London Conference crisis and the Manchurian incident, there was an unprecedented production of such books. The main theme was a future war with the United States, Russia, or both. In 1934, at least eighteen such books appeared, and few readers of magazines and newspapers could miss the advertisements for them.[6]

Although much of the scare literature dealt with the danger from Russia, a great amount of it warned of a coming clash with the United States. This fear of the United States stemmed partly from Secretary of State Stimson's criticism of Japan during the Manchurian incident, and also from his nonrecognition policy. Moreover, the Japanese press followed American naval developments closely and gave them broad coverage. For example, in mid-1934 the *Yomiuri* gave front page coverage to the United States' proposed naval building program and to its naval maneuvers. Other publications followed suit. Voices raised against this general crisis psychology were scarce. Vice Foreign Minister Shigemitsu Mamoru warned that there was too much talk of an expected crisis in 1935 and that there would probably be no such emergency, but his was a lonely voice.[7]

Between 1930 and 1934, then, the atmosphere in the mass media had changed from internationalism to militarism. The depression and the right wing terror had thrown the Minseitō and the bureaucratic cabinets on the defensive. International isolation meant that Japan would have to manage alone in a world that was divided into hostile economic blocs. The military would maintain peace in East Asia and ensure the progress of Japan's new economic bloc. For their part, Japan's ordinary citizens would have to follow the example of the military heroes and help Japan weather the emergency. Thus, international and internal events together with military propaganda had made the media amenable to the navy's coming campaign against disarmament. And censorship ensured that the media would be even more receptive to the navy's arguments.

CENSORSHIP BY SUGGESTION

According to the Meiji Constitution, all Japanese had freedom of expression "within the law." The succession of vague publication laws passed by the Diet over the years, however, had made it possible for the Interior Ministry to ban any article it disliked. Furthermore, all articles had to be brought to the Interior Ministry for approval three days before publication. In general, the ministry banned anything that would reveal military secrets, arouse the people against the constitutional order, injure public morals, or show disrespect to the imperial family. In practice, much left and right wing material was banned, and offenders were punished by fines or short jail sentences. In 1934, the number of books and articles banned had dropped to 1,700 from a high of 4,000 in 1933. According to the lists compiled by the staff of the National Diet Library, however, only two publications had been stopped because their authors advocated disarmament too vigorously.[8] The censors' real interest seems to have lain in the fields of revolutionary socialism, radical nationalism, and common pornography.

Although the censors did not prohibit free discussion of the naval problem, the Japanese navy made sure that most writers would follow the lines of their policy. In December 1933, the navy proposed to the Foreign Office that close liaison between the two ministries be established to handle information about the disarmament negotiations. The navy officials insisted that they should have the deciding voice in the announcement of national defense policy.[9] The Foreign Office resisted on this point, but by March 1934 the problem had evidently been solved, for on March 27 of that year the first liaison committee meeting of military and civilian press personnel from the various ministries was held at the Foreign Office to coordinate policy for announcements to newspapers.

At the end of April, this committee met with newspapermen and instructed them to handle their reports cautiously and to preserve close contact with naval officials. In June and again in August, the censors at the Interior Ministry banned articles dealing with building programs, renovation of older ships, and existing naval strengths, and they tightened such restrictions further when the Second London Naval Conference opened. Consequently, all discussion of the naval problem had to be rather abstract, since the press was not allowed to compare the actual naval strengths of the United States and Japan.[10]

The liaison committee met again on October 12, 1934, in order to establish the propaganda line for the various ministries to follow during the conference, and the policy adopted mirrored the navy's wishes. The committee decided that the press secretaries should insist that Japan desired a disarmament agreement which would reduce existing levels of armaments drastically. At the same time, the committee concluded that appropriate officials should explain that Japan could provide for its own defense even if new limits on arms were not established. Press secretaries should keep in touch with magazine and newspaper correspondents, the committee indicated, and also send speech makers, pamphlets, and films around the country. Finally, the committee warned that the various press bureaus should maintain liaison and avoid discrepancies in the government's arguments.[11] In fact, most newspaper and magazine articles did follow the line drawn by the liaison committee. The unification of public opinion was to be accomplished by suggestion, rather than prohibition.

NAVAL INFLUENCE ON PUBLIC OPINION

The navy itself was well prepared to convey its viewpoint to leaders of opinion in the media and around the country. The Navy Ministry had a special bureau, the Naval Affairs Reporting Division, nicknamed the *chindonya* (an itinerant advertising band of musicians and hawkers), to manage its public relations and make announcements. The first section of this bureau handled the navy's contacts with the newspapers. Most major newspapers had reporters assigned to naval matters. Reporters from most of these newspapers, such as the *Asahi, Yomiuri, Mainichi,* and *Hōchi,* as well as from all of the wire services, belonged to the "Japan Current" club, an organization with a close relation to the Navy Ministry itself. The newspaper section of the ministry's Reporting Division supplied data to the members of this organization for articles on the navy. In all, reporters from twenty-six newspapers were members of this association.[12]

The second section of the Naval Affairs Reporting Division handled both the publication of pamphlets and liaison with various independent naval organizations around the country. About ten main groups were engaged in urging the expansion of Japanese naval power through public meetings and publications. In 1932, the Navy Ministry also listed more than one hundred sympathetic youth groups, shrine groups, and sailors' organizations. The two most important associations were made up of retired and reserve officers: the Navy League and the Yūshūkai (Perfection Society). In the early thirties, the latter seems to have been the most active: it published a monthly magazine and yearly naval review, besides holding public lecture meetings. These lectures were frequently based on pamphlets published by the Perfection Society and the Navy Ministry. In 1934, the head of the Navy Ministry's Reporting Division estimated that it had arranged for three thousand speeches against disarmament.[13]

The Perfection Society and the Navy Ministry published at least fourteen pamphlets on the disarmament problem in 1934, almost all appearing from September to December when the preliminary negotiations were under way. The Perfection Society put out an early example of this type of pamphlet in February 1932, in which a retired admiral declared that Japan should get rid of the treaties and demand equality in the right to armaments. Advances in airplane and ship technology made Japan more vulnerable than it had been earlier, he explained, while changes in the international situation meant that Japan needed an independent imperial defense. He claimed that Japan did not need to fear a naval race, for the empire had defeated larger fleets in the past, and the greatly increased power of smaller weapons, such as destroyers, submarines, and airplanes, meant that the prospects for a similar victory in the future were good. Although there was no reason for a Japanese-American war, he maintained, such a conflict was continually in the offing, the basic reason for this unfortunate situation being that the United States did not understand Japan. It was the job of the diplomats, the admiral concluded, to clear up this misunderstanding.[14] Similar pamphlets became the basis for numerous magazine articles and speeches.

NAVAL PRESSURE ON THE SAITŌ CABINET

In the fall of 1933, the navy began to urge the Saitō cabinet to agree to end the "unfavorable" restrictions of the naval treaties. When this initiative did not bring results, Navy Minister Ōsumi asked the government to allow the navy to make public announcements on the disarmament problem, explaining that the navy wished to make clear to the general public the empire's views on security needs, equality of the right to armaments, the nature of real disarmament, and the end of the treaty restrictions.[15] The final result of Ōsumi's efforts probably was the joint liaison committee of press section personnel that warned the editors to cooperate with the navy in April 1934. The navy press bureau subsequently assumed leadership of the campaign against disarmament, making frequent announcements of its own versions of proper national policy. Most newspapers carried these announcements on their front pages under provocative headings.

In mid-May, Navy Minister Ōsumi began a strenuous press campaign for treaty abrogation and naval equality. Prince Konoye was traveling to America to see his son graduate from preparatory school, and apparently Ōsumi was worried that during his stay Konoye might discuss disarmament with American officials. Harada arranged a breakfast send-off party at which the top naval officials met with Konoye. Ōsumi intimated that the navy did not really want revision of the existing treaties but rather an outright abrogation. According to Harada, he said in essence, "It will be all right to make a settlement if by any chance what Japan wants goes through, but if it turns out that there is no hope at all of it going through, it is advisable for Japan to abrogate the treaties." When Harada

suggested that Prime Minister Saitō might want to seek revision of the treaties, not abrogation, the admirals were "somewhat displeased." They replied
that Germany's right to equality in armaments was gaining recognition while
Japan still suffered inequality. Ōsumi also claimed that in a five ministers' conference in the preceding year, Finance Minister Takahashi had agreed to a policy
of seeking naval equality. The Navy Minister added, however, that the cabinet
members had not recorded the agreement in the minutes of the conference because they feared a leak to the press.[16]

Following this somewhat acrimonious breakfast, Ōsumi told reporters that he
had asked Konoye to explain the navy's desires to the Americans. These desires,
Ōsumi said, were clear: because of Japan's need for security and its desire to support peace in the Orient, the navy was determined to seek to "the bitter end"
both equality of the right to arms and an end of the treaties. Japan was willing to
make a new agreement, but only on these terms. Ōsumi added, however, that
Japan was not seeking "parity." As the month wore on, the navy further elab-
orated this somewhat vague statement. When Japanese newspapers reported
that the American navy saw no need to change the naval ratios, the navy's press
bureau replied with an "informal announcement." The Japanese navy spokesman
said that all countries had an equal right to the arms that would ensure their security, and because of the great changes in the international situation and in technology, the navy could no longer defend Japan under the ratio system. It was natural, he concluded, that the empire should seek a new, just settlement and that the
people should firmly support the navy's position.[17]

By early June 1934, the fleet faction's campaign was in full progress. Okada
told Harada on May 30 that Katō and Suetsugu were holding meetings in the
Akasaka geisha district and "seducing" fleet commanders to their view. Katō
and Suetsugu were arguing that it was disgraceful to have important national
defense matters formulated by other countries; it would be better to build freely
within the limits of Japan's finances and not to "do everything this way and that
according to a treaty.'" Okada concluded, "We must be careful, because their
unity appears very strong." Admiral Nomura Kichisaburō also told Harada that
the fleet faction was in a state of "euphoria" and that it would be "dangerous"
to nominate the moderate Admiral Kobayashi Seizō as the next Navy Minister.
On July 7, after a conference with Ambassador Saitō, who had returned from
Washington for consultations, Ōsumi again publicly demanded an end to the
ratio system, and four days later the navy called for an increase in its budget for
the succeeding year.[18]

American and British actions probably aided the navy's efforts somewhat. On
June 17, when the Japanese navy announced that its leadership was united in the
belief that the ratio system had to be abolished, Anglo-American preliminary
naval talks were then under way in Washington, and the British and American
officials announced their opposition to any change in the naval ratios. When the
press played up this announcement, the Japanese navy leaders saw their chance.

They stated that they were "firmly determined to demand a change in the ratios" and added that "the establishment of our right to equality of armaments is our firm demand." Both the *Hōchi* and the *Asahi* newspapers had already come out for replacing the ratio system with equality of armaments; now the *Yomiuri* and the Tokyo *Mainichi* joined them. The *Yomiuri* declared that the ratios injured Japan's feeling of security. The *Mainichi* claimed that the "right to equality in national defense . . . is the natural right . . . of an independent nation." [19] Thus, by the end of July the major Tokyo newspapers had all come out for ending the treaties.

During these same days, the Saitō government was collapsing, and competition sharpened in the race for the prime ministership. Katō Kanji, the leader of the fleet faction, began campaigning to end the disarmament treaties and establish a strong cabinet. On July 2, the Tokyo *Mainichi* reported that sixty officers of the combined fleets had sent a petition to the Chief of the Navy General Staff, Prince Fushimi, through their commander, Admiral Suetsugu. They called for the abrogation of the Washington naval treaty at the earliest possible moment, the establishment of Japan's independent right to armament equality in the coming disarmament conference, and the formation of a strong cabinet. The *Mainichi* warned that this petition would have to be handled carefully, since it represented the feelings of the young officers. [20]

THE NAVY SEEKS ARMY SUPPORT

During these same months, the Navy General Staff was working to secure army support for abrogation of the Washington naval treaty. Even before the navy had broached the subject of treaty abrogation, the major division chiefs of the Army General Staff were fully in favor of an upward revision of Japan's ratio, thus continuing the army's sympathy for an increased ratio that Araki had expressed in the fall of 1933. The Army General Staff called for complete unity with the navy, efforts to guide public opinion through manipulation of the large newspapers, and determination to abrogate the treaty if the powers did not agree to a revision. They explained that their reasons for backing the navy were two-fold: first, the treaties endangered Japan's security, and second, because feelings in the navy had been rising higher since the May 15 incident, the army must keep the navy from running wild and jeopardizing Japan's important goals, such as the construction of Manchukuo. [21]

The Army General Staff officers did have some reservations, however. They asked that the navy begin considering what arms would be needed in the period of free competition. They also urged that a way be found to preserve limitations on fortifications and to limit air base construction in China and the Philippines. A Japanese attack on the Philippines, in particular, would be difficult if the islands were fortified. The army also asked that measures be taken to avoid responsibility for a breakup of the conference, as well as that efforts be made to keep England and the United States apart, since Japan did not have the naval strength to oppose both of them at once. Most important to the army, however, was the stipulation that Japan should insist on confining the conference solely to naval matters and refuse to discuss any East Asian problems. The navy agreed at once to exclude such matters from the negotiations, but it was not particularly enthusiastic about pressing the problem of fortifications at the conference. The army then urged that the Washington naval treaty be abrogated and that the conference consider limits on both navies and fortifications at the same time. Thus, the Army General Staff had jumped ahead of the navy in formally proposing an end to the existing treaty structure.[22]

On June 27, a member of the Navy General Staff Strategy Division came to ask formally that the Army General Staff support the navy in abrogating the treaty "quickly (at the latest, by the end of the year)." In return, the navy would agree to exclude political problems, such as the recognition of Manchukuo, from the conference. The navy representative stated, however, that the admirals would not accept restrictions on Japan's naval strength in order to secure continued limitations on fortifications, and that they would not agree to restrictions on land-based aircraft establishments; thus, the navy refused to accept two of the army's requests. After the abrogation of the Washington naval treaty, he declared, Japan should call for a new limitation system, in which all countries would establish a common upper limit at a low tonnage level, and within that limit, each country would be free to adopt those weapons necessary to its defense. Should an agreement not be reached on these terms, the navy admitted, a construction race would probably begin. The navy assured the army that, although Japan could not remain equal "in volume" to Britain and the United States, "by providing weapons which have special worth for us, we have confidence that we will ensure our national defense."[23]

Between the latter part of June and the early part of July, all the officers of the Army General Staff considered the navy's proposals. The intelligence section of the Army General Staff backed the navy from the outset, and in ten days all of the major General Staff officers had agreed to quick abrogation and to any naval strength that the navy felt necessary. They decided that the army should support the navy in seeking a completely new agreement, and they stated that Japan should withdraw from the conference if the delegates could not make a treaty guaranteeing Japan's security or if the powers insisted on raising East Asian problems. The General Staff officers still wanted an agreement limiting fortifications, but they agreed with the navy that a restriction of Japan's naval strength was too high a price to pay for such a nonfortification treaty.[24] Thus, by early June, the navy had been able to get the Army General Staff's approval for a policy of quick abrogation of the Washington naval treaty and complete naval equality.

Although the talks with the Army General Staff had gone smoothly, the navy still had to get the approval of the War Ministry for its policy. The War Minister, Hayashi Senjurō, had appointed Nagata Tetsuzan as chief of the Military Affairs

Bureau in order to draw up plans for a general economic mobilization and the development of key industries. As the implementation of such plans would require a great deal of money, Nagata thought that large sums should not be poured into needless naval building.[25] Thus, when the head of the Navy Ministry's Military Affairs Bureau, Yoshida Zengo, called on Nagata, he was given a cold reception.

Nagata asked almost immediately what effect the abrogation of the Washington naval treaty would have on naval expenses. Yoshida replied that there would be no great difference between the expenditure needed for ship replacement under the Washington naval treaty and the sums required for competitive building. Nagata then asked why the present ratios represented a danger to Japan and why the navy needed equality, to which Yoshida gave what were to become the navy's standard replies: the international situation had worsened; technological progress in naval craft, particularly the increase in cruising radii, endangered Japan's position; there could be no security without equality; and if a naval race did begin, it would not be too expensive. Finally, in exasperation, Nagata asked, "Do you judge that with this proposal there is in reality a prospect of agreement?" Yoshida admitted, "There is no such prospect." [26]

On July 12, Nagata's section informed the Army General Staff that it was opposed to the navy's proposals. Although the War Ministry officials admitted that the new agreement should not endanger Japan's security, they maintained that the navy should ensure the success of the conference. "However," they continued, "if we proceed according to the navy's present proposals, we recognize that the breakup of the conference will be the inevitable result." The navy, they continued, should consider the economic burden "that will accompany the worsening of the international situation and the competition in naval construction which will come with the breakup of the conference." Because of this economic burden, Nagata argued, some new agreement should be found, even if the existing treaties were scrapped. Six days later, the Army General Staff drew up a reply denouncing the War Ministry's objections as "unprofitable" and "meaningless." The General Staff officers said that it was "natural" to support the navy's demand for equality in the right to arms.[27] Thus, the navy had been able to secure the help of the Army General Staff, but they had not succeeded in persuading the Hayashi-Nagata leadership at the War Ministry of the need to support their position. Yet Ōsumi would need Hayashi's help, or at least his neutrality, in the five ministers' conference.

By mid-July, the Japanese navy had made substantial progress in its campaign to end disarmament. It had frightened Saionji and Saitō by its public intransigence, and it had gathered unanimous editorial support through a combination of public statements and private pressure. Its own propaganda organization was working smoothly. At the same time, the Army General Staff had agreed to support the navy's campaign. Thus, the admirals were ready to strike as soon as a new cabinet was formed.

THE MAKING OF THE OKADA CABINET

Amō's provocative declaration in April had added to the troubles of the Saitō cabinet. Sensing the opportunity, many candidates for Prime Minister stepped forward. Suzuki Kisaburō, the leader of the majority Seiyūkai faction, was especially vigorous in his efforts to replace Saitō. But the opposing faction of the Seiyūkai, led by Tokonami Takejirō, combined with the party elders to block Suzuki's drive for a showdown. War Minister Hayashi began campaigning for the right wing leader, Hiranuma Kiichirō, and when Hayashi's first efforts came to nothing, he combined with Hiranuma to boost the head of the fleet faction, Katō Kanji. But Saionji did not welcome the news of these right wing candidacies. On the other hand, a party cabinet under Suzuki carried an even greater danger, for it might give the military a greater influence in matters of government and still provoke a coup attempt by the radical right. Consequently, Saionji decided to continue steering a middle course between the parties and the military.[28]

On July 4, Saionji heard the Emperor's wishes: the new Prime Minister should be a man who would preserve the constitution and would do nothing rash in internal or external policy. Harada and Saitō both agreed that Admiral Okada Keisuke was the best choice in view of the coming naval crisis. Harada then began a series of meetings to prepare the way for Okada, culminating in a conference of former Prime Ministers. At this meeting, Saionji finally prevailed on the leader of the Minseitō, Wakatsuki Reijirō, to support the new cabinet.[29]

Okada Keisuke was a small, red-nosed man who looked like an elf. The son of a low-ranking shogunal retainer, he had been a completely faithful naval officer. His life style was frugal, and his manner careful and rational, his only recreation being to drink sake and swap stories with fellow officers. Unlike many high-ranking naval men, he had not traveled to the West. Okada enjoyed giving the impression that he was just a simple sailor. When he appeared for photographers as the new Prime Minister, for instance, his borrowed top hat fit neatly over his head and rested on his ample ears. Yet Okada was a good negotiator, skilled in the construction of compromises. At the time of the London Treaty crisis he had mediated successfully between Katō Kanji and the government. In his memoirs he recalls that at times he agreed with Katō and pressed the fleet faction's views on the government, but then he appealed to Katō's common sense and was able to get a temporary compromise; "my tactic," he wrote, "was evasion." [30]

The making of the cabinet presented many problems, and the resulting line-up was considerably weaker than that of the Saitō government. All the ministers connected with national security policy remained: Hirota, who was increasing in confidence and stature at the Foreign Office; Hayashi, who was growing bolder as Army Minister; and Ōsumi, who remained as the clumsy Navy Minister. Okada had hoped to replace Ōsumi with a moderate, Admiral Kobayashi Seizō, but he found that this was impossible because of the Katō-Suetsugu group. As

Okada told Harada, "Their unity is extremely solid and we'd better be careful."
Ōsumi also attached a condition to his acceptance of the Navy Ministry, namely,
Okada would have to abide by the decisions supposedly made by the five ministers' conferences of the previous year. Okada agreed. Gone from the cabinet was
the leading champion of disarmament and reduced military spending, Finance
Minister Takahashi; his replacement was a Finance Ministry bureaucrat who was
unable to cross swords with the military in the cabinet or even to keep control of
his own department. [31]

The Okada cabinet was weaker still in relation to the Diet. Thanks to Saionji,
Okada was able to count on the support of the minority Minseitō, but Suzuki, the
leader of the Seiyūkai, refused to cooperate, and he carried his majority faction
with him. Okada outmaneuvered the embittered Seiyūkai leader by inviting the
leaders of the minority Seiyūkai factions to join the cabinet. When they did so,
Suzuki and his followers announced a policy of noncooperation with the government. Okada, however, was able to count on a shaky majority in the Diet, made
up of the Minseitō and the dissident factions of the Seiyūkai. Suzuki retreated to
a policy of obstruction and watchful waiting, hoping for an issue with which he
could unite his party, topple the government, and assume the prime ministership.
A crisis over the naval treaties might provide such an issue, and the Seiyūkai had
already used the London Treaty to attack the Hamaguchi government in 1930.
Harada thought that the government would have to watch the Seiyūkai carefully
and move cautiously. [32]

A CONSENSUS ON CHINA POLICY

The Okada cabinet pledged to continue the foreign policies of its predecessor.
One of the main questions during the 1933 policy debates had arisen over the future of North China. Saitō subsequently turned the issue over to a committee of
high-ranking bureaucrats, composed of section chiefs of the army, navy, and
Foreign Office. They held meetings on China policy from June to early December 1934, when they finally agreed on a forward step in China. It is possible
that the navy agreed to the proposed action in China in return for army support of
its drive against disarmament. And it is probable that Okada and Hirota accepted
the new policy because they were not strong enough politically to resist it. [33]

The new initiative had two major aims: first, Japan would secure East Asian
peace by leading a cooperative system composed of Japan, China and Manchuria; second, Japan would expand its economic rights in North China. To these
ends, the empire would use internal Chinese conflicts to end anti-Japanese movements and to protect its rights and interests. In particular, the Japanese government would demand that the Nationalists promote pro-Japanese elements in their
administration. Most important, Japan expected that a situation would evolve in
which the writ of the Nationalists would not run in North China.

This policy of strictness toward the Nationalists and the separation of North
China contained the possibility of war on the continent and a subsequent collision

with the West. But the axiom of strictness had a corollary, which promised trouble with the West for Japan even were there no Sino-Japanese collision on the battlefield. Japan would end China's bad habit of ''dealing with those distant and opposing those nearby''; moreover, ''by positive diplomacy and by economic measures,'' it would ''by all means eliminate aid to China from foreign countries.'' [34] Against this background of increasing danger in China and trouble with the West, the Japanese navy decided to demand the end of disarmament. As 1934 progressed, it became less likely that Japan would remain within the naval limitation system. With the establishment of the new Okada administration, Admirals Katō, Suetsugu, and Ōsumi decided that the new government would soon have to choose between keeping domestic peace and preserving the disarmament treaties.

4 The Navy's General Offensive

The weak Okada cabinet was only five days old when the Prime Minister told Harada, "the advance guards have clashed." On July 13, 1934, Navy Minister Ōsumi handed the Prime Minister a three-point program for disarmament, claiming that this new policy was based on a decision made by the inner cabinet during the previous December. Ōsumi went on, "I must ask you to agree to this. If the Prime Minister does not agree, I will not be able to remain in my post." Okada replied that he could not agree in haste and that he would first have to hold another five ministers' conference. Ōsumi retorted that Prince Fushimi, the Chief of the Navy General Staff, had already reported the policy to the Emperor and secured his approval, which was "the end of the matter." Harada thought that Okada was determined to find a solution to the disarmament problem, but he was also disheartened by receiving such a challenge when his cabinet had just been formed.[1]

Harada suspected, however, that the navy had not received imperial sanction for its policy, since he recalled that the fleet faction had tried a similar ruse during the London treaty crisis. Consequently, he called his friend, Marquis Kido Kōichi, the chief secretary to the Lord Privy Seal. Kido learned that Prince Fushimi had asked to present a personal memorial to the Emperor, on the strength of being a member of the nobility and a naval officer. A court chamberlain had then arranged an audience for Fushimi over the Emperor's objections. During his audience, Fushimi left the navy's proposal with the Emperor, commenting on it, "There is no other choice but to discard the customary principle of a ratio and vigorously pursue a policy of equality; otherwise, the navy will not be able to control its officers." The Emperor said nothing but was angry, and later had the Imperial Household Minister remonstrate with Fushimi. Harada was able to tell Okada that the Emperor had not yet approved the navy's policy.[2] Ōsumi and Fushimi had thus tried to involve the Emperor in policy making. Even more disturbing, however, were the facts that Ōsumi had threatened to resign and bring down the cabinet and that Fushimi had raised the specter of a naval rebellion.

The exact nature of the navy's three-point program is unclear, but it certainly included a request for speedy abrogation of the Washington naval treaty and a call for naval parity. While Harada was investigating the question of Fushimi's memorial, Ōsumi continued to urge a reluctant Army Minister, General Hayashi, to support such a policy. There were three main reasons for abrogating the treaty as soon as possible, Ōsumi stated. First, the treaties threatened the national security. Since the Americans were planning to complete the greater part of their auxiliary ships by the end of 1939, "it would be unprofitable for us . . . to delay the beginning of free . . . naval building." Ōsumi's second reason for a speedy abrogation was the internal political situation of the empire. Since "the prospects for the establishment of an amicable agreement at the next naval disarmament conference are not great, the notification of abrogation simply becomes a problem of timing." But, he continued, "if we try to make an abrogation notice after there has been no agreement at the conference, we can imagine many difficulties internally." To give notice of abrogation before the conference, however, would clear the way for a new settlement, unify public opinion at home, express the government's "unshakable resolve" abroad, and "strengthen our position in the conference." Finally, a swift abrogation would have a smaller adverse effect on American and British public opinion than would an abrogation that took place after the negotiations had broken down. Ōsumi also made clear that the navy wanted equality, too. "After the expiration of the existing treaties," he concluded, "the empire will not be able to accept anything that would continue restrictions unfavorable to us." [3]

Meanwhile, Prime Minister Okada had begun his search for a solution. On July 13, when Ōsumi first made his proposal, Okada held an informal meeting with the Navy, Foreign, and Finance Ministers. Okada asked whether the other ministers could agree to Ōsumi's request for naval equality, provided that the navy were willing to build up to parity over a period of "perhaps eight years." But the Finance Minister would not agree. On the following day Okada held a five ministers' conference, which lasted five hours; the star performer was Ōsumi, who reviewed the Saitō cabinet's foreign policy decisions. Although Ōsumi and Finance Minister Fujii told the press that there had been no objection to continuing the policies of the Saitō cabinet, in actuality the Army, Foreign, and Finance Ministers had not accepted the navy's position. The meeting had broken up to let each minister consider what would happen if the naval negotiations ended in failure. [4]

After encountering this initial opposition, Navy Minister Ōsumi arranged a second meeting of the navy's Military Council in order to demonstrate the unity of the admirals. Before the meeting, on July 13, Ōsumi announced that opinion in the navy was united on the need for equality and for completion of the proposed building plans. Navy officials believed, the *Asahi* reported, that Okada would heed Ōsumi's advice, "in view of today's international situation and internal relations." Harada arranged to meet with one of his contacts in the navy, Admiral Kobayashi, following the councillors' meeting, in order to find out whether the navy was united in reality or just in public. Even before the conference, however, Kobayashi was pessimistic about the "atmosphere that had been created" among the higher naval officials.

When Harada met Kobayashi at the Tokyo Club after the meeting, the admiral told him that the fleet faction had succeeded in shutting off all hostile questions. Ōsumi first explained the navy's proposals to the assembled officers and then said that he made acceptance of this policy a condition for his remaining in office. When one of the councillors attempted to question him about the policy, the Navy Minister asked that all opinions be stated in written form, since an argument over the proposals was undesirable. With all debate thereby cut off, Katō Kanji, the leader of the fleet faction, rose to read a prepared statement. He first thanked Ōsumi for persevering in his post in a difficult time for the nation, and then said, "We want to support the minister completely." The meeting thus ended with the fleet faction still at the helm.[5]

After the councillors' conference, Yoshida Zengo, head of the Navy Ministry's Bureau of Military Affairs, told the press that the navy was united in its determination to have its policies adopted. The *Asahi* reported the navy's position under the front page caption, "Heads of the Navy Unite Behind Withdrawal from Unequal Treaties." Yoshida said that the councillors' meeting had decided: "1. In the coming disarmament conference, we will seek to the bitter end a withdrawal from the restrictions of the unequal treaties with the aim of securing our right to an independent defense; 2. we will seek to the bitter end the fulfillment of our previously determined plans for building up our national defense, which will prepare us for the crisis immediately facing us; 3. we expect to have our proposals for the 1935 budget accepted."

The navy declaration ended with a ringing call for a "united nation policy to meet the time of emergency." In its editorial column, the *Asahi* supported the navy's quest for unity, urging the army and "the entire people" to unite behind the navy's policy. All of the large papers carried the navy's demands on page one, and the *Hōchi* reported that the commanders of all fleets and bases were explaining the situation to their men. The whole Navy, the *Hōchi* indicated, was tense.[6]

Yoshida's announcement was not the navy's only venture into the public arena during these days. On July 13, the navy had announced its own national defense policy: an end to the disarmament treaties; a return to independent defense; retention of the mandated islands; development of Manchukuo, and completion of the navy's building plans. When Admirals Suetsugu Nobumasa and Takahashi Sankichi arrived in Tokyo for the admirals' conference, they called publicly for the abrogation of the treaty.[7]

During the following days the navy continued its pressure, which seemed to be having some effect. When Ambassador Saitō returned home to report on American disarmament policy, Harada warned him not to say anything rash, for the right wing had been trying to use young naval officers to change the political situation—a reference to the fleet's memorial supporting a Katō Kanji cabinet. After Ambassador Saitō met with the leaders of the navy, the navy's press bureau reported full agreement. The spokesman explained that the navy just wanted to get rid of the "unjust" restrictions of the treaties and replace them with real disarmament; the powers would have to cast off their "unnatural feeling of superiority" and cut back their navies. He also said that Saitō had agreed to return to America and work for these aims. Actually, a few days later, Saitō told the Emperor that the United States would not agree to "unconditional parity." [8]

FLAWED RESISTANCE

Okada could expect help in opposing the navy from the Foreign Office, the Treasury, and the Army Minister; aid from other areas would not be forthcoming. There was the possibility that he might have the Emperor order the navy to obey the government. If Ōsumi did resign, the Emperor could command the navy to produce another minister. But for twenty years no such rescript had been granted, and the Emperor's advisers opposed imperial intervention in politics on any question. Saionji himself believed that the Emperor should remonstrate with the navy chiefs, but Kido was opposed to this action. Ōsumi warned Okada through Harada that, "if by any chance the general desire of the navy vis-à-vis disarmament were checked by an imperial edict, this would be a big affair . . . the genrō and the *jūshin* [former Prime Ministers], etc. would probably not try such a trick, but . . ." Harada assured Okada that no one was considering such a plan. [9]

Okada might also have dissolved the Diet and tried to defeat the pro-navy Seiyūkai in the ensuing election. But the genrō would probably have opposed this course as inviting a direct clash between the Minseitō and the military. The dissident Seiyūkai leaders, who had just entered the cabinet, would also oppose such a dissolution; and worst of all, the Seiyūkai might run on a platform of naval equality and win. [10] Thus, the burden of supporting Okada against the navy's campaign fell on Finance Minister Fujii, Army Minister Hayashi, and Foreign Minister Hirota. But Fujii was new to cabinet councils and weak in debate in comparison to his predecessor, the vigorous old politician Takahashi. Moreover, General Hayashi's opposition to the navy was weakening.

Despite pressure from the Army General Staff and the navy, the Hayashi-Nagata leadership at the Army Ministry had been resisting the demand for abrogation of the naval treaty, because they feared that free naval competition would make their national mobilization plans economically impossible. On July 19, Hayashi re-evaluated his position, perhaps because the navy's campaign was heating up and perhaps because the Army General Staff still supported the navy. Hayashi stated that conciliation of China, Russia, Britain, and the United States was the way to achieve security while constructing Manchukuo. But if Japan could rid itself of the naval restrictions without causing a worsened international situation and increased expenditures, he would have no objection. Consequently, he hoped that the navy would abrogate the Washington naval treaty only after giving careful consideration to the proper time and method. After deciding to let the navy have its way, Hayashi invited Ōsumi to his residence on July 20 in order to exact these conditions from him.[11]

Navy Minister Ōsumi arrived the next morning full of reassurances for the worried Army Minister. To be sure, he declared, the navy officials were planning to insist on the establishment of equal ratios "to the last," but they were not necessarily hoping for the breakup of the conference. Moreover, since Japan would propose a large cutback in arms, it would be able to appeal to American public opinion. Hayashi asked what would happen if the negotiations broke down. Ōsumi replied, "I think there is an eighty percent chance that things will be alright, although there may be some worsening in the international situation, and it will probably cause some competition in naval construction." Then Hayashi asked what the navy's attitude toward an increase in army spending would be. Ōsumi replied that the navy recognized that the development of Manchukuo might require further increases in army expenditures. When Hayashi pressed Ōsumi further about what the navy planned to spend if the conference failed, Ōsumi said that, although it was hard to speculate about the future, the navy did not plan to ask for large budget increases. Although reassured that he would have navy support for army spending, Hayashi again told Ōsumi that the army agreed with the navy generally, but that it was concerned about the effect a naval race might have on international relations, on Japan's economy, on its naval construction program, and on army expenditures.[12] In reality, however, Hayashi had given up the fight. On July 23, he told Harada that, although he thought the navy's proposals extremely dangerous, the army as a whole would support them completely.[13]

THE VIEW FROM THE FOREIGN OFFICE

After Hayashi's defection, Okada had only the Foreign Office and its head, Hirota Kōki, as an ally. Despite the wreck of his American-Japanese rapprochement policy on the rock of the Amō doctrine, Hirota was still determined to seek good relations with the United States. He assigned the framing of the Foreign Office position to the research section of the European-American division. The director of this section was Tōgō Shigenori, an old friend of American-Japanese rapprochement and a supporter of the disarmament treaties. Tōgō found his task "extremely difficult," partly because the navy was taking such a hard line in the press. Moreover, he believed that the navy was making proposals profitable only to Japan, which left little hope for settlement. Tōgō pointed out that such a policy would cast doubt on Japan's peaceful intentions. Consequently, he began making compromise proposals, but the navy did not respond. He then tried to stir up opposition from the Army and Treasury Ministers, but they both said that, while recognizing the bad effects which the navy's policy would have, they did not think it possible to offer any opposition.[14]

In spite of these setbacks, Tōgō continued his resistance over a period of two or three months, and in one day he had three fiery interviews with the navy leaders. Admiral Yoshida Zengo, director of the Navy Ministry's bureau of military affairs, claimed that the United States and Japan might tangle over the China problem and consequently Japan had to build up its fleet. Tōgō replied that naval competition would only increase the possibility of war. In the following days Kuriyama Shigeru, the Foreign Office treaty bureau head, appealed to Harada to ask the government not to abrogate the Washington naval treaty, since this act would recreate an atmosphere similar to the withdrawal from the League. Ōsumi complained that, although Hirota was being understanding, the heads of the bureaus at the Foreign Office were opposing the navy. On July 23, the Foreign Office released its own public statement to counteract the navy's press campaign. The Foreign Office spokesman said that the navy's call for an end to naval limitations and for equality with the United States required careful consideration. The diplomats were worried about the international effect this demand might have, especially if the conference broke up because of it. Therefore, they urged that the new disarmament policy proposed by Japan be a reasonable one, in order to secure a new general agreement. And they warned against abrogating the Washington naval treaty prior to the conference.[15]

On July 24, the Prime Minister held a second five ministers' conference, at which he attempted to make Ōsumi moderate the navy's position. Okada told the Navy Minister that the preparatory negotiations for the naval conference had to succeed for financial reasons. Both the Finance Minister and the Army Minister supported this statement. Ōsumi replied that, although the navy officials hoped the preliminary talks would prove successful, they also believed it was necessary to consider the possibility that they would not. It was imperative, Ōsumi maintained, to consider proposals that would eventually yield a balance of power. Foreign Minister Hirota then saw his chance to urge Okada's original proposal: a new disarmament agreement that would grant Japan equality, but which would also regulate the building necessary to achieve a naval balance. Hirota suggested that Japan's navy be increased gradually in two or three stages. At the coming conference, then, Japan would seek a recognition of its equality and permission for the first stage of construction. The Navy Minister replied that they could consider such a proposal, since the navy was also mulling over a five-stage process. Prime Minister Okada then said that five stages were not enough and that the navy should accept a ten-stage process, if necessary, to make a compromise possible.[16]

Okada was perhaps pleased with Ōsumi's conciliatory attitude, for he urged that the navy and the Foreign Office cooperate to have "both the navy's hopes accomplished and the negotiations succeed." But Ōsumi quickly dispelled any false optimism by urging that Japan seek the total abolition of capital ships and aircraft carriers. Okada reminded him that a number of nations had refused a similar proposal during the 1932 Geneva Disarmament Conference. Worse yet, the Navy Minister was also adamant on the problem of abrogating the Washington naval treaty. The Prime Minister said that Japan should wait until the end of the year, in order to see the outcome of the preparatory negotiations. Although the rest of the cabinet supported Okada, Ōsumi said that it would be difficult to pacify opinion in the navy if the treaty were not abrogated soon. The conference ended with the Prime Minister again urging the Foreign Minister and the Navy Minister to compromise. Thus, the navy had demanded the immediate abrogation of the Washington naval treaty, and had asked that Japan seek naval equality and the complete abolition of capital ships and aircraft carriers. Okada and Hirota feared that acceptance of this bargaining position would ensure the breakdown of negotiations, and they called for the navy to accept a more moderate course of action. Japan, they maintained, should seek equality after a period of years, and it should wait before abrogating the Washington naval treaty.[17]

FURTHER PRESSURE BY THE NAVY

The navy stepped up its efforts during the hot days of August. Prime Minister Okada made the mistake of telling foreign correspondents that a solution of the naval problem would not be difficult if the powers would only recognize Japan's stabilizing position in East Asia. The navy declared that the Prime Minister had agreed that the Washington naval treaty must go, and the *Asahi* editors stated that inferior ratios threatened Japan's security. Two days later, the newspapers reported that the American Secretary of the Navy had called for the continuance of the existing ratios and an overall twenty percent reduction of tonnage. The navy authorities immediately announced that they were "completely opposed" to the self-serving American proposal. The Osaka *Mainichi* joined the other large newspapers in protesting the continuance of the ratios. It stated that the American proposal would hurt Japan more than the other powers, and that the Americans were seeking a navy second to none. Japan, they stated, should demand parity. On August 6, the navy declared that it had already decided to abrogate the treaty and that it was only discussing the timing with the Foreign Office. On August 19, the *Hōchi* reported that the genrō and *jūshin* were opposing a quick abrogation of the treaty, but that Ōsumi was willing to resign to achieve that end.[18]

The navy's campaign began to have an effect on the Emperor's advisers and the Prime Minister. When Prince Konoye returned from the United States on August 1, Harada rushed to Yokohama, took a launch to the prince's ship, and warned him not to mention the disarmament problem to the press, since it was "particularly delicate." Harada added that the Foreign Office hoped that Konoye would not be too pessimistic in public about American-Japanese relations. On August 2, Admiral Kobayashi told Harada that opinion in the combined fleet was united: the fleet officers wanted an abrogation of the treaty and a return to an independent defense. On the same day, Okada assured two members of the right-wing Kokumin dōmei party that he had not ruled out seeking parity, and after leaving the Prime Minister, the two men announced this fact to the press. On August 5, Okada himself told the press that he thought the future of the conference looked bleak. Okada and Hirota told Harada that Ōsumi, on a special trip to observe maneuvers of the combined fleets, had assured the younger officers that the government's policy had already been decided in favor of abrogation. Finally, on August 10, Okada came out against continuance of the ratio system because it injured Japan's self-respect. He was quoted as saying: "In general, ratios are no good because they are like having to use a bow and arrow against a cannon." [19]

The defection of the Prime Minister left only Hirota and the Foreign Office opposed to abrogation of the treaty. On August 10, the diplomats again crossed swords with the navy in the public opinion arena. A Foreign Office spokesman suggested that, since an immediate abrogation would cause unnecessary damage to Japan's foreign relations, Japan should wait until the end of December before taking such action. By August 23, the Foreign Office had gained the reprieve it desired; Okada and Hirota convinced their colleagues to avoid immediate abrogation of the Washington naval treaty. The Prime Minister told the Emperor that the five ministers' conference had decided to withdraw from the naval treaties, but at the proper time. The Emperor responded, "Because the military is demanding it, we have no choice," but he warned that the abrogation should be done in the least antagonizing manner possible, and the blame for a breakup of negotiations should not fall on Japan. Although the Foreign Office had won this point, in the next few days it was to lose the game. [20]

In spite of Hirota's entreaties, the navy refused to consider building up to parity over a period of ten to twenty years, insisting instead on immediate equality in terms of overall tonnage. On August 25, Admiral Suetsugu told the Greater Asia League (Dai Ajia kyōkai) that a strong navy was necessary to safeguard Manchuria and that the naval question was "now becoming the central problem of the emergency." He continued: "The fundamental policy of our navy vis-à-vis naval disarmament is the abrogation of the ratio requirements as provided in the Washington and London treaties, and the establishment of a new treaty based on the principle of equality in the right to arms. If this demand is not accepted, we will not shrink from the breakup of the conference. All countries should lower their arms to a common level, and within those limits, each country should decide on its arms by its own law." Although an agreement had been reached to abrogate the treaty by the end of the year, Suetsugu preferred to see it done "as soon as possible." Then he uttered the ultimate threat: "if these demands are not accepted, we will not be able to take responsibility for national defense." [21] In other words, the central figures in the fleet faction, Ōsumi and Suetsugu, would resign; and the effect of their resignations on naval discipline would be calamitous.

At this point, the Seiyūkai threatened to become involved. On August 24, the Suzuki leadership began pressing for a special session of the Diet to deal with the agricultural problem and with naval policy. On August 26, the Seiyūkai leaders met with Okada to urge their views. According to the newspapers, Okada told them that the cabinet was agreed on the need for abrogation of the treaty. The Seiyūkai had cooperated with the fleet faction during the London Treaty crisis and there is little doubt that they were ready to do so again. When the party decided its policy on the naval question on September 5, it came out for a quick abrogation of the Washington naval treaty and naval equality for Japan.[22]

There is little evidence of publicly expressed opposition to the navy's campaign. With few exceptions, the natural leaders of such resistance were quiet. The Prime Minister blurred his statements to avoid antagonizing excitable elements in the navy. The previous champions of disarmament in the Minseitō were silent, because they were pledged to support the Prime Minister. The army had decided to support the navy, although Hayashi and Nagata voiced doubts. Only the Foreign Office had raised any arguments for caution.

A few smaller newspapers sounded rare conciliatory notes. The *Chūgai shōgyō shinpo* urged on July 18 that the government adopt a policy which would make success at the conference possible. The *Miyako* had already come out against any unreasonable proposals that would cause a naval race. On July 18, it urged the government to resist navy pressure. By August 23, however, the *Miyako* had completely reversed its position. It now followed the navy line, calling for the maintenance of Japan's "feeling of security" by withdrawal from the Washington naval treaty.[23] Thus, by using the newspapers to threaten the Okada cabinet with talk of resignation, the navy leaders achieved quick results: the major newspapers fell into line behind their position, and only a few smaller papers showed signs of resistance.

The navy's publicity campaign also had an effect on the editors of magazines. The great majority of magazines, which aimed at mass readership, did not allot much space to the naval problem, but more specialized journals, which aimed at an elite audience, did treat the disarmament question at length. For example, the *Diplomatic Review,* written by and for members of the foreign policy elite, declared that the Western powers should withdraw from the Asian lands which they had subjugated and abolish the naval treaties which injured Japan's feeling of security. With one exception, financial journals predicted that little would come from the negotiations.[24] Owing to the navy's campaign against naval disarmament, Okada and Hirota received little aid from the elite press.

Prime Minister Okada and the civilian members of the government thus faced an impossible situation. They had to accept the navy's demands or have Ōsumi and Suetsugu resign. If such a resignation took place, the imperial advisers would not allow the Emperor to force the navy to supply a minister. Nor would the army aid Okada in opposing the navy. And the Prime Minister could not seek support in the Diet: if he called an election and tried to help the prodisarmament Minseitō win, the young naval officers might try another coup. Consequently, the genrō would probably veto such a plan. In any case, the Seiyūkai might win such an election by campaigning for "naval equality." The only active opposition to the navy during August had come from the Foreign Office, which had no constituency in the country. And the diplomats' only debating weapon was the possibility of worsened international relations, but the danger of war with the United States and Britain apparently did not worry the navy or its supporters in the media. Thus, Okada and Hirota were generals without allies or an army and at the end of August, they surrendered.

THE DECISION

On August 29, Okada, Hirota, and Ōsumi reached fundamental agreement on the policy to be presented to the cabinet. Before the meeting, Hirota warned Okada that he would resign if the new policy allowed "no leeway" in his instructions to the delegates; he also said, however, that he would be able to continue in office if there were some flexibility. Consequently, although the three ministers decided to seek an abrogation of the Washington naval treaty by the end of the year, they also agreed to let Hirota seek a cooperative abrogation by all the signers of the treaty. Moreover, while the navy succeeded in gaining agreement to its demand for naval equality, Hirota's negotiators would be able to accept a parity reached in stages. In return for these concessions, however, Okada and Hirota had to seek the abolition of capital ships and aircraft carriers.[25] Thus, Okada and Hirota would demand the end of the old system of disarmament and the substitution of Japanese naval parity. Although the civilians had accepted the basic position of the military, they had managed to soften it somewhat. By not abrogating before negotiating, Japan's position would be more flexible. Moreover, if the navy would really allow the negotiators to make an agreement that controlled the stages of Japan's naval growth, perhaps some treaty would be possible.

The leaders of the navy accepted these slight modifications of their proposals because they believed that the policy adopted was sufficient to break up the conference. The United States and Britain would first have to accept the end of the old ratio system. Then they would have to agree to an overall tonnage equality for Japan and possibly other countries as well. Finally, they would have to accept the abolition of capital ships and aircraft carriers. The navy, of course, did not believe that this final demand could be accepted. The Chief of the Navy General Staff, Prince Fushimi, told the Emperor that Japan would propose the complete abolition of capital ships "as a conference measure according to the situation." He explained, however:

> "Capital ships are the nucleus of seaborne military power. The complete abolition of these would be unprofitable from the standpoint of maintaining our position as a great naval power and of eliminating any large difference in our mutual naval ratios in both war and peace and in view of our strategy; our real intention is not to bring about the realization of this proposal. But we will propose this in case the situation demands it, in order to strengthen the empire's demands.
> We recognize that the possibility of realizing the complete abolition of capi-

tal ships is extremely small in view of England and the United States' past demands and in view of their relations with the various countries which have capital ships, such as Germany, France, Italy, and the Soviet Union.''

Fushimi also made clear that the navy did not in actuality want the abolition of carriers: ''as long as there is a balance of military strength, the complete abrogation of aircraft carriers would not be advantageous from the standpoint of imperial strategy, but we will insist on these as an offensive craft, in order to strengthen the fundamental demands of the empire vis-à-vis the conference.'' The navy believed that it had won its victory; in future months it would concentrate on preventing a change in this policy and keeping the negotiators in London from reaching a compromise.[26]

By the summer of 1934, the Japanese government had turned its face against cooperation with the West, and this change seemed fairly permanent. Although the civilian ministers were somewhat reluctant to break with Great Britain and the United States, the military leaders had few doubts. And it was the generals and admirals who held both the whip and reins; not only did they manage the media, but they could also threaten a coup d'état when thwarted.

The leaders of both services decided in 1933 that the army should continue to expand in north China, in spite of Japan's obligation under the Nine-Power Treaty to respect China's administrative and territorial integrity. They agreed that Japan would have to construct more weapons to support its independent diplomacy. Although such a buildup might invite a naval race, Japan's admirals were confident that, if only their hands were freed from naval limitations, they could match the Western powers. It remained to be seen whether or not the Americans and British could frame a diplomatic strategy that would deflect the Japanese from their course and save the Washington and London naval treaties.

PART TWO   United States Policy

5 Roosevelt's Foreign Policy and Japan

The President of the United States is never free to make foreign policy as he wishes, but in 1933 and 1934, Franklin D. Roosevelt faced an exceptional number of difficulties. The previous administration had dredged a narrow channel within which Roosevelt must steer, for Hoover's Secretary of State, Henry L. Stimson, had made a strong legal case against Japan's behavior in Manchuria, and he had ended by convicting the Japanese of deliberate and malicious transgressions against the Washington treaty system. Another formidable obstacle to change in America's basic East Asian policy was the bipartisan isolationist coalition in Congress. In foreign affairs the legislators confined the President to a narrow territory, and they patrolled its boundaries alertly against any efforts to resist Japan. Moreover, Japanese actions in 1933 neither encouraged the President to generosity toward Japan, nor frightened him into reversing Stimson's support for the Washington system. Consequently, he neither sought a fundamental compromise with Japan at the expense of China, nor did he risk war to preserve the Washington treaty system. Instead, out of the exigencies of domestic maneuvering and the pressure of foreign developments came the cautious stance that the Roosevelt administration took toward Japan in 1933 and, later, toward the questions of naval construction and disarmament. Roosevelt's caution, which continued until 1940, meant that the United States would neither run a hard-paced naval race with Japan nor forsake its commitments in Asia. The eventual price paid for this hesitation was high indeed.

STIMSON'S WEB

When the Japanese army invaded Manchuria and the Japanese navy fought in Shanghai, Henry L. Stimson read Japan out of the international community. During the Manchurian incident, Stimson warned Japan that the United States would continue to insist on its rights under the Washington treaty system and that it would not recognize the fruits of Japan's aggressions. Stimson argued that the Japanese had transgressed both against the integrity of China, which they had pledged to respect in the Nine-Power Treaty, and against the renunciation of war that they had promised in the Kellogg-Briand Pact of 1928. After the outbreak of the Shanghai incident, Stimson reaffirmed his support for the treaties and cautioned that the United States might consider itself released from the naval and fortification limitations of the Washington naval treaty if Japan did not end such aggression. Stimson's threat received almost unanimous public support.[1] The United States, with Stimson in the lead, had stepped forth as defender of international law.

The American people, however, showed little desire to make Stimson's paper defense of the treaties effective. President Hoover had Under Secretary of State William R. Castle assure the world that America would not use economic pressure or military threats in the conduct of foreign affairs. Nevertheless, during the presidential campaign of 1932, Stimson made another attempt to rally American opinion to active support of the treaties. In a speech on August 8, he said that the United States would have to consult with other nations if there were a transgression against the Kellogg-Briand Pact, and he declared that the country could not remain neutral in the face of such violations. Although many newspaper editors had supported Stimson's earlier declarations, they criticized this latest effort severely. Moreover, Congress was hostile to all military spending in 1932, and in January 1933, it showed its isolationist inclinations by passing the bill establishing Philippine independence over President Hoover's veto. The voting margins were large: 274 to 94 in the House and 66 to 26 in the Senate.[2] Clearly a Congress that was unwilling to pay for the defense of America's only East Asian possession would not welcome new Asian initiatives.

Thus, the public believed that treaties were sacred, but it was unwilling to assume the burden of upholding them. Stimson had nevertheless woven his case against Japan so tightly that he had made it "very difficult to alter the basis of Far Eastern relations without appearing to approve Japanese aggression." Roosevelt had to reconcile this devotion to the Washington treaties and distaste for foreign commitments in a policy that would be viable in both the United States and East Asia. On January 9, 1933, Roosevelt met with Stimson at Hyde Park in order to discuss foreign affairs. When questioned later by reporters about the meeting, Roosevelt wrote out a public statement in which he announced that "American foreign policies must uphold the sanctity of international treaties." In this minimal way the Democratic President-elect endorsed the Republicans' East Asian treaty system but avoided any specific indication of the measures he would take to support it.[3] Such a careful political move was entirely in character for Roosevelt.

ROOSEVELT AND FOREIGN AFFAIRS

President Roosevelt had an acute political sense, which he had developed over a lifetime of public service. He moved carefully to maintain personal control over foreign policy. Although he was willing to confer with almost anyone, he kept his own counsel and made up his mind independently. He was particularly wary of the isolationists in the country and in Congress. In order to keep his finger on the pulse of the nation, he read the major newspapers, including those most belligerently isolationist in sentiment, such as the *Chicago Tribune*. When dealing with Congress, he was particularly careful because he considered the isolationist leaders to be irreconcilable to opposing views.[4]

The President's caution was the result of painful personal experience. Roosevelt had been the vice-presidential candidate in 1920 when the Democratic candidates supported the League of Nations. Although he had hoped that this campaigning would lead to victory, Harding rolled up sixty percent of the vote and swept leading Democrats out of Washington for more than a decade. In fact, in the years from 1896 to 1932, the Democratic party had been the weak political sister of the Republicans. Woodrow Wilson had been elected President only because of a split in the Republican ranks, and the isolationist reaction to the League of Nations had brought this brief period of Democratic prosperity, as well as Roosevelt's career as Assistant Secretary of the Navy, to an abrupt end.[5] Roosevelt, having seen "public opinion" led by maverick and partisan senators rise up and destroy his party at the polls, had good reason for care in dealing with Congress.

As Governor of New York and during the campaign of 1932, Roosevelt avoided questions of foreign policy much as a colt avoids the bridle. William Randolph Hearst, editor of a chain of isolationist newspapers and a power in the Democratic party, nevertheless forced Roosevelt to speak out on the League issue when he demanded a public declaration of the policy that Roosevelt would follow toward the League. The candidate responded that, as the League had not measured up to Woodrow Wilson's hopes, the United States had no place in it. Roosevelt's compromise turned out to be extremely important, since it enabled Hearst's ally, William G. McAdoo, to provide the margin for victory at the Democratic convention by bringing Texas into the Roosevelt column.[6] The power of the isolationists was obvious, even in the party of Wilson.

Although Roosevelt's political experience dictated caution, he leaned toward adopting the policies of a great power. While at the Navy Department during the Wilson administration, Roosevelt had made speeches favoring a larger navy, despite the disapproval of the Secretary of the Navy. Roosevelt's enthusiasm for naval power dated as far back as his youth. He had been an avid yachtsman and collector of lore on the United States Navy, and as Assistant Secretary, he sometimes took command of navy ships himself. During his years at the Navy Department, he also acquired a knowledge of naval strategy. In 1915, for example, when various amateurs were suggesting that the American navy should divide its forces to cover both coasts, since it could reunite them in time of danger by using the newly opened Panama Canal, Roosevelt undertook to silence the heresy. He arranged for former President Theodore Roosevelt and naval strategist Alfred Thayer Mahan to write articles stressing the need to keep the fleet concentrated, since it was Mahan's axiom that a fleet should never be dispersed and laid open to piecemeal destruction by a superior enemy force. Roosevelt's love for the navy was so marked that George C. Marshall, Chief of Staff of the army during

World War II, once protested, "At least, Mr. President, stop speaking of the Army as 'they' and the Navy as 'us.' " [7] Thus, during his political apprenticeship Roosevelt had been both an internationalist and an advocate of a great navy. But even though the President may have wished to conduct a strong and internationalist foreign policy, political realities and past experience kept him on a more circumspect course.

THE DOMESTIC EMERGENCY AND ISOLATIONISM

When Franklin D. Roosevelt took office, the nation's economy was approaching collapse: national income had dropped by half; five thousand banks had failed, destroying nine million savings accounts; and more than fifteen million workers had lost their jobs. The economic crisis absorbed the attention of the new administration and Congress. For example, in 1934, Roosevelt published a short book describing the accomplishments of his first two years in office, and twelve of its thirteen chapters dealt with his domestic program. In order to handle the emergency effectively and to mollify Congress, Roosevelt played the role of a bipartisan leader. In November 1934, he declared that it was the duty of the President to "find among many discordant elements that unity of purpose that is best for the Nation as a whole." He told the members of his administration that he was operating between the fifteen percent of the nation who were on the extreme right and the fifteen percent on the extreme left. [8]

Roosevelt's legislative coalition was in fact bipartisan. Some of his most loyal supporters on the domestic front were liberal western Republicans, often known by the nickname, "Sons of the Wild Jackass." In the Senate, men such as William E. Borah, Robert M. La Follette, Hiram Johnson, Gerald P. Nye, Lynn Frazier, George Norris, and Bronson M. Cutting were welcome additions to the New Deal ranks, but often these men were also captains of the isolationist legions. There were other progressive isolationists in the Senate, such as the Democrats Homer T. Bone, Burton K. Wheeler, Huey Long, and the Farmer-Laborite, Henrik Shipstead. In fact, until late 1939 the isolationist bloc of liberal and conservative Republicans combined with their Democratic colleagues to control Congress. In order to maintain a bipartisan consensus, Roosevelt strove for good relations with Congress by allowing some inflationary measures to become law. But in 1933 and 1934, Congress threatened to outflank the President on the left by spending large sums for the relief of veterans, farmers, laborers, and homeowners. [9] The President lacked the resources to get his own program through, keep the spenders in check, and challenge Congress on foreign policy as well. Such a challenge might endanger his large recovery program and destroy the consensus that he was so carefully constructing.

Congress itself was in no mood to tolerate any defiance on foreign policy. In fact, the depression exaggerated the prevailing isolationism of the legislators and their constituents. By December 1936, when the first public opinion surveys on foreign policy were taken, ninety-five percent of those polled opposed *any* participation in another European war. The respondents ranked unemployment and economy in government, rather than foreign questions, as the most important issues facing the nation. In addition to the economic crisis, there were a number of other reasons for the strength of isolationist sentiment. Since the time of Washington's Farewell Address, it had been the traditional policy of the United States to avoid entangling alliances, and Wilson's venture into European politics appeared like a brief and painful aberration. A number of Americans had not been eager to go to war, and most citizens of German extraction resented the anti-German hysteria that had swept the country in 1917. Nor were the former allies universally popular. Irish-American workers in the cities joined the farmers on the plains in their suspicion of imperial Britain, international bankers, and the gold standard. Since the New Deal was particularly aimed at winning the farm vote to the Democratic standard, Roosevelt was sensitive to expressions of agrarian prejudice.[10]

The nature of Wilson's peace treaty gave the Republicans an opportunity to blend tradition, ethnic resentments, and fears for the future into a winning campaign against the Treaty of Versailles. The tenets of isolationism acquired new authority in the Republican years from 1920 to 1933, aided by a largely Republican press. In 1926, for example, Congress freighted its acceptance of the World Court with so many reservations that the other members of the Court would not seat the American representatives. Confronted with this tide of feeling, the Democratic party first split and then regrouped under the banner of isolationism. After the Democratic presidential defeat of 1924, Roosevelt and his loyal retainer, Louis M. Howe, surveyed the leaders of their party as to the reasons for the weakness of their party. From both city and country, the Democrats replied that the party of Wilson was too internationalist. By 1928, in an article for the journal *Foreign Affairs,* Roosevelt had backed away from endorsing American entry into the League.[11]

Throughout his first term, Roosevelt moved very carefully, following a line only slightly less isolationist than his predecessor. The depression had forced most European nations to end their payment of war debts, causing resentment throughout the United States. Roosevelt responded by refusing to accept a currency stabilization agreement at the London Conference of 1933, thereby preserving his freedom to manipulate the price of gold at home. In the spring of 1934, Congress showed its hostility to Europe by passing the Johnson Act, which prevented Americans from lending money to any nation in default on its war debt. Although the law would prevent England and France from financing a new war effort in America, Roosevelt showed no inclination to attempt a settlement of this problem.[12]

When he did make a slightly internationalist gesture, Roosevelt suffered severe criticism. In an attempt to save the deadlocked Geneva Disarmament Conference, Roosevelt allowed the American representative, Norman H. Davis, to make two promises: if the European nations would agree to a real measure of disarmament, the United States would consult with the other powers when peace was threatened, and more important, if it concurred with the majority of the powers consulted, it would try not to interfere with sanctions against an aggressor. Roosevelt also personally appealed to the heads of fifty-four nations to enter a nonaggression pact. A storm of criticism followed. John Bassett Moore, a leading authority on international law, denounced these moves as "the greatest danger to which the country had ever been exposed, a danger involving our very independence." [13]

The isolationists in the Senate, led by Hiram Johnson, attacked the proposal. The Senate Foreign Relations Committee had been considering a resolution to stop American arms shipments to aggressors, but after Davis' statement, the Senators decided to make the embargo apply both to the aggressor and to the nation attacked, thereby ending the possibility that the President might use it to reinforce League sanctions. Roosevelt backtracked on the arms embargo and also had Davis reassure the nation that the United States make "no commitment whatever to use its armed forces for the settlement of any dispute anywhere." Thus, when Roosevelt forgot to act cautiously, Congress reminded him. Roosevelt's initiative at Geneva was not a total failure, however, for he demonstrated that he was as concerned about disarmament as Hoover had been, and disarmament was extremely popular with Congress. Progressives of both parties were happy with the successful naval disarmament conferences of the twenties, since they believed that limiting arms removed one of the causes of war and freed needed funds for domestic spending. Some conservatives also welcomed the agreements as a way to save money. In 1932, peace groups had held an automobile procession of over a mile in length to the White House to present a peace petition bearing hundreds of thousands of signatures, to which Hoover had responded by proposing an immediate one-third reduction in all armaments. [14]

Roosevelt, in his turn, pledged on March 17, 1933, to "use every possible means" to make the disarmament conference a success. His call for a nonaggression pact and the scrapping of offensive weapons drew bouquets from his liberal supporters. Lillian D. Wald called Roosevelt's appeal "soul-satisfying"; James G. MacDonald, chairman of the National Peace Conference, sent the President a message of gratitude for his "courageous and constructive leadership." Yet while Roosevelt's initiative won support at home, it failed to resolve the deadlock at Geneva, and the conference broke up. [15]

In sum, because of the domestic emergency, Roosevelt had to put his major effort into a recovery program, and in order to maintain support for that program, he had to preserve his bipartisan majority in Congress by appealing to the increasingly isolationist legislators. At the same time, Roosevelt could not jettison the treaty structure that the Republicans had constructed during the twenties. In fact, Roosevelt and his advisors sensed little need for appeasing Japan.

IMAGES OF JAPAN

Despite the popularity of disarmament and the need to placate Congress, there was little chance that Roosevelt would accept Japan's dominance in East Asia, even if by doing so he could have preserved the naval ratios. When Roosevelt took office in 1933, Japanese troops were pushing south of the Greal Wall toward Peking. At the end of May, the League adopted the Lytton Commission Report, which condemned the Manchurian invasion, and Japan announced that it was withdrawing from the League. At the same time, Japanese armies in China succeeded in having Chinese troops withdrawn from the Peking-Tientsin area, creating a demilitarized zone in North China. Japan's defiance of the League and its aggression in China certainly did not encourage the Roosevelt administration to adopt an understanding tone toward Japan.

By nature, Roosevelt's subordinates were unlikely to favor the surrender of American rights and interests under the Washington treaties. His Secretary of State, Cordell Hull, stated repeatedly that treaty obligations were sacred. Hull had made a career of politics, starting in the Tennessee State Legislature at the age of twenty-one and becoming a judge by the time he was thirty-one. A hill country Demosthenes, Hull had sufficiently overcome a speech impediment to permit a political career. Hull's self-discipline was notable: after having smoked fifteen cigars a day for thirty-five years, he paused to consider whether or not the habit was necessary and then quit entirely. As a judge, he held offenders to the same strict standards he held for himself, recalling once that he "made short shrift of law violators, especially if they were chronic. This policy met with general approval except on the part of the lawless element." On the basis of his judicial record, he won a seat to Congress and eventually moved on to the Senate.[16] In the thirties, Hull applied his stern sense of moral outrage to the Japanese, who were breaking international law.

Although wary of committing himself in favor of policies, Hull knew well what he opposed: aggressors and high tariffs. He had devoted his career to putting Jeffersonian political principles into practice, and in foreign affairs he preached respect for the Jeffersonian "axioms of organized domestic and international society." He also sought an overall reduction of tariffs, because he had come to the conclusion during the horrors of World War I that "unhampered trade dovetailed with peace." [17] Thus the Japanese army's actions in China and its monopolistic practices in Manchuria ran against the grain of Hull's most cherished convictions. Because he feared the isolationists in Congress, Hull did not ask for any decisive démarche toward Japan, but he also would not recognize any Japanese claim to supremacy in the Orient. An increasingly hostile world and a dangerous domestic situation only increased the usual caution of this stern political professional.

Hull relied on his division chiefs for advice on foreign policy, and he later described the head of the Far Eastern Division, Stanley K. Hornbeck, as "capable, experienced, and dependable." Hornbeck, the son of a minister, recalled that there "were instilled in me principles of good behavior," and he had little patience with others who seemed to lack such a background. After teaching in China for five years, he lectured on the Far East at Wisconsin and Harvard before entering the State Department in 1928. Hornbeck dominated his division and aimed a steady stream of memoranda at his superiors. Although he was an isolationist in policy, Hornbeck retained a basic sympathy for China.

Hornbeck was the high priest of the traditional American policy in the Far East. Before entering the State Department, he had explained in a number of publications that the East Asian policies of the United States stretched back into the previous century and had always embraced "equality of commercial opportunity" in China and "maintenance of the administrative and territorial integrity of China." He noted that these axioms had received international assent in 1900 and treaty status in 1922, thereby attaining a "quasi-legal international status." Moreover, Hornbeck argued, the American public had a benevolent, if vague, desire to aid the Chinese. Hornbeck was eager to see the American tradition in East Asia upheld against the pretentions of an increasingly ambitious Japan. At the time of the Manchurian incident, he urged economic sanctions against Japan, and he was a staunch supporter of the nonrecognition policy.[18] Undoubtedly, this defender of principle found a congenial companion in Judge Hull.

The third man in government sounding this theme was the American ambassador in Tokyo, Joseph C. Grew. Although Grew occasionally urged conciliation for the sake of the Japanese moderates, he was never far out of harmony with his superiors in Washington. During the thirties, he never asked Washington to abandon the Washington treaty system, in order to accommodate itself to Japan's hegemony in the Orient. He was addicted to a nineteenth century optimism and believed that war was a rare abnormality in the modern, rational age; consequently, he hoped that Japan would soon come to her senses and resume cooperation with the powers. Grew did not probe deeply in Japan but limited himself to contact with prominent people, such as high-ranking diplomats, wealthy businessmen, and the court circle. Among the military, he knew only a few moderate admirals and almost no army officers. Grew's contacts assured him that moderates would soon regain control of the government, and despite repeated disappointments, he frequently accepted and reported their views to Washington.[19]

Grew's misinterpretation of Japanese political realities encouraged his superiors to adopt a negative policy toward Japan. Rather than warning of the real dangers and forcing Hull, Hornbeck, and Roosevelt to come to grips with the problem of Japan's ambitions, Grew urged them to sit tight and wait out the storm. Stimson's notes and declarations to Japan, after all, had done little good; even Hornbeck was tired of fruitless protests.[20] Consequently, Roosevelt's East Asian advisers argued that America should stand by its principles, but take no decisive action.

Roosevelt's own image of Japan also encouraged him both to caution and rigidity. He pictured the Japanese as an aggressive people whose ultimate aims were unworthy of trust. In a letter of April 5, 1933, to Colonel House, Woodrow Wilson's adviser on foreign affairs, Roosevelt described a meeting with Matsuoka Yosuke in uncomplimentary terms and likened the Japanese Empire to imperial Germany. Matsuoka had advised the United States to withdraw its fleet from the Pacific, a suggestion that brought, Roosevelt reported, "thousands of protests" to the White House. The President speculated whether Matsuoka had said this "to ingratiate himself against assassination by the Junker crowd when he gets home." [21]

After the Amō statement, Roosevelt told Stimson that he had met a young Japanese at Harvard who revealed that Japan had a long-range plan for taking over the Orient, the Pacific islands, Australia, New Zealand, and a few outposts in Latin America. The President assured Stimson that he would not abandon the nonrecognition doctrine. In November 1933, Roosevelt also pinned the blame for the failure of the Geneva Disarmament Conference on Japan and Germany in a letter to his ambassador to Berlin, William E. Dodd: "Walter Lippmann was here last week and made the interesting suggestion that about 8 per cent of the population of the entire world, i.e., Germany and Japan, is able, because of imperialistic attitude, to prevent peaceful guarantes and armament reductions on the part of the other 92 per cent of the world." [22] In Roosevelt's eyes, then, Japan was an unstable, aggressive, and dangerous country with long-range plans to establish a vast empire and with no compunctions against defying the desire of the world for peace and disarmament.

In the first days of his administration, Roosevelt was concerned about the danger of war with Japan. Carl Vinson, chairman of the House Naval Affairs Committee, had warned that the navy had fallen far below treaty limits, and Roosevelt himself had earlier argued that, with both Japan and the United States at peak treaty strength, there was a strategic deadlock in the Pacific. In other words, at its existing strength, the American fleet could not advance immediately against Japan with any hope of success. At the first working cabinet meeting on March 7, 1933, Roosevelt discussed a possible war with Japan in terms of a short-range defeat and an eventual victory. America would be obliged to abandon the Philippines, he said, because the fleet could not operate efficiently over long distances. His political adviser and Postmaster General, James A. Farley, remembered Roosevelt's explanation: "For every thousand miles the fleet moved away from its base . . . it would lose 10 per cent of its efficiency . . . [and] thirty per cent of the fleet would have to be diverted to furnish supplies and maintain communications." Thus the navy would have to operate at first from Hawaii and the Aleutians and gradually enforce a blockade on Japan. Farley recalled, "There was general agreement that we could defeat Japan by starvation, but that it would take from three to five years to do so." [23]

Roosevelt's conception of the probable course of war with Japan stayed with him. On December 18, 1937, after Japanese planes had attacked the U.S.S. *Panay* in the Yangtze, Roosevelt explained that the United States Navy could blockade Japan on a line from the Aleutians through Hawaii to Guam and that the British could take over the patrol from Guam to Singapore. As Harold Ickes, Secretary of the Interior, noted: "This would be a comparatively simple task which the Navy could take care of without having to send a great fleet. Blocked thus, the President thinks that Japan could be brought to her knees within a year." [24] The President thought that Japan might be formidable in East Asian waters over the short run but would ultimately prove vulnerable to the gradual economic pressure of a blockade.

Roosevelt's advisers shared and reinforced this view. On May 27, 1933, Stanley K. Hornbeck and Cordell Hull strongly endorsed and transmitted to the President a dispatch from Tokyo in which Ambassador Grew described Japan as a great power in terms of land mass, industry, and national spirit, which "probably has the most complete, well balanced, coordinated and therefore powerful fighting machine in the world today." The Japanese were superior on land and equal on sea to the United States, he reported, and they would permit no interference with their East Asian policy. Grew did add, however, that Japan might not have the strength for a long war. Under Secretary of State Phillips put his finger on one of Japan's major weaknesses: a lack of oil. Japan, he pointed out, depended on crude oil supplied by British, Dutch, and American companies. [25] In the eyes of America's leaders, therefore, although Japan was dangerous and would require careful handling, the United States did not need to change its position on the treaties, since in any conflict it could be sure of eventual victory. Given a modest amount of American naval strength, Japan would be blockaded into submission.

Out of these contradictory factors came a simple formula: the Americans would, when necessary, remind the Japanese of their treaty obligations, but at the same time they would do their best to avoid any crisis with Japan. When Japan left the League, Roosevelt asked his advisers whether the United States should press the Japanese to return the Pacific islands that they held in trust from Geneva; Phillips and Hornbeck argued that it would be better to wait for the League to take the lead, and Roosevelt followed their advice. The President also refused Chinese requests to mediate between the combatants in North China. As Japanese troops neared Peking, T. V. Soong, the Nationalist leader, had personally appealed to Roosevelt to "do something," but the President refused. [26] If in spite of Roosevelt's best efforts, a crisis did come, however, the President would have to rely on the United States Navy to blockade Japan. And in 1933, the American fleet seemed weak indeed.

NAVAL BUILDING AND RECOVERY

After the signing of the disarmament treaties in 1922 and 1930, Congress had been reluctant to provide funds for naval construction, and this reluctance increased with the onset of the depression. President Hoover responded to the economic crisis by cutting funds earmarked for naval building in 1931 and eliminating them entirely in 1932. The Navy League, a weak lobby comprised of a few wealthy men, a small staff, and no mass base, caused a mild sensation by accusing Hoover of "abysmal ignorance" of naval affairs, but the press came out against the League's challenge to the President by a margin of five to one.[27] Rearmament, then, was not likely to be popular with a depression-ridden Congress.

Even before Roosevelt's inauguration, however, the chairman of the House Committee on Naval Affairs, Carl Vinson, reminded the President that the United States fleet was dangerously weak compared to the Japanese navy. In 1932, Vinson had introduced a bill that called for spending $616 million for naval construction in a long-range, orderly program to bring the American navy up to treaty limits. On December 28, 1932, he told Roosevelt that the United States had tried in vain to encourage further disarmament by not building or replacing the ships to which it was entitled under the treaties. Vinson added: "Since the Washington Treaty of 1922, we have provided for but 40 ships, of a total of 197,640 tons, as compared with 148 ships of a total of 472,311 tons, for Great Britain, and 164 ships of 410,467 tons for Japan. During that period, France has provided for 196 ships of 507,737 tons, and Italy, for 144 ships of 297,072 tons." It was time, he implied, to abandon disarmament by example.

American strength in capital ships was satisfactory, Vinson wrote, but the United States did not have a full complement of lighter craft, and those that it did have would soon be obsolete. He pointed out that "we have less than one-half of our authorized strength in light cruisers and are greatly inferior in this type to both Britain and Japan," for Britain had thirty-four light cruisers, Japan had eighteen, and the American navy had only ten. The state of destroyer strength was even worse: all underage American destroyers had been built during the First World War, so that they would all become overage at the same time; in addition, only eight new contracts for destroyers had been let between 1928 and 1932. Consequently, on January 1, 1935, Vinson pointed out that the United States would have five underage destroyers to Britain's forty-five and Japan's sixty-three. The United States faced a similar problem in the submarine class: on January 1, 1936, Vinson revealed, it would have only twenty underage submarines, compared to thirty-six for Britain and forty-seven for Japan. Vinson concluded that, unless remedial steps were taken immediately, in 1936 the United States would have "a total underage tonnage smaller than that of Great Britain, of Japan, and of France."

Vinson argued that the United States should therefore adopt a long-range program which would provide for the yearly expenditures necessary to build a treaty navy "in a given length of time," and he recommended that the administration back his $616 million appropriations bill. He added that the "enactment of this bill would greatly strengthen the hands of our delegates at the Limitation of Armaments Conference, which must meet in 1935.'' Although he admitted that the Roosevelt administration would have to bear a ''heavier burden than it should normally have to bear . . . [since the Hoover administration had] not authorized a single new ship during its tenure of office,'' he pointed out that eighty-five percent of the total cost of ships ''goes directly into the pockets of labor,'' thereby aiding recovery. In fact, Vinson encouraged spending only the moderate sum of approximately $62 million a year over a period of ten years for naval construction.[28]

Vinson's points were well made. The strength of the American navy relative to Japan had fallen seriously. Moreover, the race in lighter naval armaments between France and Italy had the incidental result of threatening Britain's position in the Mediterranean, which forced Britain to weaken the strength of its East Asian fleet, thereby leaving Japan and the United States increasingly alone in the Pacific. Yet, Congress, suffering under the repeated shocks of the depression, was in no mood for large expenditures for naval armaments, and the isolationists tended to suspect that any increase in military strength presaged intervention in foreign troubles. Once more Roosevelt found the best alternative: a policy that provided both a naval buildup and a recovery from the depression.

In order to pacify Vinson, Roosevelt had the new Secretary of the Navy, Claude Swanson, announce that the policy of the administration was to bring the navy up to treaty strength. This pledge, however, conflicted with Roosevelt's initial recovery program, which involved cutting the budget. The navy, in fact, was expected to pare $53 million from its operating expenses. The fiscal executioner, Lewis Douglas, therefore decreed that one-third of the navy should be put on reserve; that is, the fleet would be divided into three parts and rotated, with one-third of its ships idled in the ports at all times. The Chief of Naval Operations, Admiral William V. Pratt, ordered the rotation system put into effect on July 1.[29]

Vinson reacted angrily to this new obstacle to the promised buildup. On March 27, he successfully appealed to the Navy League to fight the rotation plan. The Navy Department protested the budget cuts: on April 13, Swanson sent Roosevelt letters of protest from Admiral Pratt, Chief of Naval Operations, and from Admiral Frank B. Upham, head of the Bureau of Navigation. The Navy League campaign and the navy's protest had the desired effect as the President withdrew the rotation system and eventually restored the navy budget to normal. Roosevelt nevertheless remained wary of endorsing a large-scale building program. After reading a draft of proposed radio remarks by the Secretary of the Navy, Roosevelt had his assistant secretary, Stephen T. Early, tell Swanson that the President thought ''some of the remarks about the weakness of the Navy could be 'toned down.' '' And on May 4, 1933, Henry L. Roosevelt, the Assistant Secretary of the Navy, issued a set of instructions on fundamental policy that emphasized economy.[30]

But Vinson refused to give up in his fight for more warships, and the result was a compromise. Roosevelt agreed to seek power under the proposed National

Industrial Recovery Act to spend money for a modest amount of naval construction. Since the need for relief spending was desperate, the bill sailed through Congress easily by June 16, 1933. Roosevelt immediately allotted $238 million to start the construction that Vinson wanted. Roosevelt told Secretary of the Navy Swanson, "Claude, we got away with murder that time." [31]

Roosevelt had disarmed the potential congressional critics of naval spending by tacking it onto a piece of progressive legislation, and in the desperate days of 1933, this tactic proved successful. Roosevelt's motive for seeking new naval construction seems to have been a simple fear of Japan's increasing naval strength. When the Reverend Malcolm E. Peabody protested against the naval program, Roosevelt replied:

> That Navy program was wholly mine—I must confess . . . . Somewhat to my dismay I discovered that as a simple mathematical problem of self-defense the Japanese had built and kept their Navy up to the treaty provisions. Great Britain had done so in large part but we had not kept up at all, with the net result that our Navy was and probably is actually inferior to the Japanese Navy.
>
> All this I tell you in confidence of course, and also the further fact that the whole scheme of things in Tokio does not make for an assurance of non-aggression in the future.
>
> As a matter of fact our building program, far from building us up to our Treaty quotas, will barely suffice to keep us almost up to the ship strength of the Japanese Navy and still, of course, far below the British Navy. I am not concerned about the latter, but I am about the first. [32]

Clearly the NIRA building program would be insufficient, and Roosevelt would soon face the problem of securing additional building. Yet Peabody was not alone in opposing naval appropriations during the depression, for the announcement by Swanson in March brought a storm of protest in April and May. Many women's groups, such as the Women's Civic League, the YWCA, and the National Council of Jewish Women, sent letters and petitions of protest. Other groups favored naval construction, most notably the American Legion, retired naval officers, and labor organizations. On April 3, for example, the San Francisco local of the International Brotherhood of Boiler Makers, Iron Ship Builders, Welders, and Helpers urged the President to build more ships. However, the hostile letters outnumbered expressions of support by five to two. In spite of the President's reluctance to stir these resentments further, Vinson and the navy continued to press for the adoption of a long-term building program that would bring the navy up to treaty limits. [33]

Roosevelt had held a characteristic middle course by tacking back and forth between preparedness and economy. He had assured funds for some naval construction and promised eventually to bring the navy up to treaty limits. But he had also resisted congressional and Navy Department pressure for large expenditures to prepare for the naval negotiations. Moreover, what funds he did spend were labeled "recovery," not "rearmament." In this way he avoided rending his domestic coalition on the rocks of a foreign policy debate, and he escaped a long-range commitment to spend large sums of money.

THE VINSON PROGRAM AND DISARMAMENT

The basic problem would not disappear: the United States' need for new destroyers and submarines in order to replace its aging auxiliaries. On January 5, 1934, Henry L. Roosevelt told the President that the Navy Department wanted to continue building the ships called for in the eight-year program that Admiral Pratt had outlined during the previous year. The new administration had already made a good start with the NIRA funds, and the Assistant Secretary wanted to lay down one aircraft carrier, sixty-five destroyers, and sixteen submarines by the end of 1936.[34] The President, he emphasized, would have to make some provision for long-term building if the navy were to keep pace with Japan.

Roosevelt had good reason for continued caution in undertaking new naval construction. The building started in 1933 had led to such sustained protest that his principal disarmament negotiator, Norman H. Davis, asked the President to "say something about the naval building program which has been so misunderstood in certain quarters." Davis suggested that Roosevelt explain the necessity for keeping up the strength of the fleet while the search for further disarmament went on. Although Roosevelt made no public statement, he remained very sensitive to criticism of naval building. In early February 1934, he suggested to the Assistant Secretary of the Navy that Navy Department personnel should avoid debate on the question of naval construction.[35] The dilemma Roosevelt faced was the same: he could introduce costly long-term legislation to bring the navy up to treaty strength only at the risk of alienating highly vocal groups that certainly contained some of his supporters.

Another reason for the President's reluctance to start spending large sums on shipbuilding was the large federal deficit. In the spring of 1934, many special interest groups were threatening to increase the deficit by raiding the Treasury. Inflationists, agrarians, and silverites united behind a bill to sell farm surpluses abroad for silver, in order to raise the price of silver at home; the proposal would cost about $100 million a year to execute. Veterans' groups secured passage of a bill designed to force the President to pay a bonus to the veterans of the First World War, which Roosevelt had to veto. It was no wonder that in March the President looked "haggard"; his administration, Under Secretary of State William Phillips said, was "suffering all sorts of ailments." [36]

One principal cause of the administration's ills was Senator Gerald P. Nye, a progressive Republican from North Dakota. Nye generally supported the New Deal in 1933, but by December of that year he had concluded that the National Recovery Administration was probusiness. During the early months of 1934, Nye also began an attack on the armaments industry. At the suggestion of Dorothy Detzer, head of the Women's International League for Peace and Freedom, Nye introduced a resolution calling for an investigation of the munitions makers. Perhaps because of the antibusiness mood of the country, the proposal drew support from all quarters: churchmen and Marxists, pacifist groups and the American Legion, isolationists and internationalists, *Fortune* and the *New Republic*.[37]

Nevertheless, the navy needed ships, and Roosevelt decided to seek a pledge from Congress to build the navy up to treaty limits. Since this legislation was expected to run into severe opposition from the progressives, Roosevelt decided to ask for an extremely modest appropriation for construction during the following year. From Roosevelt's standpoint, the merits of this plan were numerous. A long-term authorization bill would end the debate over American naval policy that each new appropriation bill provoked in Congress. Instead, the United States would have a "treaty navy," and the adoption of this slogan would certainly blunt objections of the proponents of disarmament. Consequently, in January 1934, Roosevelt had Vinson introduce a bill authorizing the President to build the navy to treaty limits by 1942. Vinson also asked Congress to provide funds to start only four light cruisers.[38]

Despite the moderate nature of the actual spending planned, the reaction to the Vinson bill was angry. Once again, some of the most vigorous protests came from Roosevelt's supporters. Mary E. Woolley, the president of Mount Holyoke College and one of Roosevelt's delegates to the Geneva Conference, argued that the bill would have an unfortunate psychological effect on the disarmament negotiations. Another woman protested, "I feel that it is wrong to spend money on armaments that is so much needed for direct relief." On February 21, Secretary of State Hull warned Roosevelt that the State Department was receiving about two hundred letters and telegrams a day on the subject, more than ninety-nine percent of which were opposed to the bill. In March Senator Nye voiced similar thoughts in the Senate. Vinson had, he said, presented "a bill for the relief of the munitions makers of the United States." [39] Although his opponents were upset, Roosevelt had the votes, and by the end of March both the authorization and appropriations bills had passed through Congress.

Nevertheless, Roosevelt could not ignore the hostility that passage of the Vinson bills aroused, and he argued that no ships would be built unless absolutely necessary. On March 23, he explained at a news conference that the public did not understand the great difference between an authorization bill and an actual appropriation. He reminded the reporters that "it depends on the action of future Congresses as to whether the ships will be actually started or not." In the announcement handed to the press on March 27, he explained further that it was his "personal hope" that the coming naval disarmament conferences "would extend all existing limitations and agree to further reductions." The press seemed to take Roosevelt's statement in stride, and the Vinson bill did not provoke much editorial resistance.[40]

Roosevelt paid a price for this solution, however. By not providing for the construction of any destroyers or submarines in 1934, he made it much more difficult to bring the navy within hailing distance of treaty limits by the end of 1936. Consequently, American negotiators at the approaching London Conference would be in the difficult position of having to ask Japan alone to scrap its ships. If instead the United States had laid down a large number of destroyers and submarines between 1934 and 1936, it would have been able to destroy a number of its own ships comparable to those that Japan would have to scrap under a new and more stringent treaty. Furthermore, to Japan's admirals, the Americans appeared to lack the heart for a real naval race.

Given the President's difficult economic and political dilemmas, his policy nevertheless made sense. If the Japanese and British did not agree to preserve the limitation system during the coming conference, their refusal would convince many of Roosevelt's critics that the United States must indeed build a treaty navy. Thus, if the President unequivocally championed disarmament during the approaching negotiations and lost, few people could criticize him for turning up the road to rearmament at a later date.

6   A Tentative Decision

During the spring of 1934, it became apparent that Britain would soon call for preliminary negotiations to lay the groundwork for the conference in 1935, and consequently, the Roosevelt administration had to frame a bargaining position for its representatives. In spite of growing friction with Japan and Great Britain, the President maintained his stance on the need to work for arms limitations, in order to show the public that, if the negotiations failed, the fault would not be his.

In general, American-Japanese relations were relatively friendly at this time. In February and March, Hirota and Hull exchanged innocuous statements in which both men agreed that their two countries could settle all the issues between them by peaceful negotiation. Although there were minor irritations, all seemed calm as the preliminary negotiations approached.[1]

WASHINGTON AND THE AMŌ STATEMENT

Then on April 17, Amō Eiji, the Japanese Foreign Office press secretary, reopened the whole debate on Japan's present sincerity and ultimate intentions by declaring that Japan would oppose all efforts by the West to aid China. Under Secretary of State William Phillips considered the statement to be an "alarming development," since it was a "special notice to us to keep 'hands off' in China." Hirota told Ambassador Grew that Amō had given a "wholly false impression" of Japanese policy. But this report did not satisfy the State Department, and both Hull and Phillips pressed Ambassador Saitō for further explanation. Finally, on April 16, Saitō sent Phillips a number of explanatory documents, which included, Phillips wrote, "much to my astonishment, a copy of the instruction which had been sent by the Japanese Foreign Office to the Japanese Minister in China . . . The fifth paragraph of the instructions clearly states that it is the policy of Japan to keep foreign influence out of China, etc., etc. It looks to me as though Saitō has committed a blunder."[2] Thus, Saitō's disclosure made Hirota seem disingenuous and Japan appear extremely ambitious.

The Roosevelt administration, however, was not inclined to change its cautious policies. After sounding out the British, Hull sent a message to Japan on April 29 in which he reaffirmed the American position on the China question: the United States would continue to regulate its relations with China according to the treaty system, and would not assent to any initiative by Japan that might injure the rights of other nations. According to Phillips, the reaction of the American press to this statement was "excellent." At the same time, however, the State Department decided against encouraging any future loans to China, and Hull urged reporters to play down reports of American-Japanese antagonism.[3] The United States thus minimized the affair publicly while still maintaining its support for the Washington treaty system.

Although Roosevelt's advisers had maintained public composure, they were angered by the Japanese statement. As a result, they decided to advise the President that the United States should end the limitation system and build a fleet large enough to deter further Japanese actions against China. Since reports from Tokyo indicated that the Japanese naval authorities were spoiling for an arms race, Roosevelt's Far Eastern experts wanted America to enter the contest and win it.[4]

Even before Amō's surprising announcement, Stanley K. Hornbeck, head of the Far Eastern Division of the State Department, had warned his superiors about Japan's growing aggressiveness. The Japanese, he maintained, wanted the West to stand aside as they advanced further into China and Siberia. On April 24, 1934, Hornbeck's assistant, Eugene H. Dooman, tried to enlist the aid of Norman H. Davis, Roosevelt's chief disarmament negotiator, against the Japanese. The nonfortification articles of the existing treaties, Dooman stated, freed Japan for aggression throughout East Asia. Consequently, he argued that the United States should denounce Japan's call for parity and make a new four-power disarmament pact which would exclude Japan. Then the Americans and the British could coordinate their East Asian policies. Diplomatic isolation, Dooman predicted, would bring the Japanese to their senses.[5]

On the surface, Davis was an unlikely recruit to the ranks of Hornbeck's supporters, for he was known as an internationalist. He had made a comfortable fortune in Cuba in his youth and had then returned to the United States to become an important fund raiser for the Democratic party, and Assistant Secretary of State under Woodrow Wilson. In 1928, he had worked closely with Hull and Roosevelt in funding the campaign of Al Smith, and during the twenties he had also served as an informal foreign affairs adviser to Roosevelt. When Roosevelt was in the process of preparing an article for Foreign Affairs in 1928, Davis advised him that the United States should cooperate with the League of Nations in its efforts to preserve the peace. Davis also stressed the importance of naval disarmament. The Washington treaty system was very popular, and Congress was being swamped with letters from individual citizens protesting large naval appropriations; the American people, Davis wrote, "are not afraid of some other nation having a larger navy." J. Pierrepont Moffat, head of the Western European Division of the State Department, thought that Davis was always too optimistic about the prospects for success in disarmament talks, especially when Davis was the chief negotiator. On May 28, 1934, he recorded in his diary that Davis "psychologically is like an India rubber ball. It can be downed only to bounce up again quite as if nothing had happened.'' When Davis heard of possible disarmament talks, Moffat claimed, he was like an old warhorse scenting gunpowder.[6]

Nevertheless, Davis had reasons for agreeing with Moffat and Hornbeck. In an undated request for a decision on the disarmament policy to be followed in 1934, Davis indicated that he was a firm supporter of the Washington treaty system and predicted that the Japanese might agree to continue the existing ratios if the United States signed a nonaggression pact with them. But, Davis argued, such an agreement was impossible ''so long as they continue to penetrate China and do things in flagrant violation of treaties which we have already signed with them.'' The only way to resolve the differences between America and Japan, Davis suggested, was for Japan to settle its problems on the Chinese mainland.[7] Contrary to Moffat's expectations, Davis was pessimistic about the future of naval disarmament and eager to maintain the strength of the American navy.

On April 28, two days after his meeting with Moffat and Hornbeck, Davis joined Hull and the President for lunch at the White House. While Hull sat by in silence, Davis presented the Hornbeck thesis. He suggested that the United States should build up its navy and refuse to negotiate with Japan, because the Japanese were not honoring their treaty commitments. The Japanese had violated the Nine-Power Treaty, he said, and were probably building submarine bases in their mandated islands contrary to League rules.

But Roosevelt immediately quashed the Far Eastern Division's proposal, saying that he definitely wanted to hold a disarmament conference and to propose an overall cut of twenty percent in naval tonnage, with the ratios set up by the Washington and London naval treaties remaining in effect. The Japanese would be on the defensive if they declined such an offer, he argued. If the Japanese did refuse, however, then the United States would suggest that the existing treaties remain in effect for five years longer. If Japan then rejected this offer and withdrew from the talks, the United States could negotiate a treaty with the other powers that would provide for Anglo-American parity. The new treaty would also contain an escalation clause permitting the powers to build beyond the agreed limits in order to counter Japanese construction.[8]

Undoubtedly, Roosevelt was thinking about the protests aroused by the Vinson bills and about the popularity of disarmament in Congress. Consequently, the President hoped to neutralize both Congress and the Japanese. By championing disarmament, he silenced his critics in Washington and simultaneously put the responsibility for an arms race on Japan. Even if the negotiations failed, Japan apparently had little to gain. Roosevelt could point an accusing finger at Japan and ask Congress to provide funds for a treaty navy; if Japan then built beyond the treaty limits, Roosevelt could invoke the growing Japanese threat and exercise the United States' right to build under the escalation clause. On the other hand, should the Japanese come to their senses, and agree to keep the existing naval ratios, Roosevelt would then welcome the continuation of arms limitations and the resulting financial savings.

The luncheon meeting of April 28 did not result in an immediate decision, and the State Department did not draft the instructions for the American delegation to the conference until May 24. In the interim, Ambassador Saitō proposed establishing spheres of influence in the Pacific, but Roosevelt refused to be sidetracked from his original aim. According to Phillips, the President said that "this government should have some very simple platform on which to stand which would show our desire to cooperate in world naval disarmament; his thought was that we should be willing to reduce our force by 25%, provided others did the same . . . I pointed out that the Japanese would undoubtedly refuse to go along with us on any such lines. The President replied that the next and final position would be to stand on the present ratio." [9] Roosevelt saw no reason to modify his plan because of Japan's newly revealed ambition to police the Orient. If these pretentions led the Japanese to denounce disarmament, they alone would bear the responsibility. Roosevelt remained firm throughout the spring, holding his course for further arms reduction despite the implications of the Amō statement and despite the objections of his advisers. But the President would have to pass still another reef before he could seek further disarmament in London: the anger of American admirals.

THE ISOLATED NAVY

When asked by politicians for their recommendations on disarmament, American admirals found themselves in the awkward position of criminals on the gallows being invited to trip the drop so as to rid society of a grievous burden. Undaunted, they regularly protested against disarmament for what they considered to be innocent and professional reasons, but their efforts were useless, and the public continued to suspect them of ulterior, militaristic motives. In 1934, Roosevelt wanted to avoid any repetition of the angry public debate that the navy had held over the London Treaty in 1930; consequently, he put pressure on the navy to prevent any outburst against administration policy. In November 1933, Roosevelt and Norman Davis had ordered the General Board to make a study and then unite behind a proposal to cut all navies by ten percent. In the spring, when the navy tried to replace Roosevelt's choice of the flexible Admiral Richard H. Leigh as adviser to Davis, the President interposed his veto, saying the navy's nominee "had wood in his head." [10] Roosevelt's pressure worked, and the navy finally united behind a proposal that would allow for some disarmament. The navy coupled this flexibility, however, with a rigid insistence on the need to uphold the existing ratios.

The leaders of the navy were not a happy group in 1934. During the Senate hearing on the London Treaty of 1930, there had been a major revolt against the 10/7 ratio in auxiliaries granted to Japan, and the effects of this breach in the navy's ranks lingered on. The navy's lonely position in the bureaucratic hierarchy of the government contributed to their anger. The admirals ruminated on naval problems in isolation from the real policy makers, and during the Roosevelt administration, the civilian heads of the navy provided little coordination between naval desires and national decisions. Consequently, the members of the General Board and the Chief of Naval Operations, who were the chief naval advisers to both the President and the Secretary of the Navy, made policy recommendations unilaterally on the basis of their own strategic maxims and current needs. Even when the navy's leaders held Joint Board meetings with their army counterparts in order to coordinate strategy, their isolation from the policy makers continued.[11] Military policy was evidently not important enough to warrant close coordination between national goals and strategic realities.

This neglect caused bitterness. Admiral Frank H. Schofield complained to the Chief of Naval Operations, William H. Standley, that it was "becoming the fashion to belittle technical advice, meaning the advice of naval officers, concerning naval matters. As a matter of fact, they are the only ones competent to judge the naval aspects of naval proposals . . . It is we who have to stay on the job throughout the years of our life and who have to combat the ill effects of diplomatic decisions taken years before, contrary to that advice." [12] Schofield was invoking the professional, technical lore of the naval officer, which is a mixture of scientific, pseudoscientific, strategic, and tactical formulas laced with historicism.

All of the navy leaders necessarily believed in the maxims of their shared professional knowledge. The organization of the navy ensured that challenges to orthodoxy would be few and far between, because the leadership was self-perpetuating. The Chief of Naval Operations controlled the actual movements of ships and tried to coordinate the work of the independent bureaus, which reported directly to the Secretary of the Navy. It was the duty of these bureaus to build, maintain, and staff the fleet. On the recommendation of the Secretary of the Navy, the President selected both the Chief of Naval Operations and the bureau heads, but in most cases, the Secretary of the Navy was in turn dependent on the recommendations of the outgoing Chief of Naval Operations and the bureau chiefs themselves. The Bureau of Naval Personnel, for example, automatically advanced the navy leaders' recommendations to the civilian secretary. The Personnel Bureau also selected the members of the General Board, a group that advised the Secretary of the Navy on general naval policy and on the proper military characteristics for new ships.[13] Unless the President took a special interest as Roosevelt did, the leaders of the navy selected their own successors.

According to the professional lore inherited by this self-perpetuating group, the battleship was the decisive naval weapon. Consequently, the most promising officers were selected for gunnery school and battleship command; they in turn, when appointed to lead the navy, quite naturally emphasized the special role of the battleship.[14] Thus, the bureaucratic promotion procedure reinforced rigidity in strategic thinking. Of course, battleships could not operate alone; they required the support of cruisers and destroyers to prevent attacks by the enemy's light forces and submarines, and they needed aircraft carriers to scout for the enemy and ward off air attacks. These requirements led to the concept of the "balanced fleet," comprising a superior battleship force supported by all the necessary auxiliaries.

The navy leaders in 1934 were still on the defensive against the advocates of disarmament. Isolated from national policy makers, they drew in on themselves and held rigidly to their heritage of professional lore. Suspicion and the built-in rigidity in their strategic thinking certainly reinforced the navy's resistance to any change in Japan's ratios. But there were also more substantial reasons for the admirals' inflexibility. In particular, the lack of a "balanced fleet" in the United States Navy and the difficult strategic problem posed by a war with Japan influenced the navy leaders to advise against any further concessions to Japan.

STRATEGIC DOCTRINE AND THE REALITIES OF POWER

According to its strategic doctrines, the mission of the United States Navy was to prepare a fleet that could meet the enemy's forces and destroy them or send them into hiding. In order to ensure victory, the admirals had to make certain that the American fleet, when properly concentrated at the point of contact with the enemy, was more powerful than its opponents. After the American navy had gained control of the sea in a decisive battle, it would eliminate the enemy's seaborne trade.[15] These basic goals stemmed from the strategic writings of the premier American naval theorist, Alfred T. Mahan, whose doctrines had a great effect on the navies of the world and whose perceptiveness had apparently been confirmed during the First World War.

In the all-important final fleet action, the battleship would be the decisive weapon. On October 1, 1934, the General Board told the Secretary of the Navy that the "capital ship force is the backbone of the modern Navy . . . The basic strength of the surface fleet is in its heaviest vessels, under the protection of which its lighter craft may operate." As at Jutland, the battle fleet would cruise in columns abreast and would deploy in a single line when it contacted the enemy, whereupon the cannon of the two fleets would settle the issue. Even as late as 1941, Captain W. D. Puleston, the former head of the Office of Naval Intelligence, wrote: "The relative strengths of the opposing battle lines have been the determining factor in naval campaigns of the nineteenth and twentieth centuries . . . The power of aviation is increasing, but events of the current war indicate that the strength of the battle line is still the decisive naval factor."[16]

In March 1933, President Roosevelt asked why the administration should spend its funds to modernize United States battleships, and the Chief of Naval Operations, Admiral William V. Pratt, cited a number of ratios to prove that the cost of the battleship was small. In the ratio of building costs to defensive life (defined as the ability to take blows and keep fighting), the battleship was 10, the carrier 5.7, the cruiser 2.5, the destroyer 0.75, and the submarine 0.43. The battleship was similarly superior to all other classes in striking power per ton of ship and in radius of action. Pratt concluded that the battleship was the "most useful type of fighting craft . . . It is the backbone of the fleet." [17]

The navy's professional lore was full of ratios similar to those which Pratt cited. The navy had a mathematical rationale for believing that its 10/6 battleship superiority gave it the power to meet and defeat the Japanese fleet. As Puleston explained in 1941:

> Numerical superiority in battleships is difficult to overcome. There are not only more guns that inflict damage but fewer enemy ships to be destroyed or disabled before victory is assured. The odds in favor of a fleet of 10 against 7 sister ships are 100 to 49 at the beginning of an engagement. As the superior fleet should inflict increasing damage with each salvo, the ratio would gradually rise to the cube of the number of ships engaged and the ratio of 10 ships to 7 toward the end of an engagement should increase to 1,000 to 343. Assuming equality of personnel . . . on a day of high visibility, the American battle line . . . should decisively defeat the Japanese battle line. [18]

But in order for fourteen American ships to meet their ten Japanese counterparts, the American battle fleet would have to cross the Pacific unharmed. In other words, American auxiliary craft would have to repel successfully submarine, destroyer, and air attacks, in order to ensure the success of the battle fleet's primary mission. The major threat would come from the torpedo attacks of destroyers and cruisers and the numerous assaults expected from the enemy's submarines. In each case, America's cruisers and destroyers would be the key weapons. Yet in his economy drive, President Hoover had refused all requests for new construction and had prevented any replacement of aging auxiliaries. Consequently, the navy lacked a modern destroyer fleet and the light cruisers necessary to carry out its strategic mission. [19] Since Japan had built up to treaty limits while the Americans had not, Japan already had an 8/10 ratio, and its destroyers and light cruisers were newer than those of the Americans. An upward revision of Japan's ratio would permit further Japanese building just when the Americans were trying to catch up. If the Japanese were to achieve formal recognition of their 8/10 ratio, the admirals argued, the United States Navy could not hope to succeed in a trans-Pacific advance.

Both the navy's traditional doctrine and the various war games played by the fleet pointed to this conclusion. Distance, Mahan once said, was a factor equivalent to a number of ships. This maxim was expressed differently in another traditional formula: a fleet's efficiency declined ten percent for each 1,000 miles it had to travel away from its base. Evidently, the need to conserve fuel limited the ability of the fleet to operate at full speed for long periods when it was far from home, and the fleet would not be able to bring as many damaged ships back if it went into action far from port. Since the Philippines were 3,000 miles from

Hawaii and only 300 miles from Taiwan, the Americans were at a severe geographic disadvantage.[20] Moreover, the Philippines were not equipped to handle a battle fleet, and the Washington agreements prohibited the construction of a fortified base in the islands. Consequently, the American navy faced a formidable task.

The navy's yearly maneuvers, by which the admirals tested the "Orange" plan for war with Japan, showed that a successful relief of the Philippines would be difficult. Maneuvers played in 1930 and 1932 showed both the shape of the decisive battle expected with Japan and the nature of the navy's Pacific problem. In one case the American fleet had to advance from Pearl Harbor, avoid the Japanese light craft, and escort the American landing forces to their first target. The Americans' efforts to avoid the Japanese submarines were unsuccessful, however, and the American fleet also suffered considerable losses from surface and air attacks. Trans-Pacific attrition would thus be great. In other maneuvers, the navy practiced its tactics for the decisive battle. The attacking American fleet would use carrier planes to sink or disable the enemy's carriers. Then the American fleet would use airplanes to spot for long-range cannon fire; consequently, it would be able to start firing first and to find the range more quickly. Despite this advantage, the advancing American fleet suffered cruiser and destroyer attacks at night, and in the end, the advancing fleet met defeat because it did not have an adequate number of cruisers and destroyers to prevent the attrition of its battleship forces.[21] The war games, then, confirmed the maxim that distance increased the difficulties of the advancing fleet. Since the American fleet was also dangerously weak in auxiliaries vis-à-vis Japan, the defense of the Philippines was a doubtful proposition at best.

The admirals expected Japan to take advantage of its opportunity to wear down the American battle fleet. The Marshalls and the Carolines, Japan's mandated islands, which lay across the line of advance from Pearl Harbor to Manila, would provide good bases for Japan's light forces. In 1932, Admiral Pratt warned, "The whole Japanese plan of campaign is believed to be based on the use of submarines based on their mandated islands of the Pacific . . . which threaten our communications between Hawaii and the Far East." An undated extract in the records of the General Board from what appears to be a report written in mid-1934 warned that Japanese strategists had devised plans which would allow them to keep the Americans at bay even if a naval race occurred. The report explained, "The backbone of this defense would be swarms of submarines based on many islands and backed by powerful shore naval air stations." [22]

Nevertheless, it was the navy's job to defend the Philippines, for the islands would not become independent until 1946, and even after that date it was possible that the United States would aid in their defense. From 1900 to 1941, navy planners struggled with the problem of defending the Philippines but were never able to solve it. In 1922, the men of the War Plans Division assumed that the Philippines would be lost and that a long campaign would be required to win them back, but their superiors nevertheless ruled that the United States would have to attempt an early relief. Consequently, the Joint Board approved a revised plan for war with Japan in September 1924, which called for a prompt trans-Pacific advance. The garrison at Manila would simply have to hold out until relief arrived.[23]

The revised plan drew repeated protests in the twenties. In 1928, the members of the Joint Board admitted that the advance to the Philippines would require more time than they had allotted, and in 1933 they conceded that the navy and marines would first have to seize a base in the Marshalls before advancing further. On March 1, 1934, the commander of the Asiatic fleet joined the commanding general of the army in the Philippines in a protest to their superiors. They argued that reductions in their forces had made the Philippines indefensible and that Japan's technological progress and the "spectacular rise" of Japanese military strength made the task assigned them under the plan impossible. They asked for a decision on national policy: if the United States wanted to defend the islands, then it would have to construct a fortified base near Manila. But the planners replied that the garrisons could hold out until relief arrived.[24] In order to make good the defense of the Philippines, however, the navy would have to prevent any further increase in Japan's naval strength.

America's admirals were relatively satisfied with their battleship strength vis-à-vis Japan. They believed that a 10/6 ratio gave them a "sporting chance" for victory, since they had learned from their predecessors that the effectiveness of different-sized battle fleets varied by the cube as an action progressed. But to fight a decisive battle near the Philippines, they needed carriers, cruisers, and destroyers to escort the fleet across the Pacific. They opposed further increases in Japan's naval strength on the grounds that a larger Japanese navy would make their difficult task impossible.

THE NAVY'S DISARMAMENT POSITION, OCTOBER 1934

There were still other reasons for the navy's hostility to concessions to Japan, as the admirals explained in a long report made by the General Board on disarmament in October 1934. The members of the General Board said that the navy had to be strong enough to support the national policies of the United States, to guard its homeland and territories, and to defend the Open Door for trade. But the United States' basic policies clashed directly with those of the other powers, the navy leaders pointed out. For example, the British constantly sought to maintain a naval force superior to the American fleet and to expand their commerce at the expense of American trade.[25]

According to the admirals, however, the real threat was from Japan. From 1920 on, the General Board had repeatedly warned that Japan was a feudalistic, aggressive nation bent on dominating the Orient. In 1932, the board feared that Japan's proposals to the Geneva Disarmament Conference "would relegate the United States and Great Britain to a place of secondary importance in the Far

East. They [the Japanese] seek an indisputable naval supremacy in the western Pacific and absolute dictatorship in Far Eastern affairs.'' In their 1934 report, the General Board members warned that Japan was seeking territorial expansion, the commercial and political domination of the Far East, the expansion of their world commerce, and equality of racial treatment. All of these goals, the admirals pointed out, clashed directly with American policies of the Open Door and the exclusion of Asiatics.[26]

The members of the General Board assumed that the policies of the United States would not change. They warned, however, that the international climate was growing more dangerous and that militarism was in the ascendant, while the attitude of the American people toward national policies ''and toward national defense in particular has been listless and without understanding.'' They suggested, therefore, that the administration decide whether or not it would continue to protect its nationals abroad in wartime, and whether or not it would support its policies in East Asia and defend the Philippines.[27] The obvious implication was that the administration had to enlarge the navy and build a fortified base near Manila if it were to uphold its national policies in the face of Japanese opposition.

The leaders of the navy pointed out that it was also important for the United States to maintain the existing naval limitations, since the American navy was well under treaty strength. They reminded the Secretary of the Navy that Japan had built up to its treaty limits and that the Japanese would therefore have to press for a higher ratio if they wished to improve their naval position. The General Board argued that the situation called for an overall 5/3 ratio: ''Considering the hazards that either Great Britain or the United States must meet in any naval campaign fought to defend their possessions in the Far East, far from supporting bases and with the necessity of safe despatch of the many stores and supplies needed for the upkeep of a fleet, the present ratios assuredly grant Japan adequate naval self-defense. There would seem to be no justification for any increase in the naval ratio of Japan with respect to the United States or Great Britain . . . In fact, the application of the 3/5 ratio through all categories is warranted.'' Under no circumstances, they warned, should the administration grant an increase in Japan's ratio. If the talks failed, the United States could then stand a naval race with Japan, since with ''respect to national resources, the United States and Great Britain are both more capable of large increases of their naval armaments than is Japan.'' [28]

The leaders of the navy had implied that the United States should decide whether or not it was going to play a role in East Asia and, on the basis of that decision, either withdraw or provide the military strength necessary to support its policies. The admirals expected that the United States would not withdraw, but they warned that the laxity of the past made both a large naval buildup and the maintenance of the ratios imperative. If the Japanese were dissatisfied, they could leave the conference; the Americans could then use their superior economic strength to win a naval race.

The President had his own program for disarmament, which it would have been unwise for the navy to ignore entirely. Consequently, the members of the General Board proposed that the American negotiators seek a twenty percent reduction in the tonnage limit for capital ships, and a ten percent tonnage reduction in carriers and light cruisers. The General Board vitiated this seemingly generous reduction, however, by adding a condition: the other powers would have to agree to a fifty percent reduction in their submarine tonnages. Although the British were eager to abolish submarines, the General Board had already admitted that the Japanese were basing their whole plan of campaign on these ships; as a result, there was little hope that the navy's conditions would be met. The board also advised against any overall cuts in the allowed heavy cruiser and destroyer strengths. Since these were multipurpose craft, the board argued that it needed more, not less, of them.[29] Thus, the navy resisted any real overall reduction of naval strengths.

Davis and the Assistant Secretary of the Navy, Henry L. Roosevelt, had both warned that the navy should cooperate with the British during the talks, in order to present a common front to the Japanese. The navy responded by being flexible on the light cruiser question, which had traditionally troubled Anglo-American talks. The admirals agreed that they could grant the British a higher tonnage in the light cruiser class, provided that they received compensation in aircraft carriers. Thus, the common front would probably not fall apart on the issue of cruisers.

The General Board also made what it considered to be a significant sacrifice in its proposals for qualitative limitation. The British wished to reduce the size of the battleships drastically, perhaps to 25,000 tons mounting twelve-inch guns from the existing level of 35,000 tons carrying sixteen-inch cannon. The General Board explained that such a drastic cut was difficult for the United States to accept: "Naval strength is essentially a composite of fleets and bases. The United States has few bases throughout the world and no secure base in the Western Pacific . . . In order that this handicap may be minimized, the United States needs vessels of the greatest practicable *power of survival* . . . The capital ship is the essential basic unit of a high seas fleet. Reduction in displacement vitally reduces its power of survival." A smaller capital ship would be less able to repel attacks and return home after taking punishment. It would make the smaller types of ship, the very classes in which the United States was weak, relatively more powerful. Nevertheless, the board agreed to reduce the size of the battleship from 35,000 tons to 33,000 and to accept the fourteen-inch guns in place of the newer sixteen-inch cannon. It also agreed to reduce the size of the carrier from 27,000 to 22,000 tons and to support Britain's demand for abolition of the submarine.[30]

The navy's overall position on disarmament was fairly rigid. The General

Board was absolutely opposed to an increase in Japan's ratio, and in fact, it wanted the negotiators to secure a decrease in Japan's strength relative to that of the United States. It had to take into account the administration's desire for disarmament, however, and therefore agreed to some overall reductions in battleship, carrier, and light cruiser tonnage. But it undercut this flexibility by adding the impossible condition that the diplomats must convince Japan to cut its submarine strength drastically. In order to placate the British, the navy leaders agreed to slight reductions in the size of the battleship and the carrier, and also to the proposed abolition of the submarine. But even if successfully carried out, these reductions were small indeed.

The General Board thus opposed any further gains by Japan at the bargaining table and urged the administration to build a larger fleet. To the navy, which had always considered its traditional enemy dangerous, Japan seemed particularly threatening in 1934. Yet the civilians in and out of government were ignoring the advice of the naval experts. The admirals were an isolated priesthood, refining and transmitting their strategic dogma only among themselves. They were bitter about the neglect from which they suffered and rightly fearful for the future, since the government refused to support them with the contributions they believed necessary. When consulted about disarmament, they angrily poured forth both their fears and their demands. If Roosevelt should change his mind and yield to Japan, he would have a large group of admirals making protests before congressional committees. Caught between his people's longing for further arms reductions and his navy's strategic needs, Roosevelt steered a middle course: further reductions under the existing ratios. This position would probably not satisfy the Japanese, nor keep Japan's admirals from embarking on a naval race; in short, Roosevelt refused to consider withdrawal from Asia or meaningful rearmament until after the approaching naval talks had run their course.

PART THREE   Great Britain's Dilemma

7 The Economics of Appeasement and the Politics of Defense

By the early thirties, German, Italian, and Japanese rearmament posed threats at both the European and the Asiatic poles of the British Empire. As a result, in 1933 the leaders of the British government ordered a review of defense deficiencies. Yet when professional advisers warned them that the empire was declining dangerously, they refused to approve any real measure of rearmament. Only in later years would the British come to realize that their failure to rearm had required painful compromises with Germany and Japan. At the beginning of the thirties, the British considered themselves to be one of the great Pacific powers; yet as the decade closed, they found themselves unable to deter a Japanese attack on their possessions.

WAR AND DISARMAMENT IN BRITAIN

Twenty years before the London Naval Conference of 1935, Britain's leaders had watched while their friends and relatives were dying on the battlefields of France, and when in 1918 peace finally came, the British nation had to make a grisly accounting. The toll reached three-quarters of a million dead, and one and a half million permanently weakened by wounds and gassing. The casualties were three times as heavy for sons of the ruling class in the junior officer ranks as among enlisted men. For instance, while Anthony Eden survived the war in the trenches, every one of his male relatives, including two brothers, was killed or captured during the fighting. As a result, there was in England a fervent longing for peace, which expressed itself in passionate support for the League of Nations and for disarmament. Many believed that the next war would even spread from Europe to England itself through the dread medium of the air. London, the center and soul of England, lay minutes from the Continent by bomber. In 1932, Stanley Baldwin, the power behind the government, warned: "I think it is well for the man in the street to realize that there is no power on earth which can protect him from being bombed. Whatever people may tell him, the bomber will always get through." [1]

Throughout the early thirties the British hoped that the League could preserve peace without involving them in another war, but during the Manchurian incident they found that the process of collective security was not easy. For a variety of reasons the Foreign Secretary, Sir John Simon, tried to follow a course that was "*pro* League" rather than "*anti* Japan." He and his colleagues knew that they could not rely on the American navy for help against Japan, and the Admiralty assured them that Britain alone could not fight the Japanese. Moreover, the economic crisis made hostilities in East Asia seem a frivolous expenditure of blood and treasure. Consequently, the British ignored the option of economic sanctions against Japan, supported the League in not recognizing Manchukuo, and avoided unnecessary criticism of Japan.[2] Fear of a new world war lay like a dead weight on the shoulders of Britain's statesmen in these years.

Compounded with England's horror of past and future wars was its guilt about the allies' treatment of Germany. John Maynard Keynes and other Britons agreed that at Versailles England and France had handled the Germans too severely. In 1933 and 1934, the British tried to bring a rearming Germany back under the net of disarmament restrictions, but the French exacted conditions that seemed to doom German acceptance.[3]

In England all political parties, reflecting the electorate's beliefs, extolled the virtues of arms limitations, and Britain led the world in disarmament by example. Indeed, in 1934 the personnel of the Royal Navy hit a forty-year low. The reason for this decline was political. From 1931 on, the ruling National coalition had included both Liberals and Conservatives, who stood together against the weak and leaderless Labour party. In 1929, the Liberals had fought for the last time as a united, affluent, hopeful party, and they had lost decisively. After that election, their leaders combined with Labour to form a government. Then in 1931 they abandoned their faltering allies and joined the Tories. This policy of shifting alliances brought the Liberal leaders cabinet portfolios but cost them rank-and-file seats, and in 1931, the Liberals held only thirty-three places in Parliament, as against 471 Conservatives. These figures are misleading, however, for in many constituencies Liberal voters had no candidate of their own and consequently voted solidly for the Tories.[4] The Liberal party traditionally stood for disarmament, while the right wing of the Tory party had always pressed for military strength. If the coalition were to last, Baldwin would have to please the Liberals and muzzle the Tory right. The demands of coalition, the desires of the electorate, and the remembered toll of war combined to make disarmament a Tory policy.

In fact, the past decade showed that the leaders of the National government could not heed the occasional growls of Winston Churchill and the Tory right without alienating their Liberal allies and arousing their Labour opponents. During the Geneva Naval Disarmament Conference in 1927, one of the British representatives, Lord Cecil, had resigned and blamed the rigidity of the Conservative government for the failure of the negotiations, and in 1929 Labour had used Cecil's charge as a stick to drive the Tories from office. In 1932, a member of the British delegation to the general disarmament conference had again resigned, accusing Foreign Secretary John Simon of wrecking the talks. Once more, the Labour party leaders grasped the issue and charged the national government with warmongering. Labour's leaders warned that they would oppose all armament budgets until a real measure of disarmament was achieved.[5] Though temporarily weak, Labour was a watchful and potentially dangerous adversary.

By the fall of 1933, the leaders of the national coalition began receiving reminders of Labour's influence. In October, as Germany was leaving the disarmament conference, a by-election in East Fulham resulted in a swing of twenty-seven percent to Labour. The Labour candidate had emphasized both economic and armament questions, charging that the only solution proposed by the National leaders for England's economic difficulties was the mistaken policy of war preparations. After his victory, the Labour candidate said that "the British people demand . . . that the British Government shall give a lead to the whole world by initiating immediately a policy of general disarmament." The trend continued from November 1933 to February 1934, when the national government lost seven more by-elections and the swing to Labour averaged over twenty percent. If the tide of opinion did not turn, Labour would gain a majority of 100 seats in the next general election.[6] Thus, the lessons of the past reinforced the political needs of the present. The Labour candidate at East Fulham had also touched on another reason to disarm: the limping, depressed, and delicate economy.

CHAMBERLAIN AND THE EXCHEQUER

In the early thirties, the man who had primary responsibility for Britain's economic recovery was Neville Chamberlain, youngest son of the Victorian politician Joseph Chamberlain. Unlike his brilliant older half-brother, Austen, Neville had been a diffident student, and his father had decided to prepare him for business rather than politics. Neville's first economic venture, however, was an expensive disaster: his father sent him to the Bahamas, where for five lonely years Neville struggled to build a sisal plantation, but despite his best efforts, lost 50,000 pounds. Yet he had shown the qualities on which most of his later associates were to remark: tenacity, determination, and a capacity for long-suffering stubbornness. Despite his Bahamian failure, Chamberlain returned to Birmingham and made a modest success in the brass and bedspring business. He then entered city politics, became mayor, and upheld his family's radical tradition by securing town planning and housing reform. The successes of his middle years erased the failures of his youth. As one of his associates in the National government recalled: "Steady persistence—some might say obstinacy—in the course he had adopted was a strong element in his character. He had so often found the right solution, in municipal affairs or at the Treasury, by the hard labour of his own brains, that he was inwardly confident that world problems would in the end yield to his treatment." In the early thirties, Chamberlain was both Chancellor of the Exchequer and head of the Research Department of the Conservative party. Equally in touch with government policy and party affairs, he was generally regarded as a future Prime Minister.[7]

Chamberlain had returned to the Exchequer during the financial crisis of 1931. In that year, the world depression hit England with full force, driving tax receipts down and spreading unemployment through the land. Gold drained from the country, and the budget projected by the Labour government was unbalanced by 120 million pounds. Labour ministers, such as J. Ramsay MacDonald and Philip Snowden, found their party unwilling to accept cuts in unemployment benefits, but they believed such cuts were necessary to balance the budget and restore Britain's international credit. Consequently, the Labour leaders abandoned their party and joined Liberals and Tories in the National coalition to face the economic emergency. Chamberlain then squared the accounts and secured foreign loans, but only at the great cost of raising taxes, cutting unemployment benefits, and reducing the salaries of all government employees. These severe measures were futile, however, for England went off the gold standard and the economic emergency dragged on. In October 1931, the new National government secured an election victory and remained in power to continue its fight for economic stability.[8] What had seemed like a brief, severe illness turned out to be a chronic disease requiring constant attention.

Stanley Baldwin and Neville Chamberlain, the real leaders of the National coalition, were both Tory businessmen who had acquired their economic views in the Victorian age. After interviewing the primary figures in the National government, John F. Kennedy, young son of the American ambassador, summed up their economic views as follows: Britain lived on imported food and raw materials, and in order to pay for these imports, it had to undersell its competitors in the export markets of the world, but when inflation increased the price of British goods, Britain lost markets and faced a deficit in its balance of payments; such a deficit would eventually cause another drop in the value of the pound and might bring with it economic paralysis; therefore, the budget had to remain in balance. Despite mounting criticism, the National leaders kept a heavy hand on the Exchequer in 1932 and 1933. On March 25, 1933, the coalition's critics demanded reduction of the income tax, restoration of cuts in civil service pay, and an unbalanced budget. Neville Chamberlain replied, "I find that Budget deficits repeated year after year may be accompanied by deepening depression and by a constantly falling price level." [9] Thus, for the National leaders, a balanced budget was the miracle drug that would prevent both the dangers of inflation and the perils of deflation.

By 1934, Chamberlain had achieved a moderate success: the budget showed a small surplus. But the price was great. On May 30, 1934, the cabinet endorsed Chamberlain's note explaining to the Americans that Britain would cease paying its war debts, since it had stopped requiring payments from others. The Americans, Chamberlain argued, should not be misled by Britain's budget surplus, which was owing "entirely to the unprecedented sacrifices made by the people of this country." Compared to the Americans, the burden of Britain's national debt was great, and the rate of taxation was twice as heavy as in America. He added: "This taxation, amounting to close on one quarter of the national income, has involved a prolonged period of industrial depression and the maintenance ever since the War of an army of unemployed. Yet in order to restore the national credit in 1931, the people of this country accepted further and heavy increases in taxation, accompanied by rigorous control of expenditure and cuts in salaries and allowances of all kinds." [10] Rearmament would mean renewed pressure on the suffering taxpayer and would endanger economic recovery.

Worse still, an expanded armament program would not reestablish the empire as a world power, for Britain could not match the combined rearmament efforts of Germany and Japan. In 1935, Britain's net factory production ran at about sixty percent of the combined industrial output of Japan and Germany. Although the National government could have rearmed more fully, the treasury officials were right in believing that Britain no longer had the economic strength to be a global military power. There were simply too many competitors in the field. Thus, economic realities and the political unpopularity of raising taxes combined to slow the pace of British rearmament. [11] World tensions, however, would not wait upon a recovery of Britain's economic fortunes, and the government had to respond.

THE DEFENSE DIRECTORATE

The Japanese invasion of Manchuria and the rise of Hitler set in motion the ponderous machinery of committees that comprised Britain's defense directorate. During the Sino-Japanese struggle at Shanghai in early 1932, Britain's leaders had discovered that they lacked the strength to defend Singapore, the supposedly impregnable door to their eastern empire. Consequently, the British discarded the remarkable premise, known as the Ten-Year Rule, under which they had reduced defense expenditures in the twenties; that rule had stated flatly: "the British Empire will not be engaged in any great war during the next ten years." [12] Yet a measure of the government's reluctance to rearm was the fact that it delayed a full defense review until late in the following year.

By 1933, however, the need for a defense review was imperative. In June, the Foreign Office warned that the general international situation was in serious decline. Japan's invasion of Manchuria and its temporary incursion into North China had demonstrated the weakness of the League. The future held little comfort, for Japan might again invade China and thereby injure British interests so severely as to raise the question of sanctions. Even more alarming was the appearance of another possible aggressor in the field: the Foreign Office warned that general European appeasement and international disarmament were made difficult by "the threatening and provocative attitude of Germany . . . Germany, controlled by a frenzied nationalism and resolved to assert her rights to full equality, will proceed to the building up of formidable armaments on land

and especially in the air . . . [and her actions will lead to] a bitter competition in armaments and eventually to war.'' [13]

Thus warned, the leaders of the National government turned to the Committee of Imperial Defense for a general review of British liabilities. This committee was England's highest defense directorate and contained the Prime Minister, his defense ministers, and the chiefs of staff; in addition, a permanent secretariat connected the civilian members of the committee with the service experts and controlled the flood of reports on British defense problems. The head of this secretariat was a capable civil servant, Maurice P. A. Hankey, who had gradually acquired a measure of influence with his superiors because of his expertise and even-handedness. [14] Beneath the Committee of Imperial Defense were a number of subcommittees, the most important of which was that of the chiefs of staff. In general, the members of the subcommittees were government specialists, who sent technical reports on specific defense problems to the Committee of Imperial Defense. The members of the committee then considered the report from their wider, political vantage point. If the problem was pressing and controversial, the members of the Committee of Imperial Defense might in time refer it to an ad hoc cabinet committee. By means of this special cabinet committee, the Prime Minister could achieve a compromise *in camera,* which would preserve peace in his party or in the ruling coalition. This process was cumbersome and time-consuming. Interservice rivalries, political necessities, and personal conflicts complicated the apparently rational process, and the spinning wheels of the committees often lent a comforting appearance of progress to a procrastinating government.

In October 1933, the Chiefs of Staff Subcommittee asked for a complete review of Britain's defense needs and capabilities. During the Japanese assault on North China, the chiefs of staff had warned that Singapore was "liable to capture or destruction by a *coup de main* before our main fleet can arrive on the scene.'' [15] India, Australia, New Zealand, and British trade in the Pacific would then be at the mercy of Japan. In spite of German belligerence, the chiefs of staff pointed to Japan as the most dangerous adversary for the near future. They argued that Britain's prime interests, in order of priority, were defense of their possessions and interests in the Far East, European commitments, and defense of India against Soviet aggression. The chiefs of staff added that, in order to provide sure communications and mobile defense for its widely scattered territories, Britain's prime requirement was a strong navy.

The chiefs of staff argued that England's armed forces, particularly the navy, had accumulated an alarming number of deficiencies under the rule that there would be no major war for ten years. Furthermore, increased Japanese construction added to their difficulties, for Britain had to be able to send a fleet to the Far East that would be "sufficient to meet the Japanese Fleet at her selected moment.'' At the same time, the navy would have to protect Britain's vital trade against the raids of enemy submarines, cruisers, and capital ships. If Britain sent a fleet to the East, the Admiralty would have only four cruisers left in the Atlantic and an insufficient number of battleships to deal with its European enemy. The admirals asked for at least three more battleships, twenty additional cruisers, and numerous merchant cruisers to match Japan's ships of the line and Germany's commerce raiders. Given such strength, Britain would still have to rely on the French navy to provide the margin for victory over Germany and to hold the Mediterranean against Italy.

Although Germany's growing strength worried Britain's military leaders, they considered the Nazi threat still years away. The chiefs of staff argued that it would be suicidal for Germany to attack France "for some years to come." By building the Maginot line, the French had "rendered their eastern frontier immeasurably stronger than in 1914 and probably impregnable to land attack except by extensive and elaborate siege operations." [16] The chiefs of staff concluded that a naval increase should be Britain's first order of business. Although they pointed out the growing dangers to the empire, they did not ask for a new standard of military strength; in fact, they merely sought to bring their forces up to the levels set in the early twenties. Perhaps the army and air force could wait, they surmised, but the threat from Japan was imminent. They implied that the government would be remiss if it did not rebuild the Royal Navy.

On November 9, the Committee of Imperial Defense considered the report by the chiefs of staff. But when the First Sea Lord, Sir A. Ernle M. Chatfield, asked the committee to give first priority to the navy and the Far East, he met with stern opposition from a formidable antagonist, Neville Chamberlain. The Chancellor of the Exchequer argued that Britain should limit its responsibilities: "If it were possible to improve our relations with Japan the whole problem in the Far East would be much simplified, and it even might be possible to reduce the Far East in the order of priority." In fact, Chamberlain maintained, "it might quite conceivably be found, for example, that the situation in Europe became more urgent than the situation in the Far East." A veteran member of Parliament and one of the Labour leaders who had entered the National coalition, James H. Thomas, Secretary of State for the Dominions, added that rearmament would threaten the financial balance of the government program and the economic revival so necessary to the country. These were the first notes in a long chorus calling for economy at home and peaceful initiatives abroad.

But the Foreign Secretary, Sir John Simon, and the Prime Minister, Ramsay MacDonald, warned that there were considerable barriers in the way of Anglo-Japanese rapprochement. Simon insisted that Japan was determined to seize further territory in order to make herself "a great Power in the East." MacDonald added that the Japanese were increasing their navy and would seek naval parity in 1935. Obviously, in the coming debates there would be a battle over priorities, with the advocates of economy and of preparedness against Germany ranged against the supporters of rearmament and of worldwide imperial defense. The Committee of Imperial Defense decided to refer the question of Britain's "worst deficiencies" to an ad hoc Defense Requirements Subcommittee.[17]

THE DEFENSE DEBATE

Each of the contending camps had representatives on the Defense Requirements Subcommittee. Hankey was the chairman of the committee and a supporter of Admiral Chatfield, the navy, and the Far Eastern priority. Warren Fisher, the Permanent Under-Secretary of the Treasury and head of the British Civil Service, represented Chamberlain and the advocates of economy. Fisher distrusted both Germany and members of the Foreign Office who feared the Japanese too much and the permanent head of the Civil Service too little. Strangely enough, Robert Vansittart, the Permanent Under-Secretary of the Foreign Office, was Fisher's ally; he cheerfully and openly contradicted the views of his colleagues at the Foreign Office by urging the subcommittee to concentrate on the German danger. Litterateur, socialite, and dandy, Vansittart was "a relentless, not to say ruthless, worker" for the view that Britain had to appease Japan and Italy in order to concentrate completely on meeting the threat from Germany. He injured his case, however, since "he expressed himself with such repetitive fervour that all except those who agreed with him were liable to discount his views as too extreme." [18] The army and air force chiefs of staff were also members of the Defense Requirements Subcommittee, and they were likely to sympathize with proposals to arm against the land and air power of Germany rather than the sea power of Japan. With such strong personalities and bureaucratic interests on their side, and with the shadow of the future Prime Minister, Neville Chamberlain, hanging over the proceedings, the Far Easterners faced severe odds.

The clash between the two groups came during the first meetings of the subcommittee. Vansittart argued that Britain should complete preparations for a defensive at Singapore and then make Germany the target of all subsequent rearmament. He argued: "Our resources . . . are not sufficient to meet a menace from both Japan and Germany, [and] . . . of the two, Germany [is] the greater menace." He admitted, however, that his argument did not represent the views of the Foreign Office. Fisher agreed that the "fundamental danger" would come from Germany and that Britain should confine itself to a defensive in the Pacific. The chief of staff of the army, Archibald A. Montgomery-Massingberd, happily endorsed this argument; Germany, he said, would be prepared for war in five years, and during that grace period England must create an expeditionary force for continental war.[19]

Admiral Chatfield yielded grudgingly. He conceded that it might be necessary to consider Japan and Germany as equally dangerous, but he again warned that Britain's naval strength was inadequate for a defensive at Singapore. The Japanese, he said, "ridiculed our present strength in the Far East." Hankey, the chairman of the committee, came to Chatfield's aid, warning that Japan might advance into China, Australia, and New Zealand and that Britain could not negotiate with the Japanese while its navy was so weak. "Each year," he said, "Japan becomes stronger, and we become proportionately in a worse position to obtain her friendship and good offices." [20] The lines were clearly drawn, and the leaders of the British government had to decide whether or not they could afford to prepare for war at the European and Asiatic poles of the empire.

In the end, Hankey, Chatfield, and the chiefs of staff agreed that Britain should first strengthen the Pacific position of the navy, and then equip the army and air force. The sums they asked for these purposes were not large: the admirals merely sought modernization of their aging battleships, a moderate fortification of bases, and improvement in the levels of personnel, aircraft, fuel supplies, and ammunition. The cost for easing deficiencies in all three services would come to only 72 million pounds over five years and 288 million pounds over nine years. In addition, the navy wished to increase its spending for the replacement of overage ships from 10 million to 13.4 million pounds a year. This replacement building would keep the navy up to treaty strength in all categories, and it would eventually increase British cruiser strength from the authorized level of fifty to a total of seventy light cruisers. In fact, the cost of the recommended replacement program was one-tenth the size of the five-year defense plan adopted in 1937, a program that proved entirely inadequate for its purpose.

Despite the small sums involved, Warren Fisher continued to plead poverty on behalf of his master at the treasury, Neville Chamberlain. In a letter of protest to the Subcommittee on January 30, 1934, Fisher argued that Britain's capacity for war production was limited by the amount of foreign exchange it could send abroad to pay for imported raw material. Fisher stated that Britain had only enough strength to deal with Germany and that Britain's leaders had to get "back to something like our former relations" with Japan. In order to get on better terms with Japan, he said, it would be necessary to cut Britain off from the United States, and the London Naval Conference might prove "the parting of the ways." He argued that the naval treaties poisoned Anglo-Japanese relations; by ending the pacts and standing on the defensive at Singapore, Britain could regain Japan's respect and avoid squandering its wealth on the navy. As for the Americans, they could "circle the globe with ships if they want . . . and wait and see for how many years the politically all-powerful Middle West will continue to acquiesce in paying a fantastic bill related to no real requirement but primarily to indulge the braggadocio of Yahoodom." [21]

Fisher and Vansittart made a substantial impact on the final report of the Defense Requirements Subcommittee. The members of the Subcommittee stated that the defense of the Far East should retain first priority, but they also emphasized that Britain had to prepare against Germany. Fisher was able to insert his views on the need for rapprochement with Japan: "We cannot overstate the importance we attach to getting back, not to alliance (since that would not be practical politics) but at least to our old terms of cordiality and mutual respect with Japan.'' Also, before the naval conference, the British should ''thoroughly . . . reconsider . . . our subservience to the United States.'' Finally, Fisher secured the bald statement: ''We take Germany as the ultimate potential enemy against whom our 'long-range' defense policy must be directed.'' In the Subcommittee's concrete recommendations, however, the advocates of the navy had their way. They secured full endorsement for erasing the navy's deficiencies and for the replacement program. Apparently, the army and air chiefs had backed the navy, since they too secured their main aims. The Subcommittee recommended that the army be equipped to send a modest expeditionary force of six divisions to the Continent and that the air force receive funds to complete the air program first authorized in 1923. Admiral Chatfield and Chairman Hankey also injected their views into the body of the report, which called for a naval buildup because ''at the moment we are almost defenseless in the Far East . . . the fleet is in the position today of being unable to do more than take up a severely limited defensive attitude at Singapore.'' [22]

The bureaucrats had struggled for three months but still had not solved the dilemma of priorities. Although they fought over relatively small sums, they recognized that, by calling for economy, the treasury had raised dangerous and fundamental questions of imperial strategy. Only the cabinet could decide whether or not Britain should turn its back on the United States and the naval treaties, direct most of its war preparations at Germany, and trust its empire in the East to Japan. In March 1934, the report of the Defense Requirements Subcommittee went before the Ministerial Committee on the Geneva Disarmament Conference (it was perhaps a measure of the National government's concern with the public's desire for disarmament that it debated rearmament in a disarmament committee). Since preliminary bureaucratic sparring had failed to answer the basic question, the responsible ministers would have to break the impasse.

SURGERY BY THE MINISTERIAL COMMITTEE

J. Ramsay MacDonald, the Prime Minister, was displeased with the defense requirements report, and he submitted a series of questions to the ministers that showed his anger. Could the cabinet approve a rapprochement with Japan at the expense of Anglo-American cordiality? Would a small European expeditionary force provide a deterrent? Would the public support rearmament? Was it not logical to cultivate especially friendly relations with the United States, France, and Italy, since those countries were excluded from the list of Britain's potential enemies? As a leader of the Labour party, MacDonald had twice been Prime Minister, and he was a dedicated supporter of disarmament; in fact, as Prime Minister in 1930 he had helped bring the London Naval Conference to a successful conclusion. By 1934, however, he was a pitiful figure. During the financial crisis of 1931, when he had abandoned his party and become Prime Minister in the National government, he had brought only a handful of parliamentary supporters to the coalition, and each year his influence waned. Gradually his health also began to fail, and during the summer of 1934, he had to have complete rest. Never concise (Churchill claimed that MacDonald had "the gift for compressing the largest number of words in the smallest amount of thought"), MacDonald's prolixity increased with age.[23] Throughout the debates on armaments, he tried weakly and with small effect to save the disarmament treaties.

The real powers in the National government and in the Ministerial Committee were Stanley Baldwin, the leader of the Tory party, and his heir apparent, Neville Chamberlain. Baldwin was a hereditary Tory, having inherited from his father both a share in an ironworks and a seat in Parliament. During the war he had been appalled by the bloodshed and by the burden of debt that he had helped to load on the country as Financial Secretary to the Lloyd George cabinet and after the peace, he had contributed one-fifth of his considerable fortune to decrease the national debt and urged others to follow his example. As Chancellor of the Exchequer and as Prime Minister in the twenties, he strove consistently for a balanced budget and against higher taxes, which he believed would depress trade; he also tried to reduce the national debt, since annual interest alone comprised forty percent of the budget. Despite his party's solid majority in Parliament, Baldwin played his hand conservatively. He occupied the position of Lord President of the Council, a vestigial office that allowed him to adjudicate in the committees and Commons any issues which might threaten his coalition. He procrastinated, husbanded his power, read all the political signs, and acted rarely. Foreign affairs, in particular, were *terra infirma* for him.[24] After the debate on defense requirements had dragged on in the government for ten months, Baldwin intervened and gave the resulting report a characteristically political twist.

Before the Ministerial Committee began its meetings, the full cabinet took up Fisher's suggestion of an Anglo-Japanese rapprochement. Sir John Simon, the Foreign Secretary, said with some pique that he "had been doing everything possible to improve relations with the Japanese in detail," but that major advances would be difficult. Simon was a touchy, handsome lawyer who had become a leader of the Liberal party during the twenties; in 1931 he led his followers out of a coalition with Labour and into the National government. Almost all his colleagues agreed that Simon could make "an admirable speech in the House" but that he lacked credibility. He trimmed every argument, and Lloyd George once said of him, "the right honorable Gentleman has sat so long on the fence that the iron has entered his soul."[25] Simon was not enthusiastic about an attempt at radical improvement in Anglo-Japanese relations, but since he headed only a splinter faction and was eager to remain in office, he would cooperate with his colleagues in the National coalition.

Chamberlain proposed to the full cabinet what Fisher had asked of the Defense Requirements Subcommittee. Britain should tell Japan that " we had not linked ourselves with America. If this were done Japan would be free from the fear that we might be united with America against her. Moreover, she ought to realize that if she was going to enter into a competition in armaments with America, she would reach the breaking point financially and therefore that there must be some limit to which we could adjust ourselves. He therefore suggested a Pact of Non-Aggression with Japan for a term of years.'' Chamberlain added that, in order to make such an agreement possible, the Japanese might have to promise not to resume their advance into China.[26] Thus, a deal with Japan and a split with the United States would allow Britain to concentrate on the German danger and to keep arms spending down.

MacDonald protested that the Americans would regard an Anglo-Japanese nonaggression treaty as an alliance, and he asked that Simon explore the question further. Two days later, Simon gave the verdict of the Foreign Office: ''Just possibly, but not probably'' such a pact ''might tend to moderate [Japanese] naval demands.'' But he warned that the Japanese were going to seek naval parity at the coming conference and that Britain would have to resist. Furthermore, even if an agreement could be reached, an Anglo-Japanese pact would shock China, the United States, and Canada. According to Simon and the Foreign Office, rearmament seemed the only possible course. Throughout early 1934, the diplomats were also reminding Britain's leaders of the German threat. Simon pointed to the possibility of Nazi putsch attempts in Austria and Memel. In March, he also said that ''Germany would rearm at pleasure without any stipulated limit,'' and in April he circulated a warning that Hitler would try to dominate all of Europe. On April 20, 1934, the chiefs of staff reported that the Germans had substantially increased their spending for arms.[27] According to the Foreign Office, the international situation offered no consolation to the champions of economy and appeasement: Japan would reject British approaches and the Germans were rearming.

The debate continued throughout the spring and early summer. In March, the cabinet decided to wait for the final results of the disarmament conference in Geneva before finally deciding to accept the Defense Requirements Subcommittee report. But the French and Germans remained deadlocked, and by early June the talks had collapsed. Meanwhile, in April, Amō had demanded an end to foreign aid for China. Nevertheless, Chamberlain argued that Britain would not need to outfit an expeditionary force for Europe, since the French would be safe behind the Maginot line. The chiefs of staff replied that no fortifications could hold out without the use of a field army and that the British would in any case have to send an expeditionary force to keep the unfortified Low Countries from falling into German hands.[28]

Chamberlain was unswayed, and gradually the leaders of the National government began to reveal the basic fears that underlay their reluctance to rearm. In a strong note which Chamberlain sent to his colleagues on June 20, he argued that the size of the proposals ''might lead to a revulsion of feeling and the loss of the whole [government] program.'' He added that ''the anxieties of the British people are concentrated on Europe rather than on the Far East.'' The real threat, he argued, lay in the air; a large air force would protect Britain's homeland and dominate the Low Countries. Therefore, the army could wait: "I can hardly believe it possible that . . . [Germany] will be in a condition to wage war on the West within five years." And the navy estimates, he stated flatly, could be cut by one-third; the government would have to admit "the impossibility of simultaneous preparation against war with Germany and war with Japan." In fact, he said, "we must postpone the idea of sending out to [Singapore] a fleet of capital ships capable of containing the Japanese fleet or meeting it in battle." [29]

Sir M. Bolton Eyres-Monsell, the First Lord of the Admiralty, protested that Britain's empire in the East was in "hourly danger" and that Chamberlain "would alter the whole basis of Imperial policy" by not sending a fleet to defend the dominions. But gradually the members of the National government lined up behind Chamberlain, for sizable spending on arms would be politically dangerous. MacDonald "reminded the Committee that the National Government was committed in their next budget to a restoration of the cuts in pay [imposed in 1931] and also to a further reduction in the Income Tax." He added, however, and Baldwin agreed, that a balance should be retained among the services and that the navy's appropriations should not be chopped down. The pressure for disarmament and economy continued, with lesser members of the cabinet, such as Samuel Hoare, James Thomas, and Walter Runciman, backing Chamberlain. Their fears were well grounded. The National government would face an election in 1935 or 1936, and the by-elections were continuing to run heavily against them: in April and May, the National candidates lost West Ham, Basingstoke, and Hammersmith North with swings of sixteen to eighteen percent to their opponents. Well might Chamberlain argue that "public opinion was [not] prepared for . . . a delay in the restoration of cuts, or even fresh taxation." [30]

Baldwin accepted the advice of his colleagues and on July 2 admitted that, "from the political point of view," they had to relieve "the semi-panic conditions which existed now about the Air." The army and navy could wait. Monsell protested that the effect of Chamberlain's cuts would mean that the fleet and the Singapore base would only be ready for action by 1942, while the navy would have to give up its regular replacement programs in 1935 and 1936. On July 24, an angry freeze set in. Monsell argued for the naval program, to which Chamberlain replied: "If, by the next General Election, the Government had not restored the cuts [in civil service and teachers' pay] or the Income Tax allowances, then [I think] that the public would show their disappointment accordingly." Thomas agreed that the National government "came into office in peculiar circumstances and, in the normal course of events, at the next election there might be a big swing . . . [I am] very afraid of grounds being given for an election cry . . . that the government were not restoring the cuts because they were preparing for war." And Baldwin said firmly: "Politically, it [is] of vital importance to restore the cut." [31]

On July 31, the cabinet approved a drastically revised defense requirements report. The politicians had doubled the amount to be spent on the Royal Air Force, and they had decided to cut army spending in half. Monsell and the navy suffered a worse fate than did the army, for the cabinet had postponed the question both of present deficiencies and of future replacements until after the coming naval talks. The committee's final report stressed the need to improve relations with Japan and to secure a new disarmament agreement.[32] Thus, much would depend on the coming disarmament conference and on Japan's reaction to Britain's search for a rapprochement. If Britain's negotiators could secure a rapprochement with Japan at the coming naval conference, then the leaders of the National coalition could avoid the political and economic dangers of large naval expenditures. On the other hand, should Japan publicly destroy the disarmament system, Britain's leaders might more easily secure a mandate for naval rearmament. Thus, in 1934, delay did not seem as foolish as it came to appear in later years.

The Royal Navy, Disarmament, and Anglo-American Misunderstanding

During the debate over defense requirements, Britain's ministers had to decide what instructions to give to their delegates at the coming naval talks. The admirals did their best to force the navy's view on the government, but with one eye on the Exchequer and the other on the electorate, the leaders of the National coalition framed a compromise set of instructions that left the navy dissatisfied. Britain's leaders did, however, agree to seek what the admirals had long desired: an increase in Britain's cruiser strength. This demand, together with the search for a rapprochement with Japan, seriously alienated the Americans during the talks.

THE ADMIRALTY AND DISARMAMENT

In the British Isles, the Royal Navy had always held first rank among the services. In 1905, the Committee of Imperial Defense had confirmed the long-standing rule that England would rely on the navy as its main shield rather than maintain large standing armies. Throughout most of the nineteenth century, Britain's admirals faced few challenges to their control of the sea lanes that linked the empire's scattered outposts. Toward the close of the century, however, France and Russia began to enlarge their fleets. Consequently, in 1889 the British decided that they should maintain equality with France and Russia in the heavier types of ships. As this two-power standard still left Britain without enough ships to match American, Italian, and Japanese building, the decade of the nineties found the British seeking diplomatic understandings with those powers. Although Britain was able to ally herself with Japan against Russia and France in East Asia, the British had to face an additional threat nearer to home: the rapidly growing German navy.[1] Eventually the British settled their colonial differences with France, achieved an Anglo-French entente, and destroyed the German fleet at the end of World War I. The English had preserved their empire in spite of naval weakness, but only because their diplomats had kept Italy, Japan, and the United States as neutrals or allies during the hostilities.

The Washington Conference seemed to reestablish Britain's earlier naval supremacy. The war had eliminated Germany as a naval power, and the new naval treaty allowed the British a luxury that had been beyond their means in the age of high imperialism: the strength to cover both their European homeland and their

Asiatic empire. By treaty, Britain could build a fleet larger than the navies of Japan and the greatest European naval power. Since France and Italy were both relatively friendly to Britain, the Royal Navy actually had a margin over Japan that was sufficient to provide for a defense of Singapore. Britain's admirals excluded a war with the United States from their calculations, inasmuch as such a war would absorb all of Britain's strength and make defense of the empire against other powers impossible. From 1890 on, British diplomats always tried to ensure a friendly United States at their back.

By 1934, however, reality had begun to overtake appearances. As soon as troubles began in Europe, Britain's superiority melted away, for it had assumed a friendly Italy and a disarmed Germany. As the general disarmament conference dragged to its fruitless end in Geneva, British intelligence officers warned that Germany would seek military equality with France.[2] With a hostile Japan already poised on their eastern flank, Britain's admirals had good reason to fear a serious German challenge nearer to home. Worse still, should Italy join forces with the Germans, the empire might face simultaneous perils in the Pacific, the Atlantic, and the Mediterranean.

As in all other navies in the thirties, Britain's admirals computed their strength in terms of capital ships. Throughout the twenties and thirties, British naval officers studied the battle of Jutland for tactical lessons and, with their Japanese and American counterparts, concluded that massed destroyer attacks and long-distance cannonade by battleships would comprise the battles of the future. In 1919, a postwar review board concluded that "the capital ship is the final arbiter." The First Sea Lord in the thirties, Sir A. Ernle M. Chatfield, who had been at Jutland in command of Admiral David Beatty's flagship, argued to a doubting MacDonald in May 1934 that all Admiralty studies proved the battleship to be both indispensable and impervious to air attack.[3] Thus, the ties of tradition, Mahan, and recent battle experience bound Britain's admirals as tightly as they did their Japanese and American counterparts.

Next to battleships, the Royal Navy stressed the importance of cruisers. Surprisingly enough, the admirals neglected antisubmarine weapons, such as carriers, destroyers, and corvettes, even though the German U-boat fleet had sunk large numbers of British merchantmen during the war. The reason for this nonchalance was technical: by 1934, the experts at the Admiralty had decided that the rapid development of underwater listening devices (asdic) had overcome the submarine threat. It was another menace that made the Admirals beg for cruisers: the fast surface raider. During the First World War, a single German cruiser had appeared out of the wide reaches of the Atlantic and destroyed an entire merchant convoy. Since the twenties, Japan had been building cruisers steadily, and under the Treaty of Versailles, Germany had built three pocket battleships; each of these giant German cruisers would be a match for three normal British cruisers. Since about half of Britain's cruiser force had to stay with the main fleet, the British navy lacked the ships necessary to protect both the Atlantic and the Pacific sea lanes against German and Japanese raids.[4]

Even with the somewhat artificial two-power standard provided by the Washington treaty system, Britain's naval strength permitted only a defensive in the Far East. In June 1939, Admiral Chatfield recalled the Far Eastern strategy that had prevailed during the twenties and thirties: "the role of the Fleet in the Far East was not designed to seize control of the Sea of Japan, but rather to provide a defensive 'fleet-in-being' so that before Japan could attack our main imperial interests she would have first to defeat our Fleet under disadvantageous conditions." Yet the Royal Navy was not able to send its fleet to the Pacific. In order to provide the necessary "cover" for the dominions, the Royal Navy therefore needed a secure, fortified base at Singapore, which successive British governments had refused to provide. During the debate on defense requirements in 1933, the government finally accepted the admirals' argument and agreed to provide funds for the fortification of Singapore. By 1938, the Royal Navy would be able to send a fleet to defend the East.

The admirals had solved one problem only to face another: the lack of naval strength. Since they had only enough capital ships for a tenuous defensive in the Far East, Britain's admirals insisted that they could not afford to grant Japan a larger ratio. As it was, if war came, they could send only enough battleships to the Far East to give them a margin of one ship over the Japanese fleet for they would have to retain five ships at home to deal with France's fleet. Although the leaders of the government quite rightly ridiculed the navy's fear of France, the admirals replied that since Germany was demanding equality with France in armaments, Hitler might build a fleet equal to that of the French navy. The leaders of the Royal Navy warned that, because of the threat from Japan, German equality with France would be "very undesirable." [5] Thus, Hitler's rise in the West meant rigidity on the ratios of naval strength in the East.

The admirals' prime objection to the disarmament treaties centered on the issue of cruiser strength. On March 23, 1934, Chatfield warned the government that the two-power standard in cruisers and light craft no longer existed. After the Washington Conference, Britain had almost stopped building cruisers, while Japan and France had continued their programs. Then in 1930, the London Conference compounded the difficulty. The admirals reported that "the despatch of a Fleet sufficient to meet that of Japan, combined with a distribution of cruisers to ensure the security of our sea communications against Japanese attack, would leave us with a strength in Europe and Home waters definitely inferior to that of the strongest European naval power . . . we should have a mere handful of cruisers and destroyers left to meet the powerful cruisers and submarine forces which could be brought against our Atlantic and Mediterranean trade." Although France was then the strongest European naval power, the admiralty warned that "the present position of France may be assumed by a Power [Germany] whose interests are opposed to ours."

In a Far Eastern war, Chatfield estimated that Britain would need 148 cruisers for fleet work, convoys, and raider pursuit. Since it was financially impossible to provide such a large number of ships, the admirals proposed retaining 50,000 tons of overage cruisers while building up to a level of 250,000 tons in underage ships; this construction would give the Royal Navy seventy cruisers, and in time of war, the admirals would convert seventy-eight fast merchantmen to take up the slack. This proposal had implications for Britain's defense spending, for in order to reach the level of sixty underage cruisers, the politicians would have to provide funds for twenty-five new cruisers, in addition to the regular replacement program.

Britain's admirals added, however, that the government could best satisfy the nation's longing for disarmament by qualitative rather than quantitative restrictions. They proposed cutting the size of battleships by ten-thousand tons and the size of the main cannon on capital ships by four inches, and urged abolishing the expensive eight-inch gun cruiser. These savings in tonnage and expenditure, they implied, would more than justify the needed increase in British six-inch gun cruiser strength. The Foreign Office pointed out that the navy was seeking an increase of sixty percent in Britain's light cruiser strength, and the diplomats warned that such a large demand might destroy the talks. The diplomats added that the Japanese would try to improve their ratio and that Britain would have to make some concession if an agreement were to be reached.[6] In fact, the leaders of the Royal Navy were proposing an increase of forty percent in their light cruiser strength and a drop in Japan's ratio from 7/10 to 6/10.

Thus, the Royal Navy strongly advocated maintaining the ratio system and demanded an increase in its cruiser complement to deal with Japan in the Pacific and Germany in the Atlantic. In 1922, the Washington naval treaty had returned the navy to the secure position that it had held in the nineteenth century, but continued building by Japan, France, and Italy, linked with the rise of Germany, made Britain's admirals fear for the safety of the empire. Before Britain's negotiators could meet their American counterparts, the British government would have to decide either to accept the Admiralty's version of the threat on the seas, or to turn their ear to the pleas of the Foreign Office and the Exchequer for a deal with Japan.

THE ADMIRALTY'S HOLLOW VICTORY

On April 16, 1934, the members of the ad hoc ministerial committee that was preparing for the naval conference met to discuss the Admiralty's proposal and the Foreign Office demands. The same cast that was simultaneously squabbling over defense requirements was also present as the curtain rose on this committee: MacDonald, Baldwin, Chamberlain, Simon, Thomas, and Monsell. As in the debate on defense requirements, things seemed to go badly for the admirals from the first.

MacDonald argued that Britain should yield on the ratios and allow Japan to increase her battlefleet by one capital ship. When Simon warned that the Americans wanted the British to oppose any increase in Japan's ratio, Chamberlain said that he "hoped we should do nothing of the kind." The Chancellor of the

Exchequer said that "public opinion would be profoundly disturbed at a break-down of this conference." He believed that "people would welcome" a deal with Japan which would settle Anglo-Japanese differences on spheres of invest-ment in China and on trade questions; such an arrangement, he argued, would dispose of the Japanese threat. "That," he added, "would leave America in the cold; but that might be unavoidable." Three days later, MacDonald also warned that the Admiralty might have to forego its hopes for seventy cruisers: "If the Admiralty press too far in their demands there may be political repercussions, and they may find a government returned to power who would give them nothing like . . . [what] they required . . . 70 cruisers will be a hard number to obtain from the financial point of view." [7] Once again, politics and finance conflicted with security.

The representatives of the Admiralty fought back. The First Lord, Sir M. B. Eyres-Monsell, declared flatly that Britain could not afford to let Japan increase her ratio. The First Sea Lord, Admiral Chatfield, said construction by the French and particularly by the Germans made the level of seventy cruisers indispens-able. During the First World War, he explained, surface raiders had been ex-tremely dangerous; if an attack on a convoy were made "by a force stronger than that escorting the convoy, we must expect to lose . . . the whole of the con-voy." [8] Since the attacking ship had much greater speed than the merchantmen, it could overwhelm the escort and destroy the slowly scattering cargo ships before they could escape.

But MacDonald argued that a request for seventy light cruisers would put the government "in a very bad position. It was essential that our first proposals should not come as a shock to the public." By circulating an epistle from Warren Fisher on the fragile state of the economy, Neville Chamberlain reminded his colleagues that Britain was in no position financially to outbuild Japan. Simon then proposed a compromise: the government would accept as a final goal a level of sixty underage cruisers and ten overage. During the preliminary negotiations, Britain's delegates would get the American reaction to this new level of British strength, and if the Americans objected, Britain's negotiators would then pro-pose a level of sixty cruisers (fifty underage and ten overage), which was still an increase of ten over the London Treaty. The committee accepted this compro-mise, but Monsell predicted that "Japan was going to be the trouble." Mac-Donald replied, "That was all the more reason why we should not show a card which might upset our own people." [9]

From the cruiser question, the committee turned next to the problem of an increased ratio for Japan. Although MacDonald and Chamberlain had both ad-vocated giving Japan an improved ratio, the weight of bureaucratic advice was against any concession. On May 7, Hankey circulated to the committee a report in which the British attaché in Berlin warned that Germany would soon begin building battleships and submarines; the Germans argued that the expected fail-ure of the 1935 London Naval Conference would free them completely from the restrictions of the Treaty of Versailles, since it was unfair that they should have to disarm when the other powers did not. Admiral Chatfield told the committee that if Japan improved its ratio, the Royal Navy could not simultaneously send a fleet to Asia, defend the empire's trade, and cover the German fleet. He added, "It is only the British fleet which stands between our Eastern Empire and Japan." [10]

In April, Amō made his declaration against foreign help for China, and as a result, the Foreign Office came to the aid of the Admiralty. Simon told the cabinet on April 25 that Amō's statement was "most disturbing. Japan appears to be following the German model." On May 28, the Foreign Office warned the National government that Japan's long-range aim was "the domination of Asia . . . Any comprehensive form of cooperation with Japan in China would lead us into actions which public opinion in this country would not countenance." The diplomats argued that the most hopeful course would be to encourage Japan to enter joint investment ventures with Western nations in China and to urge the Chinese to cooperate. Since the Japanese feared isolation and could not stand the financial strain of an arms race, they might accept the ratios. But in opposition to the bureaucrats of the Admiralty and Foreign Office, Warren Fisher advocated naval equality for Japan. Britain could not fight Japan and Germany at the same time, Fisher wrote, and "the very last thing in the world that we can count on is American support." Therefore, he argued, Britain should concentrate on arming against Germany and "effect a thorough and lasting accommodation with the Japanese." [11]

In the end, the leaders of the National government reached another characteristic compromise. On June 11, they accepted the navy's basic formulation of strategic needs: "We should be able to send to the Far East a Fleet sufficient to provide 'cover' against the Japanese Fleet; we should have sufficient additional forces behind this shield for the protection of our territories and Mercantile Marine against Japanese attack; at the same time, we should be able to retain in European waters a force sufficient to act as a deterrent." The Admiralty had stated that any increase in Japan's ratio would be quite "unacceptable," but the committee was of another mind: "We recommend that we should not agree to an increase in Japan's ratio without some substantial *quid pro quo*." In other words, Chamberlain and Fisher had succeeded in holding the door open for a deal with Japan. The committee decided that Britain's negotiators would appeal for disarmament as well: they would seek to reduce the size of battleships, carriers, and light cruisers and to abolish both the heavy cruiser and the submarine. The committee also accepted the compromise on cruisers that Simon had worked out: Britain would demand seventy cruisers at the outset, but would eventually accept sixty. Finally, the ministers decided to remain adamant for indecision, stating that their instructions would be tentative, and that the delegates would test them during the preliminary negotiations. [12] Presumably, if Britain's negotiating position were challenged by the United States and Japan abroad, or by the Labour and Liberal opposition at home, it would be changed.

THE SEARCH FOR A COMMON FRONT

It is often said that the citizens of the United States and Great Britain are divided by a common language, but in 1934, the American and British governments found themselves separated as well by a variety of more substantive problems. In 1933, Roosevelt had refused to fall in behind the British during the London Economic Conference. Roosevelt's independence seemed to confirm the fact that Americans of both parties were crudely nationalistic and insensitive to England's difficulties. A year earlier, Hoover's Secretary of State, Henry L. Stimson, had accused the British of refusing to maintain a common front against Japan during the Shanghai incident. Difficulties over the depression and the Sino-Japanese crisis left angry memories among the leaders of the two governments.

The fact that the British still owed war debts to their former colonial dependents made matters worse. As part of their plan for European recovery, Britain forgave Germany its outstanding reparations liabilities and, in turn, asked the Americans to cancel Britain's war debts. But the Americans refused, and the British government began making only token payments in 1933. By the spring of 1934, it was apparent that the British would soon cease all payments, and Congress passed the Johnson Act, which prohibited Americans from lending money to countries in default to the United States. This law was a serious blow to England's security, for in any future war the British government would not be able to finance her imports by obtaining loans in the United States. As a result of these differences on Asian policy and war debts, both the Americans and the British entered the preliminary naval negotiations in a state of mutual irritation. On October 7, 1933, Neville Chamberlain, who was partially responsible for the decision to end the debt payments, wrote in his diary: "S.B. [Stanley Baldwin] says he has got to loathe the Americans so much that he hates meeting them and he actually refused an invitation to dine with Ramsay [MacDonald] to meet the James Roosevelts (the President's son); I myself am going—to look at the creature." [13] Obviously, Anglo-American cooperation would not be possible at the beginning of the talks, especially since the British were eager for a deal with Japan.

In order to carry out his instructions, however, Norman Davis, the American delegate, would eventually have to secure the help of his British colleagues. If the English joined the Japanese in seeking a change in the ratios, the United States would be the only country opposing the revised disarmament system. On the other hand, if the British joined the Americans in asking for the maintenance of the existing system, Japan would stand alone facing a joint front. At best, Anglo-American pressure might bring Japan to remain within the system, and at worst, Japan would stand out as the only nation refusing to disarm. Roosevelt had decided that the United States could live with either result, though he preferred to see the negotiations succeed. But Anglo-American cooperation, which seemed likely in April and May, proved difficult by June.

Davis was optimistic about the prospects for cooperation with the British, since throughout the spring all of the British leaders whom he consulted assured him that Britain would stand by the ratios. On his way from Geneva to Washington in April, Davis stopped in London to scout the terrain, and he found himself in agreement with the British both on basic principles and on negotiating strategy. Robert Vansittart and Robert Craigie of the Foreign Office agreed with Davis that Japan was secure in its own waters and therefore did not deserve an increase in its naval ratio. According to Davis, the three men decided to seek a formal decision on the ratio question from their respective governments and then to notify the Japanese that neither Britain nor the United States considered the ratios negotiable. If the Japanese refused to bargain and withdrew from the talks, both countries could agree to maintain Anglo-American parity and to match any Japanese increase. On the basic principle of the ratios, then, there seemed to be complete agreement.

But Robert Craigie of the British Foreign Office recorded his conversations with Davis differently. According to his notes, he had warned Davis that the cabinet had made no final decision on the ratio question and that it was impossible to predict what the government's attitude would be. In any case, Craigie wrote that the British wanted no joint Anglo-American statement on the ratios; they preferred that the Japanese discover during the talks that "neither government were prepared to make any appreciable concession on this point." There seemed to be only a few minor clouds on the horizon: the British warned that their defense needs precluded any further cuts in the tonnage allowed them, and for reasons of economy, they wanted to reduce the size of the battleship and cruiser. But they said that these problems could be worked out prior to the arrival of the Japanese. The British explained that they would issue a call for preliminary negotiations, and since it would take the Japanese representatives much longer to arrive than the Americans, there would be time to settle such minor differences.[14]

When he returned to Geneva, Davis approached the British Foreign Minister, Sir John Simon, who confirmed the desire of the British to reach an understanding with the Americans before negotiations began. Simon added, "Parity with Japan would be absurd." On the basis of these assurances, Davis informed Hull that ironing out the technical aspects of the Anglo-American front would take "not more than two weeks." [15]

At first, Davis' optimism seemed justified. On May 18, the British issued the promised call for preliminary negotiations. On June 18, Davis sat down with the British to build a joint front, and during the first week of talks, all seemed to be going well. At the opening session, Prime Minister MacDonald referred to reports that Japan was considering a denunciation of the Washington naval treaty. After a brief discussion, the representatives decided that it should be their "joint policy to preserve the principles of the Washington [naval] Treaty and to discourage any denunciation of it.'' MacDonald also said that he saw no justification for an increase in Japan's ratio, and Davis declared that the Americans ''not only saw no justification [for it] but . . . we could not consent to it.'' The delegates then pledged that they would ''refuse to accept even a minor modification in the Japanese ratio without previous Anglo-American consultation.'' Davis reported that he felt ''encouraged.'' But the American representative would not have been pleased if he could have read Craigie's account of the conversation. Craigie noted only that ''it was agreed that neither side would depart from its attitude of opposition to any increase in the Japanese ratio without previous consultation with the other.'' [16] Thus, Craigie stressed the obligation to consult, while Davis emphasized resistance to any change in the ratio. In accordance with his instructions, the British diplomat was keeping alive the possibility that Britain might grant Japan an increased ratio in return for some substantial quid pro quo.

The love fest soon ended. On June 21, the British representatives revealed that their instructions called for an addition to their own light cruiser complement. They asked for an increase of 120,000 tons in that category and an end to the construction of heavy cruisers. The British argued that they had to double the number of their light cruisers in order to guard convoys in the Mediterranean and to protect the sea lanes around Australia and New Zealand from Japanese raiders.[17] In short, they insisted that England's special position necessitated an increase rather than a decrease in British naval strength while the other powers stood still.

The American delegates immediately sent an angry report home, which in turn brought back anxious cables from Washington. The question of cruisers was an old and divisive problem, which had broken up the Geneva Conference of 1927 and troubled the delegates at London in 1930. The Americans wanted a large number of eight-inch gun, 10,000-ton cruisers to aid in the advance of their fleet across the Pacific, while the British wished to build a lighter cruiser of 6,000 tons mounting six-inch guns to protect their trade. While the directors of the British navy considered heavy cruisers to be wastefully expensive, the American admirals argued that only heavily armored cruisers would be able to survive a sea battle in the western Pacific and make good their return to port.[18]

After receiving the British demand, the American delegation held a brief meeting and then urged Roosevelt not to negotiate on the basis of the British proposal. Davis argued that American opinion would not accept any new agreement which would require an increase in American armaments. More important, the British proposal would give the Japanese the excuse they needed to press for an alteration of the ratios. In a telephone call to Craigie, Davis complained that the British delegates had not warned him that Britain would seek such a large increase in their cruiser tonnage. Craigie assured Davis that the cruiser proposal did not represent Britain's final position. Scenting compromise, Davis urged Roosevelt to take a ''strong stand at the outset'' and to make the British back down.[19] Davis had understood his instructions well, for Roosevelt could not afford to send a treaty to the Senate that added to the burden of world armament.

The Navy Department and the President needed little encouragement from Davis. The General Board, Moffat recorded, had one of "its usual storms" and urged the State Department to reject the British offer and to call the delegates home. The President was also outraged. When Phillips went to talk to him about the reply to Davis, Roosevelt immediately wrote a personal message in longhand to MacDonald: "the difficult situation of modern civilization throughout the world demands for the social and economic good of human beings a reduction in armaments and not an increase . . . I am not going into technicalities of tonnage or classes or guns at this time, because these can be solved if the naval nations agree on the big basic principle." Phillips recalled: "The President then got somewhat heated and told me that if nothing came of these preliminary conversations and if it appeared that the British and Japanese intended to increase rather than decrease their navies, he would make a public appeal to the King of England and the Emperor of Japan; he outlined the type of appeal which he would make, which ended with a threat that the United States would beat them to it if the situation developed into a naval race." Hull informed Davis that the British proposal was "wholly unacceptable to the United States even as a basis of discussion" and instructed him to make no counter proposal.[20]

On June 27, Davis told the leaders of the National government that the American delegation had been "surprised and shocked" by Britain's proposals, and he declared that the Americans were "unwilling to take them as a basis for discussion." President Roosevelt, he said, wanted either a reduction of twenty percent in overall tonnage or a continuation of the existing treaties. In spite of Davis' rigidity, the British continued to seek American sympathy for their special difficulties in both Europe and Asia. They pointed out that the United States refused to ease Britain's burden in the Orient: the Americans were withdrawing from the Philippines, and they consistently refused to enter into contractual defense agreements in the East. MacDonald and Baldwin told Davis that they could not consider any reduction in naval strength. Baldwin added that "if England were to have trouble with Japan now, it is simply not in a position to deal with the situation."[21]

Prime Minister MacDonald suggested that there was a way to hold the line against an overall increase in naval strength and still allow the Royal Navy to build the additional cruisers it needed: the powers could agree to reductions in categories other than light cruisers, in order to compensate for the British increase. MacDonald also sent a mollifying message to Roosevelt, reminding the President that Britain was seeking reductions in the size of ships and the numbers of submarines permitted under the treaties. He also claimed that the British would accept an overall cut of twenty to thirty percent in naval strength if their risks were reduced proportionately. But MacDonald withdrew this offer immediately by adding that the world situation was getting worse, not better. "European maritime nations enormously increasing naval power,'' he telegraphed; ''Far East armaments also increasing our risks.'' John Simon was also disturbed by the ''extremely ineffective interview with Norman Davis and Co.'' He told Baldwin that ''the only hope would be a preliminary Anglo-Japanese negotiation which fixed the Japanese navy at a reasonable level and then to face the Americans with the prospect of losing this advantage if they do not find it possible to agree on the British level. But I doubt very much whether Japan is going to agree with us. All of which shows what a delightful job we have inherited in this naval conundrum.'' In fact, on June 8, the Admiralty had warned that the Japanese were coming to London to end the naval ratios and to exclude Far Eastern questions from the talks.[22]

After a conference with the President, Hull instructed Davis to fight on. The Secretary of State refused to consider any Anglo-American agreement for mutual East Asian defense efforts, since it ''would in effect constitute an alliance.'' He reminded Davis that ''at the very least'' the Roosevelt administration wanted an extension of the existing treaties, if a further reduction of naval strength proved impossible. Hull was not completely uncompromising, however. In an unenthusiastic way, he took up MacDonald's suggestion that increases in the cruiser category could be compensated by decreases in other categories; the Americans, he said, might accept ''minor readjustments'' within the ratios which did not lead to any increase in overall tonnage. After this reply, the discussions limped along until the Japanese provided a welcome excuse for ending them. The Japanese government announced that its representatives could not reach London before October, whereupon the Americans and British suspended their talks.[23]

After Davis left London, however, the British decided to drop back to their secondary position on the cruiser issue. The English diplomats had been most eager to send Davis home ''in as good a humour as possible,'' but the American disappointed them by refusing to sign one of those meaningless communiqués with which negotiators gloss over fundamental differences. With President Roosevelt so angry and his representative in London so adamant, the British evidently began to fear that rumors of the Anglo-American misunderstanding would soon leak to Japan's diplomats and to the British public. Consequently, Simon and Craigie decided to pacify the Americans by cutting their cruiser proposal drastically. In late July, they offered to reduce their proposal from an increase of 120,000 tons to one of only 70,000 tons in the light cruiser class.[24] This reduction meant that a compromise might be possible; by making relatively small reductions in other classes, the powers could compensate for the increased tonnage in light cruisers. Britain had made possible an agreement that would satisfy the Americans, and the powers could now write a treaty which would prevent an overall increase in naval tonnage. But the American effort to establish a common defense on the line of the ratios had failed. If the Japanese delegates were skillful, they might be able to pry the Americans and British even further apart.

Britain's leaders were caught in a difficult dilemma. Growing dangers at the extremities of the empire seemed to require an increase in naval construction. But rearmament might alienate the public and be fatal in the coming election. The masters of the National coalition avoided settling the question of Britain's naval needs during the debate on defense requirements, but they faced the problem again when they tried to issue instructions to their delegates. The Admiralty representatives argued that the government had to increase the strength of the Royal Navy or see the empire seriously endangered throughout the world. Because of financial stringency and political fears, however, the National leaders decided to try another tack: the time-honored British device of special arrangements with their colonial competitors, a method that had served the British Empire well in the years before the First World War. Britain's search for a deal with Japan would undoubtedly anger the Americans just at a time when Anglo-American relations were in a state of mutual irritation, but Britain's leaders believed that American displeasure would be a small sacrifice to make for security in Asia. To satisfy the Admiralty, the National government accepted the admirals' contentions in principle, but the politicians' preference for a deal with the Japanese was clear. And in the negotiations with the Americans, Britain's diplomats skillfully kept the door open for a compromise with Japan. Much would depend on the demands that Japan would present when the tripartite talks began in the fall.

PART FOUR   The Negotiations

9   The First Encounter

As the time for negotiations neared, the Americans found it necessary to provide instructions for their delegates. A number of circumstances, both domestic and foreign, reinforced the Roosevelt administration's inclination to take a rigid stand in support of the ratios. During the summer of 1934, the President's advisers grew increasingly pessimistic about the prospect for profitable negotiations with the Japanese, while at home the political situation was heating up with the approach of the congressional elections. As a result of these factors, Roosevelt and his advisers hammered out a negotiating position and bargaining strategy that would protect them from criticism at home and at the same time uphold the naval ratios. The British delegates received more flexible instructions. Their job was to find a compromise solution that would guarantee British security and also prevent a naval race. The Japanese Foreign Office instructed its delegates to exploit Britain's eagerness for a settlement, to keep the talks going as long as possible, and to obscure the issue of responsibility if the talks failed.

AMERICAN SKEPTICISM

Throughout the summer of 1934, Ambassador Grew sent disturbing reports to Washington of the Japanese navy's drive for naval parity. Citing these dispatches, Under Secretary of State William Phillips wrote on June 22, "The Japanese are apparently going to make impossible demands. The fate of any further naval conference does not now look rosy." The head of the Western European Division of the State Department, J. P. Moffat, told Davis, the leader of the American delegation to the talks, on August 31, "Nothing that we get from Japan gives ground for thinking that there has been a change of heart on essentials." A naval attaché report from Tokyo on September 7 seemed to confirm the diplomats' fears.[1]

At this early stage, however, it did not serve Japan's purposes to appear too intransigent, and Foreign Minister Hirota attempted to put the Americans and British in a mood to continue the talks for a reasonable amount of time. In September, Hirota sent Yoshida Shigeru, a former Vice Foreign Minister, to tell the American and British Ambassadors in Tokyo that "the Japanese position in the conference would not necessarily be so rigid or inflexible as might be assumed from the statements appearing in the press." Yoshida told Grew that the majority of government men, including Hirota, Ōsumi, and Okada, wanted to make the conference a success, but they faced opposition from a strong minority of "intransigent admirals." Yoshida added the warning that "minorities have sometimes won out over majorities." In conclusion, he advised Grew to ignore the newspapers and to be neither overoptimistic nor overpessimistic.[2]

The reaction of the State Department to Yoshida's mollifying statement was guarded. Moffat told Davis on September 13: "Our Far Eastern experts, one and all, tell us that the message thus communicated from the Japanese Foreign Office should not be taken too seriously . . . They still feel that although Hirota may succeed in bringing about some slight modification of the Japanese Navy stand, the decision will be made by the Navy." Moffat said that the Yoshida affair reminded him of the Manchurian incident in 1931 when the Japanese had attempted to ride two horses at once. Davis agreed with Moffat, having just been warned by a former ambassador to Japan, Roland Morris, that "we must not put much store in the efforts of the so-called liberals to influence Japanese Navy policy."[3]

A few days after Yoshida's conversation with Grew, Hirota confirmed the pessimistic predictions of the Far Eastern Division. The Japanese Foreign Minister admitted that Japan would abrogate the Washington naval treaty by the end of the year. Although some admirals wanted to abrogate immediately, Hirota explained, he had persuaded them to wait until after the negotiations had started. William Phillips remarked, "So the whole Yoshida business was applesauce after all." The head of the Far Eastern Division, Stanley K. Hornbeck, said simply, "I told you so." And Cordell Hull suspected that the Japanese had made a secret deal with the British that gave them the confidence to do away with the Washington system.[4] Thus, as the time approached for giving instructions to the American delegates, there seemed little chance that Japan would accept a compromise and preserve the disarmament system. In fact, it appeared likely that Japan would take the blame for tearing up the disarmament treaties. Consequently, the administration could make a strong statement in favor of further disarmament without worrying that American rigidity would blight hopes for some form of naval disarmament.

There were sound political reasons for the Americans to support the existing system of limitations during the coming talks. Disarmament remained popular as the depression dragged on. In September, Senator Gerald Nye opened hearings in an attempt to show that the arms manufacturers had corrupted the government when securing contracts.[5] By striving to secure the future of disarmament, the administration could demonstrate its freedom from the munitions lobby. Finally, the progressive wing of Roosevelt's coalition would have actively opposed the President if he had failed to seek disarmament. Thus, the administration had little to gain and much to lose if it let its delegates compromise the naval ratios.

THE DECISION

In addition to pessimism about the prospects for compromise and the public's desire for further disarmament, there was another reason for American rigidity:

the need to support American policy in the Far East. On September 26, Roosevelt's principal diplomatic advisers, Hull, Phillips, Moffat, and Hornbeck, met with the leaders of the American navy to consider what position the Americans should take during the talks. Admiral William H. Standley, Chief of Naval Operations, asked whether or not the United States planned to uphold the treaty system in East Asia. As Standley explained: "If we desire to give adequate support to the policies which we have been following in the past, such as the Open Door, the 9-Power Treaty, the Kellogg-Pact, et cetera, then we must possess adequate naval force." If not, he added, then the Americans would be wise to give up their trade and withdraw from East Asia before they were challenged. The diplomats agreed, stating that "a definite indication that we had abandoned any intention of using force for the maintenance [of our policies] would be viewed by all Oriental countries as the removal of an obstacle to further aggression . . . . It was further the consensus that Japan's policy was definitely to continue its aims at dominating Eastern Asia. In these plans she is being held up by the United States and similarly by Great Britain." Obviously, then, if the United States were to deter further aggression by Japan, it would have to maintain its strength.

Secretary of State Hull then asked whether the naval ratios were an essential part of the disarmament system, to which Admiral Standley replied that "there was a relative strength in fleets which must not be disturbed . . . it must be maintained at all costs . . . In the first place, without it, we could exercise no strength in the Far East; in the second place, we had paid for it by giving an undertaking not to fortify our possessions in the Western Pacific." However, Standley indicated that the navy might accept a pact limiting the total tonnage of auxiliary vessels for each country without regard to the type of ships, a concession which might satisfy both Britain's desire for more light cruisers and Japan's hopes for more submarines and heavy cruisers.[6] Thus, the navy was somewhat flexible. But in view of the diplomats' intention to uphold the treaty system against Japanese aggression, the navy would accept no concessions on the ratios.

The President's advisers also agreed on the strategy for the American delegation to use during the negotiations. "At all costs," they decided, "we must avoid at the next conference having the onus placed upon us for obstructing further progress." According to Moffat, "the Secretary who has about given up hope of any real outcome of the naval talks is worrying over the best way to explain our views and justify the country in what may well be a naval armaments race with Japan." The President shared Hull's desire to advertise the United States as a friend of disarmament. On October 3, he told a meeting of diplomats and admirals that the American delegates must make their position clear to the "man in the street [or] we would be flooded by adverse propaganda from British and Japanese sources."[7] He warned of the necessity "that we set forth our position in no uncertain terms to the American public and that our offer first of reduction and then of maintenance of the present treaties should be understood in their entirety by the public."[8] The President argued that Davis should make every effort to publicize the American position before either Britain or Japan revealed their own proposals.

Everyone present at this meeting agreed that Japan would seek to increase their strength to a 8/10 ratio and that the United States could not afford to modify the existing relative strengths of the navies. Admiral Standley asked whether the President would permit a slight increase in tonnage if it would secure an agreement, and the President replied, "Definitely no." Roosevelt added that "he for one was unwilling to sign a treaty or to submit a treaty either to the Senate or the people which carried with it an increase of one ton over the total figures now appearing in the Washington and London Naval Treaties." At a press conference on October 5, Roosevelt publicly said that he would try to fulfill the purpose of the Washington and London naval treaties by seeking lower naval limits at London.[9]

According to Roosevelt's plan for the negotiations, Davis was to state at the outset that the United States supported the ratios and further arms reduction. If the Japanese refused to cooperate, they would then stand out as the disrupter of the system. At a strategy meeting held on October 4, Hull, Davis, Moffat, and Admiral Standley agreed that "it would be better to have the conversations break down on a single issue than become involved in a network of disputed difficulties in which the differences of opinion between the United States and Britain might be accentuated as much as the differences between the two of us and Japan . . . Our whole strategy must be to avoid becoming involved in any other subsidiary difficulties such as excess British cruiser tonnage, the size of capital ships, etc., until after we [have] met and passed the rock of the ratios." But Hull and Davis succeeded in persuading the President that it would be unwise to announce the American position at the outset of the talks.[10] They probably feared that the American delegation would appear too rigid. Instead, Davis was ordered to reveal the substance of his instructions when a break was imminent.

Underlying the adoption of this firm position was the assumption that the United States would win any naval race started by Japan. Stanley K. Hornbeck voiced this opinion in a series of memos that circulated among the policy makers at this time. Hornbeck believed that the Japanese navy was already reaching its natural limits: "The Japanese Navy is, or by 1937 will be, as great and powerful as the Japanese Navy can induce the Japanese nation to make it. The limitation upon it would be a limitation imposed by Japan's national resources. The United States and Great Britain can afford to build beyond that strength." Hornbeck argued that Japan would "come forward asking" for new limitations "if the American government proceeded with the program of naval construction and perhaps speeded up that program." In short, America could "face with equanimity" the end of naval limitations.[11] Thus, a sense of underlying strength was a main reason for the administration's confidence, for America apparently could build enough ships to support its East Asian policies. The major danger in the approaching talks was that the identity of the villain would be blurred, causing Congress to balk at the expenditures necessary to build a strong navy.

Roosevelt, Hull, and Davis drafted a letter of instructions that could also serve as a publicity release to be used when the talks reached an impasse. In fact, Hull and Davis redrafted the instructions to make them more "belligerent" for public consumption. Roosevelt explained in the letter that the Washington and London naval treaties had provided security for all the signatories. Excessive armaments or competition in weaponry would breed only suspicion and war. Because civilized countries could not inflict such a fate on their people, the President instructed Davis to seek "a total tonnage reduction of twenty percent below existing Treaty tonnage. If it is not possible to agree on this percentage, please seek from the British and Japanese a lesser reduction—fifteen percent or ten percent or five percent . . . Only if all else fails should you seek to secure agreement providing for the maintenance and extension of existing Treaties over as long a period as possible. I am compelled to make one other point clear. I cannot approve, nor would I be willing to submit to the Senate of the United States any new Treaty calling for larger Navies." [12] The Roosevelt administration stood squarely in Japan's path to parity.

FLEXIBLE ALBION

On July 31, Hankey told Chamberlain that the government would have to provide Britain's negotiators with definite instructions as soon as the cabinet ministers returned from their holidays. But throughout the late summer and early fall, the National leaders' desire for a deal with Japan continued to block a decision on the diplomatic instructions. On July 5, the British ambassador to Tokyo, Robert Clive, reported that Hirota wanted to arrange a nonaggression pact with the United States and England. Clive also warned his superiors, however, that Okada could not accept a continued ratio system without being assassinated. From his vacation retreat, John Simon suggested that the powers might first grant Japan "equality of status" in principle and that the Japanese might then be willing to make a voluntary declaration of limits on their future building. He continued, "As regards [a] non-aggression pact, why not? . . . What would Japan want in return? Something equivalent to recognition of Manchukuo? A free hand in China would be more difficult." He asked his subordinates for comments on his two proposals.[13] Once again Simon had emerged as the constructor of a compromise: he hoped that Japan would accept limits on further building in return for recognition in principle of her equality, and in return for this small concession, the British might secure some guarantee of their East Asian interests, which would reduce their own need for naval construction.

One of Simon's subordinates at the Foreign Office, Robert L. Craigie, welcomed Simon's suggestion. "Our task," he wrote, "is to help the more moderate elements in Japan to 'save face' in this matter and so overcome the extremist elements who want no naval treaty at all.'' A nonaggression pact merited ''sympathetic consideration,'' he claimed, since it would help Hirota overcome the intransigence of the Japanese navy. If the Americans refused to accept the Anglo-Japanese settlement, he added, Britain should proceed without them. But Craigie insisted on a condition fatal to Simon's project: Japan would have to promise that its building would remain within the limits of the ratio.[14]

The acerbic Permanent Under Secretary at the Foreign Office, Robert Vansittart, attacked Simon's proposition. A voluntary limitation on building would provide no solution, he charged, because the Japanese were demanding a large increase in their ratio, which the British could not afford to grant. Vansittart also considered negotiations for a nonaggression pact ''fraught with the greatest difficulties,'' for such an agreement would give Japan a free hand to expand unless Japan specifically guaranteed the safety of China and the Dutch East Indies. Vansittart doubted that Japan would agree to any such guarantees. He bluntly informed Simon that a bilateral pact with Japan would be ''out of the question.'' [15]

Simon temporarily lost some of his enthusiasm, but the appeal of an Anglo-Japanese understanding lingered. Simon evidently rehearsed Vansittart's arguments for the benefit of Chamberlain, for on September 10, the Chancellor of the Exchequer assured Simon that he was not proposing to give Japan a free hand in China in return for a guarantee of Britain's East Asian interests. On September 25, Simon told the cabinet that Hirota had proposed a nonaggression pact twice during the summer. ''In the view of the Foreign Office,'' he continued, ''it was very improbable that Japan would put forward any proposals which we could entertain''; but, if the difficulties could be surmounted, ''the advantages . . . [of such a pact] could hardly be overestimated.'' [16] Thus, the Foreign Secretary was not optimistic but was willing to sound out the Japanese.

Chamberlain asked that the government delay any decision on naval spending until it knew the outcome of Simon's efforts. But Simon's objections had swayed the Chancellor. ''Clearly,'' Chamberlain told his colleagues, ''we could not contemplate giving Japan a free hand in China or in Shanghai or in the Dutch East Indies or to do what she saw fit by way of aggression against the Soviet.'' Evidently, Chamberlain did not realize that these conditions would make such a pact less attractive to the Japanese. Without much debate, the cabinet agreed to have Simon explore the possibility of a deal with Japan.[17]

The leaders of the National coalition had sound political reasons to persevere publicly in a quest for disarmament, for reduced naval spending, and for a stable East Asia. By mid-1934 the Labour party was well along on the road to recovery from the electoral disaster of 1931, which had left it quartered and decapitated. In a comprehensive program titled ''For Socialism and Peace,'' the new Labour leaders promised a ''peace crusade.'' In October, when canvassers for the League of Nations Union asked Britons whether or not they favored international disarmament and collective security, the response was overwhelmingly affirmative. Among the supporters of disarmament and the League were many Liberals, the fraction of electorate crucial to the National government in the coming elections. If the Tories suffered large defections from the ranks of their Liberal allies, they would lose the margin needed for victory in many doubtful districts. The signs were bad, for the by-election results during the fall of 1934 were even more disheartening for the National leaders than they had been in the fall of the previous year. On October 23, 1934, in Lambeth North there was a remarkable fifty percent swing to Labour, and on November 28 at Putney there was a twenty-seven percent loss in the National candidate's vote. Younger men in the Tory party began grumbling against their aging leaders for fear of electoral disasters that might await them in 1935.[18] Consequently, an arrangement with Japan might help to save not only disarmament but also the fortunes of the National coalition at the polls.

On October 10, the cabinet decided that a special committee of the National leaders should direct the naval talks. In the first meeting of the group, Simon, Chamberlain, and the Admiralty quickly worked out a basic strategy for the conference. On October 16, Simon and Chamberlain asked the government to seek a special arrangement with Japan, since Britain could not afford to defend both poles of its empire. But the two ministers added that any deal which gave Japan *"carte blanche* so long as she respected her promise not to attack any part of the British Commonwealth, is manifestly impossible." If "Japan declines terms which would safeguard the interests of China, then this would be fatal to the proposed pact." To satisfy the Americans, Britain would ask that the pact be tripartite in form; if the Americans refused to cooperate, Britain and Japan would then be free to make a bilateral agreement. In any case, Japan would not be able to trade "mere political assurances" for a large increase in her navy. It was agreed that Britain's delegates should "use the negotiation of a non-aggression pact as a lever for reducing Japan's naval programme."[19] Chamberlain had yielded considerably, in that Japan would have to promise to respect Chinese integrity and give up its desire to have a great navy. But while Hirota probably considered his offer of a nonaggression pact as a temporary expedient to help ease the pain caused by Japan's insistence on parity, the British hoped that such a pact would convince the Japanese that naval equality was unnecessary.

During October, representatives of the British Foreign Office and the Admiralty proposed a set of tactics for the talks. They predicted that Japan would ask for parity with the United States but not with Britain, and that the Americans would reject Japan's demand. Then Britain would step forward with a compromise: each of the naval powers would agree to exchange its building plans for a fixed number of years. Such a settlement would moderate the effects of future naval competition. If the Japanese still pressed for parity with the United States, the British delegates would threaten to agree to Japan's demand, in order to frighten the Americans into a compromise on cruisers and qualitative limitations. From the outset, that is, Britain would avoid the common front that the Americans desired. The committee concluded, "The United States representatives can hardly expect us to fight their battles for them so long as they maintain the same unreasonable attitude towards the British proposals as they adopted last summer.'' At the same time, the British delegates would avoid giving the Japanese the impression that a wedge could be driven between the United States and Britain.[20] Thus, if Chamberlain and Simon had their way, Britain's delegates would seek a deal with Japan that would provide security for Britain and China in the East and would replace the ratios with an agreement on building programs. And if the Americans were alarmed by the Anglo-Japanese rapprochement, so much the better.

But Prime Minister MacDonald objected. On October 15, he argued that Britain was committed to parity with the United States and that it could not threaten to forsake the principles established in the Washington naval treaty in order to gain additional cruisers and lower qualitative ratios. Chamberlain replied that the proposals before them offered the best hope of settlement, and he asserted that Japan was entitled to full parity with the United States. The two arguments seemed irreconcilable. In the end, the committee decided once again to procrastinate: Britain's representatives would mention the nonaggression pact only tentatively during the talks. If Japan refused to consider Britain's proposals, there would then be no need for England's leaders to fight the issue out among themselves, and Britain could once again stand with the Americans.[21] MacDonald and Monsell were mollified by being named, with Simon, as Britain's delegates.

The National leaders entered the talks still divided and worried by their waning popularity. Chamberlain and Simon favored a deal with Japan that would limit the need for great naval expenditures in the future. And Simon was willing to use the Anglo-Japanese talks to break down the United States' rigid insistence on further large reductions within the ratio system. Although they were eager for continued disarmament, MacDonald and Monsell doubted the effectiveness of Chamberlain's strategy: they feared that Britain would alienate the Americans, yet fail to satisfy the Japanese. In the end, all of the leaders decided that the most expedient course was to let Japan make the first move. As a result of British hesitancy, the Japanese delegates would have a good opportunity to split the British from the Americans, string out the negotiations, and blur the issue of responsibility. All would depend on the instructions brought by Japan's negotiators from Tokyo.

JAPAN'S INSTRUCTIONS AND DELEGATES

Although the Japanese government had finally agreed to accept the navy's demands as the basis for Japan's disarmament policy, it tried to make its position seem as reasonable as possible. On September 7, the Japanese cabinet approved the formulas on which Hirota was to draft his instructions. The government stated that it was the purpose of the empire to have the talks succeed, ''within the limits of being able to ensure the maintenance of our national defense.'' In order to provide for mutual security, the powers should establish a ''common upper limit'' on overall naval tonnage and agree to abolish all offensive weapons, such as battleships and aircraft carriers. In this way, the navy and government disguised their demand for parity by calling for severe cuts in all navies. The government also stated that ''continuance of the Washington [naval] treaty was disadvantageous from the standpoint of national defense,'' and that Japan would have to abrogate the treaty by the end of the year. The Japanese delegates were to explain the necessity of the abrogation and to ask the other powers to join Japan in ending the treaty. If the other nations did not agree, however, the empire would ''send its abrogation notice by the end of the year independently.'' [22] While striking off its own disarmament shackles, Japan would try to appear to be the champion of even tighter chains for all the naval powers.

In the detailed instructions that he drafted after the cabinet meeting on September 7, Foreign Minister Hirota repeated the main points made by the government, and he ordered the delegates to make Japan's case seem as moderate as possible. The Japanese negotiators were to press for the achievement of a common upper limit and the abolition of battleships and aircraft carriers, but at the same time, they were to avoid provoking public opinion in other countries. Hirota repeatedly instructed them to discuss in detail their own demands, the points raised by the other delegates, and the reasons for Japan's abrogation of the Washington naval treaty. Hirota also told the delegates that they could make an agreement which would bring Japan parity by stages.[23] Nevertheless, Japan's basic position remained unchanged: the powers would have to sacrifice their naval advantage and give Japan eventual parity. By having his representatives draw out the talks, Hirota hoped to blur the responsibility for the breakdown of disarmament.

Japan's delegates to the preliminary talks were likely to follow their instructions closely. The ambassador to Great Britain, Matsudaira Tsuneo, was an aristocrat and a diplomat of the old school, who loved the good things in life, especially a fine Scotch whiskey called ''Old Parr.'' He was a smooth negotiator and, with United States Senator David A. Reed, had helped to bring about the fundamental compromise that saved the first London Naval Conference.[24] Matsudaira would handle the talks with skill and would seek to soften the blow, but he could not ignore the explicit nature of Hirota's instructions.

His partner was Yamamoto Isoroku, a middle-ranking naval officer of promise. Although only a rear admiral in 1934, he was to become Japan's premier naval hero during World War II. Yamamoto's rank indicated the navy's contempt for the talks; the United States and Britain would be represented by their highest officers, but Japan was sending a man of much less stature. In any case, Yamamoto was a safe choice for the navy. Being young, he lacked political connections and was therefore less likely to make a deal in London in order to curry favor with politicians at home. In fact, Yamamoto was determined to please his superiors. During his send-off party at the Navy Ministry, he recalled that the delegates to the First London Conference had wasted a lot of money cabling requests for changes in their instructions; he promised that he would do his best to secure acceptance of Japan's original proposals and would wait until he returned to Tokyo to report the results of his efforts.

Yamamoto also had connections with the dwindling treaty faction of the navy, primarily through his friendship with Admiral Hori Teikichi. When Hori was driven from the navy in December 1934, Yamamoto told him sympathetically that the only hope for the future was to rebuild the navy after it had fallen into adversity brought on by its own "arrogance." Nevertheless, Yamamoto consoled himself during the negotiations with the hope that even if the talks failed, Japan would be secure. He believed that the empire's safety lay in carefully building up its strength: "if prewar Germany had been patient for five or ten years more, we can imagine that today it would have no equal in Europe; in view of this precedent, we should calmly and continuously endeavor to accumulate real strength today; even though the coming conference may not finally succeed, I think the day is not necessarily far off when we can make England and the United States bow to us." [25] Both Matsudaira and Yamamoto, then, would follow their instructions with skill and vigor; arguing Japan's case at length, extending the negotiations, and ultimately destroying the ratios.

INITIAL MEETINGS

In the month preceding the naval talks, Simon repeatedly tried to secure a statement from the Japanese about the terms of the proposed nonaggression pact. He authorized his ambassador in Tokyo to ask unofficially what Hirota had in mind. "Are the Japanese really so desirous of such a pact," he asked, "that they would be prepared to pay a reasonable price for it," such as a guarantee of China and the Dutch East Indies? On October 8, Simon told Matsudaira that Britain would keep the naval talks on a bilateral basis because Japan and England had a "special relationship," by which he was referring to the former Anglo-Japanese alliance and implying that England would intercede with the United States for the Japanese during the naval talks. Then Simon asked whether Japan would give the essential guarantees to Britain, Holland, and China to make such a pact possible. Matsudaira replied that he thought mutual security agreements, including a guarantee of Britain's position in China, could help in the extremely difficult naval negotiations to come. He added, however, that Japan would abrogate the Washington naval treaty and demand an end to the ratios. Nevertheless, Simon asked Matsudaira to secure a definite proposal from Hirota. [26]

When the formal talks opened, Hirota had not yet replied. On October 23, the Japanese delegates met with the British and delivered their naval proposals. Matsudaira declared that the ratios "did not satisfy national feelings and prestige." Yamamoto then explained that all countries had an equal right to possess the armaments necessary for their national safety. Consequently, each naval power should be free to select independently the weapons it needed under a "common upper limit" on overall tonnage. But in order to increase defensive capabilities, the powers should lower this limit as much as possible and drastically reduce or abolish offensive weapons, such as capital ships, carriers, and heavy cruisers.[27] The Japanese delegation had presented their government's terms in an unvarnished fashion, even adding heavy cruisers to the list of offensive weapons.

Despite their desire for cooperation with Japan in East Asia, the British could not pay the Japanese price. They replied that Britain was much more vulnerable than Japan, since it had to defend territories scattered across the whole globe. The British also argued that a common upper limit would threaten those countries which could not or would not build up to it. On the question of abolishing "offensive weapons," the British insisted that they could not abolish carriers because they had to protect their fleet against attacks by aircraft based on the European mainland. The British urged the Japanese to maintain the existing ratio system, arguing that the powers could disarm further by reducing the size of the battleship, ending further construction of heavy cruisers, and abolishing the submarine.

The Japanese delegation criticized the British proposal as offering too little disarmament and claimed that the Japanese approach provided for greater reductions. Smaller countries would not be threatened, they asserted, if the common upper limit were set low enough. Admiral Yamamoto also denied that the United States and Britain were more vulnerable than Japan. He reassured the British, however, that while the Japanese were eager to have parity with the United States, they were not so worried about the ultimate strength of the British navy. Yamamoto argued that the vulnerability of all nations, including England, would disappear if aggressive weapons—battleships, carriers, and heavy cruisers—were abolished. To this argument, Monsell replied that "a weapon was defensive if one was behind it and offensive if one was in front of it." [28] The Japanese delegation had left the door open for a special arrangement with the British, but England's initial reaction was discouraging.

When the Japanese delegation presented its arguments to the Americans on the following day, October 24, the results were even more disheartening. Davis told the Japanese that the old disarmament system had provided twelve years of security, and that the ratios reflected continuing strategic realities. American naval requirements were greater than those of Japan, since it had two coastlines to defend. He said that there had been no change in the international situation which would justify an increase in the Japanese ratio. Davis added that any attempt to distinguish between offensive and defensive weapons would surely fail, and he closed by warning that the collapse of the talks would lead to a naval race.[29]

In reply, Matsudaira pointed out that his delegation was under definite instructions to propose a new basis for continuing naval limitation, and that they could not accept a continuation of the present system. The Japanese delegates argued that they were asking only for equality, not superiority. Moreover, they said, much had changed since the Washington treaties had been signed; for example, the increased range of warships had made the attacker stronger than the defender.

The Japanese also insisted that for them the international situation had indeed changed, because of various Oriental problems and Japan's withdrawal from the League of Nations. Japan, they explained, had no desire to engage in a naval race; in fact, their country was seeking a radical cut in all navies.[30] Thus, the United States and Japan, though barely met, were already at sword points.

Throughout the preliminary talks and during the subsequent main conference, the three delegations would repeat these same arguments endlessly. Japan maintained that its proposal for the abolition of heavy vessels and the establishment of parity would provide a more equitable disarmament system than the Washington ratios, whereas the old treaties threatened Japan and made its people uneasy. The Americans replied that the old system gave each nation equality of security and that the ratios should be continued. The British repeatedly pointed out they were more vulnerable than Japan and needed compensation in the form of new security guarantees and increased naval strength. All parties were aware that if the Japanese delegates succeeded in drawing the British away from the Americans by offering them some special arrangement, the talks might continue for a long period, and the responsibility for the breakdown of the negotiations might then fall on the Americans. Under these circumstances, it was Davis' difficult task to establish a united front with the British.

On the other hand, the British role of mediator was an unenviable one, since the Americans and Japanese were very far apart. The Roosevelt administration was determined to preserve both the disarmament system and the East Asian policies that it had inherited from its Republican predecessors. Yet Japan showed itself to be intent on abolishing the old treaty structure completely. Japan's admirals clearly expected that their demand for a common upper limit, coupled with Japan's abrogation of the Washington naval treaty, would be unacceptable to the West. In view of the contradictory negotiating positions of the United States and Japan, the main question was how long Britain would continue to search for a special security arrangement with Japan and for a compromise naval agreement.

10 Britain Seeks A Compromise

With the preliminary negotiations barely under way, it seemed that the delegates were already hopelessly deadlocked. As mediators, the British sought to cut the knot, first by offering to disguise the ratios in a new agreement, and then by suggesting a modus vivendi that would limit the effects of naval competition. But as November wore on, the British efforts began to fray and ravel the Americans' patience. Nevertheless, the Japanese delegates were able to prolong the talks by relaying each British proposal to Tokyo for comment.

THE BRITISH PROPOSALS

Since the talks had begun in such an unpromising fashion, Britain's leaders met to frame a compromise proposal that might produce an agreement. Simon explained that the Japanese were insisting on a common upper limit which would either allow Japan to gain parity or require Britain to build a prohibitively large fleet. Japan's plan, he concluded, was "quite unacceptable" to the United States and the United Kingdom. On the other hand, Simon suggested Japan might be willing to join in a gentleman's agreement that would limit the number and size of the ships they would build. Chamberlain tentatively endorsed Simon's proposal.[1]

On November 6, 1934, Simon formally presented his plan to the ministerial committee. Fortuitously, Chamberlain was ill, and MacDonald used the Chancellor's absence to try to turn the government's face permanently against any change in the ratios. In fact, Simon's compromise plan required that Japan's future building "would in practice leave the present relative positions unaffected," and the Foreign Secretary had already assured Davis that in any new arrangement the ratios would be retained. MacDonald told his colleagues that Simon had defined the British attitude and that British support for the ratios seemed assured. But Warren Fisher, Chamberlain's messenger, protested that such rigidity might doom an Anglo-Japanese deal. The Japanese, he said, might be willing to allow Britain naval superiority as long as they achieved parity with the Americans. Although Fisher spoke with his master's voice, he lacked Chamberlain's bite, and the committee approved Simon's initiative.[2] The keepers of the purse had once again failed to ease the strain of Britain's responsibilities in the East.

Actually, Simon had already broached his plan to Matsudaira on October 29. He offered to combine the old ratios with equality for Japan in an informal agreement. In this new pact, the powers would declare that all nations were equal in their right to security, which would ensure that all countries would also be equal in prestige. The three powers would then add a nonaggression clause to the new treaty, in which Japan would guarantee that it would not make any hostile moves against China or against Britain's possessions in East Asia. Presumably, such a guarantee would also extend to the Philippines. Thus, the Japanese would have equality of prestige, and they would pay for it by promising to give up their new China policy. After Japan's prestige and security had been established on the foregoing basis, the three powers would make "a secret gentleman's agreement" regulating the amount of naval construction each nation could start within a fixed period. Simon asked that this proposal be kept absolutely secret and that his name not be attached to it. Although Matsudaira replied that Japan was seeking equality of armaments rather than equality of prestige, he promised to relay the proposal to Hirota.[3]

At first glance, the British offer seemed to open the way for an increase in the relative strength of the Japanese navy, but as Matsudaira investigated the proposal, he found the door to the ratios still shut and locked. Under questioning, Simon admitted that the "secret gentleman's agreement" on construction plans would have to retain the Washington and London ratios; thus, Japan would only be able to build three capital ships for every five battleships that the United States and Britain laid down. The purpose of this proposal, Simon said, was to preserve "the kind of proportions which at present exist," although there might be "adjustments here and there." Matsudaira again asked for time to consult his government.[4]

Hirota rejected both the nonaggression pact and the limitation of building programs. He did, however, instruct Matsudaira to continue dangling the bait but to keep it out of Simon's grasp. When the talks began, Hirota told Matsudaira that the Japanese government wanted to exclude all East Asian problems, particularly the question of China, from the discussions. Hirota explained that the Japanese government was trying to make the British recognize Japan's new position in East Asia. Consequently, although the Japanese did not wish to threaten Britain's interests in China, they could not accept any agreement that would tie Japan's hands in the future. Hirota was reminding his ambassador that Japan had recently assumed the role of the stabilizing power in East Asia and that the Japanese army planned further penetration of China. Rather than giving any specific guarantees for British interests in China, Hirota indicated, the Japanese government wanted to discuss an agreement that would cover all aspects of Anglo-Japanese relations and maintain the guarantees of the Four-Power Pact signed during the Washington Conference. Still, he asked his ambassador to remain responsive to Simon's suggestions.[5] In the days ahead, Matsudaira was able to keep the talks alive, but Hirota's refusal to guarantee peace in China had smothered the Anglo-Japanese rapprochement in its cradle.

With equal firmness Hirota disposed of the proposal for limiting construction programs. Japan, he stated, could not consider continuing the ratios in disguise. On November 19, Matsudaira dutifully informed Simon that Japan required real parity, not merely equality in principle. He added that the Japanese were unwilling to deal with the question of China during the talks "for fear of confusion." Instead of a nonaggression pact, Matsudaira suggested a reaffirmation of the mutual obligations assumed by Japan in the Four-Power Pact.[6] This treaty, of course, did not guarantee Chinese security.

The first British compromise proposal was consistent in principle with Mac-Donald's pledge to the Americans that Britain would fight for the ratios during the talks. But after the Japanese had rejected the disguised ratios, the British began searching for a stopgap agreement that would limit the effects of a naval race, even at the expense of the old ratio system. Admiral Chatfield, warning that the prewar naval race had produced the dreadnought and superdreadnought, argued that "almost any limit is better than none." Since quantitative naval competition alone would be difficult to cope with on a global scale, the British were eager to prevent a simultaneous qualitative naval race in which all countries would secretly develop and build new types of ships.

On November 21, therefore, Simon proposed that each country promise to notify other powers informally when it began construction of a new ship, a duty specified in the previous treaties; furthermore, Simon wanted to maintain the treaty limits on the size and armament of each type of warship. If Japan accepted these restrictions, the United States and Britain would know in detail the extent to which Japan was increasing its naval strength, and the Western powers could then lay down the number and type of ships required to maintain or improve their old ratio vis-à-vis Japan. Presumably, Japan would therefore hesitate before abandoning the ratios. Nevertheless, this British proposal was a long step away from the old treaties. Simon offered a worm to bait his hook: if Japan agreed to retain the qualitative aspects of naval limitations, the Western countries would continue to refrain from fortifying their bases in East Asia.[7]

The Japanese delegates relayed the new British proposal to Tokyo, but they kept up a discouraging tattoo of remarks in London while awaiting Hirota's reply. Matsudaira explained informally that Japan did not favor continuing any qualitative restrictions on warships, because Japan wanted each country to be free to build the types of ships necessary for its defense. He added that this freedom would not lead to a naval race, since the common upper limit would be set so low that no country could possibly be threatened by free building. The Japanese delegates also said that they could not accept the British proposal unless Japan first received parity. Under questioning by Yamamoto, Simon admitted that the British proposal would tend to preserve the existing ratios of naval strength.[8] By early December, it was clear that the Japanese delegates' instructions were explicit and rigid. Nevertheless, the British continued to wait for a final rejection from Hirota.

From the English point of view, there was some reason to hope for a change of heart in Tokyo. Before the naval talks began, for example, the Western countries had decided not to raise the issue of Japan's violations of its pledges to China under the Nine-Power Treaty. Moreover, the British proposal for a modus vivendi ended the contractual nature of the ratios and gave Japan the freedom to attempt a quantitative race with the Western nations. If Japan agreed to qualitative limits, the Western nations would refrain from fortifying their East Asian bases. And Matsudaira continued to feed the faltering British optimism as best he could. On November 15, he told Craigie via messenger that "at Tokyo the omens were on the whole favourable to the suggested compromise," although the Japanese government was "meeting with strong resistance from the extremists in the navy." Although Craigie was impressed, Simon was not as sanguine: "this is all very well," he minuted, "but Mr. Matsudaira's *job* is to keep us hoping that Japan is not far off agreeing. *Sed maximo dubito*." [9] The dragging talks were not only bothering Simon but also irritating the Americans. The British had moved a great distance from rigid adherence to the treaties, and the Americans were growing nervous.

THE AMERICAN REACTION

At first, the American government was relatively pleased with the way things were going in London. If the treaties had to be killed, it was best that Japan be the assassin and that the weapon be Japan's demand for a common upper limit. From the first, the Japanese navy had made clear to the American public that Japan was indeed insisting on parity. On the evening of October 23, the Japanese chargé in Washington invited a number of leading American newspaper correspondents to the Japanese Embassy, where the Japanese naval attaché gave them a formal explication of the empire's position. Six of the correspondents trooped through Moffat's office the next morning and reported that the attaché had said "the prerequisite to any agreement was absolute equality, not theoretical equality, not concealed equality, but an absolute equality." According to a State Department survey, the reaction of the American press to this announcement was, from the State Department's standpoint, gratifying. On October 29, Moffat concluded that "there is a unanimity of opinion all the way over to any but the most pacifistic circles that the Japanese are adopting an unreasonable, not to say offensive, position and that she has clearly shown her hand at desiring one thing, overlordship in the Far East, which means the expulsion of American rights and the closing of the Open Door." Japan, then, would probably be the villain of the piece. On November 1, Secretary of State Hull urged "patience, self-control, and skill" during the London negotiations. Not only had a "young, wild, and lawless group of Japanese" seized the government and begun "a course of conquest by force," but now Japan was demanding naval equality as well. [10] The United States should move carefully, he implied, and supply the Japanese with enough rope to hang themselves in public.

Though the Americans were initially confident that Japan would drive the British to their side, they soon were disillusioned. On October 29, Davis told Mac-Donald that the coming Japanese denunciation of the Washington naval treaty made any discussion of Anglo-American naval differences "academic." But the British Prime Minister insisted that his country needed more cruisers, and he warned that Britain was discussing a new building program arrangement and a tripartite nonaggression pact with the Japanese. He ignored Davis' appeal for a joint front against Japan, arguing that, if the Western powers appeared to be the "enemies" of Japan, success would prove difficult.[11] MacDonald was following the strategy suggested by the British Foreign Office, by which the English would try to use their mediating position to press the Americans into making concessions on cruisers.

On November 9, Roosevelt returned from Hyde Park to Washington, where he found a confidential report on Davis' talk with MacDonald. The British, Davis explained, were "just as opposed to the Japanese demands as we are but they are more inclined to give and take . . . and there is a slight possibility that they might possibly be in favor of agreeing to what would be in effect some increase in the Japanese ratio." William Phillips had been afraid that the British, in their mediation attempts, would go over to the Japanese, "putting us out on the end of a limb should the conference fail."[12] Now Davis himself was running up this storm signal.

The President reacted violently. He told Davis: "Simon and a few other Tories must be constantly impressed with the simple fact that if Great Britain is even suspected of preferring to play with Japan to playing with us, I shall be compelled, in the interest of American security, to approach public sentiment in Canada, Australia, New Zealand, and South Africa in a definite effort to make these Dominions understand clearly that their future security is linked with us in the United States." Roosevelt also told Davis that he thought the Japanese were bluffing and that they could not stand the cost of a naval race.[13] Obviously, then, Davis would have to hold to his instructions, secure an Anglo-American front, and place the blame for the breakup of the talks on the Japanese.

Four days later, on November 13, Davis reported that the Japanese had rejected the first British proposal and were soon intending to abrogate the Washington naval treaty, thus destroying the original basis for the naval talks. It was even possible, he indicated, that the negotiations might break up. If the talks came to an end, Roosevelt replied, Davis should release the letter of instructions in which Roosevelt had so forcefully stated the American desire for disarmament.[14]

The Americans had responded strongly to Davis' report of British flexibility because they were receiving warnings that the British and Japanese might make a deal. Before the negotiations began, Grew reported that Britain might seek security guarantees from the Japanese in return for granting parity, and Hornbeck voiced similar fears. Lord Lothian, an independent Liberal who had arrived in the United States during October, reinforced these warnings. The British must keep the major part of their fleet in European waters, he said, and if Germany and

Japan joined forces, Britain would have to leave Australia and New Zealand exposed. Since the Americans would offer no aid in the Far East, the British might jump at a chance to keep Japan and Germany apart and at the same time get a Japanese guarantee for continued peace in East Asia.[15] Under these circumstances, it was natural that there should be concern in Washington. If Britain joined Japan, the Americans would seem to be standing out against a revised disarmament agreement. From the American standpoint, then, it was necessary for Britain to stop wavering and break off the talks when the Japanese abrogated the Washington naval treaty.

But instead of agreeing to end the talks with Japan's denunciation, the British made their proposal for a qualitative modus vivendi. Davis transmitted the terms of this British overture and attempted to convince his superiors that the American delegation should not protest, arguing that the Americans had little choice but to go along if they wished to keep the British from proposing "something embarrassing" later on. But Hull told Davis that he wanted the negotiations to end with the Japanese abrogation of the Washington naval treaty, so as to make clear that the Japanese were responsible for the collapse of the talks. Hull said that a "clean break" in the negotiations and a joint Anglo-American warning that the two powers would build their navies up to treaty strength would bring the Japanese government to its senses. Moreover, he warned that a "continuation on the part of the British to endeavor to play the role of middle man will only result in increasing suspicion and resentment here."[16]

Hull saw no justification for any deal with Japan. On November 12, Hornbeck sent the Secretary of State a fifty-four page memo expounding the obligations that Japan had assumed and the sacrifices that America had made during the Washington conference. The following day, Hull stated that "the naval discussions are merely symbols of a greater issue, namely whether developments in Asia will be marked by equality of security, the Open Door, fair treatment, and a sense of international solidarity or whether, on the other hand, Japan can obtain undisputed overlordship to play a lone and selfish hand." William Phillips joined Hull in fearing that the British were swinging toward the Japanese and might try to blame the Americans for the failure of the London talks.[17]

On November 20, Hull decided to act. He called in Arthur Krock, the *New York Times* columnist in Washington, and vented his accumulated anger at the British. In his column published the following morning, Krock wrote that the Roosevelt administration "is irritated over the failure of Great Britain thus far to range herself on the naval disarmament question decisively with us against Japan," and he added that the highest American officials were revealing impatience with Britain's Foreign Secretary, Sir John Simon. Hull's newspaper attack backfired, however. Roosevelt had no special love for Krock, and he asked Hull for a copy of Krock's column. Ignoring Hull's weak excuse that "things did need being brought to a head among our British friends in London," the President forced Hull to express American apologies to Simon, and Roosevelt also wrote to the publisher of the *New York Times,* Arthur Ochs, asking that in the future his paper be more careful.[18]

Meanwhile, Davis had been doing his best to keep the door to an Anglo-American front open. On November 16, Simon had pointedly asked whether the United States would grant Britain an addition to its cruiser strength if the Japanese agreed to accept the old ratios in the disguise of fixed building programs. Davis replied that the Americans would indeed grant Britain a cruiser increase as long as the British accepted compensatory cuts in other classes. Davis protested, however, that Britain's proposal "represented . . . a tremendous come down from the whole [Treaty] structure." On November 23, Davis objected to negotiating while Japan was threatening to denounce the Washington naval treaty; the American government, he explained, "considered it inadvisable to proceed with the setting up of a substitute for the Washington Treaty while this sword of Damocles hung over our heads . . . the only hope of solution lay in close Anglo-American cooperation." He warned that the Hearst press was attacking the American delegation and that the United States could not continue negotiations so long as to obscure the seriousness of Japan's denunciation. He concluded that "there should be no further appearance of solicitude for Japan's action either in the British or the American camp."[19]

Gradually, Roosevelt, Davis, and Hull began to receive some support from within Britain. Using information apparently leaked by a friendly source in the Foreign Office, the *Daily Herald* published Britain's compromise proposal on November 7. Roosevelt then engaged in some newspaper signaling of his own, with better results than Hull's earlier venture. The President called in the London *Times* correspondent and warned the British against a deal with Japan; the *Times* published the warning, followed by a sympathetic editorial. During the next week, Jan C. Smuts, the South African delegate to the talks, and Lord Lothian, the Liberal spokesman, publicly attacked the idea of a separate Anglo-Japanese arrangement. Both were former allies of Lloyd George and both represented British hopes for the success of collective security and disarmament. Although they seemed outdated figures, their former mentor, Lloyd George, and the dissatisfied Liberals who had left the National coalition might still be dangerous at the next election. Consequently, MacDonald stated publicly that Britain had made no secret deal with Japan, and Simon told the cabinet that the British delegates were taking steps to dampen Davis' fears.[20]

Despite British reassurances, Hull continued to press for a clean break in London. By late November, Japanese publicity efforts and the long negotiations were beginning to affect American opinion. On November 28, Phillips noted in his journal that "the Japanese are very successful in their propaganda seeking to throw the blame on the United States for the failure of the London naval conversations." On the same day Hull warned Davis: "Senator Nye's recent public espousal of the thesis that Japan is right in demanding equality of naval armament may tend toward crystallizing a considerable section of pacifist sentiment throughout the country . . . the fundamental issues at stake have been obscured during the talks of the last 6 weeks and the unceasing efforts of the Japanese propagandists have made some headway, which may be one reason for Matsudaira's desire to keep the conversations going and to prevent an actual breakdown with a clean break." Hull told Davis to make greater efforts to publicize the American position and to secure British agreement to end the talks when Japan abrogated the Washington naval treaty.[21]

Davis dutifully took his case to the British. He argued that a Japanese abrogation of the Washington naval treaty would destroy the basis for continuing the talks, and he insisted that the Western powers should adjourn the talks when the Japanese gave notice of abrogation. But despite American anger and domestic pressure, MacDonald and Simon vigorously rebutted Davis' argument. They pointed out that, before the Japanese went home, it was vitally important to lay the groundwork for a new agreement by exploring the British proposal for a modus vivendi. The Japanese government could then confer with its delegation and decide to compromise at the formal conference. The British did agree, however, to ask that the Japanese delay their abrogation notice until the end of the year. They also asked the Americans to reconsider their request for adjournment, arguing that the talks should be recessed only until the actual conference met. Two days later, on December 6, Matsudaira assured the British that his government's procedures for framing the abrogation notice would take at least two weeks longer.[22] Thus, the Japanese provided Britain with a reprieve, and the talks went on.

At the same time, President Roosevelt had a change of heart. When Davis explained the British case to Washington, Roosevelt and Hull agreed to continue the negotiations and to accept a recess, rather than adjournment, when Japan abrogated. He told Secretary Hull to inform Davis that "we think you should do nothing further before December thirty-first, as a result of which the Japanese could use that as a reason . . . for denunciation. In other words, we are in an excellent position at the present time. Even if it involves keeping the conversations going until December thirty-first, it is worthwhile to do it in order that the whole onus of denunciation can be placed on the Japanese without giving them any excuses." Hull's subordinates at the State Department were unhappy. Phillips wanted to send the Japanese home after having denounced the Washington naval treaty, "without having anything else of advantage in their pockets." Moffat and Hornbeck wanted to end the negotiations completely after the Japanese denunciation. But they all yielded to the President's wishes.[23] Thus, the British had gained the time they desired: Japan would not abrogate before the end of the year, and the Americans would continue to talk.

CONTINUED ANGLO-JAPANESE TALKS

While the Americans fretted, the Anglo-Japanese tête-à-tête continued. On November 21, the British cabinet decided that its delegates should keep talking until it was clear "beyond possibility of doubt that there was no hope of reaching any satisfactory agreement." Britain's representatives asked the Japanese delegates to discuss the question of fixing actual fleet strengths in a new disarmament agreement. The British wanted to maintain the existing 10/6 ratio with Japan in capital ships; they also hoped to retain their fifteen battleships, five aircraft carriers, and fifteen heavy cruisers, while increasing their complement of light cruisers from thirty-three to sixty. Admiral Yamamoto replied that Japan wanted equality with the British and the abolition of all capital ships; if, however, these ships were retained, he argued that Japan and Britain should both have six battleships, six carriers, and six or eight heavy cruisers. Moreover, if Britain increased its number of light cruisers, Yamamoto warned that Japan would have to undertake compensatory cruiser construction.[24] Japan's demand for complete naval equality remained firm, and the English and Japanese seemed as far apart as ever.

If the talks were to continue, the Japanese delegates needed to make some counterproposal. Matsudaira told Craigie that Yamamoto's position on parity should not be considered final; he then trotted out Hirota's compromise plan: Japan would reach the common upper limit by stages, and at the coming conference Japan would accept a naval limit short of full parity. Chamberlain considered the Japanese idea "most important," and although MacDonald, Monsell, and Chatfield maintained that the old ratio provided a minimum "gap of safety," Chamberlain prevailed. The committee agreed that Britain should probe Japan's suggestion further.[25]

On November 30, Yamamoto outlined his offer. In essence, he proposed that Japan should achieve parity with the United States after six years, while Britain would retain a slight naval lead by adding 150,000 tons of light cruisers to its fleet. When the blunt Admiral Chatfield pointed out that the Americans were unlikely to accept this proposal, Yamamoto laughingly agreed. Undaunted, the Japanese admiral explained that Japan would increase its strength in battleships, heavy cruisers, submarines, and destroyers to match the United States strength in these classes. At the end of six years, Japan would have eleven battleships to Britain's fifteen; evidently, the Americans would have to reach the level of eleven battleships by scrapping. In 1948, Japan would also reach full parity with Britain in battleships. In closing, Yamamoto reminded Chatfield that "this conversation was purely private, that it was his own personal idea, and not that of his government." [26] The Japanese admiral was attempting to lure the British away from the Americans by offering them special treatment.

But Yamamoto's proposal disappointed the British. Chatfield told the cabinet committee that acceptance of parity was "strategically impossible." Under the Japanese proposal, "at the end of the six year period we should have to be prepared to send 13 ships East as against the Japanese 11, leaving us an inferiority of 2 to 6 in Europe." Chatfield argued that Britain simply would not have enough ships to contain Germany in the Atlantic. Consequently, the committee decided that Japan should only retain two additional battleships if the craft were demilitarized; moreover, the Japanese would have to give up any increases in light craft. British optimism was flagging, and indeed, the time for pessimism had come. When the British presented Japan's proposals to the Americans in tabular form, they were forced to add that "this table was prepared solely as a concrete illustration . . . The Japanese representatives are particularly desirous that the figures in it should not be quoted. They have not retained a copy of it and regard it as nonexistent." The Japanese delegates said that they expected Hirota's comments on both Britain's qualitative proposal and their own "nonexistent" offer in about two weeks.[27]

As the days passed and no answer came from Tokyo, the British began talking of a recess. Craigie assured Davis on December 12 that the British were not yielding to the Japanese; they were "not agreeing to any change of substance in the present basis and principles of limitation." He added that the British wanted to recess the talks on December 20, but to continue informal discussions until the end of the year or until Japan had abrogated the Washington naval treaty. By this time, Hirota had had three weeks to comment on the British proposal but had failed to do so. Consequently, the British accepted the American contention that there should be a clean break when Japan served notice of abrogation. They still hoped that in the interval between abrogation and the subsequent main conference, late in 1935, Japan might decide to accept restrictions which would minimize the damage of a naval race. On December 13, MacDonald told Davis that the British "had no intention of giving the Japanese anything to take home other than an understanding of what they would have to do later if they wished to get an agreement." [28]

Secretary of State Hull agreed to have the British adjourn the talks on December 20. He told Davis that the twentieth would be sufficiently close to [the] Japanese denunciation to make the connection between the two events clear in the public mind without the need of its being openly stressed." Hull warned, however, that the British would have to agree not to continue "informal talks" after Japan's denunciation of the treaty.[29]

THE JAPANESE DECLINE

On November 26, the Japanese representatives had dutifully reported the terms of the British proposal for a modus vivendi, namely, that Japan would have to continue the qualitative restrictions on the size and armament of its warships and report the construction of any new vessels laid down, while the Western countries would maintain the same limits and refrain from fortifying their East Asian possessions. In their dispatch, Matsudaira and Yamamoto advised Hirota that agreeing to retain some parts of the Washington naval treaty might improve the international atmosphere if negotiations broke down. The delegates urged their government to give "careful consideration" to this question and suggested keeping the nonfortification agreement and Articles 14, 17, and 18 of the naval treaty. These sections prohibited the arming of merchantmen, the sale of naval vessels in wartime, and the use by one country of naval vessels under construction for another country.[30]

The move suggested by the Japanese delegates was merely tactical and cosmetic, since Matsudaira and Yamamoto expected the naval negotiations to break up in the near future. The exemption of a few parts of the Washington naval treaty from the abrogation notice might confuse the issues in the public mind but could not save the talks. On December 1, and again on December 11, the Japanese delegates warned that the collapse of the negotiations could not be far off. Neither Britain nor the United States, they explained, would grant Japan parity. The Americans, fearing for the future of their East Asian interests, were trying to preserve the military advantages given them by the treaty ratios. The American delegates were showing no hope of reaching a settlement and, in fact, were simply trying to avoid any responsibility for the breakdown of the talks. On the other hand, the British were striving to reach some agreement, since they wanted to prevent any sudden changes in the military balance. But, Matsudaira and Yamamoto added, the British were also completely opposed to reducing their strength relative to Japan's navy, so that the gap between the British and Japanese proposals was as wide as ever.[31]

Because of the deadlock, Matsudaira and Yamamoto requested special instructions on December 11. They told Hirota that there seemed to be only two alternatives: they could continue to insist on parity until the talks failed, or they could agree to a recess. The British wanted a recess, they said, and the Americans would not insist on a complete end to the talks, since such an action would cause a "sensation." They asked permission to agree to a recess on the understanding that the negotiators at the main conference would concentrate on Japan's wish for a common upper limit as well as on Britain's proposal for continuing qualitative limits and declaring building plans. Meanwhile, the Japanese delegates continued to throw cold water on British hopes. On December 14, Yamamoto told the British that the powers would have to accept the common upper limit before Japan would agree to reveal its building plans. He added, however, that Hirota had as yet sent him no official reaction to the British plan.[32]

On December 8, the British ambassador had warned Hirota that the "unyielding attitude of Japan might result in conversations breaking off with little prospect of success for next year's conference." Clive urged Hirota to accept the British compromise, but Japan's Foreign Minister confessed that, "in view of the intransigent attitude of the navy and the present internal position in Japan, it had been impossible to allow any discretion to the Japanese delegates." But Hirota did not preclude compromise during 1935, for once the Washington naval treaty "was denounced and the ratios eliminated, the navy would be more reasonable." Although the ever sanguine Craigie said that Hirota had opened up "interesting possibilities," the acidic Vansittart minuted, "this reads rather like 'Jam tomorrow.' " [33]

The talks had dragged on for two months. At the outset, Hirota had instructed his delegates to keep the negotiations going in order to blur the issue of responsibility. The British had aided the Japanese in this effort by making two counterproposals: Hirota held on to the first for a month and the second for a month and a half, while Matsudaira and Yamamoto skillfully spun out the talks and waited for instructions. The long delay had begun to tell on the Americans, who had first pressed the British to refrain from making a deal with the Japanese, and had then urged the British to end the talks when Japan abrogated the Washington naval treaty. In early December, however, it appeared that the talks would continue long enough to end almost simultaneously with Japan's denunciation of the treaty. Consequently, the Western countries could claim that Japan had destroyed the disarmament system, while the Japanese could point out that they had made every effort to explain their needs to the West and had been forced to abrogate the treaty by Western rigidity.

Under these circumstances, the Americans and the Japanese were willing to have the talks recessed. When the delegates went off for the Christmas holidays on December 20, they issued a communiqué stating merely that the British would invite the representatives to further talks at a later date, after they had a chance to confer with their governments. The Americans refused to set a definite date for resuming the discussions, because they did not wish to lessen the seriousness of Japan's abrogation notice. In private, the British warned that Japan would have to reconsider its position. Prime Minister MacDonald told the Japanese, "We cannot yield on any essentials; don't assume that it is only a matter of pressure or time; that is not the case. We must look out for our self-defense." [34] Thus, the Japanese would have to convince their government either to give up hope of parity or to accept a modus vivendi that would limit the harm of a naval race. The Americans left for home, but the Japanese and British continued informal talks for the rest of the month in case Hirota decided to answer the British proposal.

After the holidays, the answer came. On December 28, the day before Japan served its abrogation notice, Yamamoto called at the Admiralty and told Chatfield that he had received further instructions. He "regretted the answer was not favorable," but "the Imperial government had no desire to change its demands." The Japanese were standing by "their original plan," still demanding parity and a drastic cut in overall naval strengths. Japan would not agree to exchange building plans, since such an arrangement would only preserve the ratios. Yamamoto admitted that there was a gap between the hopes of Britain and the ambitions of Japan, but he added, "I have no definite plan for a solution to this." The English, he told Hirota, showed "extreme disappointment and perplexity." Perhaps as a result of this British reaction, Yamamoto assured them that "he himself sincerely wished for agreement" and that his instructions were not "final." He concluded that "it would be best if he returned to Japan to explain . . . [the British] proposal to his Government more fully, and he would do his best to secure agreement." [35] The British were indeed upset. In order to lay the basis for further talks, they had abandoned the Washington system and angered the Americans. At worst, they had expected the Japanese to take more time to consider both the compromise proposal and the consequences of Anglo-American hostility. Now all hope of a modus vivendi seemed to rest on Yamamoto's slender shoulders.

On January 16, 1935, the British gave Yamamoto a memorandum restating the requirements "below which the British Empire cannot feel a sense of security." Because Germany was building capital ships, they wrote, Britain's needs had increased, not decreased, since 1930. Consequently, Britain had to retain its margin over Japan in capital ships and increase its strength in light cruisers and destroyers. Yamamoto dutifully carried Britain's plea home with him. On March 28, 1935, however, he called in the British naval attaché and told him that "he had completed his report to the [Japanese] government and was going away for a holiday 'as he was very tired because there were too many die-hards in [the] Japanese Navy.' " [36] Meanwhile, Japan's admirals were rejoicing.

THE JAPANESE ABROGATION

While the Japanese delegates were talking at London, the Imperial Navy was pushing the abrogation of the Washington naval treaty through the various procedural channels of its government. The admirals' main aim was to rid themselves of the treaty restrictions, but their efforts had the useful side effect of keeping the cabinet on course during the talks. On October 29, the leaders of the navy held an admirals' conference at which they agreed to abrogate the treaty. During this conference, navy officials explained that when the treaty limits expired, they would be able to build the type of ships most suited to Japan's defense. They added that this kind of naval construction would not be much more expensive than the replacement construction necessary under the treaty. [37]

After uniting the navy behind them, Ōsumi and the other leading admirals had to convince the Privy Council to advise the Emperor to abrogate the treaty. Actually, the navy had no reason to worry, since its audience would probably be most sympathetic. The rising power on the Privy Council was Baron Hiranuma Kiichirō, who became President of the Council in 1936. Hiranuma, who saw the world in terms of a conflict between the white and colored races, opposed cooperating with the West in China. In 1930 he had used his position in the Privy Council to aid Katō Kanji during the debate on the London Treaty. [38]

With a sympathetic audience and assurances that the proceedings would be secret, the leaders of the navy explained to the Privy Council's research committee their reasons for wanting the treaty abrogated. Naval Minister Ōsumi remarked that increased international tension and the advances of science meant that "in order to provide for the empire's security," Japan needed "military strength actually equal to that of America [or] England." [39] Ōsumi repeated the arguments about technological progress that the Navy had used in its propaganda pamphlets. Japan's basic strategy was to ambush the enemy fleet and preserve command of the western Pacific, but technological progress had rendered the execution of this plan difficult. Improvements in cruising range, speed, gun power, armor, communications, and surveillance capacity gave decisive advantages to the attacking force. Moreover, the international situation was worsening, with England and America strengthening their bases at Singapore and Hawaii, while Russia was increasing its naval and air strength in the Far East, and China was building its own air force. In combination with the Western powers, Russia and China would be dangerous. No one on the Privy Council's research committee asked Ōsumi why the technological advances he had mentioned would not aid the defender as much as the attacker, nor did they point out that abrogating the treaty would tend to drive the West, China, and Russia together against Japan.

The Japanese navy remained confident that it could ensure Japan's defense, in spite of a naval race with the West. On December 2, Captain Oka Takasumi, the head of the navy's special Research Bureau, explained that Japan did not intend to match American building in each type of warship; rather, the navy planned to develop only those weapons that fitted its strategic purposes. In any case, he said, naval construction capacities of the Western countries were limited. In fact, the United States probably would not build many more ships than it was allowed to replace under the existing treaties. According to the replacement building allowed in the treaties, the United States could lay down 70,000 tons of warships every year, and England could lay down 80,000 tons. But ship-building capacity in the two countries was only 80,000 tons for the Americans and 100,000 tons for the British, and any construction beyond those figures would require great outlays for expansion of shipyard facilities. The Navy Minister added that the Americans would have to build numerous merchant ships in order to provide the fleet train necessary for trans-Pacific operations. Oka concluded that Japan had the financial, material, and strategic ability to handle the small-scale naval competition which might occur.[40]

In their report to the Privy Council, the Research Board followed the navy's reasoning and wording closely, concluding that "abrogation is truly inescapable." On December 30, when Japan announced that it was abrogating the treaty, Katō Kanji made a joyful trip to the grave of his former commander, Tōgō Heihachirō, the naval hero of the Russo-Japanese War. Katō reported the good news and, on his way home, told a friend they were "greeting the dawn of the regeneration of the Imperial Navy." [41] While there was gloom in London and joy in Tokyo, ambivalence reigned in Washington. Given the Japanese intransigence, the Americans thought that the talks had ended satisfactorily. The news that the Privy Council had decided for abrogation appeared in the same newspapers which brought word of the recess from London. When Ambassador Saitō arrived at the State Department to present Japan's notice of abrogation, "the corridors were crammed with correspondents." At his press conference on December 21, the President said that he was "very much disappointed" with the talks in London.[42] The implication was clear: Japan was destroying the old system and breaking up the efforts to extend limitation.

At the same time that the Americans were enjoying this favorable publicity, they felt both fear and confidence about a final break with Japan and a possible naval race. At one time or another, Roosevelt, Hornbeck, and Grew had argued that the Japanese could not afford a naval race and that their demand for parity was merely a bluff. Even Norman Davis, who was in contact with the Japanese in London, wrote to the President: ''I agree with you that Japan is unable to keep up in a naval race. I understand that they have now reached the point where they cannot continue military expenditures through internal loans and that they will have to resort to increase in taxation.'' If the bluff failed, Davis implied, the Japanese would moderate their position before the main conference. On January 8, 1935, Davis reported on the London talks to the effect that, since Japan's threat to denounce the Washington naval treaty had produced no concessions, the Japanese might revert to ''a more reasonable viewpoint.'' [43]

But for the first time there was fear that the Japanese might be willing to begin a costly naval competition in order to back up their aggressive foreign policy. Under Secretary of State William Phillips wrote in his diary that ''the press reports from Japan announce readiness and almost desire to undertake a naval race; they certainly have got their blood up.'' From Tokyo, Ambassador Grew warned that for the present, Japan's mood was uncompromising. Since America was determined to defend its rights and interests in East Asia, Grew wrote, it would have to speak softly and carry a big stick, as certain powerful elements in Japan wanted ''to obtain trade control and eventually predominant political influence in China, the Philippines, the Straits Settlements, Siam and the Dutch East Indies, the Maritime Provinces and Vladivostok one step at a time.'' Japan's liberals would require a long time to regain their strength, and ''the press and the public . . . have . . . been valiantly boasting that the Japanese Navy is today stronger than the American Navy.'' Consequently, unless Americans were willing to submit to a *Pax Japonica* in Asia, ''we should rapidly build up our Navy to treaty strength, and if and when the Washington Naval Treaty expires we should continue to maintain the present ratio with Japan regardless of cost.'' [44]

Japan's delegates had done their job. They had prolonged the talks until their position gained some support both in England and the United States. The British, worried about their imperial defense, nagged by economic weakness, and teased by Japan's offers, had hastened after an ever-receding agreement with Japan. In spite of all the English courting, however, in the end Britain found herself embarrassed and disappointed. During the coming conference, wiser from experience, they would be more cautious.

At the start of a sailing contest, the race committee fires two warning guns and then a third gun to signal the start; there were similar warnings at the beginning of the race to Pearl Harbor. When Japan abrogated the Washington naval treaty, it fired the first gun. The Japanese had served notice that they were ready to sail, but the Western countries still hoped to avoid the trial or to run the race under their own rules. Nevertheless, the time for the main conference was approaching, and the British and Americans were soon to find out if the second gun would really sound.

11   The Second London Naval Conference

As the year 1935 wore on, the darkening international scene again compelled the British to search for some way to limit the effects of future naval competition. By a skillful set of moves, Britain's diplomats isolated Japan on the question of qualitative limitation in 1935, just as they had done on the problem of ratios in 1934. The American government yielded somewhat grudgingly to Britain's qualitative proposals in order to maintain its long-sought united front against Japan. When the London talks finally began, Japan's delegation, led this time by the blunt and forceful Admiral Nagano Osami, came to them eager for the naval race to begin, with results that were both expected and inevitable.

ENGLAND'S STRUGGLE TO CONTAIN NAVAL COMPETITION

The London Naval Conference opened in December 1935 under highly unfavorable conditions. During that year, the Japanese army had expelled the Kuomintang from two northern Chinese provinces, where Japan's generals then replaced local Nationalist rulers with puppet governments. Japan's latest forward move took almost a full year, keeping Japanese policy constantly in the limelight and increasing fears that there would be even more trouble in Asia after Japan had freed itself from the disarmament restrictions. International stability was dissolving in Europe as well. The General Disarmament Conference held at Geneva in 1932 had failed, and an arms race was under way in all types of weapons. Italy and France were beginning a construction race in 35,000-ton battleships while continuing their competition in auxiliary craft. Hitler had ended the limits imposed by the Versailles Treaty on the size of Germany's armed forces. In March, Hitler repudiated the disarmament provisions of the peace treaty, and in April the Germans announced that they were building twelve submarines.[1] During the fall of 1935, Mussolini invaded Ethiopia, to which England replied with sanctions and a naval concentration in the Mediterranean.

Because of these varied tensions, the path to European unity on naval limitation was strewn with obstacles. As in other international questions of the period, France's fear of German revival was a major difficulty. The French were determined to maintain a two-power standard against both Italy in the south and Germany in the north, but they could not persuade Mussolini to surrender the parity with France that Italy had secured at the Washington Conference. Consequently, after the close of the preliminary naval talks, the French abrogated the Washington naval treaty, thereby ending the limits that had held its navy down to equality with Italy. The French nevertheless remained willing to accept low qualitative limits and to discuss limiting construction programs.[2]

If there were to be any hope for quantitative or qualitative limits, Britain would first have to drive a stake through the heart of the growing German navy. Should the Germans accept a moderate percentage of the British fleet, a slow rate of naval building, and low qualitative figures, the French might conclude that Anglo-French naval strength in Europe was sufficient to handle the combined threat of Germany and Italy. Moreover, the Admiralty and Foreign Office argued that the United States and Japan might join a limitation system if each of the European nations had agreed to Britain's terms before the talks began.[3] In the first half of 1935, therefore, the British sought to turn the German key to a European naval settlement.

The British asked Hitler to endorse the compromise position that they had offered Japan in the fall. Each nation would fix its building program for a six-year period and agree to limit each category of ship to a small size. On March 26, 1935, Hitler told Simon that he would accept a building program which would bring the German navy to thirty-five percent of Britain's fleet strength. Because the Admiralty had estimated that Britain could tolerate a German navy fifty percent as large as the British fleet, the offer was attractive. Since the French already had fifty percent of British strength, they too might find the proposal interesting. The Germans were also asking for parity in submarines, but this problem was not insoluble, for Britain's admirals believed that the invention of sonar had drawn the teeth of the submarine. Moreover, since Britain's own undersea fleet would be small, Anglo-German parity would impose its own low limit on the German fleet. An earlier unhappy experience with the Nazis counted too, for Hitler had made a similar self-limiting offer on land armies and had subsequently withdrawn it; consequently, Britain's delegates wanted to accept his present offer of a ratio "while it is still open." Finally, the Plans Division of the Admiralty predicted that if Britain's ratio with Japan were preserved, and if Germany accepted thirty-five percent of British strength, "we can face hostilities against Germany in Europe, with France as our ally, and at the same time preserve a defensive position against Japan."[4] Consequently, despite French displeasure, Britain agreed to Hitler's terms.

The British diplomats then turned to the task of securing European agreement on sizes of ships. In August, the British circulated figures for tonnages and guns on all classes of ships, and in spite of French pique at the Anglo-German naval agreement and tension with Italy over Ethiopia, by September they were able to secure general agreement. In this plan, however, the English projected a battleship size that was 10,000 tons under the displacement which the Americans desired; furthermore, the British proposed that cannon on capital ships be reduced by four inches in caliber. The British predicted that, if they could secure American agreement to these qualitative limits, the Japanese might also yield, since they would face a united front.[5]

THE WESTERN FRONT ACHIEVED

The European agreement posed a problem for the Americans. On the one hand, Roosevelt could continue to insist that the United States needed large ships that had trans-Pacific cruising capacities, but he would then stand out as the wrecker of the limitation effort; on the other hand, he could accept the smaller battleship and allow the American fleet to suffer the possible consequences in a war with Japan. At first, the Americans declared that the British had deceived them by securing European agreement to these "unacceptable" qualitative limitations behind their backs. In the end, however, Roosevelt decided that he had to accept Britain's figures in order to secure an Anglo-American front and to make clear that Japan, and not the United States, was the obstacle to disarmament. The Americans agreed to accept the smaller battleship and to grant the British an increase in their light cruiser complement. Craigie was delighted. "For all practical purposes," he told the cabinet, "we are justified in counting on American cooperation in the forthcoming conference." [6] When the Japanese came to London, they would face the united pressure of Britain, the United States, France, and Italy.

During the summer of 1935, the British diplomats also tried to get the Japanese to accept their schedule of qualitative figures, and they continued to argue that each country should agree to declare unilaterally the nature of its long-term building program. On August 9, the British gave the Japanese a list of suggested limits for each type of ship and stated that the French, Italians, and Germans had all given tentative approval to it. But once again, on August 26, Hirota replied that Japan would not discuss qualitative questions without first obtaining an agreement on quantitative limits. Japan's Foreign Minister followed up his instructions with a further warning on October 15. Japan would agree to notify other countries of its building plans only after all nations had accepted the common upper limit. [7] Hirota thus shut the door, not only on qualitative limitation, but also on the possibility of open building programs. In spite of the united Western pressure, the Japanese were determined to free their hands to build giant battleships.

Because of Japan's intransigence, the British had little hope of success, and consequently they agreed with the Americans not only on ultimate goals but also on the strategy to be followed during the talks. Since there was no possibility of the Japanese accepting the old ratios, the British indicated that they wanted to dispose speedily of the problem of quantitative limitation. Then the five nations could start to discuss qualitative limits. Craigie assured the Americans that Britain was still faithful to the ratio system, but he added, "every opportunity should be accorded to Japan to negotiate . . . [beyond] a reasonable doubt. Hence the emphasis had been shifted to qualitative limitation and announced building programs. But if Japan refused to accept any such reasonable offer as a basis for negotiations she would on her own initiative at some time thus eliminate herself from the picture." If the Japanese walked out, he continued, the United States and Britain could then agree to continue Anglo-American parity and to construct enough ships to maintain their 5/3 ratio vis-à-vis Japan.[8]

If Davis had written such a scenario, he could not have outlined more clearly the way in which the Americans wanted to handle the Japanese. But after Hirota had officially declined the compromise proposals, the British sought to play down the negotiations and thereby minimize the friction that the inevitable breakdown would produce. They therefore suggested that the five powers refrain from sending full delegations to the conference and negotiate instead through their ambassadors in London. This proposal met with little favor in Washington, since the Roosevelt administration was anxious to avoid any criticism of its disarmament policy; in order for it to be absolutely clear that Japan was the villain, the footlights must shine brightly on a full-dress conference. In Meredith W. Berg's words, if disarmament were going to die by violence, then Roosevelt wanted "to identify the killer for the benefit of interested spectators." Roosevelt told his ambassador in London: "I feel that we must not only make the greatest possible effort to negotiate a new naval treaty, but that we should in every way make our desire to do so manifest. While it is important that our public must not be led to expect too much from such a conference, it is equally important for us to do nothing that would make it appear that we are taking this naval conference casually . . . and thus run the risk of being blamed for failure." Roosevelt said that he would send a special delegation to the conference, and he expected other countries to follow suit.[9]

The British finally agreed to hold the talks because of domestic politics. The ministers decided that, "from the political point of view the importance was emphasized of issuing the invitations to the conference before the date of the General Election." Such an announcement would provide "a counter to talk of rearmament." MacDonald warned that the delegates would have to make clear that the failure to secure quantitative limits could not be laid at Britain's feet. The English leaders also agreed that a qualitative agreement would decrease the expense of a naval race and put Britain "in a much stronger position as regards public opinion." Consequently, they decided to propose their old building program scheme, and when Japan, Italy, and France rejected the ratios, they would then offer a qualitative agreement. If the Japanese again refused to negotiate on qualitative matters without a prior quantitative agreement, the four other nations would proceed without them.[10] Japanese intransigence over the year since the talks had begun thus helped to produce a stiff British position at the conference. The English attitude hardened further in November, when the National government won a surprisingly comfortable victory in the general election.

THE AMERICAN POSITION

On November 19, 1935, the President gathered the American delegates at the White House in order to discuss their instructions. Norman Davis read a memorandum stressing the fact that Japan's demand for parity made any quantitative agreement unlikely. Consequently, he remarked, the British were planning to concentrate on securing a qualitative agreement, and they were still hopeful that Japan would accept qualitative restrictions without a prior quantitative settlement. Davis asked permission to help the British seek a limited agreement, "which will prevent a naval race and tend to prevent any undue tension or effort to alter the *status quo* until a more opportune time for a new conference to negotiate a comprehensive agreement." [11]

The President agreed that a quantitative agreement seemed beyond the realm of possibility, since the United States could not accept the common upper limit or the abolition of battleships, carriers, and heavy cruisers. But the President urged Davis not to agree immediately to give up the quest for quantitative disarmament, and Davis promised to make "every attempt to obtain as much quantitative restriction as possible." The President then agreed to let Davis negotiate a tripartite qualitative agreement if the Japanese walked out of the talks, but he also insisted that any such agreement should have an "escape clause" which would be designed to let the signatories meet any "undue construction by a noncontracting power." [12]

Thus, Roosevelt had endorsed the British compromise proposal, thereby abandoning the Washington ratio system that the Americans had jealously defended throughout 1934. A major reason for the President's action was the desire to limit naval competition and to preserve the country's shrinking lead in the older types of weapons. One of the navy's disarmament specialists, Commander R. E. Schuirman, had explained in April to the Chief of Naval Operations, Admiral William H. Standley, that the United States would have the lead in a race involving standard types of ships but that it would start out equal in a competition involving new weapons. He also pointed out that in an all-out race, American ships might be "entirely outclassed . . . by the introduction of some new type." [13]

The Americans accepted the British plan for other reasons as well. They were eager to preserve parallel Anglo-American action in both London and the Far East. As Hull told the delegates, they were to "emphasize the inevitable and growing community of interests of the British Empire and the United States throughout the world and particularly the Far East (maintenance of treaties . . . stabilization of political and economic relations, maintenance of Open Door, opposition to expansion by military means of aggression, et cetera)." [14] If a naval race started and Japanese aggression continued, Anglo-American unity, which was important tactically during the talks in London, might also become strategically vital on the world stage.

Moreover, if the President did not accept the British proposal, he might find himself blamed for the failure of the negotiations, a charge that he had good reason to avoid. Owing to the continuing economic stagnation, Congress had become increasingly restive when dealing with matters of foreign policy. Conservative Democrats, led by Al Smith, had already broken with the President, and the progressive left remained suspicious of his foreign policy. When the Japanese gave notice that they were abrogating the Washingtion naval treaty, Admiral J. M. Reeves, commander of the United States fleet, announced that the navy would conduct large-scale maneuvers in the northern Pacific during 1935. Pacifist groups mounted a campaign against the maneuvers, labeling them provocative and likely to cause an incident. The President was annoyed, but he allowed the maneuvers to go on, arguing that the site of the American war games was two thousand miles from the Japanese fleet. Nevertheless, thousands of letters of protest poured into government offices from individuals, schools, temperance organizations, churches, and pacifist societies.[15] To satisfy such demanding critics, Roosevelt had to try every door to disarmament, and the Japanese would have to prove themselves guilty of starting the naval competition.

Senator Nye also contributed to the President's worries. After calling for the Roosevelt administration to grant Japan parity, Nye began investigating the connection between the shipbuilding industry and previous administrations. His committee, after calling numerous witnesses, issued a report in June 1935 charging that the shipbuilders had agitated constantly for an unnecessarily large navy. These findings confirmed Nye's view of December 1934 that, "until we can have a disarmament conference . . . divorced . . . from those who have selfish purposes to serve, we are not going to make much headway in international agreements." [16]

The President was particularly sensitive to criticism from Nye and the other progressives in the Senate. In spite of large expenditures for relief, ten million Americans were still without jobs in 1935, and the popularity of Huey Long and his share-the-wealth program was growing. A Democratic party survey showed that Long might draw three or four million votes from the Democrats with a third-party ticket in 1936. Roosevelt told Henry L. Stimson in early 1935, "these are not normal times; people are jumpy and very ready to run after strange gods." In fact, Nye and other progressives, such as Senator William E. Borah, toyed with the idea of creating a third-party movement, but Roosevelt outflanked them on the left by using their clamor to push through the social legislation of the Second Hundred Days. Roosevelt courted the progressives from early 1935 until close to the election of 1936, and he was able to ensure the support of some progressive Republican Senators and the neutrality of others, including Borah and Nye.[17] Thus, Roosevelt had a double reason for avoiding conflict with the leaders of the Senate on the disarmament question: such quarrels might interfere with passage of his domestic legislative program, and they might provide an added excuse for a bolt by the progressives from the ranks of his bipartisan coalition.

The Senators were also taking foreign policy very seriously in 1935. In January, after a campaign led by Senators Borah and Nye, the publisher William Randolph Hearst, and the radio priest Father Charles E. Coughlin, the Senate defeated an administration attempt to bring the United States into the World

Court. Roosevelt told Ambassador Dodd on February 2 that he expected "a period of non-cooperation in everything . . . for the next year or two." From June to September, the Senate wrote a set of neutrality acts preventing the export of goods to all nations at war, whether attacker or attacked, and Roosevelt did not dare fight what he considered a serious inroad by Congress on his freedom of action.[18] The Senate, hearing the unrest in the land, was asserting its prerogative to supervise foreign relations.

Consequently, Roosevelt attempted to minimize criticism not only of his disarmament position but also of his entire foreign policy. His response to continued Japanese penetration of China was extremely cautious: he told Hull to request information from both parties to the dispute and to register United States interest, but also to avoid comment and action. Roosevelt did allow a moderate increase in the navy, but he refused to issue an executive order setting aside bases in the Philippines for use by the American navy after the islands became independent. The Secretary of the Navy and the admirals argued that such bases were "a vital necessity" for supporting the open door, the integrity of China, and the security of the Philippines. But Roosevelt refused the request, stating that such a base might become a liability in wartime. He added that, "pending further knowledge on whether the Washington and London Naval Treaties will be extended or not, an Executive Order of this kind would undoubtedly be regarded by Japan and other nations as contrary to our determined position in favor of extension of the Treaty." [19]

JAPAN'S NEGOTIATING POSITION

In 1935 there was no repetition of the struggle to determine Japan's disarmament policy that had vexed Okada in 1934, for the Prime Minister and the Foreign Office accepted the navy's suggestions virtually in toto. In fact, during the summer of 1935, Foreign Minister Hirota made an attempt to downgrade the disarmament talks in order to minimize the effects of their probable failure. On July 18, he told Ambassador Grew that, unless there were some prospect of success, the London Naval Conference should be held in as quiet a manner as possible. He hoped that the conference "could be a purely *pro forma* meeting and could adjourn for a year or two in the hope that in the meantime some satisfactory arrangement could be evolved." [20] Roosevelt rejected this proposal.

On October 28, two weeks after Hirota had rebuffed Britain's compromise proposal, the Japanese navy completed its draft of suggested instructions for the delegates. The navy wanted equality with the United States: "The purpose of the empire's naval armaments is to provide enough military strength to control the western Pacific, to protect the seaborne lines of communication necessary for the existence and progress of the nation, and to maintain the empire's position as the stabilizing influence in the Orient. For these reasons, it is absolutely necessary for the empire to establish its right in a disarmament agreement to be able to build and maintain naval power equal to that of the world's largest naval power.'' [21]

In the actual instructions, the Foreign Office was able to add that the delegates should conduct the negotiations carefully in order to avoid angering other countries. Otherwise, the Foreign Office had to accept the navy's demands. Hirota instructed the delegates that all nations would have to agree to a common upper limit which would be reached gradually. The delegates could also seek the abolition of such offensive weapons as battleships and carriers, ''as a conference countermeasure.'' The Chief of the Navy General Staff, Prince Fushimi, explained to the Emperor that the Imperial Navy ''really did not desire the complete abolition [of capital ships],'' but that the delegates would propose this abolition ''as the situation requires, in order to strengthen the empire's fundamental demands.'' If the Western nations refused to abolish capital ships, the empire would advocate reducing their number as much as possible under a low gross tonnage limitation. There was one significant departure in the new instructions: the delegates could make adjustments in the common upper limit for certain countries, but Japan and the United States had to be equal. This restatement of Yamamoto's proposal was designed to split the British from the Americans. Most important, Hirota specifically instructed the delegates to reject any qualitative limits or any proposal for an exchange of building plans as long as Japan's demand for parity was not met. He also warned the delegates to seek a quick conclusion to the talks, since Japan had to make a decision on its naval construction plans.[22]

The only hint of flexibility in the Japanese instructions was the willingness of the navy to make adjustments in the common upper limit for countries other than the United States. But Japan's chief delegate, Admiral Nagano Osami, would make only temporary, tactical use of that flexibility. Nagano was a protégé of Admiral Katō Kanji, and when the conference began, he seemed eager to end the talks, return home, and take advantage of Japan's new freedom from armament restrictions.[23]

THE CONFERENCE

Norman Davis approached the main conference with some reluctance and little hope. On November 4, 1935, he told reporters that ''there was little chance for a renewal of the London and Washington Treaties and certainly no prospect of any naval reductions.'' A few weeks later, he cheered up somewhat, telling a friend that a ''comprehensive naval agreement now is practically hopeless. I do hope, however, that we can at least prevent a naval race.'' Pessimism extended to the President himself, who at the end of the conference on instructions held on November 19 said jokingly that ''he felt as though he were sending the Delegation on a Cocos Island treasure hunt.'' [24]

The results of the first plenary session of the conference, which met on December 9, 1935, did little to dispel the gloom. The previous day, the British and Americans had met informally at the Admiralty to reconfirm their opposition to the common upper limit and to any change in the ratios. The delegates also agreed that they would not allow the issue of qualitative restrictions or the British desire for more light cruisers to come between them. During the first session of the conference, the British emphasized the need to avoid an all-out naval race. The new British Prime Minister, Stanley Baldwin, said that "the evolution of new types and increased sizes . . . [is] the most expensive and dangerous of all types of naval competition." But the Japanese declared that they still sought a common upper limit, which was necessary to ensure mutual security. The American delegation reacted with exasperation. Under Secretary of State William Phillips, a new member of the delegation, said that the Japanese had made "what we all thought a somewhat silly statement . . . They must have had their tongues in their cheek when they referred to their needs for security at a moment when they are over-running all of North China." [25]

During the next three sessions of the conference, Admiral Nagano set forth Japan's position in full detail. Japan, he explained, wanted parity, a great reduction in overall tonnage, and the total abolition of battleships and aircraft carriers; furthermore, Japan would not accept qualitative limitation without a prior quantitative agreement. The low common upper limit would apply to Japan, the United States, and Britain, while the European powers could make their own settlement within that limit. The largest naval powers, including Japan, would thus have to sacrifice a major portion of their fleets, but they would be secure, since the common upper limit would be low and offensive weapons would be abolished. Once again, Japan's terms met rejection. The French and Italians protested their exclusion from the common upper limit and refused even to consider Japan's proposal. Both the Italians and the French also joined the British in arguing for the continuation of qualitative limits.

In their reply, the Americans and British used the same arguments they had repeated so many times during the preparatory negotiations. The Americans asserted that the existing treaties ensured security for all nations. The British were finally becoming impatient. The First Lord of the Admiralty, Viscount Monsell, argued that naval equality and equality of security were two different things. Since Britain had global possessions, he said, it was more vulnerable than Japan. The Washington system had provided for such differing degrees of vulnerability, but the Japanese proposal did not. Under the common upper limit, the larger naval powers would be hamstrung, while the smaller naval countries could build up to equality. This situation, Monsell stated, would be "absurd." Sir Ernle Chatfield, admiral of the fleet, noted that a low common upper limit would result in an Anglo-Japanese ratio of 2/2, but that the European countries would also want a strength of 2. Consequently, Britain should have a ratio of 4, since she was both a European and a Pacific power.[26]

The negotiations were clearly deadlocked only a few days after they had begun, and a solution seemed to become even more difficult when on December 13 the Japanese assured the Italians that the common upper limit could apply to all five naval powers. Nagano tried to counter the growing British impatience with an offer to make adjustments for each country's vulnerability, but only after the principle of the common upper limit had been accepted. The British held a private meeting with the Japanese delegates in order to explore this new proposal. Nagano suggested that the powers set up a special committee to investigate the nature of vulnerability, but the British explained that they were vulnerable simply because they could never send their whole fleet to the Pacific, and they asked whether the Japanese were willing to adjust the common upper limit to compensate for this difficulty. Nagano replied that Japan would make such an adjustment, but he added that such arrangements would be difficult to conclude. In any case, Nagano insisted, Japan would have to retain parity with America. Under the Japanese proposal, Britain, with the largest navy, would provide the measure for the common upper limit. The British warned that the other nations would probably object to any special Anglo-Japanese adjustment and that the French and Italians would oppose any exploration of the problem of vulnerability. Consequently, the British urged the Japanese to check with the other delegations before formally proposing the establishment of a special committee on vulnerability.[27]

Three days later, Nagano withdrew his offer. At a meeting with the other heads of delegations on December 16, he stated that, after all nations had agreed on a common upper limit, certain countries might be permitted to retain special types of weapons required by their respective defense needs. The other delegates, however, refused to consider accepting the common upper limit even with such a condition. Consequently, at another private meeting with the British, Nagano said he would postpone asking for a committee to investigate vulnerability, since the other powers did not seem interested in it. "It is better to wait for . . . spring before sowing the seed," Nagano concluded. Admiral Chatfield urged the Japanese to make some compromise proposal, but Nagano replied, "the realization of parity is basic to our demands." He and his relatively silent partner, Nagai Matsuzo, Japan's ambassador to London, said that they could not change this basic policy, and that it was up to the British to make a counterproposal if the talks had in fact reached a deadlock.[28]

The British decided to move the discussion on to the question of exchanging building programs, so as to avoid a final confrontation on the question of parity for Japan. They trundled out their old compromise proposal to the effect that all nations should voluntarily fix the limits of their naval construction over a period of years. To ensure that each country lived up to this agreement, each power would promise to notify the others of its building plans. While the Americans, British, and French gave tentative approval to the British proposal, the Japanese remained opposed. When pressed by Nagano, Craigie admitted that the limits on future building programs would have to conform to the treaty ratios.[29]

On December 19 and 20, Admiral Nagano made the same counterproposal that Yamamoto had used during the preparatory negotiations. Japan would agree to announce its building plans if the other nations would agree to a 5/5 ratio. He pointed out that the British system would simply continue the existing ratios in a disguised form: "The object of the British proposal appears to us to be, generally, to preserve the existing relations between the naval forces of the Powers concerned . . . [and therefore] we cannot see our way to accepting the British proposal in its present form." Nagano asked repeatedly whether a country with a naval force of inferior size could defeat a stronger power, and he refused to listen to British claims that a fleet sailing long distances required greater numbers on its side. Monsell replied in exasperation that "in the opinion of every expert in the world, a country defending itself in its own territory has an inherent advantage over an attacking force and therefore can defend itself in its own territory with a lesser force than that brought against it." Nagano retorted, "I do not feel that the answer given by the chairman is a complete and satisfactory answer." Davis thought the meeting "a childish affair" and told Roosevelt that the British "did not take the bait" of a larger ratio offered by Japan and that they were cooperating "one hundred percent." [30]

The negotiators recessed for Christmas, with the British intending to continue the discussion of building programs and qualitative limits in January 1936. During the recess, the Japanese delegates reassessed their position. On December 24, they notified Hirota that "it will be extremely difficult to get all countries to accept the empire's proposals." According to their instructions, they were not supposed to discuss qualitative restrictions without first securing parity. But the delegates reported that if they continued to block qualitative negotiations, the other representatives would criticize them severely. However, if they did discuss qualitative matters and again stood alone, they would be branded as "the complete destroyers of the disarmament endeavor." For these reasons, only fifteen days after the talks had begun, the Japanese delegation asked to leave the conference. If Hirota granted them his permission, they would refuse to begin qualitative negotiations and would make a final and complete explanation of their basic position. If the other powers still refused to grant Japan parity, they would then try to terminate the talks in the most amiable manner possible.[31] Hirota evidently refused this request, however, because the delegates returned to their task when the talks reopened.

The four Western naval powers were determined to end the repetitious battles they had been fighting against parity. When the conference resumed on January 6, 1936, the British explained more fully their proposal to limit building programs for a period of years. The Italians and French then insisted that the unstable international situation and the rapid rate of technological development required that naval construction programs be subject to frequent modification, and they therefore proposed that the building programs be agreed on and exchanged yearly. They also argued somewhat weakly that such a short-term agreement would not result in a continuation of the ratios.[32]

Ten days later, as the representatives of the Western powers continued discussing these proposals in an atmosphere of mutual admiration, Nagano protested. He insisted that the question of quantitative limitation had to be settled before he could participate in a discussion of building programs, and he rejected the British assertion that the Western countries had indeed made a counterproposal involving quantitative limits. William Phillips thought that the conference was at an end, the Japanese statements being "almost impertinent." The Japanese told Hirota, "We recognize that our opposition to the discussion of . . . the compromise proposals has caused a shock generally and brought about a pessimistic outlook on the future of the conference." [33] The Japanese delegates continued to wait for permission to withdraw.

After reading the discouraging reports from Davis, Secretary Hull was worried that further talks in London would "only result in confusion in the public mind." Although Hull was concerned, the President believed that the Japanese had made little impression on the American public. The President wrote to Davis on January 14: "Over here, the general tenor of press dispatches continues to give the impression that it is Japan and not any other power that is blocking some sort of agreement, even a *modus vivendi*." But James C. Dunn of the State Department explained: "We were all particularly anxious not to have the main issue—that is, the discussion of the Japanese demand for a 'common upper limit'—postponed too long, as otherwise, by giving even apparently serious consideration to the proposal, it seems to acquire a better position than if it were rejected immediately, thus showing up the impossibility of even giving it any serious attention." After conferring with the President, Hull instructed Davis on January 8 to ask the British to seek a definite Japanese response to the compromise proposal. If Nagano's answer were negative, Hull wrote, the Western nations should proceed without Japan.[34] Thus, on the same day that the Japanese rejected the compromise proposals and insisted on a final disposition of the common upper limit, the Americans decided that the negotiators should try to pass the rock of parity.

After some debate, the British had come to the same conclusion. Robert Craigie was an exception. He argued that the powers should try to keep the Japanese in London by agreeing to some sort of tripartite pact, such as Hirota had suggested in the fall of 1934; the powers would thus give "Japan a face-saving device on which to proceed in their discussion of qualitative limitations." Monsell wanted to bring matters to a head, however, and Anthony Eden, the new Foreign Minister, leaned toward Monsell's opinion. One possible reason for Eden to take this strong line was that he had replaced Samuel Hoare, who had been branded an appeaser for trying to end the Italo-Ethiopian war on terms favorable to Mussolini.

When Phillips met with Eden and Craigie on January 8, he found the debate in full swing. Craigie suggested establishing a tripartite nonaggression pact or a simple consultative pact, but Eden was unenthusiastic. When asked his opinion, Phillips said that it was impossible for the United States to sanction further Japanese aggression against China or Russia by concluding a nonaggression pact with Japan; furthermore, a vague, consultative pact would have difficulty passing through the American Senate. On January 9, when Davis presented Hull's request for a decision on the common upper limit, he found that Eden had already decided to tell the Japanese that Britain wanted to end the parity debate once and for all.[35]

That same afternoon, the British asked the Japanese whether or not they could agree to the compromise proposals even if parity were rejected, and the Japanese replied that they could not. Nevertheless, the British said that the Western powers were determined to dispose of the common upper limit and move on to discuss exchanges of building plans and qualitative limitation. In that case, Nagano replied, "there would be nothing [for Japan] to do but withdraw from the conference." If the Japanese left, Eden warned, the other four powers would remain in London and negotiate a treaty that Japan could accept later, but which it would not be able to help write. Eden told Davis that the Japanese appeared "disconcerted." [36]

The Japanese delegates advised Hirota that "there is nothing to do but withdraw." Hirota evidently agreed, for Japan's delegates told the British that they wanted to have a final vote taken on January 15, and they asked that, if their position were not then accepted, the talks be adjourned indefinitely. But the British replied that the remaining four powers would negotiate an agreement without Japan. On January 15, 1936, the delegates repeated their shopworn arguments, whereupon the four Western nations rejected Japan's proposal. The Japanese delegation withdrew, pledging that Japan would not start a naval race.[37]

After the Japanese had left, Britain, France, the United States, and Italy negotiated a new treaty, and the British began talks to secure German and Russian participation in this vestigial limitation system. All six powers agreed to keep the size and armament of their ships within qualitative limits, which were occasionally even lower than the figures prescribed in the former treaties. In addition, each of the powers agreed to notify the others of its annual building program. But the effectiveness of the treaty depended on the restraint of those countries not covered by it; if Japan, for example, were to exceed the limits, any signatory could withdraw from the treaty and increase the size of its own ships.[38] Thus, the Japanese could decide the fate of these modest limitations. In the race to Pearl Harbor, the final warning sounded on the day that the Japanese delegates walked out of the London Conference. In less than a year, on January 1, 1937, the contest would begin.

PART FIVE   The Race

12 The Japanese Navy Charts a New Course

During the last months of 1936, the sun sank on disarmament, and in the long night that followed, Japan's admirals built a new fleet suited to their growing ambitions. After Admiral Nagano returned from London in February 1936, the leaders of the navy had just ten months before the naval treaties expired. In that time, they set long-range political goals, planned the shipbuilding schedules necessary to carry out their foreign policy program, and secured enough financial support to build the warships that the new policy required. Fortuitously, an army revolt aided the leaders of the navy in their efforts by throwing the army into confusion and by making the civilian leaders fear for their lives as well as for the constitutional system.

THE POLITICAL SITUATION

The Okada cabinet had suffered heavy attacks throughout 1935. The Seiyūkai, the military, and right wing groups united in an effort to topple the government by making an issue of the constitutional role of the Emperor. Both military ministers applied pressure to the government, which finally led Prime Minister Okada to issue statements reaffirming the doctrine of imperial divinity. Only at the cost of some prestige and the purge of a few professors did Okada avoid a collapse of his cabinet and the advent of a right wing government. In early 1936, Okada counterattacked. He called a general election and strongly supported the Minseitō, which used the slogan, "What shall it be, parliamentary government or Fascism?" On Saionji's advice, Okada got a contribution of one million yen (approximately $250,000) from the Sumitomo industrial combine in order to aid the Minseitō. The result of the campaign was a reversal of the parliamentary situation: the Seiyūkai fell from 301 to 174 seats, and the Minseitō rose from 146 to 205 seats. The forces of moderation now had a solid parliamentary base from which to repel the campaigns and enthusiasms of the military and the right wing.[1]

But only a week after Okada's success, disaster struck. There had been great uneasiness in the army because its soldiers in Manchukuo lacked the weapons necessary to meet an attack by Russia's growing Far Eastern forces. The Emperor's military attaché warned Kido that all factions in the army wanted to establish a strong cabinet and to carry out the necessary buildup of tanks and planes in

Manchuria. Two junior officers decided that the moment had come for a coup. In the early hours of February 26, they led 1,400 soldiers into the central government district of Nagatachō and sent out squads of assassins to attack the leading civilian politicians. For three days, the young captains held the Prime Minister's residence and the Diet. Their assassins murdered former Prime Minister Saitō, Finance Minister Takahashi, and the army's Inspector General of Education, General Watanabe; they also wounded an Imperial Chamberlain and mounted unsuccessful attacks on Saionji and Okada. In their appeal to the people, the rebels claimed that the senior statesmen and court officials had joined hands with financiers to usurp the imperial prerogative and exploit the nation.[2]

The attacks threw the government into confusion. Since Okada's fate was as yet unknown, Prince Fushimi, the Chief of the Navy General Staff, urged the Emperor to appoint an interim Prime Minister. On the same day, Navy Minister Ōsumi appeared at court and sought the Imperial Household Minister's help in selecting Fushimi as the acting head of government. But Okada had escaped his attackers by hiding in his maid's quarters and leaving his residence with a group of his own mourners.[3] His successful escape foiled the navy's attempt to exploit the coup.

Nevertheless, the military continued to play on the fears of the surviving civilian leaders. After Prince Konoye declined the uneasy post of Prime Minister, Saionji checked with the Army and Navy Ministers before selecting Foreign Minister Hirota as the new Prime Minister designate. When Hirota presented his cabinet list to the military, however, there was trouble, for he had made the mistake of selecting a well-known moderate diplomat, Yoshida Shigeru, as Foreign Minister and a number of party politicians as lesser cabinet members. The new Army and Navy Ministers objected, and they vetoed five of the proposed candidates, including Yoshida. Hirota was also forced to agree to provide large sums for military spending and to accept Katō Kanji's protégé, Nagano Osami, as the new Navy Minister. Throughout the spring of 1936, Saionji and Harada followed the rumors of further coups closely, and on at least one occasion they reminded Hirota that it was vital to meet the military's demands with good grace.[4]

Thus, just after the breakdown of the London Conference, the navy found itself in an unexpectedly strong position. The army revolt had eliminated the moderate civilian leaders at the very moment of their revival at the polls, and the Hirota cabinet became increasingly a creature of the military. The army was now on the defensive, having to restore order in its own house while asking for funds to meet the increasing threat from Russia. Consequently, the navy could use the fears of the civilians and the divisions in the army to work its will with national policy.

THE ARMY'S DILEMMA

After 1932, Russia had begun preparing for a war on two fronts; by the end of 1935, it had more than twice as many divisions in the Far East as Japan had, three times as many men, and five times as many planes. After a full mobilization, the Japanese army would have only twenty-eight divisions with which to meet forty Russian divisions. This development worried Ishihara Kanji, the new Strategy Section Chief of the Army General Staff. Ishihara was a leading example of the new type of military intellectual and economic planner who had come to power under Generals Hayashi and Nagata. In 1933 he had been the primary exponent of forming an East Asian league stretching from Siberia to Australia under the domination of Japan, which if successful, would have given Japan the economic strength for an epochal war with the Anglo-Saxon powers.[5]

But in late 1935, Ishihara decided that the construction of such a large Japanese Empire would have to wait until the Russian threat had been met and eliminated. In order to secure the proper economic base for the buildup against Russia, Ishihara advocated adopting an economic mobilization plan for both the homeland and Manchukuo. He also suggested that any advance in China or the South Seas be restricted to peaceful economic penetration. In order to prevent excessive strain on the budget, he proposed that the army be given the lion's share of the first five-year economic plan, and that the navy wait for the output of the second five-year program. He did predict, however, that the army would return to his original idea of an East Asian league: "After the Northern threat has been eliminated, we shall actively accomplish our national policy vis-à-vis China and the South Pacific by force." [6]

These proposals met with hostility on the part of the field armies in China, since Ishihara projected a long economic buildup before risking action against Russia. The Kwantung army leaders wanted quick military reinforcement, since they expected trouble with Russia in the near future; they also wanted to secure their Chinese flank by action in North China. On January 13, 1936, the Japanese government authorized its commanders in North China to add three additional provinces to the two already in the new "self-government area." It indicated that all five provinces of North China should eventually have Japanese advisers at the top levels of the new government; the Japanese army attachés in Nanking were to persuade the Nationalist government to recognize this new situation.[7] But in order to complete a buildup against Russia and to advance into North China at the same time, the army would require large sums, which it could only get through the good will of the navy.

On December 17, 1935, Ishihara went to the Navy General Staff and asked his counterpart, Strategy Section Chief Fukudome Shigeru, to approve a policy of dealing first with the north. Fukudome refused, arguing that Japan should stand on the defensive in the north and advance to the south. Ishihara had made a mistake in showing his hand to the navy, for on his return from London, the new Navy Minister, Nagano Osami, set up an ad hoc committee of navy leaders to investigate the problem of national defense and to propose an overall policy that would prevent the army from stealing the navy's appropriations. The members of the committee included Vice Minister Hasegawa Kiyoshi, Vice Chief of the Navy General Staff Shimada Shigetarō, and Kondō Nobutake and Fukudome Shigeru of the Strategy Section.

The mission of the committee was to "consider the changes that will take place in the international situation after the lapse of the disarmament treaties and . . . to think about the empire's important role as the stabilizing power in East Asia; we must first establish a firm national policy, create a national consensus on this policy, and then . . . carry out this long-range one-hundred-year plan." The basic policy had already been decided before the members met: the crux of the new initiative was to be "internally, a reform of all phases of government; externally, while maintaining the empire's foothold on the continent, we will make it our fundamental policy to advance to the south and work for the development of our national strength and the expansion of our national rights; thereby, we shall establish peace in the Orient, contribute to the prosperity of mankind, and give reality to [our role as] the stabilizing power of the Orient." The committee was also to consider what sort of fleet would be needed for the southern advance and how much it would cost.[8]

While the members of the committee were deliberating, Nagano received a remarkable telegram from the Commander of the Third Fleet, Oikawa Kojirō. Oikawa took the side of the army. After talking with officers of the Kwantung army, Oikawa concluded that a large Japanese buildup against Russia was imperative. In order to secure the Manchurian flank and acquire further economic resources, Oikawa wrote, Japan should also advance into the five North China provinces. He added that the Kwantung army officers believed that "the United States and Britain are not in a position to use troops in the Far East," and that Japan should take advantage of its opportunities in order to build a self-sufficient empire.[9]

The necessary future steps were clear to Oikawa:

> The national policies that the empire should adopt are the southern advance and the northern advance. No problem would arise if we [could advance] . . . peacefully in all directions, but when the powers are raising high tariff barriers as they are today and are preventing artificially the peaceful advance of other countries, we must of necessity be prepared and determined to use force in some areas and eliminate these barriers.
>
> Thus, the southern advance will result in England and the United States being our opponents, and a northern advance means a collision with Russia. Although we must make our final advance to the south where the pickings are great, the empire has not yet reached the time when we can happily bring about a collision with England and the United States. Rather than that, we should advance to the north even though it causes a collision with the Soviet Union and settle [the threat from] the north; we should completely build up Manchukuo and develop our national strength; after ending the threat in our rear, we should quickly turn to the southern advance.

The leaders of the Kwantung army estimated that they would be ready to deal with Russia by 1940. During the intervening years, the navy would evidently prepare for the advance to the south.[10]

The members of the new policy committee were not pleased with Oikawa's venture into high policy. They agreed that the empire had to advance both in China and the South Seas, but they feared that placing emphasis on a first blow against Russia would give the army too large a slice of the budget. On April 16, 1936, they explained their own ideas on the proper policy, in order to gain Oikawa's understanding and support. They argued that Oikawa's plan entailed the danger of war with two or more powers, and therefore meant that Japan would have to build up both its army and navy simultaneously. In doing so, the Japanese leaders would have to be wary of exceeding the limits of their nation's strength; if possible, the advances to the north and the south should be made "peacefully." In particular, the Kwantung army should restrain itself, and Japan should make it a basic principle "not to undertake a policy of attack." [11]

The advance into China, they noted, would have to be gradual, in order to avoid provoking the Western nations. Slow penetration would lead peacefully to the independence of the five northern provinces, and eventually China would be made "an ally completely dependent on Japan." The increasingly delicate situation in Europe would keep Britain occupied and make economic infiltration into Central and South China easier, while the United States would be deterred by an increase of armaments, which would induce it to approve the empire's position in East Asia. Thus, the north was to be put on ice; Japan would exercise absolute restraint against Russia and would proceed with caution against China.

The leaders of the navy wanted to turn Japan's main thrust to the South: "The southern countries are the most important region from the standpoint of strengthening our imperial defense, solving our population problem, and developing our economy; our government of these [areas] is indispensable for the rapid promotion of our policy vis-à-vis Manchuria, China, and Russia. In short, it is the inevitable mission of the empire to plant and extend our influence in the southern countries [by action] based on the imperial way, and to increase the people's wealth in that region and hope for the realization of coexistence and coprosperity." Internally, the leaders of the empire would have to prepare for the advance by setting up special organizations and by strengthening Japan's position in Taiwan and the mandated islands. "Externally," they wrote, "we should, *for the time being,* plan a gradual advance in both emigration and the economic field, and on the other hand, we should always face with cautious preparation the pressure and resistance of England, the United States, and Holland, which we must naturally be ready for, and moreover, we should complete our military preparations in case the worst should occur." In short, the army should grant the navy sufficient funds to build the ships necessary to carry out its southern stroke. The leaders of the navy warned Oikawa that they were about to present this proposal to the cabinet. [12]

The differences between Oikawa and his superiors in Tokyo were ones of emphasis, for they agreed that Japan should advance to the south after a period of preparation, and that the Japanese penetration of China should continue. The members of the new policy committee warned Oikawa, however, that the army should restrict itself to the defensive in Manchuria and that the field generals should only use peaceful means to expand Japan's foothold in China. They insisted that the south was "the most important region from the standpoint of strengthening our imperial defense." [13] Although the navy leaders did not spell out their reasons for considering the South Seas important to national defense, it is probable that oil was the primary motive. Japan's fleet had been running on fuel produced in the United States ever since the Japanese navy converted its ships to oil in the previous decade. In order to guarantee that the western Pacific would be secure, Japan would not only have to build a great fleet, but would also have to obtain the oil with which to run it. Throughout the latter part of April, the navy negotiated unsuccessfully with the Army General Staff. Success first came on another front, when the army and navy agreed on a new Imperial Defense Policy.

THE NEW IMPERIAL DEFENSE POLICY

The Imperial Defense Policy outlined Japan's basic military posture as sanctioned by the emperor. The first version of this policy, established in 1907, listed Japan's most probable enemies as Russia, the United States, and France. With the collapse of Russian power after the First World War, the army and navy agreed that the United States should go to the top of the list, and the emperor so proclaimed. The Imperial Defense Policy was a serious point of contention between the services, since it established the upper limits of Japan's military strength in terms of ships and men.[14] By revising the Imperial Defense Policy in 1936, the navy hoped to be able to satisfy the army's desire for more weapons and at the same time secure the ships necessary to carry out its plans for the south.

The navy insisted that the United States be retained as the primary enemy, but it agreed to give the army ten more divisions and a total of 142 air squadrons. The army would thus be able to meet the Russian threat in Manchuria. On this basis, the two general staffs reached agreement. The new policy read:

> The empire's national defense policy . . . is to prepare the national strength, and particularly the weapons, [which we should have] to be the stabilizing power in the Orient in fact as well as in name; we should also adapt our diplomacy to this purpose; through these measures, we will ensure the progress of the nation and if some day there is an emergency, we will take the initiative and quickly achieve our war aims . . . in view of our national situation, it is especially important for the empire to expand its strength for initial operations as much as possible. Moreover, because we fear that a future war will be a long one, it is necessary to make preparations and be ready to weather it.
>
> Our national defense policy . . . takes as its standards [for determining Japan's own military strength] the United States and Russia, since there is a

great possibility of a clash with them and since they have great national strength, particularly in weapons; we shall also prepare against China and England. For these purposes, we must provide military strength for the defense of the empire that will be sufficient to control the East Asian continent and the western Pacific and to achieve demands based on the empire's defense policy.[15]

This new document offered something for both the army and the navy. Ishihara and the economic mobilization planners in the army could take heart from the agreement to prepare for a long war, while the navy could interpret preparation for a long war to mean acquisition of resources in the south. In the third paragraph, the two staffs agreed to build weapons that would make possible the achievement of demands based on Japan's defense needs; this phrase also could be construed as a commitment to have the forces necessary to back up a slow Japanese expansion into the South Seas or into North China.

In any case, the army agreed to allow the navy to build enough ships to defend the western Pacific, an area that presumably included the Dutch East Indies, Malaya, and the Philippines. The new official force levels for the navy were twelve battleships, twelve carriers, twenty-eight cruisers, ninety-six destroyers, seventy submarines, and sixty-five air groups. This new fleet would be much larger than Japan's treaty navy. The two new battleships would outclass any ship afloat in size, speed, and fire power. There would also be two additional first-line carriers and five smaller carriers converted from merchant ships then under construction. The navy could also construct another twenty destroyers and numerous large submarines. By these acquisitions the navy hoped both to maintain a 7/10 ratio in tonnage vis-à-vis the United States as well as to meet the larger quantity of American building with superior Japanese quality.[16] At last the Japanese navy would have the surface craft, airplanes, and fast battleships it needed to carry out its attrition strategy.

On May 11, the Chiefs of the Army and Navy General Staffs presented this new policy to the Emperor for his approval, but he objected to the addition of England to the list of hypothetical enemies. The Chief of the Navy General Staff, Prince Fushimi, succeeded in having the military councillors back up the proposed policy. On May 13, Fushimi again sought the Emperor's approval, and again failed. The Emperor asked that the military leaders consider whether or not Japan could bear the burden of building the large military forces proposed, and he reminded Fushimi that the United States and Britain were planning great naval expansion. The military then secured Hirota's support, and on May 29 they sent the Prime Minister to press their proposal on the Emperor. Inasmuch as all of the constitutionally responsible ministers now backed the proposal, the Emperor ceased his protests.[17]

It is possible that Hirota was willing to lend his support to the military because he had been reassured that the Americans would not counter Japanese naval construction with any massive military buildup or radical international initiative.

Hirota had been worried that the United States might respond badly to the end of the naval limitation system, and on January 20, 1936, he asked the Japanese ambassador to Washington, Saitō Hiroshi, what the American leaders were planning to do. He told Saitō: "What direction the United States takes in the future will have a great effect on Japanese-American relations. In particular, whether or not the United States will both build up its naval and air arms and also make some sort of special agreement or understanding with England are of course matters that require close attention." Hirota asked Saitō to suggest ways to improve Japanese-American relations.[18]

Saitō's reply was generally reassuring. He reported that the Americans were concentrating on fighting the depression and that they were therefore withdrawing further into isolation. The United States had opposed Japan during the naval negotiations simply because of its "conceit," Saitō argued. Although the Americans also maintained that they were going to build up their fleet to treaty limits to support the open door, they were gradually realizing that they would have to go to war if they opposed Japan directly in Asia. Consequently, they were slowly coming to the conclusion that they did not have real interests in the Orient and that they "should take their hands out of Asia." Most important, Saitō assured Hirota that the American leaders were making no great increase in their naval program and that they would make no special agreement with Britain, although there had been a rapprochement between the two countries.[19]

Throughout the summer of 1936, the battle over national policy and money for new weapons continued, although Hirota repeatedly played down the seriousness of the debate when talking to Harada. He told Saionji's messenger that the revision of the Imperial Defense Policy was a run-of-the-mill affair. In mid-July, however, he admitted that he was having trouble with the budget. At the end of the month, the Chief of the Military Police told Harada that young naval officers were threatening to attempt another coup. By mid-August a compromise had been reached on the budget. The admirals would have the funds necessary to carry out their Third Replenishment Program by December 31, 1941, with the 1937 appropriation permitting them to start construction of two battleships, two large carriers, fifteen destroyers, and thirteen large submarines. Hirota reported to Harada that the budget would again be in the red.[20] During these same months the navy secured another victory for its southern policy.

NORTH AND SOUTH

While the admirals were winning the fight for money and ships, they continued the debate with the army over foreign policy. Once again, the army leaders proposed dealing with Russia first. They did agree with the navy that Japan should gradually build up the necessary strength to become "the protector and leader of East Asia," but they argued that the empire should deal with its enemies one by one. They wrote, "We should first concentrate all our strength on securing Russia's submission, since at present there are many areas in which our preparations for a long-term war are inadequate, and if we do not preserve friendly relations with England and the United States, or at least the United States, it will be difficult to fight a war against Russia.'' The army added a new element to their policy for handling Russia: a deal with Germany. If the Germans made an agreement with Japan that was directed against Russia, the Soviet army would have to send even more troops to its western borders, thereby reducing its Far Eastern strength.[21]

But the army was quick to reassure the navy that, after the solution of the Russian problem, Japan would turn its attention to the south. When the Russians surrendered, the Japanese army would willingly agree to destroy British influence in East Asia. Given a favorable opportunity, the army wrote, ''we will attack their bases and liberate the oppressed Asian races and make New Guinea, Australia, and New Zealand our territory.'' But the army leaders warned that, ''although we will take into account [the possibility of] American participation in the war, we should work for their neutrality to the best of our ability.'' Only after the surrender of Russia and England would Japan unify East Asia into a strong bloc and ''prepare for the coming great, decisive war with the United States.'' The army leaders warned, however, that until Russia had been beaten, ''it is necessary to limit our political moves in China and the various maneuvers in the South Seas area to those that will [allow us] to preserve good relations with England and the United States, particularly the United States.'' [22]

The navy flatly refused to put Russia first. The admirals countered with their own position paper and, after a month of debate, were able to secure agreement to it from both the Foreign Office and the army. The result was a new national program adopted by the five ministers' conference on August 7 under the heading ''Fundamentals of Our National Policy.'' The leaders of the navy had to concede that the buildup against Russia was of equal importance with the move to the south. But in the preface of the program they were able to secure army approval for their basic aim: ''the fundamental diplomatic and defense policy that the empire must establish is to advance into the South Seas while maintaining the empire's foothold on the continent.'' In the body of the document, the navy agreed to undertake the southern advance in a peaceful manner: ''While avoiding the provocation of other countries as much as possible, we will undertake our national and economic advance into the South Seas, particularly the outer South Seas regions, and we plan to build up and strengthen our national power through advancing our influence [there] by gradual and peaceful means, as well as by completing [the construction of] Manchukuo.'' Most important, the army, the diplomats, and the Prime Minister agreed that the navy could ''prepare and build the military strength sufficient to maintain command of the sea in the western Pacific against the United States.'' [23]

The generals did not come away with empty hands. They were allowed to build up their forces in Manchuria and Korea in order to counter Russian strength. The five ministers also promised to make political and economic reforms that would enable Japan to stand the strain of a large armament program. Most important from the army's standpoint, however, was the willingness of the navy and Prime Minister to approach the Germans for an agreement against Russia. In a separate statement of diplomatic policy, the inner cabinet agreed that, "if necessary . . . we should check Russia . . . by taking steps to give reality to Japanese-German cooperation." [24] The army probably did not get all of the weapons and men it desired, but it would have compensation on the diplomatic front.

The navy also insisted on bringing Japan's basic diplomatic policy into line with the new military consensus, and the five ministers adopted a new Imperial Diplomatic Policy on August 7. Hirota evidently took this opportunity to stress that Japan should seek its goals peacefully. In fact, the army was willing to have the diplomats seek a negotiated agreement with Russia on troop strengths in the Far East in order to establish a balance of power. The army leaders promised to use "exclusively" peaceful methods vis-à-vis Russia, although one Japanese diplomat recorded that there was a limit of four years on the negotiations, during which time the army would make its military preparations.[25] If in the meantime, however, the diplomats secured reductions of Russian troop strength and the establishment of demilitarized zones on the borders of Manchukuo, the army would agree to a nonaggression pact with the Soviet Union.

The military ministers also agreed to promote better relations with the United States through improved trade relations. The army even promised that, "for the time being, we will honor United States trade interests in China." The Japanese military hoped that a favorable trade policy would keep the Americans both from increasing their armaments and from aiding China to resist Japan. Peaceful relations with England would also result, they hoped, from a similarly favorable trade policy. Thus, Hirota was able to obtain promises from the military that the diplomats would have a chance to seek peaceful relations with the West and Russia.

But Hirota's success was extremely limited, since the diplomats had to accept a continued drive in China, a new initiative in the south, and a deal with Germany. These policies were certain to undercut the efforts of the Foreign Office to maintain friendly relations with the powers. An agreement with Germany aimed at the Soviet Union would certainly render a Russo-Japanese détente unlikely. The southern advance, no matter how peaceful and gradual, would alarm the colonial powers. Hirota did get the navy's permission to offer a nonaggression pact to the Dutch and to guarantee the security of the Philippines after independence, but such promises would only be repetitions of the commitments Japan had made during the Washington Conference. Finally, and most fateful for the immediate future, was the decision to continue Japanese pressure on China: the Chinese would be pressed to agree to tripartite cooperation with Japan and Manchukuo against Russia, and the five northern provinces would become a special defensive buffer against the Soviet Union and a close economic partner of Manchukuo.[26]

While Hirota would be turning a friendly face to the West and Russia, the military would be stockpiling arms and filtering gradually into China and the South Seas.

THE PAKHOI INCIDENT

The navy's new confidence took another form in September. It was the navy's duty to protect Japanese interests and nationals in Central and South China, and on September 3, an unidentified man killed a Japanese citizen in the town of Pakhoi on the Chinese coast north of Hainan Island. This incident was one among many such cases with which the Japanese had to deal in China in 1936. As soon as the navy leaders heard of this incident, however, they began planning to dispatch ships and men to conduct an investigation. On September 26, when the Chinese government seemed reluctant to cooperate, Navy Minister Nagano advocated the use of force, and he was backed up by the Vice Chief of the Navy General Staff, Shimada Shigetarō. If China did not respond favorably, the navy leaders proposed that the army should advance in North China while both the army and navy were defending Shanghai and occupying Tsingtao. The navy would also blockade Central and South China and bomb the major air bases and military installations in that region.[27]

The real aim of the navy in advocating military action seems to have been the acquisition of Hainan Island. When the proposal was first discussed by the Navy General Staff, included in the area of protective occupation was Hainan, which was close to Pakhoi and convenient for implementing a naval blockade of South China. Japanese naval bases on Hainan would surely alarm the British, because they would offset the British position at Singapore. The navy leaders were apparently quite serious about this first step in the southern advance, for they advocated mobilization of their second and third fleets against British and American intervention. But the army was not enthusiastic about a war with China, and the Chinese solved the problem by acceding to Japanese demands during the local negotiations for settlement of the incident.[28]

The navy had to settle for lesser steps on the path to the south. Hirota agreed to let the navy take over the government of Taiwan, although it had been run by civilians for twenty years; navy officers would thus have the power to construct the bases that were necessary for action in the south. In addition, the navy took over the administration of communications in Japan's mandated islands. This authority would allow the admirals to prepare for the construction of air bases and radio stations in the Marianas and Carolines. Finally, the navy budget provided for subsidies to companies that would engage in economic development of the South Seas.[29] The Pakhoi incident and the navy's new responsibilities in Taiwan and the mandates indicated the seriousness of the navy's desire to secure the resources of the south.

In the debate on national policy during 1936, the navy had thus seized the initiative from the army. Although the struggle with the army and the diplomats had been long and hard, Nagano and Shimada had finally seen their efforts crowned with success. It was a victory, however, for which the Japanese nation was to pay a heavy price. The Japanese government had accepted the major policies advocated by both of its services. The army had agreed to retain the United States as Japan's primary enemy and to allow the navy to initiate a building race with the United States and to begin moving into Southeast Asia. In return, the navy had agreed to an army buildup against Russia, the adoption of economic planning at home, and the establishment of an entente with Germany against Russia. After the military staffs had made these trades, the Army and Navy Ministers united in pressing Hirota to accept the new policy. In four years, after the onset of war with China and following the success of German aggression in Europe, these policies would lead to the Pacific war.

The belligerence of the navy leadership is the most remarkable aspect of these decisions. In 1933, it had been the army that forced the reorientation of Japan's foreign policy, but in 1936 the navy took the lead. Underlying this new aggressiveness was the assumption that the Japanese navy could build the ships necessary to hold the western Pacific against the United States and that a sphere in the western Pacific would include the oil fields needed to provide the new fleet with fuel. The Nagano-Shimada leadership had taken advantage of the army coup to set their course for the ensuing five years, a course which included a naval race with the United States and expansion to the south.

13   Britain's Sun Sets in the Pacific

Although the Japanese navy viewed the end of disarmament as the start of a new era of opportunity, the British government considered the onset of full naval competition a grievous and insupportable burden. Through the remaining years of peace, the leaders of England struggled with a complex of fears that prevented them from keeping pace in the naval race. In the end, the National leaders admitted that Britain could not defend its empire alone, and they tried to shift the responsibility for the defense of the Pacific onto the shoulders of the reluctant Americans. The Royal Navy resembled an aging concubine, forced to join hands with her French and American peers in order to counter the powers of her younger, more vigorous rivals—Japan, Italy, and Germany.

FINANCIAL AND ELECTORAL HURDLES

In the spring of 1934, the National government had postponed its decision on naval rearmament for reasons of finance and politics. Similar considerations continued to hem in the government during the succeeding years. In July 1935, the arms race in Europe led the National leaders to appoint a special group to assume the former functions of the Ministerial Committee on Defense Requirements, which they named the Subcommittee on Defense Policy and Requirements. Baldwin, soon to be Prime Minister, and Chamberlain, still Chancellor of the Exchequer, were appointed to help the Foreign and Service Ministers keep "the defensive situation as a whole constantly under review." At their second meeting, however, they agreed that their reconsideration of defense plans would be subject to an important limiting condition: "The financial situation does not justify the assumption that within the next few years large sums can be found for the defense services in addition to the total sums already provisionally approved." [1]

It became obvious that Britain could not pay for an arms buildup from existing tax receipts. The cabinet's military advisers warned that Germany would be ready to fight by 1939 and that the government could only hope to be prepared if it floated a defense loan. But the Subcommittee on Defense Policy refused to consider such an unorthodox measure; in fact, the British government had not borrowed money to purchase arms in peacetime since 1889. Consequently, the cabinet held the line. In the spring of 1935, the National leaders issued a white paper in which they went to great lengths to justify a very small increase of ten million pounds over the expenditures for rearmament of 1934. [2] The rules of conventional finance would prove a high hurdle to jump when British rearmament began in earnest.

Even the modest rearmament paper that the government issued in March called forth a salvo of criticism, for 1935 was expected to be an election year. Labour and Liberal leaders argued that real collective security would render rearmament unnecessary. In June, the League of Nations Union reported that large majorities of its eleven million respondents favored universal arms reductions, economic sanctions, and collective security. The opposition claimed that the National government was secretly planning to impose large defense efforts on the nation.[3]

During the election campaign itself, in the fall of 1935, the National government, now led by Stanley Baldwin, came out firmly for disarmament and collective security. None of the party manifestoes called for rearmament, and one of Labour's posters showed a baby in a gas mask, evidently demonstrating what would result from the National government's warmongering policies. Baldwin was equal to the test: he kept the support of Liberals throughout the country by supporting the League against Mussolini in Ethiopia and by calling for a renewal of the search for disarmament. On October 31, 1935, he told the British Peace Society: "We mean nothing by the League, if we are not prepared, after trial, to take action to support its judgement . . . You need not remind me of the solemn task of the League—to reduce armaments by agreement . . . I give you my word that there will be no great armaments." On November 14, the election showed that Baldwin had calculated correctly, for despite the limping economy, Labour's charges of warmongering, and the earlier series of byelection disasters, the Liberals did not desert the coalition candidates. The National government retained 428 seats, of which Baldwin's conservatives held 385, while Labour and the opposition Liberals won only 171.[4] At the price of further delay in rearmament, Baldwin had pulled his government through.

Although the coalition had jumped the electoral hurdle, it still had to steer safely between its campaign promises and financial limitations. The government did spend small sums to carry out parts of the deficiency program that the Subcommittee on Defense Requirements had outlined in 1934. But the National leaders insisted that rearmament could be carried out only if normal trade and the social services were also maintained. Then in June 1936, the cabinet had to consider reducing unemployment assistance, despite warnings that such cuts might produce violent criticism or even rioting. Budgetary limits were restrictive indeed. In late 1936, Chamberlain warned that "the cost [of rearmament] was rising at a giddy rate . . . Before long . . . people would be talking about an unbalanced budget, and we might find that our credit was not so good as it was a few years ago." A few months later he told a friend: "If we were now to follow Winston [Churchill]'s advice and sacrifice our commerce to the manufacture of arms, we should inflict a certain injury on our trade from which it would take generations to recover, we should destroy the confidence which now happily exists, and we should cripple the revenue." Samuel Hoare, First Lord of the Admiralty, admitted in November 1936 that ''it would be necessary to assume for a long time that we should be [militarily] unprepared.'' Consequently, he argued, Britain's diplomats must reduce the number of the country's enemies.[5] Thus, through 1935 and 1936, the National leaders refused to prepare for war for fear that they would antagonize their constituents or disorganize the economy. Yet during these years there were additional reasons that the government starved the Royal Navy: a fear of bombardment from the air and a low estimate of Japan's capabilities.

THE AIR SCARE AND THE EUROPEAN THREAT

In the years after World War I, aircraft grew rapidly in size, speed, range, bomb capacity, and reliability. But this growth, though remarkable in itself, provoked a disproportionate amount of fear in England and funneled British rearmament spending increasingly into the Royal Air Force. British anxiety centered on Germany's air buildup, to which the Nazi leaders gave great publicity. In November 1934, after receiving alarming information on the growth of the German air corps, the cabinet decided to step up Britain's air rearmament. But Germany's pace seemed too quick for Britain, and Hitler boasted in the spring of 1935 that Germany had achieved parity in the air with England. Although the government ordered still another increase, reports continued to flow in concerning the Germans' ''tremendous efforts and sacrifices.'' By early 1937, in spite of the government's best efforts, the Royal Air Force had fallen two years behind their German counterparts. Consequently, even though in 1935 the navy had received four times the appropriation of the Royal Air Force, by 1939, the navy had fallen to second place.[6]

The British revised their priorities because they feared that Germany's strategic bombers could make the people of Britain's thickly settled cities their primary target. Moreover, as the Italians had demonstrated in Abyssinia, the bombs could contain poison gas rather than explosives. In late 1935, the government decided that it had to expand its air buildup because Germany, at the outset of hostilities, might conduct air attacks ''on such a scale that a few weeks of such an experience might so undermine the morale of any civilian population as to make it difficult for the government to continue the war.'' In 1938, Neville Chamberlain explained that he had been forced to limit spending on the navy even though it prevented England from sending a formidable force to the Far East. His reason was simple: England had to concentrate on its air force because ''London was now the most vulnerable capital in the world. Within 24 hours of warfare London might be in ruins, and most of the important industrial centers in Great Britain as well.'' [7]

What made the bomber so terrifying to Britain in the hands of its enemies, however, also made it attractive as a deterrent, and Neville Chamberlain soon joined the ranks of the air advocates. By concentrating on the air force while stinting the navy and neglecting the army, Chamberlain could also save considerable amounts of money, but he clearly believed that building a large bomber force made strategic sense as well. In a prescient moment, he predicted that Germany would "throw a highly mobile force round the end of the long line of French and Belgian fortifications and . . . advance through Holland . . . with lightning speed." The Germans, he indicated, would complete their conquest of the Low Countries before a British expeditionary force could intervene. Chamberlain concluded, "If this reasoning be correct, it surely stands to sense that our policy should be to construct the most terrifying deterrent we can think of, and recent advances in design of aircraft and engines give us the weapons best calculated to effect that purpose." A strategic bombing force might turn back the German thrust without the aid of an expensive British army. Both Stanley Baldwin and Anthony Eden supported the construction of strategic bombers in place of an expeditionary force. All agreed that there was a popular demand in the country for the government to match Germany stride for stride in building a strategic air force.[8] Thus, between 1934 and 1939, for reasons of economy, strategy, and politics, the Royal Air Force moved to the head of the line and received the largest share of assistance doled out by the National government. In the competition for support, Britain's admirals did poorly, although they did not suffer to the same degree as did the army.

THE JAPANESE NAVAL THREAT

Although the major responsibility for Britain's failure to meet the Japanese challenge must fall on the government, the admirals also showed a lack of imagination by underestimating Japan's capabilities. In late 1934, the First Sea Lord, Admiral Chatfield, assured the dominion representatives at the naval talks that if the conference failed, Japan would not try to match British or American building: "All that Japan wanted was to secure her defensive position in the East and so have a free hand with regard to China. She would not rival the United States of America in, for example, battleships or aircraft carriers, but she would build a defensive fleet to cope with those ships in Japanese waters. She would probably build submarines and destroyers and make increases in her shore-based aircraft."[9] In other words, England's Pacific dominions would be secure, since Japan would only build a defensive fleet of light forces.

Britain's admirals also neglected the Japanese threat because they did not think the Japanese were the stuff of which resourceful sailors are made. In February 1935, Britain's naval attaché in Tokyo claimed that Japan's navy was inefficient because "the Japanese have peculiarly slow brains." In complete seriousness, he explained that to learn written Japanese required the memorization of six thousand characters, and he argued that such an exertion strained the developing mind of a school child. As a result, the Japanese could learn only one task at a time, and consequently, training methods in their navy encouraged complete specialization. Similarly, Japanese naval officers lacked the ability to improvise when their plans failed. Such a result was inevitable, he claimed, because the officer corps was recruited democratically and peasant boys lacked the "power of command." The Admiralty greeted this report with a show of interest leavened only slightly by skepticism. The Director of Navy Intelligence warned that the Japanese navy might be rather efficient when mobilized. But someone at the head of the Admiralty, probably Chatfield, believed that the supposed slowness of the Japanese capacity for decision might prove useful. He therefore asked the President of the Royal Navy College to study the possibility of a feint by British light forces into Japanese waters at the start of an Anglo-Japanese war; if the Japanese had a tendency to panic, he argued, they would send their fleet to hunt the British raiding force and delay their southward advance against Singapore.[10]

In addition to these handicaps, Japan had another, even more telling weakness in Britain's view: it was vulnerable to blockade. In June 1937, the Chiefs of Staff Subcommittee informed the leaders of the National government that Britain could win a war with Japan: "We must primarily rely upon the exercise of economic pressure to enable us to defeat Japan. With our fleet based at Singapore . . . the restrictions which we could impose on Japanese trade give good prospects of breaking Japanese powers of resistance in the course of two years, provided we can sever her trans-Pacific trade." With the cooperation of the United States, Britain could sever Japan from the resources needed to sustain her war industries: "She would have to find alternative sources of supply for nearly all her wool imports, over half her jute, lead, zinc, tin and manganese imports, nearly half her rubber, aluminum, iron-ore, and raw cotton imports, or else cut down consumption accordingly." And by reducing Japan's exports drastically, the Anglo-American blockade would undercut Japan's capacity to import such raw materials from the Continent and Russia.[11] Throughout the thirties, the image of Japanese economic fragility and racial inferiority helped to blind the Royal Navy to the danger in the Pacific.

THE SEARCH FOR A TWO-POWER STANDARD

During the debate on defense requirements, the National government had refused to set the new standard of naval strength that Britain would need if the treaty limits ended in 1936. Despite the discouraging failure of the preliminary naval talks in the fall of 1934, the national government was also content to let naval policy drift in a pool of indecision. In July 1934, Neville Chamberlain had forced the Admiralty to postpone consideration of both its 1935 building program and its deficiency budget until after the diplomats had tested Japan's willingness to compromise. Even after the preliminary talks failed to revive the Anglo-Japanese entente, Chamberlain refused to approve a large battleship replacement program or new construction of cruisers. In December 1934, after negotiations between the Admiralty and the Treasury, the cabinet approved the "normal replacement program" of three light cruisers, a flotilla of destroyers, and three submarines. Chamberlain not only held the line on new construction but was also able to secure a cut in the navy's deficiency budget.[12] Finance and politics kept arms expenditure low in the year before the general election.

Hankey, Chatfield, and the other chiefs of staff persisted in their efforts to secure more naval construction. Despite the image of Japanese weakness that prevailed in their own and higher circles, they were not above pointing to the growing strength of the Japanese fleet when justifying their requests to the government. In November, the chiefs of staff warned the cabinet through the Committee of Imperial Defense that Japan would reach peak strength relative to Britain in 1936, by which time the Japanese would have modernized their entire battle fleet and increased their personnel by twenty percent; and that by 1938 they would also have quadrupled their fleet air arm. In April 1935, the chiefs of staff repeated their warning and concluded that the growth of the Japanese and German fleets required the adoption of a two-power standard. Nevertheless, Chamberlain continued to resist any commitment to a large construction program.[13]

Two developments changed Chamberlain's mind: the Italian invasion of Ethiopia and the electoral success of the National coalition in November 1935. By attacking Haile Selassie's kingdom, Mussolini challenged the League members to make good their pledges of support for collective security. Britain joined in economic sanctions against Italy, but the National leaders were embarrassed to find that they lacked the naval strength to enforce a blockade in the Mediterranean. Actually, if the admirals had been able to ignore the German and Japanese navies, they could have faced a war against Italy with confidence; they feared, however, that the losses incurred in a war with Italy would make it impossible to send a fleet to the East at a later date.[14] Losses of capital ships could not be replaced within four years, and as Chatfield had frequently reminded his superiors, Britain had in 1935 a fleet barely sufficient for a tenuous defense in the Pacific. At a time when Britain's admirals were begging the government for a two-power standard of construction against Germany and Japan, they could not afford to add Italy to their list of enemies.

In the fall of 1935, with the elections approaching and the fear of Italy reaching its peak, the chiefs of staff and Hankey decided to press for the two-power standard. Chatfield told the Subcommittee on Defense Requirements that a war with Germany would require the withdrawal of some naval forces from the Pacific and that Britain would have "to remain on the risky defensive in the Far East" until the war in the Atlantic was won. When Monsell asked for two destroyer flotillas in the 1936 program, even Chamberlain admitted that "the state of the world was such that financial considerations might have to be reviewed in a different light." In late November, the new Foreign Minister, Samuel Hoare, warned the cabinet that in North China Japan was "exploiting the situation while other countries were preoccupied elsewhere," but still the government hesitated. Although the November election victory freed their hands, the National leaders decided that they should wait for the breakup of the London

Naval Conference before adopting and announcing a large program of naval construction.[15] Such a delay would provide a decent interval between their election promises of disarmament and the start of an arms race.

In November 1935, when the members of the Subcommittee on Defense Requirements had reintroduced their naval program, they warned that Germany, Italy, and Japan were all building up their navies. "The world," they cautioned, is "more dangerous than it has ever been before . . . Japan means to dominate the Far East, as Germany means to dominate Europe." If the British Empire were going to survive, they argued, Britain's diplomats would have to appease Italy and avoid a simultaneous conflict with Germany and Japan. If appeasement failed, however, Britain would need a navy that was adequate to deal with Germany and Japan at the same time, while the French navy held down the Italians. To that end, the Subcommittee recommended that Britain lay down in a three-year period seven battleships, four carriers, fifteen light cruisers, twenty-nine destroyers, and nine submarines, the same list that the Subcommittee had first sent to the cabinet in February 1934. Even if the government accepted this large construction program, the Admiralty admitted that Britain might still fall below the necessary two-power standard. Should Japan and Germany build at their full capacity, they would have eighteen modern capital ships to Britain's thirteen in 1942 (Britain would also have eight relatively weak, unmodernized battleships). Therefore, the admirals argued, Britain would have to get on good terms with Germany or Japan in order to persuade those countries to moderate their building.[16] Obviously, the two-power standard was a minimum that the British government would have to provide if it hoped to defend the Atlantic and Pacific poles of its empire.

In fact, on January 20, 1936, Chatfield told the cabinet Subcommittee on Defense Policy and Requirements that the naval program he had requested would not be large enough to match Japan in the Pacific and Britain's potential enemies in the Atlantic: "The important point [is] . . . that today, owing to the lack of light forces, a combined threat from the East and the West would force us to abandon control in the Far East." Soon, he warned, Britain would have to raise its naval sights above the levels requested in the subcommittee report. In response to this loud and fearful chorus, the Defense Policy and Plans Committee members yielded a little, recommending to the cabinet the full replacement program set forth in the Subcommittee on Defense Requirements report of 1934. The government also allowed both the modernization of Britain's older battleships and an increase in the fleet air arm. In March 1936, the cabinet asked Parliament for an increase of fifty million pounds over the defense expenditures of the previous year, and the Admiralty received enough funds to begin the construction requested by the subcommittee. But the cabinet ignored Chatfield's warning that the subcommittee's program might no longer be adequate.[17] Thus, the failure of the London Conference, the continued Japanese, German, and

Italian naval building, the crisis with Italy, and success in the election had finally induced the British government to choke forth funds for a moderate naval program.

For the first time the Tory right, led by Austen Chamberlain, Neville's older half-brother, and Winston Churchill, the erratic, brilliant historian and politician, began in mid-1936 to criticize the government consistently for the tepid pace of rearmament. The cabinet responded by appointing a Minister for Coordination of Defense, but it allocated only enough funds to provide him with a ministry of one private secretary and two typists. Even worse, it appointed as minister Thomas Inskip, a mild-mannered lawyer who considered it his duty to help the Chancellor of the Exchequer guard the public purse from the military. One commentator declared that Inskip's appointment was the most remarkable since Caligula made his horse consul. Baldwin replied that there was always "a time of year when midges come out of dirty ditches," but that he always ignored them. He thereupon took a three-month vacation on doctor's orders.[18]

When the Prime Minister returned in the fall of 1936, he found his critics even angrier. Churchill led the attack on the government's air program. In typical cadences, he intoned: "The responsibility of Ministers for public safety is absolute and requires no mandate . . . The Government simply cannot make up their minds, or they cannot get the Prime Minister to make up his mind. So they go on in strange paradox, decided only to be undecided, resolved to be irresolute, adamant for drift, solid for fluidity, all-powerful to be impotent. So we go on preparing more months and years—precious, perhaps vital—to the greatness of Britain—for the locusts to eat." Baldwin replied "with an appalling frankness," declaring that he could have sought a mandate for rearmament from the electorate in 1933 or 1934, but could not "think of anything that would have made the loss of the election . . . more certain." Baldwin's admission produced a temporary outcry, but the useful debate on rearmament soon sank beneath the waters of controversy swirling about the King's abdication. Always a romantic, Churchill took the part of Edward VIII and his mistress, an act that brought discredit on the strongest advocate of rearmament.[19]

Yet the struggle over rearmament had some fortunate effects on naval policy. In June, 1936, Samuel Hoare, the new First Lord of the Admiralty, sought permission to accelerate the building schedule of the Subcommittee on Defense Requirements; he wanted to add three carriers, six light cruisers, three flotillas of destroyers, and twelve submarines to the longrange program already approved. On July 2, Chamberlain approved the acceleration of the program, but only for 1937. The crusade of the Tory right, however, gained converts within the National camp itself for Anthony Eden began asking his counterparts in the government to "do all we can to increase the *tempo* of our own re-equipment." [20] Even though Churchill's drive yielded few other results in 1936, it did prepare the way for a larger effort in 1937, the year in which the Admiralty decided to press for a new standard of naval strength with which it might meet the naval challenge of Germany, Italy, and Japan.

THE STRUGGLE FOR A NEW STANDARD

On the surface, it appeared that the government had responded to the collapse of naval disarmament by building a navy which could deter threats on the eastern and western flanks of its empire. In early 1937, construction began on the fleet recommended by the Subcommittee on Defense Requirements, and the cabinet appropriated funds sufficient to continue building through 1938. But as Chatfield had warned, the ships sought by the Subcommittee soon proved inadequate to match German and Japanese production.

Economically, England had recovered some of its strength by 1936, and under the critics' lash, the National leaders decided in February 1937 to adopt a large five-year rearmament program. The navy received funds sufficient to continue the Subcommittee program, with which Britain started construction in that year of five battleships, four carriers, seven cruisers, and seven submarines. Samuel Hoare told his colleagues that this program represented the maximum which could be achieved without cutting into civilian shipbuilding. But even this moderate program meant payment of a high price economically. The government raised taxes in 1936 and 1937 from four shillings six pence in the pound to five shillings, an unprecedented peacetime rate of twenty-five percent. Even more disturbing to advocates of orthodox finance was the issuance of a 400 million pound defense loan. Over a five-year period, the National government planned to spend a total of 1,500 million pounds on rearmament. Admiral Chatfield's warnings proved correct, however, for it soon became apparent that the Subcommittee program would be inadequate to maintain equality with Japan and Germany. When it was completed in 1940, Britain would have only fifteen battleships, seventy cruisers, and sixteen flotillas of destroyers—a navy that the Admiralty thought barely adequate to match Japan and Germany in 1936.[21]

Britain was losing ground to Japan qualitatively as well as quantitatively. The London Treaty of 1936 provided that all nations would build only 35,000-ton battleships mounting fourteen-inch guns, unless Japan or another country refused to accept these limits. Since the Japanese were planning to build an eighteen-inch gun battleship, they would not make such a promise, but the Admiralty still respected the London treaty restrictions when laying down its first five battleships in 1937 and 1938. This new unit of capital ships would match the new fifteen-inch gun battleships that Germany and Italy were already building. Although the five new British ships were primarily for Europe, the Admiralty believed that they would also be a match for any battleship the Japanese might build. In 1936, the controller of the Admiralty claimed that a Japanese sixteen-inch gun battleship would be inferior to its British fourteen-inch gun counterpart. The Admirals also chose to ignore a "reliable" report that Japanese technicians were building an experimental eighteen-inch gun. In 1938, the government tried to respond to Japanese building by having their sixth and seventh ships displace only 40,000 tons and mount only nine sixteen-inch guns. Even though the Americans were building 45,000-ton ships with twelve sixteen-inch guns, the First Lord of the Admiralty, Duff Cooper, preferred the smaller ship, since Britain did not have the docks for anything larger.[22] Consequently, the Japanese super battleships displaced almost twice the tonnage of the newest British battleships, and the Japanese ships were far more heavily armored and gunned. Japan's admirals, so long the tutees of their British counterparts, could look with scorn on these inferior products of British naval science.

The Royal Navy nevertheless made some important improvements in their fleet before war came in Europe. During World War I, German submarines had threatened Britain's supply lines, but by the thirties, the Admiralty believed that it had solved the submarine threat. The British led the world in the development of sonar, a device that bounced sound waves off the hulls of attacking submarines to receivers aboard Royal Navy ships. The British made another important breakthrough in the development of radar, which eventually rendered great service in wartime.[23] But sonar and radar by themselves could not redress the balance of actual strength in the Pacific, which was turning decisively against Britain.

In naval air development, Britain fared poorly. As in the United States and Japan, the battleship advocates in Britain successfully insisted that aircraft could not intervene decisively against a battle line of capital ships. They believed that improve protection by carrier planes, antiaircraft guns, new antitorpedo bulging, and compartmentalization put aircraft in the category of a nuisance rather than a major threat. In part, Britain's lag in air development was caused by bureaucratic infighting, for the Royal Air Force had responsibility for designing naval airplanes from 1918 to 1937, and its leaders concentrated on land-based aircraft. The British decreased the fighting quality of their planes by designing them to serve multiple purposes, and their own carrier-based fighter, the Fulmar, was much inferior to Japan's Zero.[24] In both quantity and quality, then, the Royal Navy was falling behind.

By the spring of 1937, the men at the Admiralty knew that they were losing ground in the naval race, and consequently, they sought funds from the government for a new standard of naval strength. The Admiralty proposed increasing authorized levels for battleships from fifteen to twenty-one, for cruisers from seventy to one hundred, and for destroyers from one to two hundred. Between 1939 and 1942, if the National government accepted this new standard, it would have to build four battleships more than it had planned, and many more light craft. The members of the Admiralty Board justified the new program by pointing to German and Japanese building in the posttreaty period and claiming that the Anglo-German naval agreement made the standard set by Subcommittee on Defense Rquirements inadequate: ''When the capital ships now building in

Europe are completed, it would not be possible, on our own existing standard of naval strength, to safeguard the Empire in the Far East if already engaged in war in Europe; even with Germany limited to 35 percent of our own strength, we could never take the risk of despatching to the Far East a sufficient fleet to act as a deterrent to Japanese aggression.'' Even granted the new standard, the admirals still warned that ''the fleets proposed would give a smaller margin over Germany than was ours in 1914, and would involve the acceptance of inferiority in the Far East.'' In 1942, if Japanese and German building continued at a moderate pace, Japan and Germany would have twenty battleships, while Britain, with the new standard fleet, would also have twenty.[25] The Admiralty was correct: if the British were to maintain a decisive superiority over German raiders on their home sea lanes, they would have to weaken their eastern fleet and accept inferiority to Japan.

The Admiralty proposal met with cold rejection. Neville Chamberlain, who was about to become Prime Minister, warned that the burden on the taxpayers was near the ''breaking point.'' A month later, his successor at the Exchequer, John Simon, flatly stated that the existing 1,500-million-pound program represented the limit of Britain's financial capacity. Eventually, he argued, the government would have to relate defense expenses to British export earnings, but for the present, he urged the cabinet to put a definite ceiling on defense spending. On June 30, 1937, the cabinet adopted this expedient, which was later called rationing. Each service was required to submit cost estimates for its program through 1940. Simon would then be sure that the service ministers were not able to expand their programs piecemeal. The new Chancellor of the Exchequer continued to be as concerned about financial stability as Chamberlain had been. In July, he warned that the costs of maintaining the defense forces after completion of the programs would necessitate annual borrowing, and in October, he told his colleagues that further borrowing for defense would be difficult.[26] If rationing were enforced, however, the Admiralty could not hope to reach the new standard, which it needed to defend the East.

During 1937, the Royal Navy received alarming reports about Japanese naval building. British intelligence warned that under its Third Replenishment Program, the Japanese navy had enough funds to build four battleships by 1943, which would give Japan a fleet of fourteen capital ships, only one less ship than Britain had in its battle line. The admirals warned that Japan's ships would be larger than their British counterparts. Furthermore, the Admiralty feared that Germany might denounce the Anglo-German naval agreement; given its freedom, the German navy had the capacity to build a fleet of fourteen battleships by 1942. Britain would then face fleets at each end of the empire almost equal to its planned navy. Consequently, at the end of October 1937, the admirals once more sought a new standard fleet of twenty-one battleships, to be completed by 1944.[27] The fight over the two-power standard entered a second phase.

Thomas Inskip reacted to the Admiralty request with a scolding. Economic stability, he explained, was "the fourth arm of defense," for Britain's credit had to be good enough to sustain imports through a long war. Yet Inskip admitted that the armed forces also had to be kept strong enough to prevent a blow which would knock Britain out of the war before it could mobilize. But inasmuch as only German air power could deliver such a blow, he continued, the government should devote any increase in arms spending to its air force. The navy would have to be content with the Subcommittee fleet, and the army would have to give up the idea of an expeditionary force. If the navy insisted on the new standard, the government would have to add new taxes to the already "grievous burden" of taxation. At this point, the Admiralty had the misfortune to be represented by Duff Cooper, a young politician without independent standing in the Tory party. On December 22, 1937, Cooper let Inskip persuade the cabinet to postpone consideration of the new standard for a year.[28]

In 1938, however, Cooper tried to circumvent the problem of rationing and secure additional funding by introducing construction programs that would eventually mount up to the new standard fleet. On February 11, 1938, Cooper asked for construction in 1939 of three battleships, two carriers, seven cruisers, eight destroyers, and seven submarines. Simon warned that further borrowing would be difficult, however, and asked the cabinet to set a final limit on defense spending at 1,650 million pounds; he cautioned that any increase beyond that level would result in "financial disorganization." Although Eden and Hoare supported Cooper, Simon carried the day. The decisive voice was that of the Prime Minister, who said, "if we accepted the advice of the Defense Departments an unbearable strain would be placed on our financial resources, whereas if we cut them down we run into the possibility of danger of war." Chamberlain consoled himself with the hope that Hitler might agree to abolish offensive air forces and accept a stable European settlement. The cabinet accepted Simon's spending limit and sent Cooper off to negotiate the 1939 construction program with Inskip and Simon.[29]

The talks continued from February to May with increasing acrimony, as Cooper fought for a reduced version of the new standard. In March, Hitler took Austria, and Cooper once again asked the cabinet to build to the new standard. The cabinet secretary recorded laconically, "The Prime Minister himself had also reflected on the possibility of increasing the Defense Programmes, but his mind had turned towards the Air Force rather than the Navy." In fact, when it became apparent that Hitler would continue to expand into eastern Europe, the British government decided to let the air force purchase twelve thousand planes by 1940. By May, Cooper had become desperate. He warned that, because of rising costs, the sums which Simon offered were inadequate to build even to the Subcommittee fleet of fifteen battleships. Yet Britain's admirals said they needed twenty-one battleships by 1944. In reply, Simon told Chamberlain that the Admiralty was trying to repudiate rationing and warned that the Exchequer doubted whether Britain could stand the strain of a two-power standard.[30]

On July 20, 1938, Cooper made his last try. He warned the cabinet that the public would drive the National government from office if its leaders rejected "the advice of a singularly strong, efficient and experienced body of Sea Lords thereby risking the security of the Empire." The whole policy of rationing was wrong, he argued, for the defense requirements of the empire were absolute. "Except in capital ships," he maintained, "we [are] in a position of numerical inferiority to Japan. Over Germany, we only [show] a small margin. Italy was left out of the calculation altogether." But Simon stood by the rationing system, and Chamberlain supported him. Once again the cabinet rejected the new standard, sending Cooper back to negotiate the 1939 program with Inskip. Although Cooper warned Inskip that the Admiralty's reaction was one of "profound disgust," he finally accepted a reduced program. From 1939 to 1942, Britain would build at levels only slightly above those of the subcommittee fleet. Instead of seven battleships, the National government would give the navy four. The Admiralty estimated that in 1942 Japan would be superior to Britain in the Pacific by four battleships, four carriers, fifteen cruisers, and eighty destroyers.[31] Thus, in 1938 the leaders of the British government decided that England could no longer support its worldwide imperial burden. They therefore began to concentrate on the German threat and ignore their possessions in the Pacific.

During these same months, the twin issues of rearmament and appeasement began to tear apart the small British ruling group. Anthony Eden left the government early in the year, and after Munich, Duff Cooper joined Eden's small antiestablishment group known irreverently as "The Glamour Boys." Churchill, Eden, and Cooper did not accept the government's plea of poverty, and they could not understand Chamberlain's timidity when the Tories commanded such a large majority. In May, Hankey told Inskip: "Parliament has rather lost its head and everyone one meets, even in one's own family and private circle, are saying nasty things about the insufficiency of the Government's Defense Programmes and their execution."

Yet the government tried to assure the nation that all was well. On March 7, 1938, Chamberlain announced that "the almost terrifying power that Britain is building up has a salving effect on the opinion of the world." On October 26, Inskip referred to a "stream which might fairly be called a flood of . . . armaments and equipment." While the empire slipped deeper into peril, the National leaders' social life also went on unabated. Henry "Chips" Channon, a wealthy American who had married into British society and become a junior member of Chamberlain's Foreign Office staff, told his diary on June 22 at the height of the debate on the new standard: "We dined with the indefatigable Laura Corrigan, a festival of 137 people, all the youth and fashion of London . . . There is a new dance called the Palais Glide which smacks of the servant's hall, and, lubricated with champagne, the company pranced about doing this absurd 'pas' till 4 a.m. Leslie Belisha [Secretary of State for War] was in the gayest of moods and 'cracked the dawn,' as did half the cabinet." [32]

Even after the Munich crisis, the British government held the line on defense spending in order to facilitate its search for appeasement. Chamberlain argued that further expansion of Britain's arms programs would inflame German and Italian suspicions, causing yet another spiral in the arms race, which Britain could not afford financially. And in early 1939, Chamberlain resisted a moderate appropriation with which the army hoped to meet the increased costs of its existing program. "As a former Chancellor of the Exchequer," he warned, "the financial position [looks to me] extremely dangerous." Simon explained that, as there had been a recession and tax receipts were falling, an economic collapse might be imminent if defense expenditures continued to rise: "During the previous autumn he [Simon] had been faced with serious difficulties in maintaining the level of the pound. Once a loss of confidence showed itself on a wide scale, there would be no means of arresting it. We might be faced with a financial crisis as grave as that of 1931, but with the added difficulty that the foreign situation was now far more serious." [33] Although the small army appropriation in question went through, Britain's leaders continued to fear financial collapse more than foreign enemies.

In spite of British restraint the Germans were not helping to limit the arms race. In December 1938, Earl Stanhope, Cooper's successor at the Admiralty, told the cabinet that Germany was going to build up to parity with Britain in submarines. As a result, he asked for sixteen destroyers and twenty corvettes in the program for 1939. Though he could make a case for building more than two battleships, he claimed, "at the moment it was impossible to build more." In order to ease the bind at the Exchequer, the government decided to delay construction of the second battleship until March 1940 and to retain two overage capital ships. Even so, the government acknowledged that the fleet would be inferior to the combined navies of Germany and Japan.[34] After March 1939, Germany's aggression against Czechoslovakia and its threats against Poland succeeded in concentrating British defense efforts almost entirely on Europe.

Then, in retaliation for Britain's pledge of aid to the Poles, Hitler repudiated the Anglo-German naval agreement. At the end of June 1939, Stanhope warned that Britain was rapidly falling behind in the naval race. The Germans were to build two battleships a year, the Japanese at least one, while Italy would increasingly pull ahead of France in the Mediterranean league of capital ship competition. In order for England to hold its own in the race against Germany and Japan, Stanhope concluded that Britain would have to build three battleships a year beginning in 1940. Such a high level of construction would require economic and labor controls and an increase in shipbuilding capacity. Even after such sacrifices, he warned, the British navy would have a deficit of three ships after 1944. Stanhope's request came at a bad time, for the financial crisis that Simon had earlier predicted seemed to have arrived. In May, the Exchequer reported that England was losing gold "heavily," and in July, Simon told the cabinet that the country had shipped forty percent of its gold stock abroad in the previous fifteen months to pay for imports for the armament program. Further borrowing was impossible, and Britain had only sufficient credit to finance a short war.[35] Consequently, nothing could be done about the inadequate naval program. In order to defend the empire, Britain would have to seek help from the United States.

ANGLO-AMERICAN NAVAL COOPERATION

When Stanhope had asked for more ships in June 1939, he told his colleagues: "It has long been accepted that it is beyond the capacity of this country and France alone to provide adequate naval forces to deal simultaneously with a major war with Germany, Italy, and Japan." [36] As a result of their weakness, the British began seeking Anglo-American naval cooperation against Japan in the Pacific in 1937. President Roosevelt, harried by the isolationists, made no definite commitment to come to Britain's aid, but he did allow some tentative planning. As the Anglo-American strategists reviewed their strength, it became increasingly clear that, if a world conflict came, the United States would have to assume the burden of fighting Japan.

The Sino-Japanese war, which began in the summer of 1937, caused the first real moves toward Anglo-American naval cooperation in the Far East. Anthony Eden suggested that the Western powers could best protect their interests in China by a joint naval demonstration at Singapore. Chamberlain agreed that England "could not put forceful pressure on the Japanese without [the] co-operation of the United States," yet he doubted that the Americans would be helpful. Although admitting that Britain sorely needed allies, he added, "The Power that [has] the greatest strength [is] America, but he would be a rash man who based his calculations on help from that quarter." [37]

Still, Britain had nowhere else to turn for aid in the East. After the Panay incident in December, 1937, Eden tried again to secure a joint naval demonstration. The Americans replied that, "though the President and the Secretary of State . . . had been doing their best to bring American public opinion to realize the situation, they were not yet in a position to adopt any measures of the kind now contemplated." Instead, the President suggested a joint Anglo-American blockade, to be enforced if Japan again attacked Western troops in China; in the meantime, Roosevelt proposed naval staff discussions on the problem of Pacific defense. Roosevelt's reply dampened Chamberlain's temporary enthusiasm for a joint demonstration, and the Prime Minister concluded that "it is always best and safest to count on nothing from the Americans but words." [38]

In spite of Chamberlain's doubts, the staff talks began. In 1938, hope still existed that an Anglo-American front in the Pacific would be sufficient to deter Japan. The director of the Admiralty's Plans Division concluded that an Anglo-American battle fleet, cooperating tactically, would "face the Japanese with an overwhelmingly strong line of battle." When Captain Royal E. Ingersoll of the United States Navy arrived in London, he agreed with the British admirals that both the United States and Britain would have to send battle fleets to the Pacific.

The Americans would send ten capital ships to Singapore, while the British agreed to send nine. If Britain had to fight Japan, Germany, and Italy simultaneously, however, the British worried that "it would most certainly be necessary to effect a considerable reduction in the British [contribution to Anglo-American] strength in the Far East." The admirals explained that in such a war they would have to let the French deal with Italy in the Mediterranean while they tried to cope with German surface raiders in the Atlantic.[39] If all went well, however, the Anglo-American Pacific fleet would boast nineteen capital ships to Japan's ten.

But by 1939, not only had the danger of war in Europe increased greatly, but German, Japanese, and Italian naval construction had further outstripped Britain's shipbuilding efforts. In January 1939, the Admiralty informed the American naval attaché: "In view of the developments in the European situation that have taken place in the past year some reduction has had to be made in the strength of the British fleet that would be sent to the Far East." The leaders of the Royal Navy suggested that, instead of nine battleships, they would only be able to send seven or eight. When during the spring of 1939, Japan began to put increasing pressure on the British position in China, Chamberlain asked the Americans for help in deterring Japan from moving south. At Roosevelt's request, the Admiralty sent Commander T. C. Hampton, traveling as a [real] estate agent, to concert plans for fighting a three-ocean war.[40]

Just before Hampton met with the Americans, the British decided that they could no longer shoulder the burden of Pacific defense. In February, the chiefs of staff stated that Britain could not defeat Germany, Italy, and Japan through its own efforts, and that victory would depend "upon other powers, particularly the United States of America, coming to our aid." In March, the Admiralty concluded gloomily that Japan would be superior in the Far East "for many years." In June, the chiefs of staff warned the government that Britain's position in Europe made the dispatch of a large force to the East impossible. The Royal Navy would have to keep six battleships in the Atlantic to patrol against German raiders and three capital ships in the eastern Mediterranean to help the French tie down the growing Italian fleet. Consequently, the maximum number of battleships available for Far East duty in 1939 would be two. Chamberlain decided that all conflict with Japan had to be avoided.[41]

In late June 1939, Commander Hampton told Admiral William D. Leahy that the situation had changed since the Ingersoll talks. The British government could no longer promise what size fleet would go to Singapore or when it would arrive. In reply, Leahy first warned Hampton that his thoughts were "purely personal," but then the American Chief of Naval Operations comforted the worried British by explaining: "Broadly speaking, [if America entered the war] the U.S. fleet should control the Pacific and the allied fleets should control European waters, the Mediterranean and the Atlantic . . . The U.S. fleet should move to Singapore in sufficient force to be able to engage and defeat the Japanese fleet if met with on passage." If the United States remained neutral, Leahy continued, the

President would hold the American fleet at Pearl Harbor, where its flanking position would keep Japan from attacking Australia and New Zealand. The President also tentatively promised American aid in the Atlantic. On July 1, 1939, Roosevelt called the British ambassador to the White House "most secretly," and in the presence of the Secretary of State, the Secretary of the Navy, and the Chief of Naval Operations, he said: "In case of [a] war in which the United States would be neutral, it would be his desire that the United States government should establish a patrol over the waters of the Western Atlantic with a view to denying them to warlike operation of belligerents." [42] The Americans, then, would help the British to meet the naval challenge in both the Atlantic and the Pacific.

Thus, between 1934 and 1939 the National government despite its large Parliamentary majorities and contrary to the warnings of its admirals, reached the conclusion that Britain could no longer defend its empire in the Pacific. At first, the National leaders had delayed naval rearmament in the hope that Japan would accept further limitations and guarantee Britain's Asian possessions. Even after the collapse of the London Conference had given them a reason, and the election of 1935 had given them the votes, however, Britain's politicians refused to respond to the Japanese naval challenge. In part, the admirals failed to urge their views strongly enough because they had a low opinion of the Japanese navy. But even if the Admiralty Board had resigned en masse, the government would probably not have adopted a two-power standard. The fear of economic collapse was too great, reinforced by a horror of German strategic bombing. Consequently, the British ignored their critics and confined their naval building to a replacement fleet barely adequate, both qualitatively and quantitatively, to counter the German and Italian fleets. What funds they did allow to the armed services went to the Royal Air Force. By 1939, the Royal Navy had traveled far down the road to impotence in the East, and Britain had become more of a liability than an asset to the Americans. On the last lap of the race, the United States found itself alone with Japan.

14   A Steady Pace and a Sudden Sprint

During the five years from 1937 to 1941, the Japanese government gradually carried out the programs it had outlined in 1936. The navy built the ships that the army and government had granted it in the revised National Defense Policy, and in 1939 the admirals began moving south. The army continued infiltrating North China until the Nationalist government reacted, which began a major war in 1937. The expansion of the fighting in China consumed some of the funds designated for the army's buildup against Russia, but by 1941, the army had returned to its plan and begun mobilizing for a final battle with the Soviet Union. After much internal debate, Japan also made a firm connection with Germany through the Axis alliance. Thus, although the war with China drew most of the public's attention, it did not interfere with the fundamental policies adopted in 1936. The army still was preparing for a war with Russia, while the navy kept building the ships that it needed to fight the United States. But as the years passed, the navy found itself caught in a spiraling naval race with the United States. In 1937, the Japanese navy started a major program of naval construction. In order to avoid provoking a reaction from the Americans, the Japanese built their ships in strict secrecy and refused to reveal the extent of their naval programs. The result was a fatal lag in United States construction of capital ships, a delay that resulted in a temporary Japanese lead in the naval race.

JAPAN'S THIRD AND FOURTH REPLENISHMENT PLANS

After 1937, the basic aim of the Japanese navy's construction programs was to provide the ships necessary to defend the western Pacific. Japan's admirals set out a plan that would allow them to maintain a 7/10 ratio with the United States in tonnage, as long as the Americans adhered to the first Vinson program which would bring the United States up to the limits set in the Washington and London naval treaties by 1942. The leaders of the Japanese navy believed that maintenance of the 7/10 ratio, Japan's special geographic position, and the superior size and firepower of Japan's warships would provide a real degree of security in the western Pacific, as long as Roosevelt did not accelerate the pace of United States naval building.[1]

The Third Replenishment Program was extremely large-scale: by 1942 the Japanese navy would build seventy-two ships, including two giant Yamato-class battleships, two aircraft carriers, fifteen destroyers, and thirteen submarines. The builders laid down the first super battleship in November 1937, and the second in March 1938. From 1936 to 1940, Japan's building increased by five times, and during these same years the Japanese builders launched 420,000 tons of warships. Japan's admirals dropped a veil of secrecy over the construction of the giant battleships, building high fences around the ways, allowing the construction personnel to see only small sections of a ship, and clearing the harbors when the ships were launched.[2]

Possibly because of this secrecy, the Americans hesitated for a year before accelerating the pace of their own building. Finally, in early 1938 Congress passed the second Vinson bill, which increased the authorized strength of the American navy by twenty percent, and the legislators provided funds for two battleships in 1937 and four battleships in 1938. In reporting on the new building proposed by the Americans, Japan's naval attaché in Washington reassured his superiors that the Americans could not achieve a 10/6 ratio even if they did increase their navy by twenty percent. According to a chart sent to the Foreign Office by Japanese Navy Intelligence, the actual naval construction that the Americans had started would not even replace the ships which would be overage, and presumably scrapped, by 1942. Although the United States would be up to treaty strength in underage carriers and cruisers, it would be seriously weak in destroyers, submarines, and battleships. By 1942, seven of America's fifteen battleships would be overage, while Japan's capital ships would be modernized and strengthened by the addition of the two Yamato-class battleships.[3] Since the Americans were building only six new capital ships, their battleship strength would presumably decline by one in 1942.

The second Vinson bill, however, authorized the United States Navy to build up to a total of eighteen battleships, and in 1939 the legislators provided funds for two more battleships and for the modernization of five older capital ships. The Japanese navy countered with a building program of their own, the Fourth Replenishment Program, which was larger than their third plan. This new schedule added two more battleships of the Yamato class and one carrier, five cruisers, twenty-one destroyers, and twenty-five submarines to the construction already begun. The Japanese also planned to double the size of their air arm by the end of 1943. In May and November of 1940, the two new Yamato-class battleships were laid down.[4] Thus, up until 1940, the Japanese navy was moving ahead in its building competition with the Americans. It was building one vastly superior battleship for every two inferior American capital ships, was far ahead in the race to modernize capital ships, and was maintaining its margin in light craft.

A FATEFUL DELAY

Nearly all of the United States' leading policy makers had said, at one time or another, that their country could and would outbuild the Japanese after the treaties lapsed. But from 1935 to 1940, Roosevelt refused to start any large American naval program. There were many reasons for this delay. In governmental circles, and even in the upper ranks of the navy, there was a genuine reluctance to provoke a naval race, and Japan's refusal to reveal its building plans made it difficult for the United States to justify a large program. The political strength of the isolationists and Roosevelt's strained relations with Congress reinforced this reluctance. Thus, between 1937 and 1939, the President was able to secure from Congress only one naval increase, the second Vinson authorization bill, and only moderate sums for actual ship construction.

In the spring of 1935, the American navy conducted large-scale maneuvers in the Pacific, which indicated clearly that the defense of the Philippines would be impossible unless the government immediately started a prohibitively expensive naval program. Admiral J. M. Reeves used many elements of the United States fleet to recreate a trans-Pacific American advance against Japanese forces. The hypothetical American fleet was superior in the strength of its battle line, but greatly inferior in speed, light surface forces, submarines, and aircraft—an exact reproduction of the existing balance of naval strengths between the United States and Japan. In the first phase of the operation, the American fleet sortied from San Diego to Pearl Harbor but in the process suffered heavy damage from attacks by Japanese submarines.

In the second phase, the American fleet left Pearl Harbor with an invasion force bound for Midway, with the Americans pretending that Pearl Harbor represented Manila and that Midway represented an island in the Ryukyus. Again the battleships suffered damage from submarines during their departure from harbor. In the decisive battle off Midway, the Japanese destroyers inflicted further harm on the American battleships, and the Japanese battle line then used its superior speed to cross the American ''T'' and wipe out the remains of the crippled fleet.[5] Thus, the Americans had simulated in rough outline the Japanese plan of campaign. Japan's admirals would use their submarines to wear down the American fleet, and they would use the superior speed of their ships to concentrate their guns on the head of the American battle line. Both Japan's admirals and their American counterparts agreed that the result would be the annihilation of the Americans.

The weakness of the American navy meant that the military's plan for a war against Japan, known as the Orange Plan, had to be revised. The navy and the war secretaries asked the State Department to help them make the plan more realistic because ''successive developments during the past two decades have so weakened our military position vis-à-vis Japan that our position in the Far East may result not only in our being forced into war but into a war that would have to be fought under conditions that might preclude its successful prosecution.'' The army representatives argued that the Philippines could not be defended and that the United States should therefore retreat to a strategic triangle running from Alaska to Hawaii to Panama. But the navy resisted, and the debate went on until 1938. Finally the army accepted the navy's argument that the United States was obliged to defend the Philippines, but the two services still left the timing of a relief expedition undecided.[6] Naval weakness cast a pall of futility over any large building plans. Moreover, by the time the Americans could build enough ships to make the defense of the Philippines possible, the islands might be independent.

Consequently, in late 1937 and early 1938, the navy evolved a new strategy, which gave some promise of securing victory over Japan. The genesis of the idea seems to have appeared in a letter from the commander of the Asiatic fleet, Admiral Harry E. Yarnell, which was forwarded by the Chief of Naval Operations to Roosevelt. Yarnell pointed out that the United States would have Britain, France, Russia, and Holland as either active or passive allies in a war with Japan. "With our allies," he wrote, "we would control roughly ninety per cent of the world's reserves of iron, coal, and oil as well as a major portion of other raw materials." Thus, American and British light forces could use their bases in the western Pacific to blockade Japan at long range. As Yarnell concluded, "some nations can be strangled to death." Roosevelt told Leahy, "Yarnell talks a lot of sense . . . it goes along with that word 'quarantine' I used in the Chicago speech last month." Leahy hastened to assure the President that the army and navy had recently agreed on a plan of campaign similar to Yarnell's proposition.[7]

Yarnell's plan eventually became known as Rainbow Two, one of a new set of war plans that the Americans were making in response to the outbreak of war in China and to the increasing threat of hostilities in Europe. Since the old war plans for individual countries were "color" plans (orange for war with Japan and black for war with Germany), the new plans for global war were, ipso facto, rainbow plans. Early in the debate on the new plans, it became apparent that America would not have the naval strength in the foreseeable future to fight alone in both oceans. The navy decided that it would need forty battleships, eighteen carriers, over one hundred cruisers, and three hundred destroyers if it were to take the offensive in both oceans. An offensive in the Atlantic and a defensive in the Pacific would require twenty-seven battleships, twelve carriers, sixty-nine cruisers, and almost two hundred destroyers.[8] In 1938, the American navy was only one-half the size required by the latter, more modest program and less than one-third the size required by the former, more ambitious program. Consequently, the Americans had to rely on the help of allies in order to maintain a viable defensive in the Pacific.

The rainbow planners, therefore, assumed that in some cases the United States would have foreign help. According to Rainbow Two, the British and French would defend a line drawn from Singapore to Timor, with the Americans and Dutch helping. The allies would prevent Japan from taking the Dutch East Indies, and they would then blockade Japan at long range and wait for her war machine to grind to a halt. Finally, the Americans would take bases in the Marianas, advance to retake the Philippines, and then attack the Japanese homeland. In January 1939, the President sent Captain Ingersoll to London in order to make sure that the British would cooperate in Rainbow Two by sending a division of capital ships to Singapore on the outbreak of war. The President evidently was confident in the prospects for victory under the new plan. In the fall of 1939, Ambassador Grew, who was on home leave, warned Roosevelt against cutting off Japan's oil. If the United States proclaimed a complete embargo, Grew said, the Japanese would send their navy to take the Dutch East Indies. The President replied, "Then we could easily intercept her fleet." [9]

Weak as the Americans were in the western Pacific, they were still confident that Japan did not have the capability to reverse the naval balance completely. The American leaders thought that Japan was simply not strong enough to drive the United States and her allies out of the western Pacific and then threaten Hawaii or the West Coast. In the spring of 1937, Roosevelt asked Hull whether Japanese finances would permit large military building. Hull replied that Japan was suffering no decisive financial weakness and that the Japanese military could continue its buildup as long as it retained the support of the people. Thus, the President's doubts about Japan's economic strength, which he had expressed in 1934, continued into 1937. American naval intelligence records show that the navy did not underrate Japan's shipbuilding capacities, but that it seriously underestimated the type of building which Japan was undertaking. In January 1937, a report predicted that Japan might build four battleships of 35,000 tons each, when in actuality the Japanese were planning two battleships of 70,000 tons apiece. Moreover, the informant cautioned that his estimate was probably too high. In July 1937, another report showed that the Japanese were undertaking a large aircraft buildup, yet the writer concluded that "a natural inaptitude in this field will keep them somewhat behind the more progressive occidental countries, but the difference will steadily decrease as the limits of material and performance are closely approached." [10] Because the Americans underestimated the Japanese challenge, they assumed that they had plenty of time in which to right the strategic balance.

Japan's continued refusal to reveal its building plans compounded the Americans' uncertainty and left the Roosevelt administration without an obvious reason for undertaking large-scale construction. In early 1937, the Americans and British asked the Japanese to maintain the qualitative limits set in the new London Treaty of 1936, but the Japanese refused. In May 1937, the Tokyo correspondent for the *New York Times,* Hugh Byas, reported that Japan was not planning a great navy program. When Byas had questioned Admiral Yonai Mitsumasa, Japan's Navy Minister, about reports that Japan was building huge ships with guns larger than sixteen inches in caliber, Yonai had replied, "Those press reports are sheer speculation with no foundation whatever and the Japanese navy is prepared to deny them." Finally, in February 1938, the United States, Britain, and France sent an identical note to Japan, asking assurance that Japan was adhering to the qualitative treaty limits. Without such a promise, the note continued, the Western nations would have to scrap their own limits and resume freedom of action. The Japanese navy recommended an answer that rejected the American request completely, and Hirota accepted the navy draft. The Japanese replied that there was no reason for the Western governments to assume that Japan was violating the treaty limits simply because Japan kept its plans secret; rather, it was Japan's naval inferiority which made secrecy necessary.[11] Japan's evasion worked. It would have been difficult to explain to the American people that they should run a race with an invisible opponent.

Thus, the strategic balance, the image of Japan as economically weak and technologically backward, and the uncertainty about Japan's actual building plans all contributed to Roosevelt's lack of enthusiasm for a large naval program. But the political situation also made naval construction unattractive. Throughout the summer of 1935, the domestic crisis continued to have top priority, and Roosevelt concentrated on broadening his support for the presidential campaign of 1936. The President was especially careful to cultivate the support or neutrality of Republican progressive leaders, such as Gerald Nye, with the result that he sounded occasional notes on the isolationist horn. Campaigning as a bipartisan leader, he undercut the appeal of the Union party on the left while retaining the support of moderates by promising to balance the budget.[12]

Given this political strategy, rearmament was out of the question, since it would absorb funds needed for relief and would unbalance the fiscal seesaw. In any case, the administration had to seek new taxes in 1936 for the relief agencies, which faced repeated economic crises. Roosevelt's political strategy resulted in a landslide victory in 1936 and a seemingly unshakable congressional majority. After the election, Roosevelt appeared to have legislative strength comparable to that of the National government in Britain. But then the President miscalculated by starting a battle to reform the Supreme Court, which had been vetoing much of the administration's domestic program. As a result of this fight, the President found himself facing a hostile coalition in Congress. Since economic conditions were improving, the congressional leaders demanded that Roosevelt honor his campaign promises by balancing the budget. Roosevelt responded by cutting expenditures, but a recession in the fall of 1937 decreased tax revenues even further.[13] As a result of these political exigencies, neither money nor votes were available for a large naval program.

The debate on the Supreme Court issue in 1937 also influenced the conduct of foreign policy. Fearing a campaign by Roosevelt for a third term, conservatives in Congress increasingly charged that Roosevelt had dictatorial ambitions and that he was seeking to distract the people from the administration's domestic failures by irresponsible attempts to embark on foreign adventures. Roosevelt opened himself to this criticism after the outbreak of Sino-Japanese hostilities by calling for the quarantine of aggressors, to which the isolationists reacted angrily. When Japanese planes sank the U.S.S. *Panay* on the Yangtze, Congress did not call for strong measures against Japan; instead, the House debated the Ludlow amendment to the constitution, which required a nationwide referendum on any declaration of war, and the administration had to make a strong effort to beat back the measure.[14] Roosevelt would have to overcome violent domestic criticism if he were to secure the funds for further naval construction, because his critics would charge that he wanted to use the ships to sail into foreign seas searching for trouble.

A MODERATE PROGRAM

As a result of these factors, Roosevelt contented himself with continuing gradual naval armament under the Vinson authorization of 1934. In June 1935, Congress had passed the naval supply bill for 1936, which granted funds for one carrier, two light cruisers, fifteen destroyers, and six submarines. The General Board was at that time also urging Roosevelt to provide for the immediate construction of a battleship, in order to replace the ship that would be overage in 1938, but Roosevelt told Swanson that the navy should give no publicity to the matter, although he allowed work to go ahead on the designs. Swanson wanted to use Public Works funds to accelerate the pace of naval building, and Cordell Hull, Norman Davis, and Key Pittman, the Chairman of the Senate Foreign Relations Committee, supported him. But Admiral Standley, the Chief of Naval Operations, advocated continuing regular building under the Vinson plan, and Roosevelt followed his advice.[15]

In 1936, with the election approaching, the President did ask for funds to start two capital ships in 1937, promising that the administration would build the ships only if other nations had already started constructing their own new battleships. This bill also allowed the navy to replace six destroyers and twelve submarines. Despite its extremely limited nature, the proposal provoked sharp debate. Representative Fred J. Sisson, a Democratic supporter of the New Deal, proposed cutting the navy budget by twenty percent. Walter W. Van Kirk, the director of the National Peace Conference, personally presented an appeal to Roosevelt against the "tremendous increase" in military spending, which had been signed by college presidents, businessmen, and church leaders. Other pacifist and church groups made similar appeals.[16] Although the naval bill went through, the nucleus of opposition remained, and a larger proposal might provoke even greater debate.

Roosevelt was waiting until Japanese action made it obvious to Congress and to the people that large naval increases were necessary. On February 13, 1936, he wrote, "Heaven only knows I do not want to spend more money on our Army and Navy. I am initiating nothing new unless and until increases by other nations make increases by us absolutely essential to national defense. I wish England could understand that—and, incidentally, I wish Japan could understand that also." A month earlier he had explained why the army could not have more money with which to increase its air strength: "the amount of increased appropriations for the Army and Navy have mounted each year during the past three years to such an extent that it is unwise, from the point of view of the national finances, and, incidentally, from the point of view of public opinion, for me to recommend additional increases over those contained in the budget." [17] But throughout 1936 and early 1937, the Japanese would not provide the President with evidence that the naval race was on. In the spring of 1937, the Japanese government refused to release any information about their naval program. Consequently, Roosevelt had to wait for a political hook on which to hang a request for a naval increase.

There was also surprisingly little enthusiasm for a naval race evidenced by the higher officials in the navy. In May 1935, the General Board outlined a very modest program for 1937 of one battleship, twelve destroyers, and six submarines. The members of the board explained, "The General Board assumed that the United States will not initiate a building race, and, if present treaties lapse, will not exceed present treaty limits unless the situation is disturbed by the building of some other power." They argued that the navy should not try to achieve a full treaty navy in one leap; instead of a massive program, slow, staggered construction would allow the builders to take advantage of design improvements, and it would avoid straining either the nation's finances or its limited building capacity. In 1936, the General Board did recommend that Congress supply funds for two more replacement battleships in the 1938 program, and the Chief of Naval Operations, William H. Standley, replied that the Navy Department was already committed to the Vinson program, which called for only one battleship in 1938. He added that since the United States had not built any battleships since 1923, "it is considered advisable to take advantage, to as great an extent as possible, of the experience to be gained by the building of the two battleships already appropriated for." [18] The leadership of the navy, then, did not twist the President's arm; after the famine of the Hoover years, they remained satisfied with the hors d'oeuvres that Roosevelt provided.

Roosevelt's time of watchful waiting continued through 1937. The President announced on January 8, 1937, that the United States would indeed build the two battleships appropriated for in 1936, but he denied that a naval race had begun. Caught in the toils of the divisive debates on neutrality legislation and Supreme Court reform, Roosevelt sent through Congress his smallest naval proposal, asking for eight destroyers and four submarines.[19] The United States was adhering to the Vinson plan, which provided for a treaty navy by 1942, while the Japanese were forging beyond the treaty limits in 1937.

For three years the President had been avoiding a large naval increase. During the naval talks, he had kept actual construction down, in order to provide a proper atmosphere for the discussions. In 1936, the President wanted to avoid controversy during an election year, and in 1937 his strained relations with Congress made it difficult to propose any large increases. Throughout these years, the economic emergency, budgetary limitations, and the perfunctory attitude of the admirals toward the Japanese challenge contributed to the delay. Finally, in December 1937, the Japanese provided a convenient reason for large American naval building, when the Japanese campaign in China led to the sinking of the American gunboat *Panay* on December 12, 1937. Roosevelt seized the incident as an opportunity to expand the navy's authorized limits.

By December 18, the President had decided that he should ask for four new battleships rather than two in the budget for 1939, and in January 1938, he had Vinson introduce a bill which raised the authorized strength of the navy twenty percent above treaty levels. In a special message to Congress, Roosevelt urged passage of the new Vinson bill, stressing that the United States could not defend the hemisphere by protecting only one coast. The United States, he said, had to cover both coasts and also ensure the safety of the Panama Canal. Roosevelt was wise to stress hemisphere defense in supporting the Vinson bill, since his opponents were quick to accuse him of a desire to intervene in European and Asiatic wars. They also charged the administration with making secret agreements to help Britain against Japan in Asia. Many Senators claimed that the existing strength of the navy was sufficient for hemisphere defense. But Roosevelt's strategy worked, and the ranks of his opponents split. Many isolationists were attracted by the argument that the United States needed more ships to defend the Monroe Doctrine unilaterally, and in the end, isolationist papers, such as the *Chicago Tribune, Los Angeles Times,* and *Indianapolis Star,* supported the second Vinson bill.

The Roosevelt administration also made a final appeal to Japan for specific information on Japanese building, and Japan's refusal to adhere to treaty limits further strengthened the administration's hand in Congress. Even Representative Louis Ludlow, the sponsor of the war referendum amendment to the Constitution, confessed that he was convinced. On January 9, 1938, he said, ''I shall vote for naval expansion but I regret . . . that other nations force us to do it.'' After a delay of four months, the Vinson authorization passed through the House by a vote of 294 to 100 and through the Senate by a vote of 56 to 18.[20]

The second Vinson bill authorized only very moderate increases above former treaty levels. Provided that Roosevelt could secure the money from Congress, the Vinson authorization would allow him to build three extra battleships, two more carriers, nine additional light cruisers, twenty-three more destroyers, nine extra submarines, and over one thousand planes. But Congress refused to appropriate funds for the two additional battleships that Roosevelt requested in early 1938. Consequently, Japan's Fourth Replenishment Program, started in 1939, was almost equal to the increase of America's naval tonnage authorized by the second Vinson bill.[21] For a variety of reasons, then, American naval building remained at quite moderate levels, and the Japanese navy was able to secure a head start in the competition.

The low rate of American expansion continued through 1939 and, in spite of the outbreak of war in Europe, continued well into 1940. In the 1938 elections, Roosevelt lost control of Congress to a coalition of conservative Republicans and southern Democrats. Although he jettisoned his domestic programs, he was not able to secure the repeal of the neutrality legislation that would keep him from extending aid to Britain and France in case of war. As Europe slid closer to conflict, the struggle over neutrality absorbed all of the President's political capital. Unless the embargo were repealed, Roosevelt would not be able to send the large numbers of airplanes America was building to aid the democracies in Europe. To satisfy the isolationists, Roosevelt had to show that he was trying to avoid war. Consequently, his armament program remained at a level sufficient for hemisphere defense, but insufficient for foreign expeditions. Thus, in May 1939, at the height of the debate over neutrality, Roosevelt secured from Congress funds to build only two battleships, two cruisers, eight destroyers, and eight submarines; at this late date, Congress also provided for the modernization of five battleships.[22]

As a result of this tardy American buildup, Japan was increasing its naval strength in relation to the United States. Japan had four battleships built or appropriated for, while the Americans had eight, but the Japanese ships were twice the size and strength of their American counterparts. From May 1933 to September 1939, the United States had built five carriers to an equal number for Japan, seventeen cruisers to Japan's twelve, sixty-five destroyers to Japan's fifty-seven, and forty-one submarines to Japan's forty-nine. The United States had a 10/8 ratio with Japan in 1936, which had steadily worsened in subsequent years.[23]

The outbreak of war in Europe solved Roosevelt's neutrality problem, but it did not answer the questions of rearmament and naval support in the East for Britain and France. Congress modified the neutrality laws in the fall of 1939, but it rejected a large appropriation bill introduced by the administration in November. The new bill would have sharply increased the pace of naval building under the second Vinson authorization bill. Since Congress had been relatively generous with funds for battleships, the administration now called for money to build three carriers, eight cruisers, fifty-two destroyers, and thirty-two submarines over a four-year period. But with the election of 1940 approaching and with foreign policy becoming a major issue in that contest, the legislators refused to act.[24] The bill was still pending when the kaleidoscopic events of 1940 drastically increased America's naval needs, and the Congress had to consider calls for a two-ocean navy.

As a result of the continuing lag in American naval construction, Japan was improving its ratio of strength not only in quantity but also in quality. Because of a lack of both funds and imagination, the American navy did not try to redress the declining quantitative balance by emphasizing superior quality in the established types of ships or by developing new weapons. Consequently, Japan's admirals could still enter the war confident that their battleships, planes, and other weapons were individually superior to those of the United States.

The American research and development effort in the thirties was weak and uncoordinated. Each bureau maintained its own development department, and the navy resisted overall coordination of the effort until 1941. Harold G. Bowen, the cantankerous chief of the Bureau of Engineering for most of this period, was able to have the Navy Research Laboratory removed from the Radio Division of the Bureau of Engineering and placed directly under the Chief of Naval Operations, but in 1939 the laboratory was still receiving less than $1 million per year. As a result, it continued to emphasize radio and sonar research. Although radar was an important exception to this unfortunate record, the Americans were still installing it throughout the fleet when war came.[25]

With the exception of the important successes in radar and sonar, the navy made few other advances during the thirties, because it concentrated on making marginal improvements in existing types of ships. Bowen himself worked on producing better engines and reducing weight, in order to widen the cruising radii of the new American craft. This effort embroiled him in a nasty fight with the General Board, but in the end he was able to install improved engines in the new ships. The new North Carolina class battleships were seven knots faster than their predecessors, and they had better armor, fire control, compartmentalization, and antiaircraft protection. Other classes of ships benefited from similar improvements. In addition, Americans produced a fast fleet train in order to fuel at sea. For the first time, Americans began building submarines with the cruising range needed for operations in the Pacific, but the engineers lacked the funds to test the torpedoes which the submarine commanders would have to use. Consequently, in the early stages of the war the torpedoes refused to explode when they hit Japanese ships. In early 1939, Charles Edison, Assistant Secretary of the Navy, confessed to the President that technical development during the naval building holiday had been "virtually stagnant." [26] In the late thirties, therefore, the Americans could not rely on superiority of type.

Although the Americans themselves continued to believe in the central role of the battleship, they did not produce a match for Japan's Yamato class. In the spring of 1937, Roosevelt decided to equip the new American battleships with fourteen-inch guns, to ensure that the United States would not be the first nation to overturn the limits established in the new London Naval Treaty. Although Rear Admiral A. C. Pickens, a Bureau of Ordnance expert, warned that the Japanese might build an eighteen-inch gun battleship, he added, "Our present superiority in the battle line is such that we can afford to let Japan take the first step." American restraint might prevent a qualitative race, he suggested, thereby avoiding the need to build a ship that was too large to transit the Panama Canal. Nor was the rate of building for the smaller battleships high: in order to incorporate design improvements, the General Board advised building only one or two battleships a year until 1949.[27]

In March 1938, Japan's refusal to divulge its building plans led the American navy to escalate the size of its new capital ships to 45,000-ton craft mounting sixteen-inch guns, but the American admirals still refused to build a superbattleship. In June 1938, representatives of the Soviet Union sought permission to build a 62,000-ton battleship mounting eighteen-inch guns in the United States, but the American navy objected. After war had begun in Europe, American interest in the superbattleship project (dramatically labeled "Ship X") revived, but the members of the General Board again advised against any action. Although they admitted that Ship X would render existing battleships "individually inferior," the admirals argued that they could not afford to interrupt construction of the smaller battleships. In any case, they explained, a superbattleship would not be able to use American harbors or the Panama Canal. Consequently, the Chief of Naval Operations, Admiral Stark, told Roosevelt that the navy opposed the plan.[28]

A similar lag occurred in the development of American naval air power and carrier doctrine. In this area, the leaders of the American navy shared with their Japanese and British counterparts doubts about the proper role for carriers. Ever since Brigadier General William (Billy) Mitchell's bombers had sunk several battleships in the early twenties, the issue of planes versus ships had been a sensitive one. The leaders of the navy claimed that the tests were inconclusive, since the older battleships had been stationary and undefended. In fact, the battleship advocates took heart in 1924 when a modern hull stayed afloat despite considerable pounding from the air. A board headed by Admiral Edward W. Eberle thereupon concluded that modern battleships would not be sunk if properly defended.[29]

Gradually the Americans evolved an important, but subsidiary, role for their carriers. The ships were to engage in reconnaissance, gunfire spotting, attacks to slow fleeing enemy ships that were outdistancing the American fleet, and protection against air and submarine attack. Since the carriers were extremely vulnerable, however, they would have to remain under the protection of the battle line during an action. American admirals considered that the role of aircraft in spotting the gunfire of battleships was especially important. In practice, until 1940 the American navy generally built one carrier for every two battleships, and they resisted suggestions to increase the production of carriers at the expense of battleship production.[30]

Because of its secondary status, the naval air force did not develop rapidly until war began in Europe, and American naval aircraft did not progress in step with Japan's planes. Since aircraft were so expensive and funds short, the Bureau of Aeronautics concentrated on improving new prototypes rather than producing large numbers of planes. As a result, the first generation of carrier planes was standardized late in the thirties. But even after production of these improved types had begun in earnest, the best American carrier-based fighter, the Grumman F-4-F Wildcat, proved inferior in several respects to the Japanese Zero. It was almost two years after the start of the Pacific war that these improved planes began to reach the carriers in any numbers. Consequently, in spite of rapidly increasing American production, in 1941 Japan's five hundred carrier planes still comprised the strongest individual shipborne air force in the world.[31]

The Americans had an advantage in one sector of air development, however, for the Army Air Force had developed medium and heavy bombers, the B-24 and B-17, which promised help in the defense of Southeast Asia. Between 1936 and 1938, maneuvers demonstrated that land-based bombers could intercept shipping far at sea, and by 1941 the Americans were in fact relying on B-17s for blockade use and defense of the Philippines if war should come.[32] Yet the B-17 and the new strategy of distant blockade could not solve the basic problem, namely, that in 1940 and 1941 the United States and its unofficial ally Britain were too weak to fight in the western Pacific.

THE NAVAL BALANCE SHIFTS

Throughout the thirties, Britain's admirals had predicted that in case of war, the Royal Navy would have great difficulty in protecting the empire, but Germany's first attacks at sea in the fall of 1939 proved that even the direst of their predictions had been too optimistic. After the outbreak of war, the Admiralty had to concentrate its strength in Europe and to cease building capital ships. But worse was to come, for the French surrender forced the Royal Navy to use its own forces to contain Italy. This new responsibility in the Mediterranean, combined with the all-consuming battle of the Atlantic, stripped away the thin veil of protection that Britain's Pacific dominions had formerly enjoyed; eventually, even the Americans had to begin withdrawing some of their ships from the Pacific in order to aid the Atlantic convoys. More important, the sharp swing of the naval balance to the Axis side led the Americans to begin a massive, emergency program of naval building.

Germany's successes at sea surprised the Admiralty. In January 1938, the British admirals had informed the Americans, "Should hostilities with Germany occur, the Admiralty is not so seriously apprehensive of German submarines, as they believe that they can successfully cope with them." The leaders of the Royal Navy expected that underwater listening devices would make attack by submarine too dangerous, but the German commanders overcame the new British detection machinery through night surface attacks. Consequently, German submarine warfare proved to be even more effective than it had been during the First World War. The Germans also broke up their small battle fleet and used their strongest ships as surface raiders. These attackers, aided by numerous armed merchantmen, tied down many British battleships and cruisers.[33] Thus, Germany's decision to concentrate its efforts against British shipping had a disproportionate effect on the distribution of the Royal Navy.

Germany's fierce attacks on Britain's supply lines also forced the Admiralty to stop all long-range naval construction. By 1940, the British were trying to complete only those ships that could be ready within two years, and they therefore stopped building the two battleships which they had ordered in August 1939. In place of the old capital ship program, Britain's admirals planned to produce masses of destroyers, destroyer escorts, and corvettes, which they could send to guard the embattled Atlantic convoys.[34] In 1939, the leaders of the Royal Navy had already admitted that they could not hope to send a fleet to the Pacific unless the government provided funds for a large new complement of capital ships. But after the outbreak of the European war, it became apparent that no battleships would be launched after 1943. As long as the war in Europe lasted, Britain would not be a Pacific power.

After the fall of France in 1940, the crisis deepened. The German navy acquired channel ports from which it could help to launch an invasion, and the German submarine fleet secured ports much closer to Britain's sea lanes. In order to guard against an invasion, the Admiralty had to decrease its guard on the sea lanes and concentrate more of its ships near home. Consequently, in 1940 and 1941, German surface raiders took a serious toll of merchantmen and tied down much of the navy. Worse still, the neutralization of the French navy forced the British to place a fleet in the Mediterranean in order to prevent the Italians from joining German operations in the Atlantic. Throughout 1940 and 1941, control of the Mediterranean remained in doubt. The British chiefs of staff decided that the defense of the dominions in the Pacific would have to depend on air power alone and that Britain would have to avoid war with Japan at all costs. The German threat to Britain's sea lanes and to the homeland itself produced a string of appeals to Roosevelt for naval aid in the Atlantic. In order to convince the President to keep his prewar promises of aid, Britain's new Prime Minister, Winston S. Churchill, painted a garish portrait of the looming threat to the United States. If the British had to surrender, he warned, the only bargaining counter they would have was their fleet. Once Hitler controlled the ships of the Royal Navy, the Americans would have to face the combined fleets of Germany, Italy, Japan, France, and Britain, and they would have to do it alone.[35]

PANIC IN WASHINGTON

Throughout the thirties, the naval balance had been tilting slowly in favor of Germany, Italy, and Japan, and after 1939, Germany's unexpected successes forced the British to concentrate on the Atlantic and to ignore the Japanese threat in the Pacific. Consequently, by 1940 Britain's critical difficulties and the growing Axis naval threat had shocked the Americans from their slumber. The Roosevelt administration and Congress realized that the United States Navy would have to fight the Japanese fleet unaided, and as a result, they hastened to put a huge number of warships on the ways.

While Churchill was sounding the emergency siren in Europe, the American office of Naval Intelligence informed the President that the threat was growing in the Pacific as well. In October 1939, Roosevelt received an exaggerated report that Japan was building eight battleships, each of approximately 40,000 tons displacement and mounting sixteen-inch guns. The report also indicated that Japan was building two battle cruisers of 15,000 tons, which would be able to overpower all American cruisers. Thus, Japan seemed to be building as many powerful battleships as was the United States. The allied collapse in Europe, combined with the threatened increase in Japanese naval strength, brought panic to Washington. The General Board informed the Assistant Secretary of the Navy that the second Vinson program was "entirely inadequate" and that the United States should build "to the utmost capacity of existing facilities." They added: "The need for this program is stressed by the knowledge that Japan is rapidly increasing her fleet, and, without extraordinary efforts on our part, will attain approximate parity during the years 1941–1943." The General Board also predicted that the United States could no longer rely on Britain and France to hold the Atlantic. Although it was impractical for the United States to build a fleet capable of taking the offensive in both oceans at the same time, the board indicated, "work should be commenced with the greatest possible dispatch to provide the United States with sufficient naval strength to provide for freedom of action in one ocean and maintain an effective defensive action in the other." But the board warned that Congress would have to authorize, and the shipyards would have to build, almost two hundred more ships if the navy were to reach even these limited strategic objectives.[36]

The President and Congress responded immediately. On June 14, 1940, Congress passed the appropriation for the ships authorized in the second Vinson bill of 1938. Three days later, Admiral Harold R. Stark, Chief of Naval Operations, asked for four billion dollars to provide a two-ocean navy by 1946, and in July, Roosevelt had Congress approve a bill authorizing an additional 1,325,000 tons of naval construction. In two months, Congress had provided funds for almost two hundred and fifty warships, nearly double the number of vessels that it had granted during the first six years of the Roosevelt administration. The two-ocean navy bill projected seven new battleships, five of which would displace 60,000 tons and mount twelve sixteen-inch guns. Although individually these new battleships would still be no match for their counterparts in Japan's Yamato class, they were almost twice the size of the first four ships that the Americans had laid down after the treaties ended. Since there were reports from Tokyo indicating that the Japanese were building battle cruisers to destroy heavy cruisers, the navy also secured funds for six battle cruisers of 27,500 tons mounting nine twelve-inch guns. The two appropriations bills also provided for nineteen carriers, over sixty cruisers, approximately one hundred and fifty destroyers, and one hundred and forty submarines.[37]

A similar effort was made in aircraft production, which had more immediate effects. English and French airplane orders had produced such an expansion of factory output that by 1941, the United States aircraft industry was producing four times the number of planes coming off Japanese assembly lines. Though much of the American production was earmarked for the Allies, it was obvious that the American navy would benefit dramatically as the years passed.[38]

In short, when naval competition had begun in 1937, Japan jumped into an early lead, both quantitatively and qualitatively. Out of financial necessity, the British government had shut its eyes to the danger in the East and built only enough ships to counter the growing threat in Europe. Nor did the Americans take up the British slack. Roosevelt faced more political opposition to rearmament than did Chamberlain, and Congress provided only enough funds to keep the Americans following in Japan's wake. After the war had begun and France fell, Britain was forced to drop entirely out of the race in the Pacific. The Americans, realizing that they would now have to face the new Axis threat to the naval balance alone, began building a huge number of warships. The lighter craft in this emergency program were to start coming off the ways in late 1942, and the battleships would be finished between 1944 and 1946. Japan's naval advantage, sought for so long and purchased at such a great price, would first be undermined and then swept away by the rising tide of this American construction. If the Japanese were going to expand according to plan, they would have to strike quickly—while they still held the naval lead.

15   Japan's Decision for War

The Japanese navy held the key to Japan's decision for war, since it was the service that would bear the major burden in a Pacific conflict. By 1940, the navy was well started on the road south, and the admirals were starting to receive ships built under the Third and Fourth Replenishment Programs. Then, the fall of France furnished the opportunity for further southern expansion, and the threat of massive American naval building provided the need for an early start. Between April and early July 1941, both the Japanese navy and the cabinet decided to risk war. There were many reasons for this decision, but running through the admirals' arguments was the contention that Japan had to strike before the Americans tipped the naval balance back against the empire.

SOUTHERN EXPANSION

The Imperial Navy, led by Navy Minister Nagano Osami and Vice Chief of Staff Shimada Shigetarō, had been eager to start expanding south during the Pakhoi incident in the fall of 1936, but the leaders of the army had objected, because they still feared the Russian threat to their northern flank. After the outbreak of war with China, the army continued to oppose opening an additional front in the south while Japan was occupied in the north. In any case, the navy was not ready to make a deep penetration into the southern seas in 1936, since it had not yet built the ships necessary to fight the Americans and British. Nevertheless, after the struggle in China had begun, the commander of the third fleet, Admiral Hasegawa Kiyoshi, occupied islands near Amoy and Hong Kong, far south from the scene of hostilities.[1]

The navy also proposed sending an expedition to establish Japan's claim to the Spratly Islands, which lie between South Vietnam and Borneo, across the sea lanes that connect Singapore to Manila. By taking the Spratlys, the Japanese navy would acquire submarine bases in the midst of the French, British, Dutch, and American territories in Southeast Asia. In 1936, the Japanese navy took over the colonial administration in Taiwan, and in that same year the Taiwan government subsidized a Japanese fishing operation in the area. In late 1937 and early 1938, the French sent warships to the island to leave claim markers. Consequently, in July 1938, the Japanese rushed their own claim markers to the island, and in the fall, the Japanese left off soldiers. On December 23, 1938, the Japanese cabinet decided to take the islands, and on March 30, 1939, the government announced the annexation. For good measure, the Japanese also claimed jurisdiction over the coral reefs in an ocean area covering approximately 100,000 square miles, stretching from Palawan in the southern Philippines to the tip of the Indochina peninsula.[2]

During the fall of 1938, the Navy Minister, Yonai Mitsumasa, was also pressing the government to acquire Hainan Island, which would provide another and better base in the south. The admirals claimed that they needed a port on Hainan to help close the southern end of their blockade against China, although Pakhoi on the coast of Kwantung would have been more suited to that purpose. Hainan and the Spratly Islands would give the Japanese navy bases that separated the Americans in Manila from the British in Singapore and which provided staging areas for further southern moves. On November 25, 1938, the five ministers also decided to take Hainan, an operation that the navy carried out on February 10, 1939. The Japanese navy placed both Hainan and the Spratly Islands under the jurisdiction of their own administration in Taiwan.[3] Thus, the pace of southern expansion was picking up as war approached in the West.

The conflict in Europe stripped from the British, French, and Dutch colonies in East Asia what little protection they had enjoyed in the days of peace. The General Staff of the Japanese navy immediately sought permission to start by November 15, 1939, the first stage of mobilization of the fleet (about sixty percent of wartime footing), but the Navy Ministry postponed the completion of this order to April 1940. The admirals nevertheless reorganized the navy in November 1939, in order to provide a new fleet for the southern operations. After the German successes in Denmark and Norway in April 1940, the Chief of the Navy General Staff secured permission to carry out the second stage of the fleet mobilization. When the Germans invaded Holland on May 10, the Japanese government sent the new southern fleet, the fourth fleet, to Palau in order to be ready to move against the Dutch East Indies if any other power decided on a preventive occupation.[4] The Western powers did not occupy the Dutch East Indies, however, and the Japanese fleet remained mobilized and poised throughout the summer.

By June 1940, it was clear that neither France nor Britain would be able to offer any real resistance to a Japanese thrust in the south, for the French surrendered to Germany on June 22, and the British were preparing to meet a German invasion. Consequently, both the Dutch East Indies and French Indochina were completely open to invasion. On June 20, 1940, the Navy General Staff and the Military Affairs Bureau of the Navy Ministry began concrete operational research on the southern advance. The participants in this work included members of the navy's Bureau of Construction and the Aircraft Board, who helped to determine when their production schedules would provide optimum naval strength. The investigators concluded that a southern advance would mean war with the United States, Britain, and Holland.[5]

While the navy debated, the army voted for the southern advance. Throughout

July, the army leaders argued that Japan should strike, thereby freeing itself from dependence on imports from the United States. In taking this line, the generals were departing decisively from their earlier preoccupation with Russia. The reasons for this change were numerous. The army leaders had been trying to subdue Chiang Kai-shek by threatening to recognize the new puppet government of Wang Ching-wei, a prominent member of the Chinese Nationalist movement who was supposed to draw his former colleagues into the Japanese camp. But by mid-July, negotiations with Chiang were stymied, and the generals faced the failure of the Wang maneuver and the prolongation of the conflict in China. In such a war of attrition, the army required a continued flow of raw materials from America, yet Roosevelt was threatening to strengthen his weak economic embargo. On the other hand, a victory in Southeast Asia would provide supplies for Japan's war industry and sever Chiang's supply line through Burma. And the generals hoped that the United States might not react to Japan's southern thrust as long as the fate of England was still in doubt. Finally, the army believed that the time was right to advance, since Russia was transferring its forces in Siberia to meet the threat of Germany in Europe. Although this shift in the army's attitude toward the southern advance provided the navy with a rare opportunity to act, the admirals at first hesitated for fear that the Americans would fight. Finally, in mid-July 1940, the two services decided to advance south and to meet the American challenge with force if necessary.[6]

As the German offensive expanded, public pressure for the southern advance also increased. However, Yonai Mitsumasa, a retired admiral who had been Navy minister from February 1937 to July 1939, became Prime Minister in January 1940, and he personally selected as his Navy Minister Yoshida Zengo, with the hope that Yoshida would oppose any hasty military moves. From 1938 on, the navy had been resisting the Axis pact, because Yonai feared that the Germans would involve Japan prematurely in a war with the United States and Britain. In 1939, Yonai did agree to the first cautious steps south, such as taking Hainan, but he continued to shun any great leap into the western colonies as long as Japan's building programs were incomplete. It is from this period of Yonai's resistance to the Axis pact that the legend of the Imperial Navy's moderation dates, yet Yonai was no moderate. Shortly after the China incident began in the fall of 1937, Yonai agreed to send marines to Shanghai, thereby decisively expanding the hostilities. Rejecting all appeals for further arms restrictions, he presided over the adoption of the navy's Fourth Replenishment Program. As Navy Minister, Yonai demanded that Japan take Hainan and the Spratlys, and as Prime Minister, he warned of Japan's interest in the Dutch East Indies, and established a puppet government for all of China. Perhaps Yonai was an unwilling medium for the militarists, but there is a point at which reluctance ends and responsibility begins; and Yonai certainly crossed that line with the attack on Hainan. In fact, Yonai was even willing to enter the Axis pact, granted one condition: inasmuch as Japan's naval building program was not complete, Germany would let the Japanese pick their own time to enter a war with the West. Hitler rejected Yonai's proposal in 1939. But in 1940, the fall of France and the approaching fruition of Japan's naval construction program rendered Yonai's hesitancy obsolete. In June, the parties in the Diet accused the Yonai cabinet of truckling to the West and called for a southern advance. In mid-July, the army lost patience, and the generals, having secured the navy's agreement, toppled the Yonai cabinet by withdrawing the army's support.[7]

The army leaders then procured the nomination of Prince Konoye Fumimaro as Prime Minister, and they reached an agreement with the navy on national policy. The two services insisted that Prime Minister Konoye, Foreign Minister Matsuoka Yōsuke, Army Minister Tōjō Hideki, and Navy Minister Yoshida Zengo unite behind the military's foreign policy before they took office. On July 19, the ministers met and agreed to strengthen Japan's connection with the Axis: they also resolved to continue building up the army to meet the Russian threat, but at the same time to seek a nonaggression pact with the Soviet Union. Finally, they decided that they would "take positive steps, in order to incorporate into the New Order in East Asia, the English, French, Dutch, and Portuguese colonies and their neighboring islands in East Asia." The leaders of the new government also endorsed the navy's warning that, in carrying out the southern expansion, Japan must accept the possibility of war with the United States. The four ministers agreed that they would try to avoid a clash with the Americans, but they also resolved that Japan would meet force with force in carrying out the southern advance.[8] Having agreed in principle to the military's wishes, Konoye became Prime Minister on July 22, 1940.

Five days later the Konoye cabinet formally adopted the policy that the four ministers had accepted on July 19. They immediately faced a new demand when on August 1 the navy advocated moving quickly against French Indochina. The admirals, who wished to start operations against French Indochina in early November 1940, argued that the territory would provide them with firm bases for the advance south, would be useful strategically in operations against England and the United States, and would allow Japan to control the resources necessary for national defense, such as coal, rice, rubber, and iron. The leaders of the navy recognized, however, that an invasion of French Indochina would "increase the probability of a tightened embargo against Japan, and the execution of an embargo on scrap iron and oil is a matter of life and death for the empire, and [if such an embargo is imposed,] the empire will inevitably have to make a firm decision to invade the Dutch East Indies in order to acquire its oil fields." In addition, the admirals admitted that such a move might provoke "hostilities with a third country." Consequently, they asked for funds to continue their military buildup and advocated starting an "emergency wartime mobilization."[9] When the Japanese army entered northern Indochina on September 22, Roosevelt ended exports of scrap iron and steel, and the circle of invasion and embargo closed.

The request of August 1 was the high point of naval optimism in 1940. As the month wore on, it became obvious that England would not surrender to Germany. Though the army continued to argue for an advance into southern French Indochina, the navy decided to delay any attack until 1941, when its Third Replenishment Program was due for completion. The admirals, who had not yet finished their operational plans, believed that they needed time to survey their stockpiles of material and the effects of the Western embargoes on Japanese production before making a final decision. Moreover, after a decision for war it would take the navy eight months to reach full mobilization. Thus, if the southern advance were to start a war with the United States, the navy would need time to get ready. Consequently, the Japanese contented themselves with negotiating the agreement for the establishment of bases in northern Indochina, and beginning economic talks with the Dutch colonial authorities in the East Indies, in order to secure a steady flow of oil to Japan. Despite this delay, the commitment to a southern advance remained firm. On August 27, the cabinet decided that, if the economic talks succeeded, the Dutch East Indies would then be made a member of the Greater East Asia Coprosperity Sphere; that is, the Indonesian people would be freed from Dutch rule, and a new, independent Indonesian government would enter into a defense agreement with Japan.[10]

Thus, the southern advance was a fundamental national policy for the Japanese nation and navy. After Nagano Osami had led Japan out of the London Naval Conference, he had pressed the southern policy on both the army and the Hirota cabinet and had gotten the navy to begin building the ships to carry it out. From 1937 to 1939, despite the distractions of the China incident, the navy made the most of its opportunities to take various bases that would be useful in a later, more extensive advance. Then in the spring and summer of 1940, the eclipse of the European colonial powers convinced the army that the southern policy offered a good chance to cut China from the West and to achieve autarchy for Japan. The army's reversal seems to have caught the navy by surprise, and although the admirals were at first enthusiastic about an immediate southern advance, they decided to avoid hasty action, realizing that a southern advance might bring war with England and the United States. Consequently, before moving south, they wished to survey their needs for materials, calculate the balance of military strength, conduct orderly planning, and mobilize fully. After careful preparations, they would decide whether or not they could go to war.

THE AXIS ALLIANCE AND THE NAVAL BUILDUP

Before moving south, the army leaders also wanted to secure the diplomatic support that an alliance with Germany would provide, believing that such an alliance would tie down Russia and make the Americans shrink from interfering with Japan's expansion. Even before the Konoye cabinet had been established, the army got approval from the navy and from the government for a firm tie with Germany and Italy. Konoye's Foreign Minister, Matsuoka Yōsuke, immediately began negotiations with the Germans. When he relayed to the cabinet Hitler's request that Japan strike against Britain's East Asian possessions as soon as possible, however, the admirals dragged their heels before accepting the pact. They wanted assurances that Japan would not be forced to fight the United States before its preparations were complete. Furthermore, the debate over the pact provided a good opportunity for the navy to seek an increased share of manpower and material in order to complete its construction programs. In the imperial conference of September 19, 1940, the Chief of Staff of the navy, Prince Fushimi, reminded the leaders of the government that the navy had accepted the Axis alliance only on condition that the army and government would provide enough funds to accelerate the navy's war preparations.[11] There was ample reason for the admirals' concern.

In 1940 and 1941, the Japanese navy was being greatly strengthened by the fruits of their Third and Fourth Replenishment Programs. By early 1942, the whole third plan would be complete, including the Yamato-class battleships, and at the same time, the new smaller craft produced under the fourth plan would become available. When in the United States Vinson introduced legislation for large naval appropriations in the fall of 1939, the Japanese navy began considering a Fifth Replenishment Program. This plan called for twice the amount of construction as had taken place under the fourth program, including three superbattleships, two battle cruisers, three carriers, thirty-two destroyers, and forty-five submarines. The superbattleships built under the new program would be even more powerful than their predecessors: they would mount twenty-inch guns instead of eighteen-inch cannon and would be armored to withstand a twenty-inch shell. The Japanese also planned to make their other classes of ship more powerful than their American counterparts, in order to overcome quantity with quality. The navy could begin building at least some of these ships in 1941, but the admirals realized that the whole plan would not be complete for a number of years.

After the fall of France, the United States Congress not only passed Vinson's bill but also appropriated funds for a two-ocean navy, with all the American building to be completed by 1948. In the summer and fall of 1940, therefore, the Japanese navy began calculating the number and type of ships it would need to match this new American buildup. Although the completion of the original fifth program by 1948 would place a great strain on Japan's shipbuilding capacity and resources, it was apparent that Japan would have to build more than double the tonnage of the fifth program by 1948 if it were going to keep pace with the Americans. In the end, the admirals decided that Japan did not have the capacity for such a massive and rapid construction program.[12]

Although Japan lacked the strength to compete with the Americans over the long term, its short-term prospects were much better. By mid-1942, the Japanese navy would reach the peak of its strength relative to the Americans. Toward the end of 1941, the major capital ships of the Third Replenishment Program would be operational, including the two Yamato-class battleships and two Shokakuclass carriers. Moreover, the reconditioning of Japan's older warships and the conversion of auxiliaries and liners into carriers would be complete by 1941. The Japanese were also reconditioning *Hiei*, the older battleship that they had been required to demilitarize and use as a training ship under the treaties, and they were rebuilding some of their light cruisers so as to make them, in effect, full heavy cruisers. Most of this work would be finished by late 1941 or early 1942.[13] Thereafter, American shipyards would outstrip the production of Japan's builders, and the naval balance would tip in an accelerating arc against Japan.

In the governmental debate of these years, the leaders of the Japanese navy clearly stated that the naval balance was a major source of anxiety. They argued that Japan should strike while it had prospects for victory, and they used the naval race to justify their demands for more labor and material. Admiral Kondō Nobutake, Vice Chief of the Navy General Staff, told the liaison conference of military and government leaders on September 14, 1940, that the navy had not yet completed its preparations for war with the United States, but he predicted that the shipyards would finish rebuilding Japan's older ships and militarizing sufficient merchant ships by April 1941. He argued, "When that is done, we have prospects of achieving victory, if we fight an early, decisive battle." Although he admitted that the situation would become "extremely difficult" if the Americans refused an early decision and adopted a strategy of attrition, he nevertheless maintained that the United States was "rapidly building ships, and the gap in the ratio will become increasingly large in the future, and Japan cannot possibly overtake them, and, in that sense, if we go to war, today would be best." [14]

On September 26, 1940, Navy Minister Oikawa Kojirō repeated Kondō's arguments in testimony before the research committee of the Privy Council. He assured the committee that, "at present we have adequate chances of victory, if we meet the Americans in an early decisive battle." But he also reported that, as the Americans were building large numbers of ships, Japan must continue its own construction programs. In August and September of 1940, the leaders of the navy, surveying their capability to withstand a long-term war, told the army that the navy could fight a long war provided that its allocations of material were increased. In other words, the admirals implied, they could build enough ships to win a victory over the United States if they received sufficient resources. It is unclear whether this argument was based on complete confidence or on a vague belief that their own attrition strategy and the superior quality of Japan's weapons would be enough to overcome the United States' increasing naval strength. Nevertheless, on December 17, 1940, the army and government fulfilled the navy's request for more supplies.[15]

There was one key resource that the navy itself would have to provide, since in any long war Japan would lack oil for its fleet. Navy Minister Oikawa assured the Privy Council research committee that, although Japan would have to control its oil consumption carefully, it would have enough to fight for a considerable period during a war of attrition. Oikawa explained that the navy had been in-

creasing the amount of its crude oil in storage and setting up facilities for artificial oil manufacture and for producing high-octane gasoline. He added that
''artificial oil alone will be insufficient, but we expect [to get oil from] the Dutch
East Indies and North Sakhalin.'' [16]

In October and November 1940, the Japanese navy began planning the southern advance. After conducting drawing board exercises, the leaders of the navy
concluded that an attack on the south would inevitably mean war with the United
States and Britain. They therefore decided that they would fight the Western
powers only after setting up a defensive sphere in the south. It was obvious that
the Japanese fleet would not be able to hang back near the Philippines, awaiting
an American advance, for the Americans might not risk crossing through Japan's
mandated islands, and in any case, the Japanese navy would have to protect the
sea lanes between the Dutch East Indies and Tokyo. Consequently, the strategic
planners moved the site of the expected decisive capital ship encounter to the
Marianas and Carolines. Even with the battle moved to the mandated islands, attrition by Japan's land-based aircraft and by submarines would still be possible,
and it was expected that this fleet encounter would preserve the integrity of
Japan's sphere in the south. On October 15, 1940, the navy ordered the second
stage mobilization to begin, with the end of March 1941 as the target date, and
full mobilization to be completed by November 15, 1941.[17]

Thus, by the end of 1940, the Japanese navy was committed in principle to advancing south in the fall of 1941 and had begun mobilizing for war. It had accepted the army's suggestion that Japan exploit the remarkably favorable international situation by seizing the derelict colonies of Europe and establishing an
autarchic empire in the western Pacific. The admirals had also agreed to link
arms with Germany, and they had used the army's new enthusiasm to extract additional resources for their construction programs. They knew, however, that
Japan's chance would soon pass, since American naval building would render
their plans impossible in the future.

THE NAVY'S DECISION FOR WAR

These were not easy months for the navy's high command. The debate over
the Axis alliance, southern expansion, operations in the south, and war with the
West produced considerable friction, which in turn led to frequent changes in
ranking personnel. Yonai's choice for the Navy Ministry, Yoshida Zengo, resigned during the debate over the Axis pact. Oikawa Kojirō, who replaced him,
continued in office until he began having doubts about the southern advance in
September 1941. His job was taken over by Shimada Shigetarō, who had been
Vice Chief of the Navy General Staff in 1936, when the navy had forced the
Hirota cabinet to adopt the southern policy. In September 1940, Ishikawa Shingo, chief of the second section (political affairs) of the Military Affairs Bureau
and a follower of Katō Kanji who had advocated ending the disarmament treaties and building superbattleships in 1933, also joined the Navy Ministry staff. A

similar change took place in the navy's General Staff when Prince Fushimi resigned as Chief of Staff in April 1941, and his place was taken by Nagano Osami, who had led the Japanese delegation out of the disarmament talks in 1936 and had been the prime mover behind the adoption of the southern advance by the Hirota cabinet.[18] Thus, as the time for decision approached, the doubters departed, and the spiritual heirs of Katō Kanji returned to power.

The navy continued to press for a slow southern advance but resisted any large-scale move before its mobilization was complete. Thus, during January and February 1941, the navy leaders tried to have the Japanese government acquire bases at Cam Ranh Bay and airfields near Saigon in French Indochina. But they refused Matsuoka's pleas for a full attack on the Dutch East Indies, Malaya, and Singapore, arguing that, although their preparations were sufficient to deal with Britain and Holland, they were not yet ready to fight the Americans. The leaders of the army at first endorsed Matsuoka's position, perhaps because they expected the Germans to invade Britain in the spring. But when the navy resisted, the generals agreed that the southern advance should take place only when the navy was ready or if the Americans forced Japan's hand by decreeing a complete embargo.[19]

In May 1941, the navy began a full review of the question of war with the United States. The leaders of the navy had decided to set up three liaison committees in November 1940, in order to coordinate the work of the Navy General Staff and the Navy Ministry. The task of the first committee was to consider matters of national policy, while the other two would coordinate the navy's military preparations and its intelligence operations. In May, the members of the first committee began a final study to decide whether or not the navy could advance south and risk war with the United States, and they completed their work by June 5. The researchers had been thorough, having studied the state of Japan's supplies, the international situation, the attitude of the army, and the availability of shipping before reaching a decision. In the end they decided that Japan had to make a firm decision to move south despite the danger of war with the United States.

One reason that the leaders of the navy were eager to secure a formal decision for war was that their mobilization was running into snags. Other sections of the government were not cooperating with the navy, and the admirals wished to settle the issue of war once and for all in order to be able to exercise their right to men and materials. There were other, more basic calculations in the report of the first committee. Its members argued that Japan could establish autarchy ''in the special resources needed in wartime for the expansion of our armaments and production capacity'' if it took control of Thailand, French Indochina, and the Dutch East Indies. By seizing bases in French Indochina, they claimed, Japan could build ''an impregnable position.'' They assumed that there was a strong possibility of Germany's attack on England succeeding. They also anticipated

that the Western powers might cut off Japan's supplies of oil and other war materials if the empire advanced into French Indochina and Thailand, in which case,
"the Imperial Navy must decide to fight without delay." [20]

The Americans and British provided yet another reason for Japan's decision,
because by spreading their ships across the globe, they had recreated as favorable
a strategic opportunity as the Russians had presented to Admiral Tōgō in 1904.
In fact, the Japanese navy could concentrate a superior fleet against the remaining English and American forces in the Pacific. For some time the British had
been begging the Americans for aid in the Atlantic, and in March 1941, the
Western nations finally worked out an arrangement that promised Britain some
relief. The United States agreed to send one-quarter of its fleet to the Atlantic,
and the British promised to send a comparable number of ships to Singapore.
However, although Roosevelt was able to bring the United States' Atlantic fleet
up to a strength of eight battleships, four carriers, and numerous light craft, the
sorely pressed British could not keep their part of the bargain. Because of losses
in the Atlantic and the Mediterranean, the English sent only two battleships to the
Pacific in the fall of 1941 instead of the six battleships that they had promised.
And the Americans could not refill this gap in the Pacific, since they found themselves fully engaged in patrols against Axis submarines and raiders in the western
Atlantic.[21]

By the fall of 1941, then, Japan had achieved absolute equality in the Pacific
with the forces of the Western Allies, as shown by the following figures on com-
parative Pacific naval strengths: [22]

	Battleships	Carriers	Cruisers	Destroyers	Submarines
United States	9	3	24	80	56
Great Britain	2	0	8	13	
Dutch and					
Free French	0	0	4	7	13
TOTAL	11	3	36	100	69
JAPAN	10	10	36	113	63

Actually, however, effective Allied strength was lower than these figures indicate throughout most of 1941, because the Allied forces were spread from
Hawaii across the Philippines to the Dutch East Indies and on to Singapore, and
the Japanese could easily concentrate superior forces against these scattered
ships. By the time the Allied fleets could recover from a Japanese surprise attack,
recall ships from the Atlantic, and launch a trans-Pacific drive, it would be the
summer of 1942, when the Japanese navy would have the new superbattleships
and additional light craft in its fleet. The Americans and British had provided an
ideal opportunity, which was unlikely to come again. And it appeared that the
Western leaders, who had haughtily kept Japan from racial and naval equality in

the past and who were enforcing an ever-tightening embargo on Japan in the present, would not fail to send a fleet to recover their colonial possessions in the Pacific. Such, it appears, were the premises on which Japan's admirals based their decision for war.

In spite of their naval weakness, the Americans were asking the Japanese in the spring of 1941 to make a critical choice: either agree to abandon the advance into China and Southeast Asia, or face an embargo that would eventually strangle Japan's military effort. Because of the increasing tension, the United States and Japan began talks to establish a temporary modus vivendi, but by June the negotiators, Cordell Hull and Nomura Kichisaburō, had reached a standoff. At the outset, the Japanese had offered to forgo a move into Southeast Asia and to stay out of the world war, provided that the Americans did not attack Germany. But the price they demanded in return was high: the Americans would have to guarantee that Japan receive war materials from the Western hemisphere and Southeast Asia and would have to insist that Chiang Kai-shek submit to Japanese rule in China. For their part, the Americans wanted the Japanese to ignore the increasing pressure that the United States Navy was putting on Germany in the Atlantic, to refrain from advancing in Southeast Asia, and to withdraw in stages from China. If Japan would give up its previous gains, the Americans would continue to provide Japan with vital supplies. By June, the diplomatic stalemate was apparent to all, for Japan would not forgo its planned empire in China, and the United States would not forsake China and Britain.[23]

From the middle of 1940 on, the Americans had been signaling that they would cut off fuel for Japan's war machine if the Japanese continued to advance. After the war began in Europe, Roosevelt began restricting the sale of strategic materials that might be needed in the United States' own rearmament program. Then after the fall of France, Roosevelt stopped the export of aviation fuel and top-grade scrap to Japan. The implication was clear: if Japan tried to exploit France's difficulties, the Americans would use their leverage as the supplier of Japanese industry to halt Japan's march.

In September 1940, when the Japanese entered French Indochina, Roosevelt cut off scrap iron and steel. Japan's attempts to find alternate sources of supply were unsuccessful. Japan also tried in vain to persuade the leaders of the Dutch East Indies to increase their oil shipments to Japan. In January 1941, the Americans gradually extended the embargo to such vital materials as copper and brass, and by June 1941, many Japanese industries were affected by the wide-ranging American restrictions. Finally on June 20, Roosevelt announced that, owing to domestic shortages, the Americans would no longer ship oil to Japan from ports on the eastern seaboard.[24]

Thus, there seemed to be little hope on the diplomatic front, and time was beginning to run against Japan. As the months went by, the embargoes would sap Japan's economic strength, and in two years the Americans would begin to overtake Japan in the naval race. But if Japan took decisive action at once, there was hope: the Japanese navy could win a decisive fleet encounter while it still had a lead over the scattered forces of its enemies.

THE CABINET'S DECISION

After receiving the first committee's report, Nagano began urging the cabinet in June 1941 to decide formally for the southern advance. As the days passed, Nagano and the navy acquired still another reason for wanting an immediate decision: reports from Germany indicating that Hitler might attack Russia in the near future had revived the desire of the Japanese army to deal the Soviet Union a decisive blow. The leaders of the navy feared that the chance for the southern advance would never return if the army opened a new front in Siberia.

The debate went on through June. The navy leaders insisted that Japan concentrate its efforts in the south and speed up its timetable for the advance. On June 11, 1941, Japan's admirals called for a quick thrust to establish bases in southern Indochina. Nagano explained: "We must build bases in French Indochina and Thailand in order to launch military operations. We must resolutely attack anyone who tries to stop us." On June 25, the army agreed to accelerate the southern advance; in return, the admirals promised to go to war against Russia after the end of operations in the south, if a favorable opportunity presented itself. On July 2, an imperial conference confirmed this basic decision. Japan would advance south in the near future, and would then turn north to deal with Russia. The Japanese leaders resolved: "In carrying out the plans outlined above, our empire will not be deterred by the possibility of being involved in a war with Great Britain and the United States." [25]

Admiral Nagano kept up the pressure during July. On July 12, he asked that Ambassador Nomura be called home from Washington. On July 21, the Japanese government received French approval for their move into southern Indochina, and Japanese troops began arriving in the former French colony on July 24. Nagano immediately called for a firm decision on Japan's next move south. On July 21, he stated:

> Although at present we have prospects for victory over the United States, as time passes the probability of our success will decrease and by the latter half of next year, we will have difficulty matching them, and thereafter things will become worse and worse; the Americans will probably prolong the issue and not settle it until they finish arming. Consequently, as time passes, the empire will be at a disadvantage. Nothing would be better than ending this without fighting. But if we decide that a clash cannot possibly be avoided, then I want you to know that we will be at a disadvantage as time passes. Furthermore, if we occupy the Philippines, the war will be easier to conduct for the navy.

On July 25, he told Admiral Kobayashi that Japan should attack before the chains of encirclement were completely forged, adding, "there is no choice left but to fight." [26] Thus, the official spokesman for the Imperial Navy demanded war with the United States four days before the Western oil embargo was announced, and he insisted that the government carry out its decision of July 2 by advancing to the south.

The Western powers responded to Japan's occupation of southern Indochina by ending all trade with the empire, including the supply of oil. Consequently, Japan's civilian leaders realized that the southern advance would almost certainly bring about war with the United States and Britain. By the end of August, the mobilization of the navy was ninety percent complete. On August 16, the leaders of the navy asked the army to agree to start operations at the end of October, until which time the Nomura negotiations could continue. On August 30, the army approved the proposed date, and on September 6, an imperial conference formally adopted the end of October as the date for beginning the war. Navy Minister Oikawa warned that the other members of the government should not open this decision to further debate in late October.[27]

Nagano explained to the imperial conference on September 6 that "the military preparedness of the [Western] countries, particularly of the United States, is being strengthened with great speed. By the latter half of next year the United States' military preparedness will have made great progress, and it will be difficult to cope with her." Nagano probably based his statement on a study done by the Navy General Staff in July and August, which concluded that Japan, by using its attrition and ambush strategy, would have a chance for victory as long as it retained a 5/10 ratio vis-á-vis the Americans. The researchers predicted that Japan would have seventy percent of the United States' strength at the end of 1941, sixty-five percent in 1942, fifty percent in 1943, and only thirty percent by 1944. Thus, by the first half of 1943, American naval strength would be approaching a 10/5 ratio. The study also estimated that Japan had only 320,000 tons of warships under construction, while the Americans had 900,000 tons on the ways. Nagano cited other reasons for haste: the Americans and British were strengthening their defenses in the south, and the Western embargo would progressively weaken Japan.[28] Clearly, time was running out.

The navy's decision for war and its operational planning for the southern advance went forward only at the cost of some internal friction. Admiral Yonai's loyal supporter at the Navy Ministry in the fight against the Axis pact, Yamamoto Isoroku, was the commander of the combined fleets in 1941. He evidently believed that carriers would play an important role in the future, and he thus had doubts about the attrition and ambush strategy of the battleship admirals. As a believer in air strength, Yamamoto and his friend Inoue Shigeyoshi, the head of the Aviation Section of the Navy General Staff, feared that Japan lacked the aircraft and carriers to defeat the Americans. But compared to the many members of the Navy General Staff, Yamamoto and Inoue comprised only a small and weak minority of two. Yamamoto warned his superiors that war with the United States was a dangerous undertaking. Japan would have to disperse its fleet in order to carry out the southern advance, he argued, and if the American fleet intervened, Japan would suffer severe losses. Therefore, Yamamoto asked permission to carry out a raid against Pearl Harbor, in order to damage the American fleet sufficiently to keep it temporarily on the defensive. Throughout the spring and summer of 1941, the General Staff resisted Yamamoto's suggestions, but Nagano finally agreed to give Yamamoto the carriers his operation required, and the General Staff's acceptance of the Pearl Harbor raid reconciled Yamamoto to the war.[29]

On September 25, both the army and the navy demanded that the government agree by October 15 to begin hostilities in November. Caught in a web of his own spinning, Prime Minister Konoye began searching desperately for a solution. He asked permission to delay the start of the southern advance while he arranged a summit conference with President Roosevelt. Both general staffs resisted Konoye's maneuver, and the Americans demanded the establishment of a common ground for negotiations before the leaders met. Nevertheless, Konoye continued to ask Japan's military leaders for more time to seek an agreement. Japan's generals, however, were growing impatient, since they wanted to finish the southern operation and concentrate on preparing for war with Russia. At an informal conference with the military ministers held at his home on October 12, Konoye pleaded for a reprieve, but the Navy Minister refused, warning that any further negotiations would have to be guaranteed of success, since Japan could not fight at a later date.

It was clear that Konoye could not pledge that the talks would succeed, for in fact the negotiators had reached a complete deadlock. In asking for the summit meeting, Konoye revealed that Japan's demands had not changed: an end of Western aid to China and settlement of the war with China on Japan's terms; a Japanese standstill in Southeast Asia in return for the renewed supply of war materials; no Japanese attack on the Soviet Union but its continued adherence to the Axis alliance. The Americans were not willing to abandon China, and Roosevelt refused to meet Konoye without first establishing some basis for successful negotiations. The Japanese and Americans were as far apart as ever, and Japan's oil hoard was starting to shrink. Finally, Konoye resigned, and War Minister Tōjō Hideki formed a new cabinet. Shimada Shigetarō, Nagano's old ally, became Navy Minister, and Tōgō Shigenori, the career diplomat, became Foreign Minister. For the most part, however, the personnel in the cabinet remained unchanged.[30]

Tōjō promised the Emperor that his government would put off a final decision while reviewing once again Japan's capacity for war. After a series of inconclusive meetings in which the participants argued over vague estimates of Japan's resources, the members of the liaison conference held a seventeen-hour meeting on November 1. Finance Minister Kaya Okinori expressed the fear that the military had not projected carefully the amounts of material Japan would need in case of war. In fact, the navy had suddenly increased its projected demand for steel for 1942. Kaya asked Nagano whether Japan would be able to defend itself after three years if it refused to go to war in 1941. Nagano replied that it would be easier to go to war immediately, because "now we have the necessary foundation for it." Kaya argued that the Americans would not attack Japan even after the passage of three years had weakened the empire, and Foreign Minister Tōgō supported him. With this, the exchange became heated: "Nagano: There is a saying, 'Don't rely on what won't come.' The future is uncertain . . . In three years enemy defenses in the south will be strong, and the number of enemy warships will also increase. Kaya: Well, then, when can we go to war and win? Nagano: Now! The time for war will not come later!'' In the end, the liaison conference decided to start hostilities in early December.[31]

The naval race, then, was one of the main reasons for Japan's attack on Pearl Harbor. The leaders of the Imperial Navy had withdrawn from the disarmament system and begun building a fleet that would allow the Japanese Empire to bring the southern Pacific under its sway. Despite the distractions of the war in China, the admirals held to their course, and in 1940 they decided to take advantage of the eclipse of the colonial powers by Germany. But at the same time, the United States responded to the Japanese challenge and to the crisis in Europe with an enormous naval building program and with full diplomatic support of China and Great Britain. The completion of the new American naval program threatened to extinguish all hope for a Japanese victory by late 1943 or early 1944. Consequently, the leaders of the Japanese navy decided to strike while they had enough ships to carry out their strategy. With the help of the army, they forced the Japanese government to risk a full American embargo by taking southern Indochina. After July 1941, the United States oil embargo added another incentive to strike quickly, before the naval balance had tipped against the empire. Less than five years after the naval treaties had lapsed, Japanese planes were leaving their carriers to attack the American battle fleet at Pearl Harbor.

Conclusion

In 1930, the Pacific was at peace. Each power lay secure within a net of treaty obligations and under bonds of mutual deterrence. By 1940, Japan's quest for an autonomous empire had destroyed the old Washington system, Japan's army had sunk into a wasting war in China, and its navy was about to fall behind in an accelerating naval race with the United States. The calm waters of 1930 had become a troubled, dangerous sea by 1940, and the failure of the Second London Naval Conference had helped to stir the storm.

It is difficult to gauge the importance of the individual events that led up to Pearl Harbor, for each must be judged in relation to the other. Japanese aggression in China and Southeast Asia brought tightened Western embargoes against Japan. In turn, these embargoes increased Japan's need to expand south, and the evolving southern drive made a Japanese connection with the Axis seem desirable. In Europe, Germany's conquest of France, its threat to England, and the early successes of its campaign against Russia turned the old international order upside down. In the fall of 1940, the Axis alliance drove the Americans, British, Chinese, and Dutch together in an entente to deter further Japanese moves. And in order to preserve the entente, the Americans endorsed China's terms for a settlement of the Sino-Japanese War, thereby closing the door to any fundamental compromise with Japan.

Japan's advance into China and Southeast Asia, coupled with the success of Hitler's attacks in Europe, reversed the flow of American public opinion, and Roosevelt, who had for so long stood helpless on the sidelines, began to provide all possible aid to the Allies short of war. By mid-1941, his naval patrols against Germany in the Atlantic and his tightening economic embargoes against Japan in the Pacific had edged the United States up to the very border of belligerency. Finally in July 1941, when Japan continued its southern advance despite Allied warnings, Roosevelt stopped supplying Japan's ships with oil. In short, great events in distant parts of the world followed so closely upon one another that it is difficult to sort cause from effect. But through this grey tangle ran the red thread of the naval race, which had begun long before these final critical years.

The naval system had collapsed, not because it threatened or discriminated against Japan, but because it assumed that Japan was a satisfied power. By 1934, however, the Japanese advocates of disarmament had fallen, and the expansionists in the army and navy had taken charge. Although their control was not absolute, they could usually push the cabinet down the road to expansion by a combination of argument, propaganda, and threats of domestic violence.

Japan's military leaders thought that expansion was both necessary and possible. They believed that the leaders of the United States and Great Britain were closing the doors of their empires to peaceful Japanese economic advances, while remaining blind to the fact that they lacked the military strength to resist any forceful move by the Japanese. Consequently, Japan's admirals believed that if they freed themselves from the restrictions of the treaties, they could build a strong fleet, secure a sphere in China and Southeast Asia, and become one of the great world powers.

Distracted by troubles in Europe, by domestic economic distress, and by extreme political partisanship, the Americans and the British refrained from entering into the naval competition until very late in the day. But by 1941, the sudden and massive entry into the naval race by the United States cast a steadily lengthening shadow over Japan's building programs. Faced with both the frustration of their plans for expansion and a counterbalance to the fleet for which they had made great economic sacrifices, the leaders of Japan's navy decided to seek battle while they were still fairly confident of victory. In December 1941, naval technology, which had been controlled until 1936 by the Washington and London naval treaties, finally seized the wheel and sailed for war.

Bibliography   Notes   Index

NOTE ON PRINCIPAL SOURCES

For information on the diplomacy of the thirties, the archives of the Japanese Ministry of Foreign Affairs are available to scholars in two places: on microfilm at the Library of Congress in Washington and in the original at the Foreign Ministry Archives in Tokyo. There are significant gaps in all of the records, especially for the late thirties; however, those engaged in microfilming the records for the Library of Congress missed some important documents, so that the most thorough research is possible only in Tokyo. Japanese military records are more difficult to use, since the papers at Japan's Defense Agency in Tokyo are presently unavailable, being organized and studied for a multivolume history of Japan's army and navy. Fortunately, Tsunoda Jun, Director of the Shidehara Peace Collection at the Diet Library, and his associates have collected and published many of these military documents in *Gendai shi shiryō,* vols. VIII–XIII, and in *Taiheiyō sensō e no michi,* vol. VIII. Private papers, such as those of Katō Kanji (Shakai kagaku kenkyūjo, Tokyo University) and Saitō Makoto (Kensei shiryō shitsu), are also helpful.

Much of the material on the American side has been published by the Department of State in its well-edited series *Papers Relating to the Foreign Relations of the United States;* the State Department records themselves merely add minor details to the story. The general records of the Navy Department at the National Archives in Washington are useful, but the records of the General Board at the Washington Navy Yard provide even better sources on the general trends of naval policy. For Franklin D. Roosevelt's first administration, selected documents appear in Edgar B. Nixon's *Franklin D. Roosevelt and Foreign Affairs.* Much of the Roosevelt collection at Hyde Park, New York, is well indexed and available, although it should be noted that materials are still being declassified. At the Manuscripts Division of the Library of Congress, the papers of Norman H. Davis are helpful, but those of Cordell Hull, William D. Leahy, and Ernest J. King are thin indeed. For the view from the State Department, the diaries of J. Pierrepont Moffat and William Phillips at the Houghton Library, Harvard University, are informative. Meredith W. Berg's dissertation on the second London Naval Conference provides a summary and analysis of the negotiations from the American side.

For the British view, the archives of the cabinet, Foreign Office, and Admiralty are available at the Public Record Office in London. The Foreign Office records are well indexed and numerous, but the key papers for understanding British decision-making in this period are in the records of the British cabinet. By comparison, the records of the British Admiralty are fairly meager.

Certain secondary sources proved essential for studying Japanese, American, and British foreign policy in the thirties. On Japan, the seven volumes of *Taiheiyō sensō e no michi* are indispensable. In English, there are the ground-breaking works of James B. Crowley and Robert J. C. Butow. For the American side of the story, studies by Selig Adler, Dorothy Borg, Herbert Feis, Waldo Heinrichs, William L. Langer and S. Everett Gleason, and William L. Leuchtenberg proved most helpful. Because British records have been open for a shorter time than the American and Japanese, key secondary works are still in preparation, with the notable exceptions of the work of Stephen W. Roskill on the Royal Navy and of William Roger Louis on Britain's Far Eastern policy.

The diplomatic history of the thirties is still being explored in a very preliminary way, and much remains to be done. The archives have barely been touched, particularly those in England and Japan. In future years there will undoubtedly be major additions to our present knowledge.

Bibliography

Acheson, Dean. *Present at the Creation: My Years at the State Department.* New York, Norton, 1969.

Adler, Selig. *The Isolationist Impulse: Its Twentieth Century Reaction.* New York, Abelard-Schuman, 1957.

―――. *The Uncertain Giant, 1921–1941: American Foreign Policy Between the Wars.* New York, Macmillan, 1965.

ADM. Records of the British Admiralty, Public Record Office, London.

Agawa, Hiroyuki 阿川弘之. *Yamamoto Isoroku* 山本五十六. Tokyo, 1965.

Aritake, Shūji 有竹修二. *Saitō Makoto* 斎藤実. Tokyo, 1958.

―――. *Okada Keisuke* 岡田啓介. Tokyo, 1956.

―――. *Shōwa no saishō* 昭和の宰相 (Shōwa Prime Ministers). Tokyo, 1967.

Asada, Sadao. "The Role of the Japanese Navy, 1931–1941." Paper presented at the Conference on Japanese-American Relations, July 14–18, 1969, Hakone, Japan.

Asahi jyānaru 朝日ジャーナル (Asahi Journal), ed. *Shōwashi no shunkan* 昭和史の瞬間 (Moments in Shōwa history). 2 vols. Tokyo, 1966.

Attlee, Clement R. *As It Happened.* London, Heinemann, 1954.

Avon, Earl of (Anthony Eden). *The Eden Memoirs: Facing the Dictators.* London, Cassell, 1962.

―――. *The Eden Memoirs: The Reckoning.* London, Cassell, 1965.

Barnes, Harry E., ed. *Perpetual War for Perpetual Peace: A Critical Examination of the Foreign Policy of Franklin Delano Roosevelt and Its Aftermath.* Caldwell, Ida., Caxton, 1953.

Beard, Charles A. *American Foreign Policy in the Making, 1932–1940: A Study in Responsibilities.* New Haven, Yale University Press, 1946.

―――. *President Roosevelt and the Coming of the War, 1941: A Study in Appearances and Realities.* New Haven, Yale University Press, 1948.

Berg, Meredith W. "The United States and the Breakdown of Naval Limitation, 1934–1939." Ph. D. diss., Tulane University, 1966.

Bloch, Charles. "Great Britain, German Rearmament, and the Naval Agreement of 1935." In Hans W. Gatzke, ed. and trans. *European Diplomacy Between Two Wars, 1919–1939.* Chicago, Quadrangle, 1972.

Blum, John M., ed. *From the Morgenthau Diaries,* vol. I: *Years of Crisis, 1928–1938;* vol. II: *Years of Urgency, 1938–1941.* Boston, Houghton Mifflin, 1959, 1965.

Bōeichō, bōeikenshūjo, senshishitsu 防衛庁防衛研修所戦史室 (Defense Ministry, Defense Research Institute, War History Branch), ed. *Daihon'ei rikugunbu, I: Shōwa jūgonen gogatsu made* 大本營陸軍部〈I〉昭和十五年五月まで (The army section of imperial headquarters, I: To May 1940). Tokyo, 1967.

―――. *Kaigun gunsenbi,* vol. I: *Shōwa jūrokunen jūichigatsu made* 海軍軍戦備〈I〉昭和十六年十一月まで (The navy's war preparations, vol. I: To November 1941). Tokyo, 1969.

Borg, Dorothy. *The United States and the Far Eastern Crisis of 1933–1938*. Cambridge, Harvard University Press, 1964.

Bowen, Harold G. *Ships, Machinery, and Mossbacks: The Autobiography of a Naval Engineer*. Princeton, Princeton University Press, 1954.

Boyle, John Hunter. *China and Japan at War, 1937–1945: The Politics of Collaboration*. Stanford, Stanford University Press, 1972.

Brodie, Bernard. *A Guide to Naval Strategy*. Princeton, Princeton University Press, 1958.

Buckley, Thomas H. *The United States and the Washington Conference, 1921–1922*. Knoxville, University of Tennessee Press, 1970.

Bungei shunjū 文芸春秋.

Bunker, Gerald E. *The Peace Conspiracy: Wang Ching-wei and the China War, 1937–1941*. Cambridge, Harvard University Press, 1972.

Burns, James M. *Roosevelt: The Lion and the Fox*. New York, Harcourt, Brace, and World, 1956.

Butow, Robert J. C. *Tōjō and the Coming of the War*. Princeton, Princeton University Press, 1961.

Byas, Hugh. *Government by Assassination*. New York, Knopf, 1942.

CAB. Records of the British Cabinet, Public Record Office, London.

Chūgai shōgyō shinpō 中外商業新報.

Chūgai zaikai 中外財界.

Chūō kōron 中央公論.

Churchill, Winston S. *The Second World War*, vol. I: *The Gathering Storm;* vol. II: *Their Finest Hour*. Boston, Houghton Mifflin, 1948–1949.

Cole, Wayne S. *Senator Gerald P. Nye and American Foreign Relations*. Minneapolis, University of Minnesota Press, 1962.

Colvin, Ian. *Vansittart in Office: An Historical Survey of the Origins of the Second World War Based on the Papers of Sir Robert Vansittart, Permanent Under-Secretary of State for Foreign Affairs, 1930–1938*. London, Gollancz, 1965.

Cooper, Duff (Viscount Norwich). *Old Men Forget: The Autobiography of Duff Cooper*. London, Hart-Davies, 1954.

Craven, W. F., and J. L. Cate, eds. *The Army Air Forces in World War II*. 7 vols. Chicago, University of Chicago, 1948–1958.

Crowley, James B. "A New Deal for Japan and Asia: One Road to Pearl Harbor." In Crowley, ed. *Modern East Asia: Essays in Interpretation*. New York, Harcourt, Brace, and World, 1970.

———. *Japan's Quest for Autonomy: National Security and Foreign Policy, 1930–1938*. Princeton, Princeton University Press, 1966.

Dalton, Hugh. *The Fateful Years: Memoirs, 1931–1945*. London, Muller, 1957.

Davis, George T. *A Navy Second to None: The Development of Modern American Naval Policy*. New York, Harcourt, Brace, 1940.

Davis, Norman H. Papers, Manuscript Division, Library of Congress, Washington, D.C.

Divine, Robert A. *The Illusion of Neutrality*. Chicago, University of Chicago Press, 1962.

Fairbank, John K., Edwin O. Reischauer and Albert M. Craig. *A History of East Asian Civilization*, vol. II: *East Asia, The Modern Transformation*. Boston, Houghton, Mifflin, 1965.

Farley, James A. *Jim Farley's Story: The Roosevelt Years*. New York, McGraw-Hill, 1948.

Feiling, Keith. *The Life of Neville Chamberlain*. London, MacMillan, 1946.

Feis, Herbert. *The Road to Pearl Harbor: The Coming of the War Between the United States and Japan.* Princeton, Princeton University Press, 1950.

Ferrell, Robert H. *American Diplomacy in the Great Depression: Hoover-Stimson Foreign Policy, 1929–1933.* New Haven, Yale University Press, 1957.

FO. Records of the British Foreign Office, Public Record Office, London.

Freidel, Frank. *Franklin D. Roosevelt,* vol. I: *The Apprenticeship.* Boston, Little, Brown, 1952.

Fukui, Shizuo 福井静夫. *Nihon no gunkan* 日本の軍艦 (Japan's Warships). Tokyo, 1956.

Gaikō jihō 外交事報.

Gaimushō hyakunenshi hensankai 外務省百年史編纂会 (Foreign Office Hundred-Year History Editorial Group) ed. *Gaimushō no hyakunen* (One Hundred Years of the Japanese Foreign Office). 2 vols. Tokyo, 1969.

Gendai 現代.

George, Margaret. *The Warped Vision: British Foreign Policy, 1933–1939.* Pittsburgh, University of Pittsburgh Press, 1965.

Gilbert, Martin, and Richard Gott. *The Appeasers.* London, Weidenfield and Nicolson, 1962.

Greene, Fred. "The Military View of American National Policy, 1904–1940," *American Historical Review* 66.2:354–377 (1961).

Grew, Joseph C. *Ten Years in Japan.* New York, Simon and Schuster, 1944.

GSS. Gendai shi shiryō 現代史資料 (Documents on Modern History), ed. Tsunoda Jun 角田順. Vols. 8–12, Tokyo, 1964–1965.

Halifax, Earl of (Edward Wood). *Fulness of Days.* London, Collins, 1957.

Halsey, William F., and J. Bryan, III. *Admiral Halsey's Story.* New York, Whittlesey, 1947.

Hanmura, Sen'ichi 榛村専一. *Shinbun hōsei ron* 新聞法制論 (A discussion of the newspaper laws). Tokyo, 1968.

Harada, Kumao 原田熊雄. *Saionji Kō to seikyoku* 西園寺公と政局 (Prince Saionji and politics). Tokyo, 1951.

Harvey, John, ed. *The Diplomatic Diaries of Oliver Harvey, 1937–1940.* London, Collins, 1970.

Hashimoto, Motome 橋本求. *Nihon shuppan hanbaishi* 日本出版販売史 (A history of Japanese publishing). Tokyo, 1964.

Havighurst, Alfred F. *Twentieth-Century Britain.* New York, Harper and Row, 1962.

Hayashi, Katsuya 林克也. *Nihon gunji gijutsushi* 日本軍事技術史 (A history of Japan's military technology). Tokyo, 1957.

Heinrichs, Waldo H. *American Ambassador: Joseph C. Grew and the Development of the United States Diplomatic Tradition.* Boston, Little, Brown, 1966.

———. "Japanese-American Relations, 1931–1941: The Role of the United States Navy." Paper presented at the Conference on Japanese-American Relations, July 14–18, 1969, Hakone, Japan.

Hezlett, Arthur. *Aircraft and Sea Power.* New York, Stein and Day, 1970.

Hirota Kōki denki kankōkai 広田弘毅伝記刊行会 (Hirota Kōki biographical association). *Hirota Kōki.* Tokyo, 1966.

Hōchi shinbun 報知新聞.

Hosoya, Chihiro, Saitō, Makoto, Imai, Seiichi, and Rōyama, Michio 細谷千博, 斉藤真, 今井清一, 蠟山道雄. Nichibei kankeishi: kaisen ni itaru jūnen (1931–1941) 日米関係史:開戦に至る10年 (Japanese-American Relations: The Ten Years to the Outbreak of the War). 4 vols. Tokyo, 1972.

Hull, Cordell. *The Memoirs of Cordell Hull*. 2 vols. New York, Macmillan, 1948.
———. Papers, Manuscript Division, Library of Congress, Washington, D.C.
Ickes, Harold L. *The Secret Diary of Harold L. Ickes*. 3 vols. New York, Simon and Schuster, 1953–1955.
Ienaga, Saburō 家永三郎. *Taiheiyō sensō* 太平洋戦争 (The Pacific war). Tokyo, 1968.
Ike, Nobutaka, ed. and trans. *Japan's Decision for War: Records of the 1941 Policy Conferences*. Stanford, Stanford University Press, 1967.
Ikeda, Kiyoshi 池田清. *Nihon no kaigun* 日本の海軍 (The Japanese navy). 2 vols. Tokyo, 1967.
———. "Rondon kaigun jōyaku to tōsuiken mondai" ロンドン海軍条約と統帥権問題 (The London Naval Conference and the controversy over the right of supreme command), *Hōgaku zasshi* 法学雑誌 (Law review) 15:2 (1968).
Ikei, Masaru 池井優. "Manshū jihen o meguru NichiBei sōgo imēji" 満州事変をめぐる日米相互イメージ (Mutual images of the United States and Japan concerning the Manchurian incident), *Kokusai seiji* 国際政治 (International politics) 2:58–74 (1968).
Iklé, Frank William. *German-Japanese Relations, 1936–1941*. New York, Bookman, 1956.
Imamura, Takeo 今村武雄. *Takahashi Korekiyo hyōden* 高橋是清評伝 (Takahashi Korekiyo: A critical biography). Tokyo, 1965.
Inō, Tentarō 稲生典太郎. "Meiji ikō ni okeru 'sensō miraiki' no ryūkō to sono shōchō" 明治以降における戦争未来記の流行とその消長 (The post-Meiji vogue for "future war" fiction and its vicissitudes), *Kokugakuin daigaku yōran* 国学院大学要覧 (Kokugakuin University review) 7:129–165 (1969).
Iriye, Akira. *After Imperialism: The Search for a New Order in the Far East, 1921–1931*. Cambridge, Harvard University Press, 1965.
Ishikawa, Shingo 石川信吾. *Shinjuwan made no keii* 真珠湾までの経緯 (The road to Pearl Harbor). Tokyo, 1960.
Itō, Masanori 伊藤正徳. *Daikaigun o omou* 大海軍を思う (Remembering the great navy). Tokyo, 1956.
Iwaya, Fumio 巖谷二三男. *Chūkō: kaigun rikujō kōgeki kitaishi* 中攻:海軍陸上攻撃機隊史 (Medium bomber: A history of the navy's land-based attack planes). 2 vols. Tokyo, 1958.
James, Robert Rhodes, ed. *Chips: The Diaries of Sir Henry Channon*. London, Weidenfield and Nicolson, 1967.
JMFA. Japanese Ministry of Foreign Affairs Archives, Tokyo.
Jonas, Manfred. *Isolationism in America, 1935–1941*. Ithaca, Cornell University Press, 1966.
Kaigunshō 海軍省 (Navy Ministry), ed. *Kaigun narabi ni kaigun kankei sono ta no dantai ichiran* 海軍並に海軍関係その他の団体一覧 (A list of navy and navy-related groups, etc.). Tokyo, 1939.
Kaizō 改造.
Katō, Kanji. Papers, Tokyo daigaku shakai kagaku kenkyūjo 東京大学社会科学研究所 (Social science research institute), Tokyo University.
Katō Kanji Taishō denki hensankai 加藤寛治大將伝記編纂会 (Admiral Katō Kanji biographical association). *Katō Kanji Taishō den* (The biography of Katō Kanji). Tokyo, 1941.
Keizai zasshi daiyamondo 経済雑誌ダイヤモンド.
Kennedy, John F. *Why England Slept*. New York, Wilfred Funk, 1940.
Kido Kōichi nikki 木戸幸一日記 (The diary of Kido Kōichi), ed. Oka Yoshitake 岡義武. 3 vols. Tokyo, 1966.

Kilpatrick, Carroll. *Roosevelt and Daniels: A Friendship in Politics.* Chapel Hill, University of North Carolina Press, 1952.

Kimball, Warren F. *The Most Unsordid Act: Lend-Lease, 1939–1941.* Baltimore, Johns Hopkins University Press, 1969.

King, Ernest J. Papers, Manuscript Division, Library of Congress, Washington, D.C.

Kingu キング.

Kirby, S. Woodburn, et al. *The War Against Japan.* 5 vols. In J.R.M. Butler, ed. *History of the Second World War.* London, Her Majesty's Stationers' Office, 1957–1969.

Koginos, Manny T. *The Panay Incident: Prelude to War.* Lafayette, Ind., Purdue University Press, 1967.

Kokumin shinbun 国民新聞.

Kokusai chishiki 国際知識.

Kokusai hyōron 国際評論.

Krock, Arthur. *Sixty Years on the Firing Line.* New York, Funk and Wagnalls, 1968.

Langer, William L., and S. Everett Gleason. *The Challenge to Isolation: The World Crisis and American Foreign Policy, 1937–1940.* New York, Harper, 1952.

Leahy, William D. Papers, Manuscript Division, Library of Congress, Washington, D.C.

Leopold, Richard W. *The Growth of American Foreign Policy: A History.* New York, Knopf, 1962.

Leuchtenberg, William E. *Franklin D. Roosevelt and the New Deal, 1932–1940.* The New American Nation Series. New York, Harper and Row, 1963.

Levine, Robert H. "The Politics of Naval Rearmament, 1930–1938." Ph. D. diss., Harvard University, 1972.

Lockwood, William W. *The Economic Development of Japan: Growth and Structural Change, 1868–1938.* Princeton, Princeton University Press, 1954.

Louis, William Roger. *British Strategy in the Far East, 1919–1939.* Oxford, Clarendon, 1971.

Lu, David J. *From the Marco Polo Bridge to Pearl Harbor: Japan's Entry into World War II.* Washington, D.C., Public Affairs Press, 1961.

McKenna, Marian C. *Borah.* Ann Arbor, University of Michigan Press, 1961.

MacLeod, Iain. *Neville Chamberlain.* London, Muller, 1961.

Mahan, Alfred T. *Kaigun senryaku* 海軍戦略 (Naval strategy), trans. Ozaki Riki 尾崎力. Tokyo, 1932.

Marder, Arthur J. *The Anatomy of British Seapower: A History of British Naval Policy in the Pre-Dreadnought Era, 1880–1905.* New York, Knopf, 1940.

———. "The Royal Navy and the Ethiopian Crisis of 1935–1936," *American Historical Review* 75.5: 1327–1356 (1970).

Maruyama, Masao. *Thought and Behavior in Modern Japanese Politics,* trans. Ivan Morris. London and New York, Oxford University Press, 1963.

Matloff, Maurice, and Edwin M. Snell. *Strategic Planning for Coalition Warfare, 1941–1944.* 2 vols. The United States Army in World War II. Washington, D.C., Office of the Chief of Military History, Department of the Army, 1953–1959.

Matsudaira Tsuneoshi tsuisōkai 松平恒雄氏追想会 (Matsudaira Tsuneo biographical association). *Matsudaira Tsuneoshi tsuisōroku* 松平恒雄氏追想録 (Reminiscences about Matsudaira Tsuneo). Tokyo, 1961.

Matsumoto Shigekazu 松本繁一 "Tōgō gaishō to Taiheiyō sensō" 東郷外相と

太平洋戦争 (Foreign Minister Tōgō and the Pacific war), *Kokusai seiji* 33: 52–67 (1966).

May, Ernest R. and James C. Thomson Jr., eds. *American-East Asian Relations: A Survey.* Cambridge, Harvard University Press, 1972.

Middlemas, Keith, and John Barnes. *Baldwin: A Biography.* London, Weidenfield and Nicolson, 1969.

Miyako shinbun 都新聞.

Moffat, Jay Pierrepont. Diary, Houghton Library, Harvard University, Cambridge, Mass.

———. Papers, Houghton Library, Harvard University, Cambridge, Mass.

Morison, Samuel E. *History of the United States Navy in World War II*, vol. I: *The Battle of the Atlantic, Sept. 1939–May, 1943;* vol. III: *The Rising Sun in the Pacific, 1931–April, 1942.* Boston, Little, Brown, 1947, 1950.

Morton, Louis. *Strategy and Command: The First Two Years.* The United States Army in World War II. Washington, D.C., Office of the Chief of Military History, Department of the Army, 1962.

Mowat, Charles L. *Britain Between the Wars, 1918–1940.* London, Methuen, 1956.

Muggeridge, Malcolm. *The Thirties: 1930–1940 in Great Britain.* London, Collins, 1967.

Nakajima, Kenkichi 中島権吉. *Kaigun senryaku yōran* 海軍戦略要覧 (A synopsis of naval strategy). Tokyo, 1939.

Nakamura, Kikuo 中村菊男. *Shōwa kaigun hishi* 昭和海軍秘史 (A secret history of the Shōwa navy). Tokyo, 1969.

NARG:80. General Records of the Navy Department, Record Group 80, National Archives, Washington, D.C.

Nihon gaikō nenpyō narabi ni shuyō bunsho, 1840–1945 日本外交年表竝主要文書 (Selected documents and chronology of Japanese diplomacy, 1840–1945), ed. Gaimushō 外務省 (Ministry of Foreign Affairs). 2 vols. Tokyo, 1966.

Nihon oyobi Nihonjin 日本及日本人.

Nixon, Edgar B. *Franklin D. Roosevelt and Foreign Affairs, 1933–1937.* 3 vols. Cambridge, Harvard University Press, 1969.

O'Connor, Raymond G. *Perilous Equilibrium: The United States and the London Naval Conference of 1930.* Lawrence, University of Kansas Press, 1962.

Odagiri, Hideo 小田切秀雄 et al. *Shōwa shoseki, shinbun, zasshi hakkin nenpyō* 昭和書籍・新聞・雑誌発禁年表 (A list of books, newspapers, and magazines banned in the Shōwa period). Tokyo, 1966.

Okada, Keisuke. *Okada Keisuke kaikoroku* 岡田啓介回顧録 (The memoirs of Okada Keisuke). Tokyo, 1950.

Ōmae, Eiichi 大前栄一. *KyūNihon kaigun no heijutsuteki hensen to kore ni tomonau gunbi narabi ni sakusen* 旧日本海軍の兵術的変遷と之に伴う軍備竝に作戦 (Tactical changes, weapons, and strategy in the old Japanese navy). Tokyo, 1956.

Ono Hideo 小野秀雄. *Nihon shinbunshi* 日本新聞史 (A history of Japan's newspapers). Tokyo, 1949.

Osaka mainichi shinbun 大阪毎日新聞.

Ōsumi Taishō denki kankōkai 大角大將伝記刊行会 (Admiral Ōsumi biographical association). *Danshaku Ōsumi Mineo den* 男爵大角岑生伝 (The biography of Ōsumi Mineo). Tokyo, 1943.

Parkes, Oscar. *British Battleships: Warrior to Vanguard, 1860–1950, A History of Design, Construction, and Armament.* London, Seeley, 1956.

Patterson, James T. *Congressional Conservatism and the New Deal: The Growth of the Conservative Coalition in Congress, 1933–1939.* Lexington, University of Kentucky Press, 1967.

Phillips, William. Journal, Houghton Library, Harvard University, Cambridge, Mass.

Pogue, Forrest C. *George C. Marshall,* vol. I: *Education of a General, 1880–1939.* New York, Viking, 1963.

Potter, E. B., and Chester W. Nimitz. *Sea Power: A Naval History.* Englewood Cliffs, Prentice-Hall, 1960.

Puleston, W. D. *The Armed Forces of the Pacific.* New Haven, Yale University Press, 1941.

Rappaport, Armin. *The Navy League of the United States.* Detroit, Wayne State University Press, 1962.

———. *Henry L. Stimson and Japan, 1931–1933.* Chicago, University of Chicago Press, 1963.

Rauch, Basil. *Roosevelt, from Munich to Pearl Harbor: A Study in the Creation of a Foreign Policy.* New York, Creative Age, 1950.

Roosevelt, Elliott, ed. *F.D.R.: His Personal Letters, 1928–1945.* 4 vols. New York, Duell, Sloan, and Pearce, 1947–1950.

Roosevelt, Franklin D. *On Our Way.* New York, Day, 1934.

———. Papers, Franklin D. Roosevelt Library, Hyde Park, New York.

Rosenman, Samuel I., ed. *The Public Papers and Addresses of Franklin D. Roosevelt, 1928–1936.* 5 vols. New York, Random, 1938.

Roskill, Stephen W. *The War at Sea.* 3 vols. London, Her Majesty's Stationer's Office, 1954–1960.

———. *Naval Policy Between the Wars,* vol. I: *The Period of Anglo-American Antagonism, 1919–1929.* New York, Walker, 1968.

———. *Hankey: Man of Secrets,* vol. I: *1877–1918.* London, Collins, 1970.

———. *White Ensign: The British Navy at War, 1939–1945.* Annapolis, U.S. Naval Institute, 1960.

Rowse, A. L. *Appeasement: A Study in Political Decline, 1933–1939.* New York, Norton, 1961.

Saitō, Makoto. Papers, Kensei shiryō shitsu 憲政史料室 (Constitutional Government Archive), National Diet Library, Tokyo, Japan.

Senshi kenkyūkai 戦史研究会 (War history research association), ed. "Hawaii sakusen to Yamamoto gensui" ハワイ作戦と山本元帥 (Admiral of the fleet Yamamoto and the Hawaii operation), *Kokubō* 国防 (National defense), December 1968, pp. 104–113.

Silverstone, Paul H. *United States Warships of World War II.* Garden City, N.Y., Doubleday, 1966.

Simon, Viscount (John Simon). *Retrospect.* London, Hutchinson, 1952.

———. Papers, Public Record Office, London.

Sprout, Harold, and Margaret Sprout. *Toward a New Order of Sea Power: American Naval Policy and the World Scene, 1918–1922.* 2nd ed. Princeton, Princeton University Press, 1943.

Stimson, Henry L., and McGeorge Bundy. *On Active Service in Peace and War.* New York, Harper, 1947.

Storry, Richard. *The Double Patriots: A Study of Japanese Nationalism.* Boston, Houghton Mifflin, 1957.

Suekuni, Masao 末国正雄. "Teikoku kaigun to nanawari" 帝国海軍と七割 (The Imperial Navy and the 7/10 ratio), *DaiTōa (Taiheiyō) sensō senshi sōsho* 大東亜 (太平洋)戦争戦史叢書 (The greater East Asia (Pacific) war history series), vol. 31 (1969).

Sugiyama memo: daihon'ei-seifu renrakukaigi nado hikki 杉山メモ:大本営・政府連絡会議等筆記 (Notes of the liaison conferences of the supreme command and the government, etc.), ed. Sanbōhonbu 参謀本部 (Army General Staff). 2 vols. 1969.

Takagi, Sōkichi 高木惣吉. *Shikan Taiheiyō sensō* 私観太平洋戦争 (A personal view of the Pacific war). Tokyo, 1969.

Tamura, Kōsaku 田村幸策. *Taiheiyō sensō gaikōshi* 太平洋戦争外交史 (A diplomatic history of the Pacific war). Tokyo, 1966.

Tansill, Charles Callan. *Back Door to War: The Roosevelt Foreign Policy, 1933–1941*. Chicago, Regnery, 1952.

Tate, Merze. *The United States and Armaments*. Cambridge, Harvard University Press, 1948.

Taylor, A. J. P. *English History, 1914–1945*. New York, Oxford University Press, 1965.

Templewood, Viscount (Samuel Hoare). *Nine Troubled Years*. London, Collins, 1954.

Thorne, Christopher. "The Shanghai Crisis of 1932: The Basis of British Policy," *American Historical Review* 75.6: 1616–1639 (1970).

Tōgō, Shigenori 東郷茂徳. *Gaikō shuki* 外交手記 (Diplomatic Memoirs). Tokyo, 1967.

Tokyo asahi shinbun 東京朝日新聞.

Tominaga, Kengo 富永謙吾. "Daihon'ei happyō" 大本営発表 (A release from imperial headquarters), *Gendai shi shiryō geppō* 現代史資料月報 (Documents on modern history bulletin), vol. 3 (1967).

Tōyama, Shigeki 遠山茂樹, et al. *Shōwa shi* 昭和史 (A history of the Shōwa period). Tokyo, 1959.

Tōyō Keizai shinpō 東洋経済新報.

TSM: Taiheiyō sensō e no michi 太平洋戦争への道 (The Road to the Pacific War), ed. Nihon kokusai seiji gakkai 日本国際政治学会 (The International Politics Association of Japan). 8 vols. Tokyo, 1963.

Tsunoda, Jun. "A History of Japan's Naval Policy," ms., Shidehara Peace Library, Diet Library, Tokyo.

Tuleja, Thaddeus V. *Statesmen and Admirals: The Quest for a Far Eastern Naval Policy*. New York, Norton, 1963.

Turnbull, Archibald D., and Clifford L. Lord. *History of United States Naval Aviation*. New Haven, Yale University Press, 1949.

U.S., Department of the Navy. Records of the General Board, Washington Navy Yard, Washington, D.C.

U.S., Department of the Navy, Naval History Division, ed. *Dictionary of American Naval Fighting Ships*. 5 vols. Washington, D.C., Government Printing Office, 1959–1970.

USCON. U.S., Department of State. *The London Naval Conference of 1935*. Conference series no. 24. Washington, D.C., Government Printing Office, 1936.

USFR. U.S., Department of State. *Papers Relating to the Foreign Relations of the United States*. On disarmament negotiations: 1933, vol. 1; 1934, vol. 1; 1935, vol. 1; 1936, vol. 1. Washington, D.C., Government Printing Office, 1950–1953. Also, *Papers Relating to the Foreign Relations of the United States and Japan, 1931–1941*. 2 vols. Washington, D.C., Government Printing Office, 1943.

Usui, Katsumi 臼井勝美. "Hirota Kōki ron" 広田弘毅論 (A discussion of Hirota Kōki). *Kokusai seiji* 国際政治 (International Politics), 1:40–52 (1966).

Uyehara, Cecil, ed. *Checklist of Archives in the Japanese Ministry of Foreign*

Affairs, Tokyo, Japan, 1868–1945. Washington, D.C., Library of Congress, 1954.

Watt, Donald C. *Personalities and Politics: Studies in the Formulation of British Foreign Policy in the Twentieth Century*. London, University of Notre Dame Press, 1965.

Wheeler, Gerald E. *Prelude to Pearl Harbor: The United States Navy and the Far East, 1921–1931*. Columbia, University of Missouri Press, n.d. [1953].

Wheeler-Bennett, John W. *Munich: Prologue to Tragedy*. New York, Duell, Sloan, and Pearce, 1948.

Woodward, E. L., and Rohan Butler. *Documents on British Foreign Policy, 1919–1939, Third Series, 1938–1939*. Vols. 3, 8, 9. London, Her Majesty's Stationer's Office, 1949–1955.

Yomiuri shinbun 読売新聞.

Yūshūkai 有終会. *Gunshuku mondai no saikentō* 軍縮問題の再検討 (A reconsideration of the disarmament problem). Tokyo, 1934.

Notes

INTRODUCTION

1. Richard W. Leopold, *The Growth of American Foreign Policy: A History* (New York, 1962), pp. 441–447.

2. Gerald E. Wheeler, *Prelude to Pearl Harbor: The United States Navy and the Far East, 1921–1931* (Columbia, n.d. [1953]), pp. 53–62, 182–183.

3. Wheeler, p. 183; A. J. P. Taylor, *English History, 1914–1945* (New York, 1965), p. 273; James B. Crowley, *Japan's Quest for Autonomy: National Security and Foreign Policy, 1930–1938* (Princeton, 1966), p. 66; Keith Middlemas and John Barnes, *Baldwin: A Biography* (London, 1969), pp. 340–341.

4. Suekuni Masao, "Teikoku kaigun to nanawari," *DaiTōa (Taiheiyō) sensō senshi sōsho,* vol. 31 (November 1969).

5. Iriye Akira, *After Imperialism: The Search for a New Order in the Far East, 1921–1931* (Cambridge, 1965), pp. 227–303 *passim.*

6. Robert H. Ferrell, *American Diplomacy in the Great Depression: Hoover-Stimson Foreign Policy, 1929–1933.* (New Haven, 1957), pp. 184–185.

7. For an overview of the debate on Pearl Harbor, see Ernest R. May and James C. Thomson, Jr., eds., *American-East Asian Relations: A Survey* (Cambridge, 1972), pp. 243–290; Charles A. Beard, *American Foreign Policy in the Making, 1932–1940: A Study in Responsibilities* (New Haven, 1946), p. 42; Beard, *President Roosevelt and the Coming of the War, 1941: A Study in Appearances and Realities* (New Haven, 1948), pp. 499–516; Charles Callan Tansill, *Back Door to War: The Roosevelt Foreign Policy, 1933–1941* (Chicago, 1952), *passim;* Harry E. Barnes, ed., *Perpetual War for Perpetual Peace: A Critical Examination of the Foreign Policy of Franklin Delano Roosevelt and Its Aftermath* (Caldwell, 1953), pp. 233–307.

8. See, e.g., Crowley, "A New Deal for Japan and Asia: One Road to Pearl Harbor," in Crowley, ed., *Modern East Asia: Essays in Interpretation* (New York, 1970), pp. 235–264; Crowley, *Japan's Quest,* passim; David J. Lu, *From the Marco Polo Bridge to Pearl Harbor: Japan's Entry into World War II* (Washington, D.C., 1961), pp. vii–viii, 238–242.

9. For answers to the revisionists, see William L. Langer and S. Everett Gleason, *The Challenge to Isolation: The World Crisis and American Foreign Policy, 1937–1940* (New York, 1952), pp. 42–53, 102–105, 576–606, 719–723; Herbert Feis, *The Road to Pearl Harbor: The Coming of the War Between the United States and Japan* (Princeton, 1950), pp. 3–7, 209–260; Robert J. C. Butow, *Tōjō and the Coming of the War* (Princeton, 1961), *passim.*

10. See, e.g., Basil Rauch, *Roosevelt, from Munich to Pearl Harbor: A Study in the Creation of a Foreign Policy* (New York, 1950), *passim;* Martin Gilbert and Richard Gott, *The Appeasers* (London, 1962), *passim;* Margaret George, *The Warped Vision: British Foreign Policy, 1933–1939* (Pittsburgh, 1965), *passim.*

1. THE BACKGROUND OF JAPAN'S
DISARMAMENT POLICY

1. Toyama Shigeki, et al., *Shōwa shi* (Tokyo, 1959), pp. 87–92.

2. *Gendai shi shiryō*, ed. Tsunoda Jun (Tokyo, 1964), VIII, 3, "Manmō mondai shori yōkō" (Summary of our policy for handling the problem of Manchuria and Mongolia), Mar. 12, 1932; pp. xxiii-xxvii; pp. 4–8, "Kokusai kankei yori mitaru jikyoku hōshin an" (Draft of a policy for handling the emergency viewed from the standpoint of our international relations), Aug. 27, 1932.

3. *Kido Kōichi nikki*, ed. Oka Yoshitake (Tokyo, 1966), I, 10–15; see also David Titus' forthcoming book on court politics in the thirties.

4. Richard Storry, *The Double Patriots: A Study of Japanese Nationalism* (Boston, 1957), *passim;* Hirota Kōki denki kankōkai, *Hirota Kōki* (Tokyo, 1966), p. 165.

5. Storry, pp. 128–135; *Kido*, I, 252–254, 260–262. For a full exploration of the roles played by the various actors, see Hosoya, Chihirō, et al., *Nichibei kankeishi: kaisen ni itaru jūnen (1931–1941)* (Tokyo, 1972), vols. 1–4.

6. Aritake Shūji, *Shōwa no saishō* (Tokyo, 1967), pp. 16–40; Harada Kumao, *Saionji Kō to seikyoku* (Tokyo, 1951), II, 377. Harada's multivolume work is actually a diary that he dictated weekly throughout the thirties.

7. Crowley, *Japan's Quest,* p. 151; Harada, II, 420–422; III, 159–160, 174–175, 182–187; *Kido*, I, 303–304; *Kido*, I, 3–4, 249; Storry, pp. 21, 46–48, 149.

8. Aritake Shūji, *Saitō Makoto* (Tokyo, 1958), pp. 3–63, 246–249; *Kido*, I, 318.

9. Crowley, p. 180; Aritake, *Saishō*, pp. 261–267; Aritake, *Saito*, pp. 185–192; Imamura Takeo, *Takahashi Korekiyo hyōden* (Tokyo, 1950), pp. 250–280; Saitō Makoto, Papers, Folder 1748, Kensei shiryō shitsu, National Diet Library, Finance Ministry memo, undated [1932].

10. Usui Katsumi, "Hirota Kōki ron," *Kokusai seiji*, 1:42–44 (1966); Storry, p. 149.

11. Harada, III, 206–207; Aritake, *Saitō*, p. 171.

12. Crowley, *Japan's Quest*, pp. 201–206; Storry, p. 311; Ōsumi Taishō denki kankōkai, *Danshaku Ōsumi Mineo den* (Tokyo, 1943), pp. 601–603.

13. *Taiheiyō sensō e no michi*, ed. Nihon kokusai seiji gakkai (Tokyo, 1963), I, 100–104.

14. Crowley, *Japan's Quest*, pp. 30–31, 43; Aritake Shūji, *Okada Keisuke* (Tokyo, 1956), pp. 177–178; *TSM*, I, 60.

15. *TSM*, I, 30, 70, 152–153.

16. Storry, pp. 104, 109; Aritake, *Saitō*, pp. 126–141; Aritake, *Okada*, pp. 59–61.

17. *TSM*, I, 58–59; Aritake, *Okada*, pp. 6–13.

18. *TSM*, I, 100–103, 120–122; Crowley, pp. 63–78; Aritake, *Okada*, pp. 143–144.

19. Aritake, *Saitō*, pp. 192–194; Harada, III, 113–116, 140–149; *Kido*, I, 263–264; *TSM*, I, 152–153.

20. *TSM*, I, 152–153; Harada, III, 172–174; *Kido*, I, 284.

21. JMFA, S 1.1.0.0–1, *Teikoku taigai seisaku ikken* (Documents on the foreign policy of the empire), Army Ministry memo, "Teikoku kokusaku" (Imperial policy), Oct. 2, 1933. The index numbers beginning with "S" refer to the checklist of documents on microfilm at the Library of Congress: Cecil Uyehara, *Checklist of Archives in the Japanese Ministry of Foreign Affairs, Tokyo, Japan, 1868–1945* (Washington, D.C., 1954).

22. JMFA, S 1.1.0.0–1, Army Ministry to Foreign Office, "Gaikō jikō: goshō kaigi giketsu rikugun shūseian" (Diplomatic questions: Army proposals for revision of the five ministers' decision), Nov. 30, 1933; *GSS*, VIII, 15, memo by Military Affairs Bureau of the Army Ministry, "Tainai kokusaku juritsu ni kansuru kokubōjō no yōbō" (National defense proposals concerning the establishment of an internal policy), Oct. 30, 1933.

23. JMFA, S 1.1.0.0–1, Army Ministry memo, "Teikoku kokusaku" (Imperial policy), Oct. 2, 1933.

24. *GSS*, VIII, 9, "Kaigun no tai-shi jikyoku shori hōshin" (Naval policy for handling the China situation), Sept. 25, 1933; JMFA, S 1.1.0.0–1, Navy Ministry memo, "Kaigun shūseian" (Navy proposals for revision), n.d.

25. JMFA, B 10.4.0.2–1, *1935 nen kaisai no kaigun gunshuku kaigi kankei ikken: gaimu, riku, kai, sanshō kaigi kankei* (Documents relating to the 1935 Naval Disarmament Conference: Meetings of the representatives of the Foreign Office, the Army Ministry, and the Navy Ministry), Navy Minister to Foreign Office, Sept. 21, 1933. No "S" number is given, because this volume was not microfilmed by the Library of Congress; the "B" series is the original prewar file number. JMFA, S 1.1.0.0–1, Navy Ministry memo, Oct. 16, 1933.

26. JMFA, B 10.4.0.2–1, Navy Minister to Foreign Office, Oct. 6, Dec. 13, 1933; Jan. 21, 1934; Foreign Office reply, Jan. 21, 1934.

27. *TSM*, I, 150; Harada, III, 110–112, 125, 152–159, 195–196; *Kido*, I, 284, 292–293; Imamura, pp. 258–268; Aritake, *Saitō*, pp. 196–206.

28. Matsumoto Shigekazu, "Tōgō gaisho to taiheiyō sensō," *Kokusai seiji* 33:54–55 (1966); Tōgō Shigenori, *Gaikō shuki* (Tokyo, 1967), pp. 82–98.

29. Harada, III, 155, 165–169.

30. *Nihon gaikō nenpyō narabi ni shuyō bunsho, 1840–1945* ed. Gaimushō (Tokyo, 1966), II, 275–276.

31. Tamura Kōsaku, *Taiheiyō sensō gaikōshi* (Tokyo, 1966), p. 87; *Nihon gaikō nenpyō*, II, 278–280.

32. Dorothy Borg, *The United States and the Far Eastern Crisis of 1933–1938* (Cambridge, 1966), pp. 55–75; *GSS*, VIII, 54–59, telegrams from Tsukamoto to Hirota, Feb. 9, 1934, Nakahara to Navy Ministry and General Staff, Feb. 17 and 20, 1934; Tayui to Navy General Staff, Feb. 22, 1934; Hirota to Ariyoshi, n.d.

33. *GSS*, VIII, xxviii–xxxi; pp. 30–32, telegram from Hirota to Ariyoshi, Mar. 19, 1934; *TSM*, III, 74–78.

34. At the end of 1934, the respective ministries reconfirmed that Japan would penetrate China. *GSS*, VIII, 22–24, memo of a decision made by the Foreign, Navy and Army Ministries, "Tai-shi seisaku ni kansuru ken" (On the question of our China policy), Dec. 7, 1934; Usui, "Hirota ron," p. 45.

35. *TSM*, III, 73–76; Hirota Kōki denki, pp. 119–121; Harada, III, 285–286; *GSS*, VIII, 27–29, 41–48; Hirota Kōki denki, pp. 121–123; *TSM*, 82–83; Borg, pp. 76–77.

36. JMFA, SP 304, *Teikoku no tai-shi gaikō seisaku* (The empire's diplomatic policy vis-à-vis China), 3, Shigemitsu Mamoru memo, September 1933; Morishima Gorō memo, "Jikai gunshuku kaigi ni oite kyūkoku jōyaku o saikakunin suru koto no fukanaru riyu" (Why we cannot reaffirm the 9-Power Treaty at the next disarmament conference), Apr. 18, 1934; JMFA, SP 304, Hirota to Saitō and Matsudaira, "Wagahō tai-shi seisaku tetteikata no ken" (Concerning the realization of our China policy), Apr. 18, 1934.

37. Borg, pp. 92–99; JMFA SP 304, Saitō to Hirota, May 20, 1934. Although Saitō reported to Hirota at the time on this interview with Hull, he made no mention of his attempt to establish spheres of influence in the Pacific; he may have informed Hirota of the matter when he returned to Tokyo in July.

38. Borg, pp. 92–99.

39. JMFA, S 2.10.4.0.3, *1935 nen kaisai kaigun gunshuku kaigi ikken: yobi kōshō kankei—Kafu jōyaku haiki kankei* (Documents on the 1935 Naval Disarmament Conference: Preliminary negotiations—Washington treaty abrogation), Matsudaira to Hirota, May 17, 1934; JMFA, B 10.4.0.2–2, *1935 nen kaisai no kaigun gunshuku kaigi ikken—*

yobi kōshō (Documents on the 1935 Naval Disarmament Conference—preliminary negotiations), Matsudaira to Hirota, May 18, June 19, 1934.

2. NEW WEAPONS, NEW STRATEGY, AND NO LIMITATIONS

1. JMFA, S 2.10.4.0.3, Navy Ministry to Foreign Office, "Shōwa 11 nenmatsu godaikaigunkoku kaigun seiryoku hikosho" (A comparison of the naval strengths of the five great powers at the end of 1936), Dec. 8, 1934; Leopold, pp. 524–525.

2. Ōmae Eiichi, *Kyūnihon kaigun no heijutsuteki hensen to kore ni tomonau gunbi narabi ni sakusen* (Tokyo, 1956); E. B. Potter and Chester W. Nimitz, *Sea Power: A Naval History* (Englewood Cliffs, 1960), pp. 341–343; Ozaki Riki translated Mahan's *Naval Strategy (Kaigun senryaku)* for the Navy General Staff (Tokyo, 1932); Nakajima Kenkichi, *Kaigun senryaku yōran* (Tokyo, 1939); Nakamura Kikuo, *Shōwa kaigun hishi* (Tokyo, 1969), p. 226; Ōmae, *passim*.

3. Potter, pp. 346–365; Nakamura, p. 277; Omae, *passim*.

4. Katō Kanji denki hensankai, *Katō Kanji Taishō den* (Tokyo, 1941), pp. 48, 127–130; Okada, pp. 52–54.

5. Katō denki, pp. 822–834.

6. Ikeda Kiyoshi, "Rondon kaigun jōyaku to tōsuiken mondai," *Hōgaku zasshi,* 15:2 (1968); Tsunoda Jun, "History of Japan's Naval Policy" (Diet Library, Tokyo; 1968).

7. Katō denki, pp. 940–941.

8. Senshi kenkyūkai, ed., "Hawaii sakusen to Yamamoto gensui," *Kokubō (December 1968),* pp. 104–113; Bōeichō, bōeikenshūjo, senshishitsu, ed., *Daihonei: rikugunbu,* vol. I: Shōwa jūgonen gogatsu made (Tokyo, 1967), pp. 251–255.

9. Takagi Sōkichi, *Shikan taiheiyō senso* (Tokyo, 1969), pp. 11–16; Potter, pp. 432–454.

10. Potter, pp. 2–10, 25–65.

11. Potter, pp. 225–227, 331–340.

12. Potter, pp. 388–392.

13. Potter, pp. 403–454.

14. Fukui Shizuo, *Nihon no gunkan* (Tokyo, 1956), pp. 1–2, 9–10, 214.

15. Fukui, pp. 45–48, 159–169, 188–192, 198–199.

16. Itō Masanori, *Daikaigun o omou* (Tokyo, 1956), pp. 327–346; Ikeda Kiyoshi, *Nihon no kaigun* (Tokyo, 1967), II, 72–73, 98, 179; Iwaya Fumio, *Chūkō: kaigun rikujō kōgeki kitaishi* (Tokyo, 1958), II, 302; Bōeichō, bōeikenshūjo, senshishitsu, *Kaigun gun senbi,* I: Showa jūrokunen jūichigatsu made (Tokyo, 1969), p. 176; also pp. 139–215.

17. Fukui, pp. 28–38, 42.

18. Interviews with Baron Admiral Tomioka Sadatoshi and Commander Sekino Hideo, Shiryō chōsakai (Historical Research Institute), Tokyo, December 1968; Hayashi Katsuya, *Nihon gunji gijutsushi* (Tokyo, 1957), pp. 206–214; Fukui, pp. 120–121.

19. Fukui, pp. 21–27, 112–114, 230–232; Itō, pp. 443–463; interview with Admiral Suekuni Masao, Senshshitsu, bōeikenshūjo, bōeichō, Tokyo, April 1969; see also Bōeichō, ed., *Kaigun gunsenbi,* I, 396–532.

20. Fukui, pp. 50–61.

21. Katō Kanji, Papers, Tokyo daigaku shakai kagaku kenkyūjo, Yamashita Chisaku and Shiotani Eisaku to Katō, "Kafu jōyaku rondon jōyaku haikigo no kenkan keisho" Building plans for the period after the abrogation of the Washington and London treaties), Sept. 10, 1934.

22. Katō Kanji, Commander Ishikawa Shingo to Katō, "Jiki gunshuku kaigi taisaku shiken" (Personal opinion on countermeasures for the next disarmament conference), Oct. 21, 1933.

23. *Ibid.;* Ishikawa Shingo, *Shinjuwan made no keii* (Tokyo, 1960), pp. 71–74; Fukui, pp. 72–74.

24. Katō Kanji, Ishikawa Shingo to Katō, "Gunshuku shiken" (Personal opinion on disarmament), Sept. 10, 1934.

25. Katō Kanji, Yamashita Chisaku and Shiotani Eisaku to Katō, "Doitsu teikei ni kansuru iken" (Opinion concerning cooperation with Germany), n.d.

26. *GSS,* XII, 60–61, "Gensui kaigi ni okeru gunreibu sōchō setsumeian" (Draft for the explanations of the Chief of the Navy General Staff to the Conference of Fleet Admirals and Field Marshals), fall 1934.

27. Ōmae, *passim;* Nakamura, p. 80.

28. Ikeda, "Kaigun jōyaku," pp. 18–35; interview with Admiral Tomioka and Commander Sekino, December 1968; Ōmae, *passim.* Admiral Tomioka was strategy section chief of the Navy General Staff, 1940–1941.

29. Tomioka and Sekino interview, December 1968; Suekuni interview, April 1969; Nakajima, *passim.*

30. Suekuni interview, April 1969.

31. Takagi, pp. 16–17.

32. Katō Kanji, Admiral Suetsugu Nobumasa memo, "Gunshuku taisaku shiken" (Personal opinion on disarmament countermeasures), June 8, 1934.

3. PUBLIC OPINION AND THE NAVY'S FIRST MOVES

1. Asahi jyānaru, ed., *Shōwa shi no shunkan* (Tokyo, 1966), I, 90–92.

2. Tōyama Shigeki, et al., pp. 87–89.

3. Arisawa Hiromi, "Dai-ei teikoku burokku ron," *Kaizō* (September 1933), pp. 37–61; Kasamatsu Kiyoyuki, "Shinkō nippon to nanyō keizai burokku," *Nihon oyobi Nihonjin* (July 1, 1934), pp. 16–18; *Yomiuri shinbun,* May 23, 1934; Ishizawa Chiko, "Gunshuku kaigi o meguru keizai kankei," *Chūō kōron* (September 1934), pp. 51–64.

4. Asahi jyānaru, I, 132–139, 148.

5. JMFA, B 10.4.0.2–3–1, *1935 nen kaisai no kaigun gunshuku kaigi kankei ikken: yoron narabi ni shinbun ronchō–honpō no bu* (Matters related to the 1935 disarmament conference: Domestic, public, and newspaper opinion), Zaigō gunjinkai (Reservist Association) memo to Foreign Office, Nov. 18, 1933; Tōjō Hideki, "Kyokutō no shinjosei ni tsuite," *Gaikō jihō* 697:68–78 (Dec. 1, 1933); Suzuki Bunshirō, "1935, 1936 nen naze 'kiki' to yū," *Kingu* (January 1934), pp. 258–261.

6. Tnō Tentarō, "Meiji ikō ni okeru 'sensō miraiki no ryūkō to sono shōchō," *Kokugakuin daigaku yoran* 7:129–165 (1969); *Kingu,* April 1934; *Gendai,* April 1934; *Bungei shunju,* February 1934; *Chūō kōron,* May 1934.

7. Ikei Masaru, "Manshū jihen o meguru Nichi-Bei sōgo imēji," *Kokusai seiji* 2:58–74 (1966); *Yomiuri shinbun,* May 18, July 20, 1934; *Kokusai chishiki* (June 1934), pp. 2–11.

8. Ienaga Saburō, *Taiheiyō sensō* (Tokyo, 1968), pp. 30–34; Hashimoto Motome, *Nihon shuppan hanbaishi* (Tokyo, 1964), p. 459; Hanmura Sen'ichi, *Shinbun hōsei ron* (Tokyo, 1968), pp. 8–9; Odagiri Hideo et al., *Shōwa shoseki, shinbun, zasshi hakkin nenpyō* (Tokyo, 1966), II, 1–4, 121, 134–139, 191.

9. JMFA, B 10.4.0.2–1, Navy Minister to Foreign Office, Dec. 13, 1933; Jan. 9, 22, 1934.

10. Ono Hideo, *Nihon shinbun shi* (Tokyo, 1948), pp. 271–272.

11. JMFA, *Records of the International Military Tribunal for the Far East,* 335, WT 45, microfilm, memo by the Liaison Committee of Press Bureau Personnel, "Shōwa jūnen kaigun gunshuku kaigi yobi kōshō ni taisuru yoron keihatsu yōkō oyobi hōshin"

(Outline and policy for the development of public opinion vis-à-vis the preparatory negotiations for the 1935 Naval Disarmament Conference), Oct. 12, 1934.

12. Tominaga Kengo, "Daihon'ei happyō," *Gendai shi shiryō geppō*, vol. 3 (1967); *Kaigun narabi ni kaigun kankei sono ta no dantai ichiran*, ed. Kaigunshō (Tokyo, 1931).

13. *Kaigun dantai; Hōchi shinbun*, Jan. 8, 1931.

14. *Gunshuku mondai no saikentō*, ed. Yūshūkai, (Tokyo, 1934).

15. JMFA, B 10.4.0.2–1, Navy Ministry to Foreign Office, Sept. 21, 1933; Navy Minister to Foreign Office, Oct. 6, 1933.

16. Harada, III, 306–307; *Kido*, I, 328–329.

17. *Tokyo asahi shinbun*, May 18, 25, 1934.

18. Harada, III, 322; *Tokyo asahi shinbun*, July 7, 14, 1934.

19. *Hōchi shinbun*, June 17, 21, 1934; *Tokyo asahi shinbun*, June 20, 1934; *Osaka mainichi shinbun*, June 22, 1934; *Yomiuri shinbun*, June 22, 1934.

20. *Osaka mainichi shinbun*, July 2, 1934.

21. GSS, XII, 12–14, memo by the Fourth Section of the Army General Staff, "1935 nen kaigun gunshuku kaigi ni taisuru hōsaku" (Policy for the 1935 Naval Disarmament Conference), May 1934.

22. GSS, XII, 15, memo by the Second Section of the Army General Staff, "1935 nen kaigun gunshuku kaigi ni taisuru hōsaku ni kansuru ken" (Concerning policy for the 1935 Naval Disarmament Conference), May 26, 1934; p. 19, memo from the Navy General Staff to the Army General Staff, June 13, 1934; pp. 20–21, memo by the Second Section of the Army General Staff, "Taiheiyō bōbi mondai" (The problem of Pacific fortifications), Apr. 5, 1934.

23. GSS, XII, p. 4, memo by the Second Section of the Army General Staff, "Kaigun gunbi seigen mondai ni kansuru keii" (Chronology of the naval arms limitation problem), October 1934; pp. 28–29, memo from the Navy General Staff to the Army General Staff, June 27, 1934; GSS, XII, pp. 28–29.

24. GSS, XII, p. 4; pp. 25–26, memo by the Second Division of the Army General Staff, "1935 kaigun gunshuku kaigi ni taisuru hōsaku" (Policy for the 1935 Naval Disarmament Conference), n.d.; p. 27, memo by the Army General Staff, "Kaigun gunshuku kaigi ni taisuru hōsaku" (Policy for the 1935 Naval Disarmament Conference), June 28, 1934.

25. Crowley, *Japan's Quest*, pp. 206–208; GSS, XII, 4.

26. GSS, XII, 16–18, memo by the Army Ministry, "Kaigun gunshuku hōshin ni kanshi rikugunshō gunmukyokuchō ni nashitaru shitsumon oyobi kore ni taisuru kotae no yoshi" (The gist of the questions concerning naval disarmament policy put by the chief of the Army Ministry's Military Affairs Bureau to the chief of the Navy Ministry's Military Affairs Bureau and the replies to those questions), June 11, 1934.

27. GSS, XII, 30, memo by the Military Affairs Section of the Army Ministry, "Gunshuku kaigi kaigunan ni taisuru shoken" (Opinions concerning the navy's proposals for the disarmament conference), July 12, 1934.

28. Harada, III, 260–263, 317–318, 320, 333, 336; *Kido*, I, 336–340, 349–350.

29. *Kido*, I, 329–330, 343–345; Harada, III, 314–315, 347–350; Aritake, *Saitō*, pp. 237–246.

30. Okada Keisuke, *Okada Keisuke kaikoroku* (Tokyo, 1950), pp. 42–43, 52–54; *Tokyo asahi shimbun*, July 5, 1934; Aritake, *Okada*, pp. 6–7, 12–13; Aritake, *Saishō*, p. 109.

31. Aritake, *Okada*, p. 241; Hirota Kōki denki, p. 130; Harada, III, 322; Okada, pp. 92–94, 99.

32. Aritake, *Saitō*, p. 250; Aritake, *Okada*, pp. 201, 244–245, 294–295, 301–302; Harada, IV, 3–11.

33. *GSS,* VIII, 22–24; *TSM,* III, 71–73.

34. *GSS,* VIII, 22–24.

4. THE NAVY'S GENERAL OFFENSIVE

1. Harada, IV, 16–17.

2. *Kido,* I, 346–347; Harada, IV, 17–19; Asada Sadao, "The Role of the Japanese Navy, 1931–1941 (paper presented at the Conference on Japanese-American Relations, July 14–18, 1969), pp. 45–46.

3. *GSS,* XII, 35–36, "Kaigun daijin yori rikugun daijin ni shukō shitaru ikensho" (The position paper given by the Navy Minister to the Army Minister), July 14, 1934.

4. Harada, IV, 19–20; *Tokyo asahi shinbun,* July 15, 1934.

5. *Tokyo asahi shinbun,* July 13, 1934; Harada, IV, 19–23.

6. *Tokyo asahi shinbun,* July 13, 16, 17, 1934; *Hōchi shinbun,* July 17, 1934.

7. *Hōchi shinbun,* July 17, 1934; *Chūgai shōgyō shinpo,* July 15, 1934; *Kokumin shinbun,* July 16, 1934; *Osaka mainichi shinbun,* July 19, 1934.

8. Harada, IV, 23–27; *Tokyo asahi shinbun,* July 20, 1934.

9. Harada, IV, 22–23, 45–50.

10. *Tokyo asahi shinbun,* July 19, 1934.

11. *GSS,* XII, 31–32, Army Ministry memo, "Kaigun gunshuku mondai ni kansuru rikugun daijin taidan yōshi" (The gist of the Army Minister's conversation concerning naval disarmament), July 20, 1934.

12. *GSS,* XII, 33–34, Army Ministry memo, "Kaigun gunshuku ni kanshi rikukaigun daijin kaidan yōshi" (The gist of the Army and Navy Ministers' talk about naval disarmament), July 20, 1934.

13. Harada, IV, 24.

14. Tōgō, pp. 105–106.

15. *Ibid.;* Harada, IV, 45, 48–49; *Tokyo asahi shinbun,* July 23, 1934.

16. JMFA, B 10.4.0.2–1, "Dainikai gōshō kaigi" (The second five ministers' conference), July 24, 1934. Okada held three such conferences, but records remain only for this one.

17. *Ibid.;* Harada, IV, 24, 27–28.

18. *Hōchi shinbun,* Aug. 3, 19, 1934; *Osaka mainichi shinbun,* Aug. 1, 6, 1934; *Yomiuri shinbun,* Aug. 3, 1934; *Tokyo asahi shinbun,* Aug. 1, 2, 1934.

19. Harada, IV, 32–35, 39, 43–44; *Kido,* I, 351–352; *Tokyo asahi shinbun,* Aug. 2, 5, 10, 1934.

20. *Tokyo asahi shinbun,* Aug. 10, 20, 1934.

21. *Tokyo asahi shinbun,* Aug. 26, 1934.

22. *Tokyo asahi shinbun,* Aug. 24, 26, 1934; JMFA, B 10.4.0.2–3–1, Foreign Office memo, Sept. 5, 1934.

23. *Chūgai shōgyō shinpo,* July 18, 1934; *Miyako shinbun,* July 15, 18; Aug. 23, 1934.

24. Ienaga, pp. 37–50; Hashimoto, pp. 318–360, 386–387; Sekine Gunpei, "1935 nen e no tenbō," *Gaikō jihō* 693:10–22 (Nov. 15, 1933); Oyama Ujirō, "Nichi-Bei kankei to beikoku no keizainan," *Gaikō jihō* 696:127–136 (Jan. 1, 1934); Yoshizawa Kenkichi, "Myōnen no gunshuku kaigi to wagakuni no taido," *Gaikō jihō* 707:14–29 (May 15, 1934); Hanzawa Gyokujo, "Gunshuku kaigi yobi kaidan," *Gaikō jihō* 709:1–4 (June 15, 1934); *Gaikō jihō* 709:210–213 (Sept. 1, 1934); Nozaki Ryūji, "Shinyosan hensei," *Keizai zasshi dayamondo* (Aug. 21, 1934), pp. 12–13, *Tōyō keizai shinpo* 1602:13–14 (June 2, 1934); 1619:5–7 (Sept. 15, 1934); *Chūgai zaikai* (Nov. 15, 1934), pp. 13–14.

25. Harada, IV, 55–57; JMFA, S 2.10.4.0.3, "Kurubeki kaigun gunshuku yobi kōshō ni taisuru teikoku seifu hōshin—naikaku kettei" (The cabinet's decision on the imperial

government's policy concerning the coming preparatory naval disarmament negotiations), Sept. 7, 1934.

26. *GSS,* XII, 45–46, "Yobi kōshō teikoku daihyō ni ataeraruru kunreichū tōsui jiko ni kanshi gunreibu sōchō sōjō no sai no sōjōsho" (The Chief of the General Staff's report to the Emperor on matters relating to the supreme command in the instructions to be given to the imperial representatives at the preparatory negotiations), Sept. 8, 1934. For a brief account of the decision from the Japanese side, see Gaimushō hyakunenshi hensankai, ed., *Gaimushō no hyakunen* (Tokyo, 1969), II, 515–522.

5. ROOSEVELT'S FOREIGN POLICY AND JAPAN

1. Armin Rappaport, *Henry L. Stimson and Japan, 1931–1933* (Chicago, 1963), pp. 107–109, 114–115; Ferrell, pp. 157, 184–185, 209–210.

2. Rappaport, *Stimson,* pp. 115, 169; Ferrell, pp. 252–253.

3. Waldo H. Heinrichs, *American Ambassador: Joseph C. Grew and the Development of the American Diplomatic Tradition* (Boston, 1966), p. 213; Ferrell, pp. 239–245.

4. Langer and Gleason, pp. 1–10; Selig Adler, *The Uncertain Giant, 1921–1941: American Foreign Policy Between the Wars* (New York, 1965), pp. 156–157.

5. Carroll Kilpatrick, *Roosevelt and Daniels: A Friendship in Politics* (Chapel Hill, 1952), pp. 70–72.

6. Adler, pp. 148–149.

7. Frank Freidel, *Franklin D. Roosevelt,* vol. I: *The Apprenticeship* (Boston, 1952), pp. 157–173, 220–235, 253–259, 304–336; William F. Halsey and J. Bryan, III, *Admiral Halsey's Story* (New York, 1947), p. 18; Forrest C. Pogue, *George C. Marshall,* vol. I: *Education of a General, 1880–1939* (New York, 1963), p. 22.

8. William E. Leuchtenberg, *Franklin D. Roosevelt and the New Deal, 1932–1940* (New York, 1963), pp. 18–19; Cordell Hull, *The Memoirs of Cordell Hull* (New York, 1948), I, 191–200; Franklin D. Roosevelt, *On Our Way* (New York, 1934); James Mac-Gregor Burns, *Roosevelt: The Lion and the Fox* (New York, 1956), pp. 167–172, 175–176, 183.

9. Burns, pp. 186–191; James T. Patterson, *Congressional Conservatism and the New Deal: The Growth of the Conservative Coalition in Congress, 1933–1939* (Lexington, Ky., 1967), pp. 3–13; Selig Adler, *The Isolationist Impulse: Its Twentieth Century Reaction* (New York, 1957), pp. 251–252; Manfred Jonas, *Isolationism in America, 1935–1941* (Ithaca, 1966), pp. 129–132.

10. Adler, *Isolationist Impulse,* pp. 32–53; Leuchtenberg, p. 35.

11. Adler, *Isolationist Impulse,* pp. 191–192, 203–217, 239–258; Adler, *Uncertain Giant,* pp. 160–161.

12. Burns, pp. 176–179, 247–251.

13. *Ibid.;* Leuchtenberg, p. 211.

14. Adler, *Uncertain Giant,* pp. 150–153; Borg, pp. 29–30; Ferrell, pp. 194–214.

15. Edgar B. Nixon, ed., *Franklin D. Roosevelt and Foreign Affairs, 1933–1937* (Cambridge, 1969), I, 25–26, 125–128, 159–160; Norman H. Davis, Papers, Box #20, Manuscript Division, Library of Congress, memo on naval conversations, Oct. 7, 1932.

16. Hull, I, 3–25, 37–44, 50–55, 129, 138; Dean Acheson, *Present at the Creation: My Years at the State Department* (New York, 1969), pp. 9–10.

17. Hull, I, 75–90, 173–180, 448; James C. Thomson, "Japanese-American Relations, 1931–1941: The Role of the Department of State" (paper presented at the Conference on Japanese-American Relations, 1931–1941, July 14–18, 1969), pp. 7–8.

18. Hull, I, 159–63, 181; Rappaport, *Stimson,* pp. 38–39, 72; Thomson, pp. 1–4, 8–10, 12–16.

19. Heinrichs, *Grew,* pp. 154–162, 180–200.

20. Borg, pp. 31–36.

21. Elliott Roosevelt, ed., *F.D.R.: His Personal Letters, 1928–1945* (New York, 1947), I, 342–343.

22. Henry L. Stimson and McGeorge Bundy, *On Active Service in Peace and War* (New York, 1947), pp. 297–300; William Phillips, Journal, Houghton Library, Harvard University, June 11, 1934; Nixon, I, 484–485.

23. Franklin D. Roosevelt, Papers, Roosevelt Library, Hyde Park, New York, PPF 5901, Carl M. Vinson to Roosevelt, Dec. 28, 1932; Borg, p. 101; James A. Farley, *Jim Farley's Story: The Roosevelt Years* (New York, 1948), p. 39.

24. Harold L. Ickes, *The Secret Diary of Harold L. Ickes* (New York, 1953), II, 274–278.

25. Nixon, I, 177–180; Phillips, Journal, Oct. 25, 1934.

26. Nixon, I, 32–34, 103–107; Borg, pp. 33–34.

27. Wheeler, p. 185; Armin Rappaport, *The Navy League of the United States* (Detroit, 1962), pp. 1–152.

28. Roosevelt, Papers, PPF 5901, Carl M. Vinson to Roosevelt, Dec. 28, 1932.

29. Burns, p. 253; Ickes, I, 11; Rappaport, *Navy League,* pp. 157–158.

30. Rappaport, *Navy League,* pp. 157–158; Roosevelt, Papers, Navy Department, 1933–1943 File, Claude Swanson memo to Roosevelt, Apr. 13, 1933; OF 18, Stephen A. Early to Claude Swanson, Apr. 22, 1933; U.S., Dept. of the Navy, Records of the General Board, 420.2, Washington Navy Yard, Henry L. Roosevelt memo to the bureau chiefs of the navy, May 4, 1933; Vinson was a political ally of the President. During the campaign of 1932, he criticized Hoover publicly and supported Roosevelt. See Robert H. Levine, "The Politics of Naval Rearmament, 1930–1938" (Ph.D. diss., Harvard University, 1972), p. 64.

31. Roosevelt, Papers, OF 18, Carl M. Vinson to Roosevelt, May 4, 1933; George T. Davis, *A Navy Second to None: The Development of Modern American Naval Policy* (New York, 1940), p. 359; Harold G. Bowen, *Ships, Machinery, and Mossbacks: The Autobiography of a Naval Engineer* (Princeton, 1954), pp. 59–70.

32. Nixon, I, 370.

33. NARG:80, Box 2A, the International Brotherhood of Boilermakers, Iron Ship Builders, Welders, and Helpers to F. D. Roosevelt, Apr. 3, 1933; Roger Baldwin to Roosevelt, Apr. 6, 1933; U.S., Dept. of the Navy, Records of the General Board, 420.2, W. V. Pratt memo to Claude Swanson, Mar. 24, 1933; Roosevelt, Papers, OF 18, Claude Swanson to Roosevelt, Apr. 5, 1933; OF 197, Carl M. Vinson to Louis M. Howe, June 3, 1933.

34. Roosevelt, Papers, OF 18, Henry L. Roosevelt to F. D. Roosevelt, Jan. 5, 1934. Roosevelt may have been exaggerating the worth of the NIRA program to the Navy. Although the Navy did get money for new ships during these years, it could not count on help from Harold L. Ickes, the Administrator of Public Works, who was hostile to the use of relief funds for shipbuilding, since the money went primarily to small numbers of shipyard workers. See Levine, pp. 1, 157–168.

35. Roosevelt, Papers, PSF Box 52, N. H. Davis to Roosevelt, Dec. 26, 1933; Roosevelt, Papers, OF 18, F. D. Roosevelt memo to H. L. Roosevelt, Feb. 2, 1934.

36. John Morton Blum, *From the Morgenthau Diaries* vol. I: *Years of Crisis, 1928–1938* (Boston, 1959), pp. 229–230; Leuchtenberg, pp. 82–83; Samuel I. Rosenman, ed., *The Public Papers and Addresses of Franklin D. Roosevelt, 1928–1936* (New York, 1938), III, 172–181; Phillips, Journal, March 16, 1934.

37. Wayne S. Cole, *Senator Gerald P. Nye and American Foreign Relations* (Minneapolis, 1962), pp. 55–59, 66–76; Nixon, II, 111–112.

38. Davis, pp. 361–385.

39. Nixon, I, 627; NARG 80 Box 6, Hallie M. Huber to Roosevelt, Feb. 2, 1934; Sara R. Beasley to Roosevelt, Feb. 17, 1934; Roosevelt, Papers, OF 404-A, Cordell Hull to Roosevelt, Feb. 21, 1934; Cole, pp. 65–66, 127–128.

40. Rosenman, III, 163–165; Nixon, II, 30–31; Borg, p. 102; Patterson, pp. 11–12.

6. A TENTATIVE DECISION

1. Patterson, p. 10; Phillips, Journal, Mar. 9, 1934; Heinrichs, *Ambassador*, p. 204.

2. Phillips, Journal, Apr. 19, 26, 1934.

3. Phillips, Journal, May 2, 1934; Borg, pp. 77–83.

4. Nixon, II, 8–11.

5. *USFR, 1934*, I, 230–231, Hornbeck to Hull, Mar. 31, 1934; Nixon, II, 53–71; Davis, Papers, Box 20, E. H. D[ooman] to Davis, Apr. 24, 1934.

6. J. Pierrepont Moffat, Diary, Houghton Library, Harvard University, Mar. 27, Apr. 26, 1934; Borg, pp. 3, 22; Davis, Papers, Box 27, Davis to Roosevelt, Apr. 12, 1928.

7. Roosevelt, Papers, PSF Box 52, N. H. Davis to Roosevelt, n.d.

8. Davis, Papers, Box 9, memo of a meeting with Roosevelt and Hull, Apr. 28, 1934.

9. Phillips, Journal, May 24, 1934.

10. Thaddeus V. Tuleja, *Statesmen and Admirals: The Quest for a Far Eastern Naval Policy* (New York, 1963), pp. 98–99; Davis, Papers, Box 9, memo of a conversation with Roosevelt and Hull, Apr. 27, 1934.

11. Raymond G. O'Connor, *Perilous Equilibrium: The United States and the London Naval Conference of 1930* (Lawrence, 1962), pp. 109–121; Fred Greene, "The Military View of American National Policy, 1904–1940," *American Historical Review* 66:354–377 (January 1961); Waldo H. Heinrichs, "Japanese-American Relations, 1931–1941: The Role of the United States Navy" (paper presented at the Conference on Japanese-American Relations, 1931–1941, July 14–18, 1969), pp. 3–4.

12. Roosevelt, Papers, PSF Box 56, Claude Swanson to Roosevelt, enclosing Schofield's memo to Standley, Nov. 19, 1934.

13. Heinrichs, "Navy," p. 3.

14. Heinrichs, "Navy," p. 10.

15. Wheeler, p. 123; Bernard Brodie, *A Guide to Naval Strategy* (Princeton, 1958), pp. 1–16.

16. Davis, Papers, Box 36, recommendations of the General Board on the 1935 Disarmament Conference, Oct. 1, 1934; Brodie, pp. 45–50; Potter, pp. 638–639; W. D. Puleston, *The Armed Forces of the Pacific* (New Haven, 1941), pp. 178–182.

17. Roosevelt, Papers, OF 18, Claude Swanson to Roosevelt, enclosing a W. V. Pratt memo to Swanson, Mar. 30, 1933.

18. Halsey, p. 120; Puleston, p. 182.

19. Wheeler, pp. 12–129; Brodie, p. 32; Heinrichs, "Navy," p. 2.

20. Harold and Margaret Sprout, *Toward a New Order of Sea Power: American Naval Power and the World Scene, 1918–1922,* (2nd ed. Princeton, 1943), intro.; Tuleja, pp. 125–126; Brodie, p. 178.

21. NARG 80, Box 65, Fleet Problem IX, Mar. 18, 1920; Box 66, Fleet Problem XII, Apr. 1, 1931; Box 67, Fleet Problem XIV, Jan. 31, 1933; Box 68, Fleet Problem XV, Apr. 24, 1934; Box 65, Fleet Problem XI, July 14, 1930; Box 65, Fleet Problem X, May 7, 1930; Box 66, Fleet Problem XIII, n.d.

22. Davis, Papers, Box 20, memo of a conversation between Davis, D. MacArthur, and W. V. Pratt, Mar. 30, 1932; U.S., Dept. of the Navy, Records of the General Board, Conference series, XIII, 7, undated memo.

23. Louis Morton, *Strategy and Command: The First Two Years,* The United States Army in World War II (Washington, D.C., 1962), pp. 21–30.

24. Morton, pp. 33–37; Tuleja, pp. 99–100, 114–115.

25. Wheeler, p. 187; Greene, pp. 362–368.

26. Wheeler, pp. 53–62; Tuleja, p. 80; Davis, Papers, Box 36, recommendations of the General Board on the 1935 Disarmament Conference, Oct. 1, 1934.

27. Davis, Papers, Box 36, recommendations of the General Board on the 1935 Disarmament Conference, Oct. 1, 1934.

28. *Ibid.;* Tuleja, pp. 101–107.

29. Davis, Papers, Box 36, recommendations of the General Board on the 1935 Disarmament Conference, Oct. 1, 1934.

30. *Ibid.*

7. THE ECONOMICS OF APPEASEMENT AND THE POLITICS OF DEFENSE

1. John F. Kennedy, *Why England Slept* (New York, 1940), pp. 35–38; Earl of Avon (Anthony Eden), *The Eden Memoirs: The Reckoning* (London, 1965), pp. 3–6, 15–18.

2. William Roger Louis, *British Strategy in the Far East, 1919–1939* (Oxford, 1971), pp. 178–189, 203–205; Christopher Thorne, "The Shanghai Crisis of 1932: The Basis of British Policy," *American Historical Review* 75.6:1616–1639 (October 1970).

3. Martin Gilbert and Richard Gott, *The Appeasers* (London, 1967), pp. 3–24; Eden, pp. 47–94; John W. Wheeler-Bennett, *Munich: Prologue to Tragedy* (New York, 1948), p. 207.

4. Alfred F. Havighurst, *Twentieth Century Britain* (New York, 1962), pp. 210–231; Keith Feiling, *The Life of Neville Chamberlain* (London, 1946), pp. 261–262; A. J. P. Taylor, *English History, 1914–1945* (New York, 1965), pp. 326–327.

5. Keith Middlemas and John Barnes, *Baldwin: A Biography* (London, 1969), pp. 368–372, 526; Hugh Dalton, *The Fateful Years: Memoirs, 1931–1945* (London, 1957), pp. 64–65, 84–85; Clement R. Attlee, *As It Happened* (London, 1954), pp. 96–104; Feiling, p. 262.

6. Ian Colvin, *Vansittart in Office* (London, 1965), pp. 30–31; Wheeler-Bennett, p. 243; Middlemas and Barnes, pp. 744–755.

7. Feiling, pp. 1–16, 118–125; Earl of Halifax (Lord Irwin), *Fulness of Days* (London, 1957), pp. 227–234; Feiling, pp. 48–117; Viscount Simon, *Retrospect* (London, 1952), pp. 275–279; Iain MacLeod, *Neville Chamberlain* (London, 1961), pp. 163–165.

8. Viscount Templewood (Samuel Hoare), *Nine Troubled Years* (London, 1954), pp. 13–24; Charles L. Mowat, *Britain Between the Wars, 1918–1940* (London, 1956), pp. 402–404; MacLeod, pp. 146–162; Feiling, pp. 189–216.

9. Kennedy, pp. 25–35; Taylor, pp. 331–341; MacLeod, pp. 166, 200–206.

10. Feiling, p. 227; CAB 23/79, cabinet meeting, May 30, 1934.

11. William W. Lockwood, *The Economic Development of Japan: Growth and Structural Change, 1868–1938* (Princeton, 1954), p. 178.

12. Middlemas and Barnes, pp. 728–730; Winston S. Churchill, *The Second World War, I: The Gathering Storm* (Boston, 1948), pp. 50–51.

13. CAB 4/22, Committee of Imperial Defence (CID), 1112-B, Papers for Chiefs of Staff, June 1933.

14. Donald C. Watt, *Personalities and Politics: Studies in the Formulation of British Foreign Policy in the Twentieth Century* (London, 1965), p. 85; Stephen Roskill, *Hankey: Man of Secrets, vol. I: 1877–1918* (London, 1970).

15. CAB 4/22, CID 1103-B, report of Chiefs of Staff, Mar. 31, 1933.

16. CAB 16/109, CID 1113-B, annual review by Chiefs of Staff, Oct. 12, 1933.

17. Watt, pp. 85–87; CAB 1/6/I, CID 216th meeting, Nov. 9, 1933.

18. Watt, p. 85; Colvin, pp. 18–21.

19. CAB 16/109, Defence Requirements Subcommittee (DRSC), Nov. 14, 1933; Dec. 4, 1933; Vansittart to Hankey, Feb. 24, 1934.

20. CAB 16/109, DRSC, Dec. 4, 1933; Jan. 18, 1934.

21. CAB 16/109, DRSC, note by N. F. Warren Fisher, Jan. 29, 1934; Fisher to Hankey, Feb. 12, 1934; report of DRSC, Feb. 28, 1934.

22. CAB 16/109, report of DRSC, Feb. 28, 1934.

23. CAB 16/111, cabinet paper (CP) 70, note by MacDonald, Mar. 12, 1934; Taylor, pp. 273–277; Havighurst, p. 216; Hoare, pp. 27–30; Mowat, pp. 397–414.

24. Middlemas and Barnes, pp. 1–74.

25. Gilbert and Gott, p. 53; Avon, pp. 23–40, 219–220; Feiling, p. 249; CAB 23/78, cabinet meeting, Mar. 14, 1934.

26. CAB 23/78, cabinet meeting, Mar. 14, 1934.

27. *Ibid.;* CAB 16/111, CP 68, Simon memo, Mar. 9, 1934; CP 80, Simon memo, Mar. 16, 1934; Vansittart memo, Apr. 9, 1934; Chiefs of Staff memo, Apr. 20, 1934.

28. CAB 23/78, cabinet meeting, Mar. 19, 1934; 16/110, Disarmament Conference 1932—Ministerial Committee (DCMC), May 3, 1934; May 10, 1934; 16/111, notes by Chiefs of Staff, May 14, 28, 1934.

29. CAB 16/111, Chamberlain memo to DCMC, June 20, 1934.

30. CAB 16/110, DCMC, June 25, 26, July 2, 17, 1934.

31. CAB 16/110, DCMC, July 17, 24, 1934; 16/111, Monsell memo to DCMC, July 18, 1934.

32. CAB 23/79, cabinet meeting, July 31, 1934; 16/110 report of the DCMC, July 31, 1934.

8. THE ROYAL NAVY, DISARMAMENT, AND ANGLO-AMERICAN MISUNDERSTANDING

1. Arthur J. Marder, *The Anatomy of British Sea Power: A History of British Naval Policy in the Pre-Dreadnought Era, 1880–1905* (New York, 1940), pp. 65–83, 105–141, 209–240.

2. ADM 116/3373, Plans Division memo, June 29, 1934.

3. CAB 29/147, Ministerial Committee for the London Naval Conference (NCM), May 31, 1934; Stephen Roskill, *Naval Policy Between the Wars, vol. I: The Period of Anglo-American Antagonism, 1919–1929* (New York, 1968), pp. 48–50, 115, 532–539.

4. Roskill, *Naval Policy,* I, 532–539, 543.

5. CAB 16/183A, historical note by Chatfield for the Committee on Defence Plans and Policy, June 23, 1939; ADM 116/3373, Plans Division memo, June 29, 1934; naval staff memo on requirements for 1935 Naval Conference, April 1934; Roskill, *Naval Policy,* I, 274–299, 419–425, 464–466.

6. CAB 29/148, NCM, Chatfield memo with comments by Foreign Office, Mar. 23, 1934.

7. CAB 29/147, NCM, Apr. 16, 19, 1934.

8. CAB 29/147, NCM, Apr. 19, 1934.

9. CAB 29/148, Warren Fisher memo, Apr. 19, 1934; 29/147, NCM, Apr. 23, 1934.

10. CAB 29/148, Hankey memo, May 7, 1934; Chatfield memo, May 18, 1934.

11. CAB 29/148, Warren Fisher memo, Apr. 19, 1934; Foreign Office memo, May 28, 1934; 23/79, cabinet meeting, Apr. 25, 1934.

12. CAB 29/148, NCM draft report, June 11, 1934.

13. Middlemas and Barnes, p. 729; Hoare, pp. 264–268.

14. CAB 29/148, report by R. L. Craigie, Apr. 12, 1934; FO 371/17597, Craigie to

Lindsay, Apr. 17, 1934; Davis, Papers, Box 9, memo of a conversation with R. Vansittart and R. Craigie, n.d.; memo of a conversation with Craigie and C. J. C. Little, Apr. 12, 1934.

15. *USFR, 1934,* I, 241–242, Davis to Hull, May 29, 1934.

16. *USFR, 1934,* I, 244–245, 259–262, Davis to Hull, June 2, 18, 19, 1934; FO 371/17598, Craigie note, June 22, 1934.

17. *USFR, 1934,* I, 267–268, Bingham to Hull, June 22, 1934; p. 269, Davis to Hull, June 22, 1934; U.S., Dept. of the Navy, Records of the General Board, Conference series, XIII, Admiral Leigh memo, June 21, 1934, included in Leigh's report to the General Board of the navy; Davis, p. 362.

18. Wheeler, *passim;* Moffat, Diary, May 21, 1934.

19. *USFR, 1934,* I, 277–278, Hull to Davis, July 26, 1934; FO 371/17598, Craigie memo, June 23, 1934.

20. Moffat, Diary, June 26, 1934; *USFR, 1934,* I, 276–278, Hull to Davis, June 26, 1934; Phillips, Journal, June 26, 1934.

21. CAB 29/149, notes of Anglo-American meeting, June 27, 1934; *USFR, 1934,* I, 279–280.

22. Nixon, II, 161–162; FO 800/271, Simon to Baldwin, June 27, 1934; 371/17598, Admiralty to Foreign Office, June 8, 1934.

23. *USFR, 1934,* I, 284, 296–297, Hull to Bingham, June 29, July 17, 1934.

24. FO 371/17598, Craigie minute, July 10, 1934; Craigie to F. D. G. Osborne, July 20, 1934; 371/17599, Eden to Foreign Office, July 19, 1934; *USFR, 1934,* I, 299–303, Bingham to Hull, July 27, 1934.

9. THE FIRST ENCOUNTER

1. Phillips, Journal, June 22, 1934; Davis, Papers, Box 35, J. C. Grew to Hull, July 17, 1934; Box 41, J. P. Moffat to Davis, Aug. 31, 1934; *USFR, 1934,* I, 303, report from U.S. naval attaché in Tokyo, Sept. 7, 1934.

2. *USFR, 1934,* I, 306–307, Grew to Hull, Sept. 11, 13, 1934. Grew believed Yoshida and speculated that Japan could not afford a naval race financially. *Ibid.,* pp. 309–311, Grew to Hull, Oct. 17, 1934.

3. Davis, Papers, Box 41, Moffat to Davis, Sept. 13, 1934; Moffat, Diary, Sept. 14, 1934; Davis, Papers, Box 41.

4. *USFR, 1934,* I, 303, Grew to Hull, Sept. 18, 1934; Moffat, Diary, Sept. 18, 1934.

5. Moffat, Diary, Sept. 14, 1934.

6. Davis, Papers, Box 35, memo of meeting at State Department, Sept, 26, 1934.

7. *Ibid.;* Moffat, Diary, Sept. 24, 1934; Moffat, Diary, Oct. 3, 1934.

8. Jay Pierrepont Moffat, Papers, Houghton Library, Harvard University, Box 23, memo of conversation at White House, Oct. 3, 1934; Nixon, II, 225–226.

9. *Ibid.*

10. Moffat, Diary, Oct. 4, 1934.

11. Davis, Papers, Box 35, Hornbeck to Davis, Sept. 26, 27, 1934; Hornbeck to Davis, Oct. 4, 6, 1934.

12. Moffat, Diary, Oct. 4, 1934; *USFR, Japan, 1931–1941,* I, 281–284.

13. FO 371/17599, Vansittart to Simon, Aug. 17, 1934; Simon to Vansittart, Aug. 20, 1934.

14. FO 371/17599, Craigie minute, Aug. 23, 1934.

15. FO 371/17599, Vansittart minute on Simon letter, Aug. 22, 1934.

16. Feiling, pp. 253–254; FO 800/291, Chamberlain to Simon, Sept. 10, 1934; CAB 23/79, cabinet meeting, Sept. 25, 1934.

17. CAB 23/79, cabinet meeting, Sept. 25, 1934.

18. Havighurst, p. 243; Taylor, pp. 379–383; Middlemas and Barnes, pp. 791–792; Robert Rhodes James, ed., *Chips: The Diaries of Sir Henry Channon* (London, 1967), pp. 136–138.

19. CAB 23/80, cabinet meeting, Oct. 10, 1934; 27/596, CP 223, memo by Chamberlain and Simon, Oct. 16, 1934.

20. CAB 29/148, memo by Foreign Office and Admiralty, October 1934.

21. CAB 29/147, NCM, Oct. 15, 1934; 23/80, cabinet meeting, Oct. 17, 1934.

22. JMFA, S 2.10.4.0.3, "Kurubeki kaigun gunshuku yobi kōshō ni taisuru teikoku seifu hōshin" (Policy of the imperial government vis-à-vis the coming preparatory negotiations for naval disarmament), Sept. 7, 1934.

23. JMFA, S 2.10.4.0.3, Hirota to Matsudaira, Sept. 7, 1934.

24. Matsudaira Tsuneo shi tsuisōkai, *Matsudaira Tsuneoshi tsuisōroku* (Tokyo, 1961), pp. 355–357.

25. Agawa Hiroyuki, *Yamamoto Isoroku* (Tokyo, 1965), pp. 3–31, 33.

26. JMFA, S 2.10.4.0.2, Matsudaira to Hirota, Oct. 8, 9, 1934; ADM 116/3373, Foreign Office to Clive, Sept. 25, 1934; CAB 29/149, Simon to Clive, Oct. 8, 1934.

27. JMFA, S 2.10.4.0.2, Matsudaira to Hirota, Oct. 23, 1934; CAB 29/149, Anglo-Japanese meeting, Oct. 23, 1934.

28. JMFA, S 2.10.4.0.3, Matsudaira to Hirota, Oct. 23, 24, 26, 1934; CAB 29/149, Anglo-Japanese meeting, Oct. 26, 1934.

29. JMFA, S 2.10.4.0.3, Matsudaira to Hirota, Oct. 24, 1934.

30. *USFR, Japan, 1931–1941,* I, 254–256.

10. BRITAIN SEEKS A COMPROMISE

1. CAB 23/80, cabinet meeting, Oct. 31, 1934; 29/147, NCM, Oct. 29, 1934.

2. CAB 29/148, draft of British position, Nov. 6, 1934; 29/147, NCM, Nov. 6, 1934; 23/80, cabinet meeting, Nov. 7, 1934.

3. JMFA, S 2.10.4.0.3, Japanese delegation to Hirota, Oct. 30, 1934.

4. CAB 29/149, Anglo-Japanese meeting, Nov. 7, 1934; JMFA, S 2.10.4.0.3, Matsudaira to Hirota, Nov. 7, 1934.

5. CAB 29/148, Simon memo, Nov. 21, 1934; JMFA, S 2.10.4.0.3, Hirota to Matsudaira, Oct. 29, 1934.

6. JMFA, S 2.10.4.0.3, Hirota to Matsudaira, Nov. 16, 1934.

7. JMFA, S 2.10.4.0.2, Japanese delegation to Hirota, Nov. 21, 1934; CAB 29/148, Chatfield memos, Oct. 30, Nov. 19, 1934; Simon memo, Nov. 22, 1934; 23/80, cabinet meeting, Nov. 21, 1934.

8. JMFA, S 2.10.4.0.2, Japanese delegation to Hirota, Nov. 21, 27, Dec. 7, 1934.

9. CAB 29/148, Craigie memo, Nov. 15, 1934; FO 371/17601, Craigie memo, Nov. 15, 1934.

10. Moffat, Diary, Oct. 24, 29, 1934; Roosevelt, Papers, PSF Box 35, Hull to Roosevelt, Nov. 1, 1934.

11. CAB 29/149, Anglo-American meeting, Oct. 29, 1934.

12. Nixon, II, 250–254; Phillips, Journal, Oct. 31, 1934.

13. Nixon, II, 263.

14. *USFR, 1934,* I, 328–331, Davis to Hull, Nov. 13, 1934; pp. 333–334, Roosevelt to Hull, Nov. 14, 1934.

15. Phillips, Journal, Aug. 21, Oct. 11, 1934; Roosevelt, Papers, PPF 222, E. M. House to Roosevelt, Oct. 9, 1934, reporting Lothian's warning.

16. *USFR, 1934,* I, 353–355, Hull to Davis; pp. 356–358, Davis to Hull, Nov. 21, 1934.

17. Cordell Hull, Papers, Library of Congress, Box 37, S. K. Hornbeck to Hull, Nov. 12, 1934; Moffat, Diary, Nov. 16, 1934; Phillips, Journal, Nov. 16, 1934.

18. Arthur Krock, *Sixty Years on the Firing Line* (New York, 1968), pp. 160, 182–183; Roosevelt, Papers, PSF, Box 56, Hull to Roosevelt, enclosing Krock's column, Nov. 21, 1934; *USFR, 1934,* I, 363, Hull to Davis, Nov. 22, 1934.

19. CAB 29/149, Anglo-American meetings, Nov. 16, 23, 1934.

20. Watt, p. 95; Taylor, pp. 82n, 133; CAB 29/151, meeting with dominions, Nov. 13, 1934; 23/80, cabinet meeting, Nov. 14, 1934; FO 800/392, Lothian to Vansittart, Sept. 9, 1934.

21. Phillips, Journal, Nov. 18, 1934; *USFR, 1934,* I, 375–376, 378, Hull to Davis, Nov. 28, Dec. 3, 1934.

22. CAB 29/149, Anglo-American meeting, Dec. 4, 1934; *USFR, 1934,* I, 381–388; pp. 393–394, Davis to Hull, Dec. 11, 1934; JMFA, S 2.10.4.0.3, Japanese delegation to Hirota, Nov. 28, Dec. 6, 1934.

23. *USFR, 1934,* I, Davis to Hull, Dec. 7, 1934; pp. 390–391, Roosevelt to Hull, Dec. 7, 1934; pp. 391–392, Hull to Davis, Dec. 8, 1934; Phillips, Journal, Nov. 22, Dec. 8, 1934; Moffat, Diary, Dec. 8, 9, 1934.

24. JMFA, S 2.10.4.0.2, Japanese delegation to Hirota, Nov. 30, 1934; CAB 29/148, Foreign Office memo, Nov. 26, 1934.

25. CAB 29/148, NCM, Nov. 27, 1934; FO 371/17602, Craigie memo, Nov. 29, 1934.

26. CAB 29/149, Chatfield memo, Nov. 30, 1934; Craigie memo, Dec. 6, 1934.

27. CAB 29/148, Chatfield memo, Dec. 7, 1934; 29/147, NCM, Dec. 10, 1934; 29/149, Craigie memos, Dec. 10, 12, 1934.

28. *USFR, 1934,* I, 395–398, Davis to Hull, Dec. 12, 13, 1934.

29. *USFR, 1934,* I, 401–402, Hull to Davis, Dec. 15, 1934.

30. JMFA, S 2.10.4.0.3, Japanese delegation to Hirota, Nov. 26, 1934.

31. JMFA, S 2.10.4.0.2, Japanese delegation to Hirota, Dec. 1, 11, 1934.

32. JMFA, S 2.10.4.0.2, Japanese delegation to Hirota, Dec. 11, 14, 1934.

33. FO 371/17602, Clive to Foreign Office, Dec. 8, 1934.

34. *USFR, 1934,* I, 381–392, Hull to Davis, Dec. 8, 1934; pp. 402–403, Anglo-American meeting, Dec. 19, 1934.

35. CAB 29/149, Craigie memo, Dec. 28, 1934; 29/148, Foreign Office memo, Jan. 17, 1935; JMFA, S 2.10.4.0.2, Japanese delegation to Hirota, Dec. 29, 1934.

36. CAB 29/148, Foreign Office memo, Jan. 17, 1935; FO 371/18732, Clive to Foreign Office, Mar. 28, 1935.

37. *GSS,* XII, 63, "Gunreibu gensui kaigi ni okeru shitsumon ōtō an" (The Navy General Staff's draft of questions and answers for the conference of field marshals and admirals of the fleet), Oct. 29, 1934.

38. Storry, pp. 33–36; Aritake, *Saishō,* pp. 143–153; Crowley, p. 77.

39. JMFA, S 2.10.4.0.3, "Kafu kaigun gunbi seigen jōyaku haishi tsūkoku ni kansuru sumitsuin shita shinsa no yōshi" (An outline of the deliberations of the Privy Council concerning the announcement of the abrogation of the Washington naval treaty), Dec. 7, 1934.

40. *Ibid.*

41. JMFA, 2.10.4.0.3, "Taisho llnen 2gatsu 6nichi 'Washington' ni oite chomei serarutaru kaigun gunbi seigen ni kansuru jōyaku haishi tsūkokukata no ken no shinsa hōkoku" (Report of our investigations into the manner in which the abrogation of the treaty limiting naval armaments signed in Washington on Feb. 6, 1922, should be announced), Dec. 14, 1934; Ōsumi Taishō denki, pp. 603–605; Ikeda Kiyoshi, *Nihon no kaigun* (Tokyo, 1967), II, 95–96.

42. Moffat, Diary, Dec. 19, 1934; Nixon, II, 325–327.

43. Davis, Papers, Box 51, Davis to Roosevelt, Nov. 27, 1934; Phillips, Journal, Jan. 8, 1935.

44. Phillips, Journal, Dec. 19, 1934; Joseph C. Grew, *Ten Years in Japan* (New York, 1944), pp. 145–152.

11. THE SECOND LONDON NAVAL CONFERENCE

1. Crowley, pp. 210–237; Davis, p. 362; Hull, I, 444–447.

2. CAB 29/149, Anglo-French meeting, July 11, 1934; Anglo-Italian meeting, July 30, 1934; Charles Bloch, "Great Britain, German Rearmament, and the Naval Agreement of 1935," in Hans W. Gatzke, ed. and trans., *European Diplomacy Between Two Wars, 1919–1939* (Chicago, 1972), pp. 125–151.

3. CAB 29/148, memo by Admiralty and Foreign Office, July 17, 1935; 24/253, CP 19, Jan. 24, 1935.

4. CAB 24/254, CP 69, Mar. 26, 1935; FO 371/18733, Little to Craigie, May 4, 1935; ADM 116/3373, Plans Division memo, May 27, 1935; CAB 29/148, report by British representatives, June 5, 1935; Eden, pp. 230–235.

5. CAB 29/148, Foreign Office memo, July 18, 1935; FO 371/18738, S. Hoare to G. Clerk, Aug. 7, 1935.

6. CAB 29/148, Craigie memo, Oct. 29, 1935; FO 371/18739, Craigie memo, Sept. 12, 1934; *USFR, 1935,* I, 87–90, Atherton to Hull, Aug. 9, 1935; pp. 85–87, 110–113, Field memos; pp. 113–115, Hull to Atherton, Sept. 19, 1935.

7. JMFA, S 2.10.4.0.2, Matsudaira to Hirota, July 4, 1935; Fujii to Hirota, July 9, 27, Aug. 9, 26, 1935; Hirota to Fujii, Oct. 15, 1935; CAB 29/148, memo by Foreign Office and Admiralty, October 1935.

8. *USFR, 1935,* I, 97–98, Atherton to Hull, Aug. 21, 1935; pp. 132–134, Bingham to Hull, Oct. 28, 1934; CAB 29/148, memo by Foreign Office and Admiralty, October 1935.

9. Meredith W. Berg, "The United States and the Breakdown of Naval Limitation, 1934–1939" (Ph.D. diss., Tulane University, 1966), p. 152; *USFR, 1935,* I, 136–138, Roosevelt to Bingham, Nov. 1, 1935.

10. CAB 29/148, memo by Foreign Office and Admiralty, October 1935; 29/147, NCM, Oct. 12, 1935; 29/148, report of the Ministerial Committee (NCM), October 1935; Hankey memo, Oct. 23, 1935.

11. *USFR, 1935,* I, 144–149, Field memo, Nov. 23, 1935.

12. *Ibid.*

13. Davis, Papers, Box 36, W. H. Standley to Davis, June 28, 1935.

14. *USFR, 1935,* I, 150–156, Hull to Davis, Nov. 26, 1935; pp. 144–149, Field memo, Nov. 23, 1935.

15. Leuchtenberg, pp. 68–69, 91–94; Tuleja, pp. 135–136; Roosevelt, Papers, OF 197-A, Box 2, R. L. Smith to Roosevelt, Mar. 4, 1935; NARG 80, Box 544, Mrs. I. F. Gifford to the Secretary of the Navy, Jan. 22, 1935; OF 18, H. L. Roosevelt to Stephen Early, Apr. 9, 1935.

16. Cole, pp. 83–84, 128.

17. Leuchtenberg, pp. 95–136; Burns, pp. 213–215, 220–226, 252; Cole, pp. 134–138; Marion C. McKenna, *Borah* (Ann Arbor, 1961), p. 319; E. Roosevelt, I, 468.

18. Robert A. Divine, *The Illusion of Neutrality* (Chicago, 1968), pp. 92–161; Adler, *Giant,* p. 158; Nixon, II, 386; III, 94–95; Leuchtenberg, pp. 216–230.

19. Borg, pp. 528, 531–533; Roosevelt, Papers, PSF, Navy Dept. 1935–1940 File, Swanson to Roosevelt, Apr. 22, 1935; Nixon, II, 495–496.

20. *USFR, 1935,* I, 79–80, Grew to Hull, July 18, 1935.

21. *GSS,* XII, 86–88, "Kaigun gunshuku kaigi teikoku zenkeniin ni ataeru kunreian" (Draft of instructions to be given to the empire's representatives at the Naval Disarmament Conference), Oct. 28, 1935.

22. JMFA, S 2.10.4.0.1, *1935 nen no kaigun gunshuku kaigi ikken* (Documents related to the 1935 Naval Disarmament Conference), "Rondon ni okeru kaigun gunshuku kaigi teikoku zenken ni ataeru kunrei" (Instructions to the empire's representatives at the London Disarmament Conference), Nov. 9, 1935; *GSS,* XII, 94–95, "Rondon ni okeru kaigun gunshuku kaigi teikoku zenkeniin ni ataeraruru kunreichū tōsui jiko ni kanshi gunreibu sōchō sōjō no sai no sōjōsho" (The report by the Chief of the Navy General Staff to the Emperor concerning supreme command matters in the instructions of the empire's delegates to the London Naval Disarmament Conference), Nov. 4, 1935.

23. *TSM,* I, 130, 134.

24. Hull, Papers, Box 38, Davis to Hull, Sept. 22, 1935; Davis, Papers, Box 2, Davis to Atherton, Nov. 4, 1935; Box 26, Davis to W. Gonzales, Nov. 21, 1935; *USFR, 1935,* I, 148.

25. *USFR, 1935,* I, 156–158, Davis memo, Dec. 8, 1935; *USCON,* pp. 44–66, Dec. 9, 1935; Phillips, Journal, Dec. 10, 1935.

26. *USCON,* pp. 86–128, Dec. 11–13, 1935; JMFA, S 2.10.4.0.1, Japanese delegation to Hirota, Dec. 11, 12, 1935.

27. *USCON,* pp. 129–143, Dec. 13, 1935; JMFA, S 2.10.4.0.1, Japanese delegation to Hirota, Dec. 14, 1935; CAB 29/157, Anglo-Japanese meeting, Dec. 13, 1935.

28. FO 371/18744, Anglo-Japanese meeting, Dec. 16, 1934; JMFA S 2.10.4.0.1, Japanese delegation to Hirota, Dec. 17, 1935; Davis, Papers, Box 37, notes of first meeting of heads of delegations, Dec. 16, 1935.

29. *USFR, Japan, 1931–1941,* I, 239–240, Davis to Hull, Dec. 17, 1935; *USCON,* pp. 144–156, Dec. 17, 1935.

30. JMFA, S 2.10.4.0.1, Japanese delegation to Hirota, Dec. 18, 20, 1935; *USCON,* pp. 157–183, Dec. 19, 20, 1935; Phillips, Journal, Dec. 17, 1935; Nixon, III, 131–134.

31. JMFA, S 2.10.4.0.1, Japanese delegation to Hirota, Dec. 24, 1935.

32. *USCON,* pp. 184–195, Jan. 6, 1936.

33. *USCON,* pp. 196–211, Jan. 8, 1936; Phillips, Journal, Jan. 8, 1936; JMFA, S 2.10.4.0.1, Japanese delegation to Hirota, Jan. 9, 1936.

34. *USFR, 1936,* I, 22–25, Hull to Roosevelt, Jan. 7, 1936; pp. 25–27, Davis to Hull, Jan. 8, 9, 1936; Davis, Papers, Box 37, Roosevelt to Davis, Jan. 14, 1936; J. Dunn to Davis, Jan. 15, 1934.

35. Phillips, Journal, Jan. 8, 1936; *USFR, 1936,* I, 24–26, Davis to Hull, Jan. 8, 1936.

36. JMFA, S 2.10.4.0.1, Japanese delegation to Hirota, Jan. 10, 1936; FO 371/19802, Anglo-Japanese meeting, Jan. 9, 1936; *USFR, 1936,* I, 29–30, Davis to Hull, Jan. 10, 1936.

37. *USCON,* pp. 212–236, Jan. 15, 1936.

38. Berg, pp. 185–203.

12. THE JAPANESE NAVY CHARTS A NEW COURSE

1. Okada, pp. 100–116, 119–126, 134–135; Harada, IV, 349–350; John K. Fairbank, Edwin O. Reischauer, and Albert M. Craig, *A History of East Asian Civilization* (Boston, 1965), II, 596.

2. *Kido,* I, 459–460; Crowley, pp. 244–246.

3. *Kido,* I, 464; Okada, pp. 137–173.

4. *Kido,* I, 474–478; Harada, V, 19, 37–42, 55, 70.

5. Tsunoda, "Japanese Navy"; Bōeichō, *Daihonei rikugunbu,* I, 338–339, 341–342, 352; *TSM,* VIII, 214.

6. *TSM*, VIII, 215–216; Crowley, pp. 284–286.

7. *Nihon gaikō nenpyō*, II, 322–323, instructions to the commander of the army in China, "Hoku-shi shori yōkō" (Outline of North China policy), Jan. 13, 1936; *TSM*, III, 206–210.

8. Bōeichō, *Daihonei: rikugunbu*, I, 380–392; *GSS*, VIII, 351–353, unsigned memo, "Kaigun seisaku oyobi seido kenkyū chosa iinkai soshiki no gyōsai" (Request for approval of the organization of a research committee to investigate naval policy and systems), n.d.

9. *TSM*, VIII, 216–222, telegram from the commander of the Third Fleet to the Navy Minister and the Chief of the General Staff, Mar. 27, 1936.

10. *Ibid.*

11. *TSM*, VIII, pp. 222–223, telegram from the Vice Minister of the navy and the Vice Chief of the General Staff to the commander of the Third Fleet, Apr. 16, 1936; pp. 223–224, telegram from the head of the Military Affairs Bureau of the Navy Ministry and from the head of the First Division of the Navy General Staff to the Chief of Staff of the Third Fleet, Apr. 16, 1936.

12. *TSM*, VIII, 222–223, italics mine.

13. *Ibid.*

14. Bōeichō, *Daihonei: rikugunbu*, I, 158–160, 392–398.

15. *GSS*, VIII, 356, "Teikoku kokubō hōshin—yōhei kōryō dai-sanji kaitei" (The third revision of the Imperial Defense Policy and the general outline of our military strength), June 8, 1936.

16. *Ibid.;* interview with Admiral Suekuni Masao, April 1969.

17. Bōei kenshūjo, *Daihonei: rikugunbu*, I, 392–398.

18. JMFA, S 2.10.4.0.1, Hirota to Saitō, Jan. 20, 1936.

19. JMFA, S 2.10.4.0.1, Saitō to Hirota, Feb. 6, 1936.

20. Harada, V, 78–80, 106, 122–123, 139; Ikeda, II, 98–99.

21. *GSS*, VIII, 357, memo by the Second Section of the Army General Staff, "Kokubō kokusaku no taikō" (An outline of our national defense policy), June 30, 1936; Harada, V, 114–115. Tōgō Shigenori of the Foreign Office told Harada that the army was anxious to get an agreement with Germany in order to check Russia in the West.

22. *GSS*, VIII, 357. For the process of the decision, see *ibid.*, pp. 359–360, memo by the First Section chief of the East Asian Bureau of the Foreign Office, "Kokusaku taikō no keii" (The chronology of the outline of national policy), July 12, 1936.

23. *GSS*, VIII, 361–362, a decision of the five ministers' conference, "Kokusaku no kijun" (Fundamentals of our national policy), Aug. 7, 1936.

24. *GSS*, VIII, 363–365, a decision of the four ministers' conference, "Teikoku gaikō hōshin" (Imperial diplomatic policy), Aug. 7, 1936.

25. *GSS*, VIII, 359–360, 363–365.

26. *GSS*, VIII, pp. 363–365.

27. *TSM*, III, 199–206.

28. Tsunoda, "Japanese Navy."

29. *TSM*, VI, 149–150.

13. BRITAIN'S SUN SETS IN THE PACIFIC

1. CAB 16/138, subcommittee on Defence Policy and Requirements (DPR), July 1, 1935; 16/136, DPR, July 8, 1935.

2. Taylor, p. 412–413; Wheeler-Bennett, p. 246; CAB 16/112, Defence Requirements Subcommittee (DRC), July 11, 1935; DRC, July 19, 1935. The DRC continued as a standing subcommittee of the CID, dealing with technical matters.

3. Avon, pp. 126–130; Feiling, pp. 262–270.

4. MacLeod, pp. 182–186; Kennedy, p. 100: Havighurst, pp. 246–248.

5. CAB 23/83, cabinet meeting, Mar. 2, 1936; 23/84, cabinet meeting, June 25, 1936; 23/86, cabinet meeting, Nov. 4, 1936; Feiling, pp. 314–315.

6. Middlemas and Barnes, pp. 787–790, 814–815, 942–943; Eden, pp. 182–186; Taylor, pp. 411–412; CAB 24/251, draft report of the Committee on German Rearmament, Nov. 23, 1934; 23/257, Hoare to cabinet, Nov. 25, 1935; 16/137, DPR, Feb. 4, 1937; 4/26, memo on Air Force, Feb. 26, 1937.

7. CAB 16/112, programs of defense forces, Nov. 21, 1935; E. L. Woodward and Rohan Butler, *Documents on British Foreign Policy, 1919–1939,* 3rd ser. (London, 1950), III, 291–292, Anglo-French conversation, Nov. 24, 1938.

8. CAB 24/260, Chamberlain note, Feb. 11, 1936; 16/123, DPR, Jan. 14, 16, 1936.

9. CAB 29/151, meeting with dominions, Nov. 13, 1934.

10. ADM 115/3862, memo by naval attaché in Tokyo, Feb. 18, 1935; Chatfield? to president of Royal Naval College, July, 1935.

11. CAB 16/182, Chiefs of Staff memo, June 14, 1937; 16/181, Committee on Defence Policy and Plans, July 13, 1937.

12. CAB 24/251, Monsell memo, Dec. 6, 1934; memo by Chamberlain and Monsell, Dec. 7, 1934; 23/80, cabinet meeting, Dec. 12, 1934.

13. CAB 2/6/I, meeting of Committee of Imperial Defence, Nov. 22, 1934; 4/23, CID 1154-B, annual review by Chiefs of Staff, November 1934; CID 1181-B, annual review by Chiefs of Staff; 29/147, NCM, June 6, 1935.

14. Arthur Marder, "The Royal Navy and the Ethiopian Crisis of 1935–36," *American Historical Review,* 75:1327–1356 (June 1970).

15. CAB 16/112, DRC, Oct. 14, 1935; 23/82, cabinet meeting, Oct. 23, 1935; 16/112, DRC, Nov. 12, 1935; Hankey note, Nov. 21, 1935.

16. CAB 16/112, DRC, Nov. 21, 1935; ADM 116/3382, building program, Jan. 1, 1936.

17. CAB 16/123, DPR, Jan. 20, 1936; 23/83, cabinet meeting, Feb. 25, 1936; Wheeler-Bennett, pp. 255–256; CAB 24/261, CP 103, building program, Apr. 7, 1936.

18. CAB 16/137, DPR, Dec. 10, 1936; Eden, pp. 478–488; Middlemas and Barnes, pp. 928–948; Malcolm Muggeridge, *The Thirties: 1930–1940 in Great Britain* (London, 1967), p. 49; A. L. Rowse, *Appeasement: A Study in Political Decline, 1933–1939* (New York, 1961), pp. 45–46.

19. Middlemas and Barnes, pp. 962–970, 1013–1017; Havighurst, pp. 250–254.

20. CAB 16/136, DPR, June 11, July 2, 1936; 24/262, Eden memo, Apr. 25, 1936; 23/85, cabinet meeting, Oct. 14, 1936.

21. MacLeod, pp. 182–186; Feiling, pp. 282–294; Wheeler-Bennett, p. 265; CAB 23/87, cabinet meeting, Feb. 17, 1937; 24/268, CP 61, building program, Feb. 12, 1937; CAB 24/268, CP 61, building program, Feb. 12, 1936.

22. CAB 23/88, cabinet meeting, Apr. 7, 1937; FO 371/19820, Craigie memo, Oct. 20, 1936; CAB 4/27, CID 1435-B, memo on size of capital ships, June 13, 1938; FO 371/19805, naval experts meeting, Jan. 23, 1936; 371/19816, Phillips to Craigie, July 2, 1936; 371/19821, Clive to Foreign Office, Dec. 9, 1936.

23. Stephen W. Roskill, *White Ensign: The British Navy at War, 1939–1945* (Annapolis, 1960), p. 27; Roskill, *Naval Policy,* I, 346–347.

24. Roskill, *Naval Policy,* I, 343–345, 532–539; Roskill, *White Ensign,* pp. 27–28; Arthur Hezlett, *Aircraft and Sea Power* (New York, 1970), pp. 112–113, 128–129, 140, 173, 214–215.

25. ADM 1/9729, memo on a new standard of naval strength, n.d.; CAB 24/268, CP 73, Inskip memo, Feb. 26, 1937; 16/181, DPP, May 11, 1937.

26. CAB 16/181, DPP, May 11, 1937; 24/270, CP 165, Simon memo, June 25, 1937; 23/89, cabinet meeting, July 29, 1937; 23/90, cabinet meeting, Oct. 27, 1937.

27. CAB 4/24, CID 1252-B, German naval construction, July 22, 1936; ADM 1/9729, building program, Oct. 29, 1937.

28. CAB 24/273, CP316, memo on defense expenditure in future years, Dec. 15, 1937; 23/90, cabinet meeting, Dec. 22, 1937.

29. Duff Cooper (Viscount Norwich), *Old Men Forget: The Autobiography of Duff Cooper* (London, 1954), pp. 1–167; CAB 16/182, DPP, Hankey note, Jan. 9, 1938; 24/274, CP 29, building program, Feb. 11, 1938; 23/92, cabinet meeting, Feb. 16, 1938; 16/182, DPP, Hankey note, Feb. 21, 1938.

30. CAB 23/92, cabinet meetings, Feb. 23, Mar. 12, 1938; Cooper, pp. 207–223; CAB 23/93, cabinet meeting, Mar. 22, 1938; ADM 3631, Cooper to Simon, May 27, 1938.

31. CAB 23/94, cabinet meeting, July 20, 1938; CAB 24/278, CP 170, Inskip memo, July 12, 1938; ADM 116/9672, Cooper to Inskip, July 21, 1938; CAB 23/94, cabinet meeting, July 27, 1938.

32. Wheeler-Bennett, p. 321; James, p. 160; Avon, pp. 3–4, 31–38; CAB 21/531, Hankey to Inskip, May 16, 1938.

33. CAB 24/279, CP 234, Inskip memo, Oct. 21, 1938; 23/96, cabinet meeting, Oct. 31, 1938; 23/97, cabinet meeting, Feb. 2, 1939.

34. CAB 23/96, cabinet meeting, Dec. 14, 1938; 23/97, cabinet meeting, Jan. 25, 1939; 4/29, CID 1521-B, CP 14, building program, Feb. 3, 1939; 24/284, meeting of Committee of Imperial Defence, Feb. 24, 1939.

35. CAB 27/625, Committee on Foreign Policy, June 9, 1939; 23/99, cabinet meeting, May 23, 1939; 24/287, CP 118, Simon memo, May 18, 1939; 16/183A, Stanhope memo, June 27, 1939.

36. CAB 16/183A, Stanhope memo, June 27, 1939.

37. John Harvey, ed., *The Diplomatic Diaries of Oliver Harvey, 1937–1940* (London, 1970), pp. 48–49; CAB 23/90, cabinet meetings, Nov. 24, Dec. 8, 1937.

38. CAB 23/90, cabinet meetings, Dec. 15, 22, 1937; Feiling, p. 325.

39. ADM 116/3922, Phillips memo, Dec. 17, 1937; Anglo-American staff conversations, Jan. 3, 5, 1938; Ingersoll draft record of Anglo-American staff conversations, signed by Ingersoll and Phillips, Jan. 13, 1938.

40. ADM 116/3922, report by Captain Russell Willson, Jan. 13, 1939; Danckwerts memo, Mar. 24, 1939; CAB 27/625, Committee on Foreign Policy, June 20, 1939; 23/100, cabinet meeting, June 21, 1939.

41. CAB 16/183A, DPP, Chiefs of Staff memo, Feb. 20, 1939; ADM 1/10141, Danckwerts minute, Mar. 3, 1939; CAB 16/183A, DPP, Chatfield memo, Apr. 19, 1939; 27/627, Chiefs of Staff memo, June 18, 1939; 16/183A, DPP, June 18, 1939.

42. ADM 116/3922, T. C. Hampton report, June 27, 1939; Lindsey reports, July 1, 7, 14, 1939; Foreign Office to Lindsey, July 6, 1939.

14. A STEADY PACE AND A SUDDEN SPRINT

1. Admiral Suekuni Masao interview, April 1969; Davis, p. 361.

2. Fukui, pp. 89–92, 102.

3. Davis, pp. 372–377; JMFA, S 2.10.4.0.4, *Shuryokkan bihō seigen mondai, Ei, Bei, Futsu no teikoku seifu ni kenkan tsūkoku yokyū kankei o fukumu* (The problem of gun limitation, including the demand of England, the United States, and France for notification of ship construction by the imperial government), Japanese naval attaché in Washington to the Military Affairs Section of the Navy Ministry, Feb. 3, 1938; memo by the Third Section of the Navy General Staff, "Beikoku kaigun gunji seiryoku" (The military strength of the American navy), Jan. 7, 1938.

4. Davis, p. 381, 390n; Ikeda, *Kaigun*, II, 99; Fukui, pp. 111–112; *TSM*, VII, 328.

5. NARG 80, Box 70, critique of Fleet Problem XVI; Box 71, J. M. Reeves to W. H. Standley, Nov. 29, 1934.

6. Morton, pp. 37–39; Maurice Matloff and Edwin M. Snell, *Strategic Planning for Coalition Warfare, 1941–1942,* The United States Army in World War II (Washington, D.C., 1953), I, 2–3.

7. Roosevelt, Papers, PSF Box 25, W.D. Leahy to Roosevelt, enclosing Yarnell's letter, Nov. 8, 1937; Roosevelt to Leahy, Nov. 10, 1937; Leahy's reply, Feb. 18, 1938.

8. U.S., Dept. of the Navy, Records of the General Board, 420.2, unsigned memo, "Rainbow Studies: Requirements for Operations in Both Oceans," Dec. 15, 1938.

9. Heinrichs, "Navy," pp. 16–22; Matloff, pp. 4–10; Feis, pp. 41–44; Morton, pp. 39–44, 104–105.

10. Roosevelt, Papers, PSF Box 13, Hull to Roosevelt, Aug. 26, 1937; NARG 38, Box 3, report on Japanese naval policy, Jan. 22, 1937; report on expansion of Japan's aircraft industry, July 21, 1937.

11. Merze Tate, *The United States and Armaments* (Cambridge, 1948), pp. 193–196; *USFR, Japan, 1931–1941,* I, 298–302, Standley to Hull, July 25, 1936; Hull to Grew, June 4, 1937; Grew to Hull, June 18, 1937; NARG 38, Box 3, report on Japanese building program, May 22, 1937; *USFR, Japan, 1931–1941,* I, 303–304, Hull to Grew, Feb. 3, 1938; JMFA, S 2.10.4.0.4, "Kaigun an" (Naval draft), Feb. 7, 1938, and "Kaigun saigo an" (Final naval draft), Feb. 9, 1938; *USFR, Japan, 1931–1941,* I, 304–306, Hirota to Grew, Feb. 12, 1938.

12. Leuchtenberg, pp. 170–187; Ickes, I, p. 661; Adler, *Uncertain Giant,* p. 184.

13. Blum, I, 175–196, 305; Leuchtenberg, pp. 232–256; Burns, pp. 303–324.

14. Jonas, pp. 91, 161–163; Langer and Gleason, II, 18–19; Adler, *Uncertain Giant,* pp. 195–196.

15. Davis, p. 365; Roosevelt, Papers, PSF Box 28, C. Swanson to Roosevelt, June 29, 1935; Nixon, II, 546; Hull, I, 456–459; Roosevelt, Papers, PPF 745, telegram from Key Pittman to Roosevelt, Nov. 11, 1935; Nixon, III, 200; Levine, pp. 292–312.

16. Davis, p. 370; Jonas, pp. 129–132; Roosevelt, Papers, OF 18, telegram from Rose C. Wolf to Roosevelt, May 8, 1936.

17. E. Roosevelt, I, 555–556; Roosevelt, Papers, PSF Box 39, Roosevelt to George H. Dern, Jan. 15, 1936.

18. U.S., Dept. of the Navy, Records of the General Board, 420.2, memo from the chairman of the General Board to the Secretary of the Navy, May 24, 1935; memo from the Chief of Naval Operations to the Secretary of the Navy, Aug. 26, 1936.

19. Nixon, III, 573–576; Davis, p. 371.

20. Ickes, II, 274–278; Jonas, pp. 132–133; Adler, *Uncertain Giant,* p. 203; Manny T. Koginos, *The Panay Incident: Prelude to War* (Lafayette, 1967), pp. 104–111, 115–122.

21. Davis, pp. 372–373; NARG 80, Box 544, Hull memo to the Secretary of the Navy, July 12, 1938.

22. Burns, pp. 358–380; Adler, *Uncertain Giant,* p. 210; Blum, II, 43–50; Langer and Gleason, II, 35–39, 48–51; Divine, pp. 239–285.

23. Davis, pp. 390–391n; Ikeda, *Kaigun,* II, 98–100.

24. Davis, pp. 383–384.

25. Bowen, pp. 1–20, 142–170, 197–198; NARG 80, Box 50, Bowen to Chief of Naval Operations, June 13, 1935; Roosevelt, Papers, PSF Navy Department, 1941, Box 23, Office of Naval Intelligence to Captain Beardall, Nov. 25, 1941.

26. Bowen, pp. 59–110; Potter, pp. 485, 796–812; Morison, I, lix; Roosevelt, Papers, PSF Navy Department, 1935–1940, Box 21, C. Edison to Roosevelt, Feb. 15, 1939. The

General Board members feared that high compression engines would suffer a high rate of mechanical breakdown.

27. Davis, Papers, Box 39, Davis memo, Mar. 12, 1937; Roosevelt, Papers, PSF Box 25, Roosevelt to Swanson, Apr. 8, 1937; U.S., Dept. of the Navy, Records of the General Board, 420.6, A. C. Pickins to General Board, Apr. 21, 1938; General Board memo to the Secretary of the Navy, Apr. 21, 1938; Roosevelt, Papers, PSF Box 25, N. H. Davis to Roosevelt, July 30, 1937; Records of the General Board, 420.2, memo from the Chairman of the General Board to the Secretary of the Navy, May 8, 1937.

28. Roosevelt, Papers, PSF Navy Department, 1936–1940, C. Edison to Roosevelt, Feb. 23, Mar. 3, 1938; Langer and Gleason, pp. 127–128; Roosevelt, Papers, PSF Navy Department, Callaghan folder, Captain D. J. Callaghan to Roosevelt, Jan. 4, 1940, reporting a conversation with Admiral Stark.

29. Archibald D. Turnbull and Clifford L. Lord, *History of United States Naval Aviation* (New Haven, 1949), pp. 186–204, 209–211, 214–215, 238–239.

30. Potter, pp. 638–639; Roosevelt, Papers, PSF Navy Department, 1935–1940, Box 23, Adm. J. M. Reeves to Roosevelt, June 5, 1936; Fleet Admiral Ernest J. King, Papers, Library of Congress, Box 5, Adm. Adolphus Andrews to King, Feb. 23, 1938; Fleet Admiral William D. Leahy, Papers, Library of Congress, Diary, Nov. 26, 1939; NARG 80, W. G. DuBose memo, May 14, 1938.

31. Potter, pp. 635–638, 694–710; Turnbull, pp. 159–160, 226–229, 284–287, 308; Hezlett, pp. 194–196; King, Papers, to A. Andrews, Feb. 17, 1938.

32. W. F. Craven and J. L. Cate, eds., *The Army Air Forces in World War II* (Chicago, 1948), I, 69–70, 125–126, 184–193; Roosevelt, Papers, PSF Navy Department, 1935–1940, W. Brown to Paul Bastedo, Nov. 13, 1936.

33. ADM 116/3922, record of Anglo-American staff conversations, Jan. 3, 5, 1938; Taylor, pp. 504–508; Stephen W. Roskill, *The War at Sea* (London, 1954), I, 73, 105–106, 195–228.

34. Roskill, *War at Sea*, pp. 114, 247–254, 287–292, 297–301, 379, 588–589; Oscar Parkes, *British Battleships: Warrior to Vanguard, 1860–1950, A History of Design, Construction, and Armament* (London, 1956), 663–669.

35. Langer and Gleason, II, 491–493; Winston S. Churchill, *The Second World War*, vol. II: *Their Finest Hour* (New York, 1962), pp. 114–115, 162–163, 219; Woodburn Kirby et al., *The War Against Japan* (London, 1957), I, 23–24, 33–36, 46–50, 75–76, 84–86.

36. Roosevelt, Papers, Safe file, Japan, naval intelligence report on Japanese capital shipbuilding program, Oct. 11, 1939; U.S., Dept. of the Navy, Records of the General Board, 420.2, memo from the chairman of the General Board to the Assistant Secretary of the Navy, May 3, 1940; W. R. Sexton to Admiral H. R. Stark, June 18, 1940.

37. Samuel E. Morison, *History of the United States Naval Operations in World War II*, vol. I: *The Battle of the Atlantic, Sept. 1939–May, 1943* (Boston, 1947), pp. 27–28; Langer and Gleason, II, 546–575; U.S., Department of the Navy, Naval History Division, ed., *Dictionary of American Naval Fighting Ships* (Washington, D.C., 1959), I, 198–199, 216–222, 249–251, 304–315; II, 468–471.

38. Blum, II, 122; Craven, pp. 79–81, 108–110.

15. JAPAN'S DECISION FOR WAR

1. *TSM*, VI, 3–5.
2. *TSM*, VI, 13–17; Heinrichs, *Ambassador*, p. 284.
3. *TSM*, VI, 5–13.
4. *TSM*, VI, 155–158; VII, 16–19.
5. *TSM*, VII, 19–20.

6. *TSM*, VII, 21–26; Gerald E. Bunker, *The Peace Conspiracy: Wang Ching-wei and the China War, 1937–1941* (Cambridge, 1972), pp. 211–244; John Hunter Boyle, *China and Japan at War, 1937–1945: The Politics of Collaboration* (Stanford, 1972), pp. 277–301.

7. *TSM*, VI, 164–166; VII, 1–14, 27–32; Lu, pp. 69–73; Frank William Iklé, *German-Japanese Relations, 1936–1941* (New York, 1956), pp. 87–118.

8. *TSM*, VII, 34–44; VIII, 319–320.

9. *TSM*, VII, 44–46.

10. *Kido*, II, 814; *TSM*, VI, 87–89, 176–185.

11. *TSM*, VII, 53–61, 65–80.

12. Bōeichō, *Daihon'ei: rikugunbu*, I, 594–607.

13. Fukui, pp. 26, 35–38, 99–100, 124–131.

14. *TSM*, VII, 79–80.

15. *TSM*, VII, 46–48, 78.

16. *TSM*, VII, 78.

17. Interview with Commander Sekino and Admiral Tomioka, December, 1968; Senshi kenkyūkai, ed., "Hawaii sakusen to Yamamoto gensui," *Kokubō* (December 1968), pp. 104–113; *TSM*, VII, 80–83.

18. *TSM*, VII, 86, 104–117, 201–202.

19. *TSM*, VII, 86, 104–117.

20. *TSM*, VII, 84–85, 204–206, 269–272, 470–473, n. 18.

21. Feis, pp. 167–169, 301; Pogue, II, 135–140; Potter, 647–648.

22. Roskill, *War at Sea*, I, 560–561.

23. Feis, pp. 171–201.

24. Feis, 95–109, 142, 150–161, 205–207.

25. Nobutake Ike, ed. and trans., *Japan's Decision for War: Records of the 1941 Policy Conferences* (Stanford, 1967), pp. 46–82; *TSM*, VII, 213–220.

26. *Sugiyama memo: Daihon'ei-seifu renrakukaigi nado hikki*, ed. Sanbōhanbu (Tokyo, 1969), I, 273–275; *TSM*, VII, 241.

27. *TSM*, VII, 241–249, 272.

28. *TSM*, VII, 322–328; Ike, pp. 138–140.

29. *TSM*, VI, 272–274; Asada, p. 37; Senshi kenkyūkai, pp. 108–112.

30. Feis, pp. 261–287; *TSM*, VII, 272–289.

31. Ike, pp. 199–207.

Index

Harvard Studies in American-East Asian Relations